KV-144-444

KING'S COLLEGE CHAPEL, ABERDEEN, 1500–2000

KING'S COLLEGE CHAPEL, ABERDEEN, 1500–2000

Edited by

JANE GEDDES

NORTHERN
UNIVERSITIES
PRESS

2000

All rights reserved: no part of this publication may be reproduced, stored in a retrieval system, or transmitted in any form or by any means, electronic, mechanical, photocopying or otherwise, without the written consent of the copyright holder. Requests for such permission must be addressed to the Copyright Section, Queen Mother Library, Aberdeen University.

Published by Northern Universities Press, an imprint of W. S. Maney & Son Ltd, Hudson Road, Leeds LS9 7DL, UK.
Telephone: +44 (0)113 249 7481
Facsimile: +44 (0)113 248 6983
E-mail: maney@maney.co.uk
Web Site: www.maney.co.uk

© The University of Aberdeen, 2000

ISBN 1 902653 19 X

This book is published with generous assistance from the following organizations:
The Anderson-Dunlop Fund
The Carnegie Trust for the Universities of Scotland
Francis Eeles Bequest, Council for the Care of Churches

Front cover: King's College Chapel, Aberdeen, from the west. Detail showing the west window, the armorials of King James IV and Alexander Stewart, Archbishop of St Andrews, the Crown Tower and the lead steeple.

CONTENTS

THE POST-REFORMATION CHAPEL

ORGANIZATION

WORSHIP

ARCHITECTURE

POST-REFORMATION FITTINGS

FOREWORD

It is not inconceivable that Bishop Elphinstone had work on King's College Chapel started in 1500 because it coincided with the start of a new century. It is more likely that he simply plunged into building as soon as he could, within the constraints of his devastatingly busy life as a statesman, churchman, and university leader. What is inconceivable is that he could have imagined the tiny new university flourishing, without a chapel which would be the visible symbol of his ambition for it, and the platform to enable King's College to realize his vision of service to the north of Scotland.

At the start of a new millennium, the chapel's quincentenary gives us a welcome opportunity to reflect on the past of one of the oldest surviving buildings in Aberdeen. It is one of the great historic monuments in the North, a monument to the whole history of the university community and its faith — indeed a monument to the way in which this whole province was brought into the European mainstream.

That historic perspective should not obscure something even more extraordinary. The chapel may be a monument, but it is also still a living building. It remains at the heart of our university community. It is a landmark and an icon through which the university is immediately recognizable by members of its extended family throughout the world. It is a place for prayer and contemplation used by students and staff of all denominations and religions, and indeed some of none.

Right at the centre of the university we are blessed by having a working church, used and loved by the academic community, by graduates, and by the people of Aberdeen. There are no more moving events in the university calendar than the services of Remembrance Sunday or the Kirking of the Trades, where we still gather to reflect on our past, on the horrifying but glorious century we have left, and on our future.

This would be an important book just because it takes scholarly stock of that first five hundred years. It is all the more important in that it does so in a way which is methodologically ecumenical. It spans a huge period of Scottish history, but it does so by ranging from liturgy, to social context, to iconography, to simple matters we learn about through the objects of everyday life. What the contributors have tried as a team to produce is a holistic history fit for our times — a great deal more than an antiquarian or pietistic account of a building which happens to carry great emotive force for our community.

Perhaps no one is better placed to understand that tension and complementarity between emotive force and scholarly precision than myself. I have said to friends, and I will now say publicly, that no moment in my life had as much effect on me as the first time I sat as Principal in the stall which has been used by my predecessors through the centuries running back to the time of our great founder. That stall, however, is itself a piece of researchable history. Generations have carved graffiti in its wood. One of the sets of eighteenth-century initials is those of two brothers 'Maver'. Their family was forced to leave the country for a time after getting on the wrong side at the Forty-Five. One of their descendants is John Mavor, my fellow Principal who sits at Napier University on the estate of the Scottish inventor of logarithms; another was a well known Aberdeen surgeon who was a colleague and contemporary of my father.

No one who has had a connection with this university will fail to understand why I speak as I do — but it would not be worth speaking about if this collection was not a rigorous contribution to Scottish historical scholarship. Because Dr Geddes has made sure that it is that, I am proud to commend the collection as a book for all who are interested in the culture of Scotland, and indeed in the five hundred years of the whole European experiment in which we are still engaged.

C. DUNCAN RICE, *Principal of the University of Aberdeen*
Aberdeen, 2000

PREFACE

This book is dedicated to celebrating five hundred years of the chapel's existence at the heart of the university. A range of dates could have been chosen, from the start of work in 1497 to the dedication in 1509, but the date of 2 April 1500, inscribed on the west front as the start of operations, has been chosen to mark its quincentenary because it was the day and month of that year specifically chosen to emphasize the theocratic significance of the event (Chapters 4 and 5). As a part of the celebration, the last survivor of the original bells paid for by Bishop Elphinstone, the founder of the University of Aberdeen, has been retrieved from two hundred years exile in Tough Church and is now replaced in the chapel tower (Chapter 8).

Earlier histories of the chapel, like those of Macpherson and Kelly, concentrated on aspects of its fabric, Eeles examined the 1542 Inventory and liturgical rules, and Macfarlane looked at Bishop Elphinstone's personal contribution.[1] This book brings together all these aspects, on the premiss that the fabric of a church needs to be understood in relation to its function as well as its contemporary artistic context. It has also involved a considerable reassessment of the original documentary evidence available in the Historic Collections of the library.

The book is divided into two parts, split by the Reformation. The first section provides an account which, for Scotland, is unusually rich in both its documentary sources and its surviving objects. The chapel, with its splendid woodwork (Chapters 6 and 11) has one of the best-preserved medieval church interiors in the country. It demonstrates the well-managed, optimistic faith which Bishop Elphinstone (1431–1514) had in endowing a community to worship God in beauty, and to pursue academic studies. The foundation bull from Pope Alexander VI, from 1495 illustrates the dire situation which Elphinstone sought to rectify:

> [King James IV] desiring that the condition of his people may be improved, and considering that in the north or north-eastern parts of the said kingdom there are some places, separated from the rest of his kingdom by arms of the sea and very high mountains, in which dwell men who are rude, ignorant of letters and almost barbarous, and who, on account of the over great distance from the places in which the universities flourish and the dangerous passage to such places, cannot have leisure for the study of letters, nay, are so ignorant of these letters that suitable men cannot be found not only for preaching the word of God to the people of those parts, but even for administering the sacrament of the church...: and therefore King James has the utmost desire that a university should be erected.[2]

It is in this cultural environment that Elphinstone's creation needs to be evaluated. The first part of the book reflects his achievement, in some respects brought to completion by his successor Bishop Gavin Dunbar (c. 1455–1532). The beauty of his building sprang from Elphinstone's desire for a rich and meaningful liturgy: the choir stalls and even the shape of the building were a vehicle for music while the altars, sacred vessels and fine vestments were essential for the mass (Chapters 2 and 3). One of the discoveries in this book concerns the woodwork: the stalls, pulpit and desk. Far from being unique and exotic, it is shown that they are rather the outstanding survivors of a richly developed local craft in Aberdeen (Chapters 6, 11, 17).

Two essential figures from the early stage have barely left a trace: the Virgin Mary, to whom the chapel is dedicated and Bishop Elphinstone himself. All medieval images of the Virgin were disposed of at the Reformation, so the gift of the fifteenth-century Virgin of the Apocalypse (Chapter 12) from Douglas Strachan in 1944, is particularly appropriate. Strachan also brought the Virgin back in some of his stained glass (Chapter 23). Elphinstone's absence is perhaps more surprising since he was the patron. His spectacular renaissance tomb effigy, commissioned by Bishop Dunbar after 1518, was destroyed (Chapter 9). Its replacement, made by Henry Wilson in 1931, had to be located somewhat ignominiously outdoors because of a misunderstanding about its size (Chapter 24). It was common for patrons around 1500 to apply at least their coat of arms to the structure, in stone, wood or glass. Elphinstone's arms, carved in wood, although now displayed in the chapel, originally came from the hall (Chapter 10). His portrait, part of an altarpiece, survives, but was not necessarily among the original chapel furnishings (Chapter 7). This evidence of Elphinstone's modesty and devotion may stem from his background. Although well born, he was illegitimate and grew up in his father's household, barely knowing his mother.[3] Instead, he showed a deep devotion to the Virgin from the age of four when he was found kneeling before her altar in Glasgow Cathedral, until his death when her name was the last he spoke.[4]

The chapel ceased to function as a religious building after only about sixty years. Its preservation for almost three hundred years while being used as a synod meeting room, masons' lodge for cutting stone, lumber room and library, was fortunate (Chapters 13 and 17). The high and continual costs of maintenance were borne, even in lean years, because the chapel, with its crown tower, remained a symbol of the university's allegiance to the monarch (Chapter 16). This royal allegiance was also demonstrated by the creation of the mace, in 1650, and the Old Testament paintings (Chapters 20 and 19). The latter have been revived from dingy obscurity. Far from being mediocre quality and too blackened to comprehend, they emerge as rare and early examples of 'painted cloths', celebratory but temporary decorations for some major occasion linking the virtues of kingship with the college. Most examples of this type of art were destroyed after the event.

The restoration of worship to the chapel in 1824 came about almost by default. For years, students had processed to St Machar's, originally Aberdeen Cathedral but then the parish church, for their Sunday service. Their behaviour on the way to church lacked 'decorum', so Reverend Murray donated money in his will for sermons to be given in the chapel, to save embarrassment in the High Street (Chapter 14). Restoration of the fabric could only begin in earnest after the library moved out of the west end in 1873, and the chapel, having escaped the fury of the Reformation and Civil War, also escaped an over-zealous Victorian revival. The repairs around 1890 and later, in the 1930s were exceptionally sensitive (Chapter 16 and 22).

The chapel today remains a beautiful building for worship, listening to music and contemplation (Chapters 15 and 25). Its quiet charm and dignity pervade the quad, providing a tangible link with the collegiate past for both students, staff and visitors. Billings observed this pervasive atmosphere during his visit in the early nineteenth century: 'For five months of the year it is indeed the noisy resort of a student crowd, whose scarlet robes, worn with more ease than dignity, give fantastic gaiety to the scene, strangely in contrast with its original solemnity; but when the mob has taken flight early in the spring, nothing can be more sweetly silent than the old carved chapel and deserted courtyard.'[5]

JANE GEDDES
Aberdeen, 2 April 2000

Notes

[1] Macpherson, 1889; Kelly, 1949; Eeles, 1956; Macfarlane, 1995.

[2] Eeles, 1956, 138–39.

[3] His father, also William Elphinstone, was in minor orders and the younger son of a knight and his mother came from a baronial family. Macfarlane, 1995, 16–18.

[4] Boece, 58–60; 108.

[5] W. Billings, *The Baronial and Ecclesiastical Antiquities of Scotland*, 1845–52, 4 vols, Edinburgh, 1, 4.

ACKNOWLEDGEMENTS

In their second year, History of Art students at the University of Aberdeen are introduced to medieval church architecture, and a tour around the chapel is a vivid part of the course. For years, they have moaned 'There is nothing to read about it'. The bibliography in Chapter 26 totally dispels this complaint, but equally demonstrates why an accessible book was needed. Most of the existing literature is fragile and not suitable for class teaching. So, this book is dedicated, in part, to the Second Years, whose needs prompted its creation.

The book has drawn on a wide range of expertise and I would like to thank all the authors for their enthusiastic and efficient contributions. The steering committee got the project off the ground: Professor Mike Meston, Dr Grant Simpson, Colin McLaren, Dr Jennifer Carter, the chaplain Gillean Maclean and Leslie Macfarlane. Leslie has been a kindly guide and companion throughout. The staff in Special Collections, in particular Myrtle Anderson-Smith and Michelle Gait, have patiently discovered documents and answered queries. Mike Craig and his team in the reprographic department have produced many of the illustrations. I am particularly grateful to the Principal of the University, Professor Duncan Rice for backing this project; and to the Dean Graeme Roberts who was involved in planning the conference and celebrations held on 1–2 April 2000. My family, Peter, Henry and David Watt have also assisted with patience and technical advice.

ABBREVIATIONS

AUL	Aberdeen University Library, Historic Collections and Archives
AUR	*Aberdeen University Review*
Boece	*Hectoris Boetii Murthlacensium et Aberdonensium episcoporum vitae*, ed. J. Moir, New Spalding Club, Aberdeen, 1894
Eeles, 1956	Eeles, Francis C., *King's College Chapel, Aberdeen: its fittings, ornaments and ceremonial in the sixteenth century*, Aberdeen University Studies, No. 136, Edinburgh, 1956
Fasti	*Fasti Aberdonenses: selections from the records of the University and King's College of Aberdeen, 1494–1854*, ed. C. Innes, Spalding Club, Aberdeen, 1854
Kelly, 1949	*A Tribute offered by the University of Aberdeen to the memory of William Kelly, LL.D, A.R.S.A.*, ed. W. D. Simpson, Aberdeen University Studies, No. 125, Aberdeen 1949
Macfarlane, 1995	Macfarlane, Leslie, *William Elphinstone and the Kingdom of Scotland, 1431–1514. The Struggle for Order*, Aberdeen, 1995
Macpherson, 1889	Macpherson, Norman, *Notes on the Chapel, Crown and Other Ancient Buildings of King's College, Aberdeen*, Edinburgh, 1889. Reprinted from *Archaeologica Scotica*, 5
Orem, 1791	Orem, William, *A description of the Chanonry, Cathedral and King's College of Old Aberdeen in the years 1724 and 1725*, Aberdeen, 1791
PSAS	*Proceedings of the Society of Antiquaries of Scotland*
SRO	former Scottish Record Office, Edinburgh, now National Archives of Scotland

LIST OF FIGURES

LIST OF COLOUR PLATES

THE CONTRIBUTORS

MYRTLE ANDERSON-SMITH is Senior Curator at the Directorate of Information Systems and Services, Special Collections and Archives, Aberdeen University.

ELIZABETH BRACEGIRDLE is a graduate in History of Art from Aberdeen University. She is currently Associate Lecturer for the Open University.

CHARLES J. BURNETT has been Ross Herald of Arms since 1988 and was formerly at the National Museums of Scotland. He is Chamberlain of Duff House, Banff, a Knight of the Order of St John and Chevalier of the Order of Saints Maurice and Lazarus. He has written *The Honours of Scotland* (1993), *Scotland's Heraldic Heritage* (1997), *The Order of St John in Scotland* (1997).

IAN CAMPBELL is Reader in Architectural History and Theory at Edinburgh College of Art. He has published on the Renaissance in Scotland and Italy. The first volume of his catalogue raisonné of the architectural drawings in Cassiano dal Pozzo's 'Paper Museum' will appear shortly.

LORNE CAMPBELL, formerly Reader, Courtauld Institute of Art, London, now Research Curator, National Gallery, London. Author of *Hugo van der Goes and the Trinity Panels* (with Colin Thompson, 1974), *The early Flemish Pictures in the Collection of Her Majesty the Queen* (1985), *Renaissance Portraits* (1990), *National Gallery Catalogues, The Fifteenth Century Netherlandish Schools* (1998).

ELIZABETH CUMMING is a Lecturer at the Edinburgh College of Art, her publications include *Phoebe Anna Traquair 1852–1936* (National Galleries of Scotland, 1993); and as co-author, *The Arts and Crafts Movement* (1991) and *The Arts and Crafts Movements in Dublin and Edinburgh, 1885–1925* (1998).

GEORGE R. DALGLEISH is Curator of the History and Applied Art Department, National Museums of Scotland, where he has responsibility for Scottish decorative arts. He co-ordinated the eighteenth- and nineteenth-century displays in the new Museum of Scotland, and has published extensively on aspects of Scotish material culture.

JOHN DICK formerly Head of Conservation, National Galleries of Scotland has contributed technical essays to several National Galleries publications including *Raphael: the Pursuit of Perfection* (1994) and *The Art of Sir Henry Raeburn* (1997).

RICHARD EMERSON is Chief Inspector of Historic Buildings, Historic Scotland. He trained at the Courtauld Institute of Art, London University, where he was subsequently employed as Deputy Conway Librarian, before joining the Royal Commission on the Ancient and Historical Monuments of Scotland in 1973. He joined Historic Scotland as Principal Inspector of Historic Buildings in 1978 and became Chief Inspector in 1999.

RICHARD FAWCETT is Principal Inspector of Ancient Monuments for Historic Scotland. He has published widely on Scottish medieval architecture, including books on Scottish architecture from 1371 to 1560, Scottish abbeys and priories and Scottish cathedrals.

JANE GEDDES, formerly an Inspector of Ancient Monuments with English Heritage now lectures in History of Art at Aberdeen University. She has written widely on medieval metalwork and manuscripts, including *Medieval Decorative Ironwork in England* (1999) and is currently exploring the architecture of Kincardine and Deeside.

JOHN HARPER is Director General of the Royal School of Church Music, and Research Professor in Christian Music and Liturgy, University of Wales, Bangor. His guide *The Forms and Orders of Western Liturgy* (1991), is used widely. He has contributed to the new history of Hereford Cathedral and is working on the use of the organ in the liturgy between 1480 and 1680.

JOHN HIGGITT is Senior Lecturer, Department of Fine Art, Edinburgh University. His research interests include medieval epigraphy and the art of medieval Scotland. His forthcoming book examines the thirteenth-century 'Murthly Hours' and he is working on an edition of the medieval library catalogues of Scotland. He chairs the National Committee on Carved Stones in Scotland.

NORBERT JOPEK, Assistant Curator, Sculpture Department, Victoria and Albert Museum. He studied art history at the universities of Münster, Munich and Hamburg. He was employed at the *Amt für Denkmalpflege* and the Cathedral Treasury in Trier, and taught at the universities of Trier and Freiburg im Breisgau.

LESLIE MACFARLANE, Honorary Reader in Medieval History, University of Aberdeen. He is the author of guides to the Vatican archives (on which he has published numerous articles) and King's College, Aberdeen and the biography *William Elphinstone and the Kingdom of Scotland*.

GILLEAN MACLEAN is Chaplain to Aberdeen University. She trained as a nurse and became a mature graduate in Divinity from Aberdeen University. She was made Assistant Chaplain to the University in 1994 and Chaplain in 1996. She is the first female Chaplain to the University and the first woman to tbe ordained in King's College Chapel. She is a regular contributor to Radio Scotland's *Thought for the Day*.

STUART MAXWELL, formerly Deputy Keeper, National Museum of Antiquities, Edinburgh. A past President of the Society of Antiquaries of Scotland, he gave the

Society's Rhynd Lectures in Scottish Silver and Silversmiths in 1956. He has pubished extensively on Scottish silver, costume and weapons.

COLIN MCLAREN, Associate Director and Librarian of Aberdeen University Director- ate of Information Systems and Services (retired). He was University Archivist and Keeper of Manuscripts, 1969–96, and University Librarian, 1996–99. Author of *Rare and Fair: a Visitor's History of Aberdeen University Library* (1995) and, with J. J.Carter, *Crown and Gown: an illustrated history of the University of Aberdeen* (1994).

JOHN REID is Senior Lecturer in Physics, Aberdeen University. He is a Fellow of both the Royal Astronomical Society and Royal Meteorological Society. He currently gives popular undergraduate courses in astronomy and meteorology, amongst more specialist teaching. He curates the university's extensive collection of historic scientific instruments.

HENRY R. SEFTON, Honorary Senior Lecturer in Church History, Aberdeen University. Formerly Master of Christ's College, Aberdeen. He is a graduate of the Universities of St Andrews and Glasgow and of Union Theological Seminary, New York. He was ordained in 1957, serving in parishes in Scotland and Nigeria. He has a special interest in worship and has published in this field.

SALLYANNE SIMPSON took her degree in History of Art at Aberdeen as a mature student, having previously worked as a secretary, with particular skills in computing. She is currently a Tax Assistant for Deloitte and Touche.

JOHN THOMAS has lectured at South Bank University since 1975. He has published on Henry Wilson, John Singer Sargent and Giles Gilbert Scott. He is particularly interested in church art and architecture of the late nineteenth and early twentieth centuries.

ROGER WILLIAMS studied at the University of Wales, Cardiff, Goldsmiths' College, London and King's College, Cambridge.and spent eight years as a professional conductor, organist, singer, composer and lecturer in London. He is currently Director of Music and Organist at Aberdeen University.

THE
PRE-REFORMATION
CHAPEL

CHAPTER ONE

THE FOCAL POINT OF BISHOP ELPHINSTONE'S UNIVERSITY

By LESLIE MACFARLANE

When William Elphinstone was consecrated Bishop of Aberdeen in the late spring of 1488, he faced a huge task of restoration and renewal. His large, scattered diocese had been without a bishop for five years. His cathedral of St Machar in Old Aberdeen was unfinished and lacked a number of its official administrators. The parish church of St Nicholas in the nearby royal burgh had run short of the funds required to extend its choir and complete its spire, while several of the more isolated rural parish churches were badly in need of repair and were pastorless. During the vacancy of the see, too, a number of church lands had been unlawfully appropriated by local landlords, thereby considerably reducing the bishop's annual income needed to meet the constant demands made on diocesan funds. Having informed himself of the actual state of his diocese within the first few months of his consecration, Elphinstone then began to plan a co-ordinated long term programme of reform intended both to protect and educate his clergy and to advance the well being of all the laity committed to his spiritual care. His most immediate task, certainly, was to retrieve those lands and that income which had been misappropriated from 1483 onwards, if not earlier, as well as to fill his vacant benefices with clergy of his own choice and to visit the outlying parishes of his diocese in order to understand their problems and needs. And it is a measure of his skills as a senior appeal judge, his familiarity with the current procedures of the Papal Curia, and of his former experience as a parish priest in a rural area, that patiently and tenaciously he was able to pursue and resolve a number of these serious obstacles to his long term plans in the early years of his episcopate. Errant landlords and the crown itself, for example, were taken to court, his diocesan lands recovered and large sums of money retrieved. Rival patrons wishing to fill his vacant benefices were fought off, and cathedral administrators and parish priests of his own choice nominated in their place. Chapter funds were pooled and the stipends of vicars choral and rural vicars stabilized. Work on a belfry and spire for the central tower of the cathedral was begun, and preparations made to extend its choir eastwards. A new choir was designed for the parish church of St Nicholas, and liturgical reforms were set in motion to improve the quality and substance of divine worship throughout the diocese.[1]

Within the framework of all this activity, however, there was one further venture which Elphinstone longed to undertake: the foundation of a university in Old Aberdeen, the heartland of the diocese. It was one which he knew would be of inestimable value to both his clergy and laity alike, but one which he recognized would strain his resources to the limit. For universities were very expensive institutions to found and maintain, and without adequate endowment could soon run into serious difficulties, as he knew from the impoverishment suffered by the Faculty of Law at Glasgow when he was a student there during its early years.[2] He was aware, then, that he would have to ingather sufficient funds to guarantee the permanent salaries of his teaching staff, the prebends of his vicars choral and choir boys for the chapel, and a number of bursaries for his poor students, not counting the university's initial building costs. But such was his skilful planning, that between 1495 and 1505 he was able to attract enough gifts in land and money from the king, his friends and relations, and the burgesses of Aberdeen, though not without considerable anxiety from shortfall crises as his expenses mounted, to create a well endowed academic community of thirty-six persons organized around a single, handsomely built college only some five hundred yards away from his own cathedral.[3] It was an extraordinary act of faith, and was to prove his greatest and most lasting achievement.

In order to ensure that his university would be academically viable, it was clearly imperative for him to select and appoint well qualified, life tenured teachers capable of providing excellent courses in the liberal arts, canon and civil law, medicine and theology, so that his students would be able to add to the professional expertise which the area and the nation still badly lacked. But over and above this essential task, it was also his firm conviction that the fitting worship of God should form an integral part of the daily rhythm of their academic studies. Indeed, this is evident in the very wording of his supplication to the Pope in 1495, where he explained that the whole purpose of founding his university was 'to praise the Divine Name, to rejoice in the Catholic faith, for the salvation of souls, and to advance the good order and profit of the local area and of the nation itself'.[4] Nor was he alone in this conviction, for by the late fifteenth century, the liturgy of the church was being sung daily, not only in all the cathedrals and monasteries throughout western Christendom, but also by the vicars choral in the college chapels of its universities, in which both their masters and students participated. Moreover, this was no mere religious formalism. Its purpose, as far as the collegiate foundations were concerned, was two fold. In the first place, it was intended to encourage within them a deep Christian piety based on community worship, private prayer and studies which, whether secular or sacred, would lead their scholars to love God and serve their fellow men. But also, given the religious ethos of the age, it encouraged them to recall with gratitude and thanksgiving the past generosity of their college benefactors and of its other deceased members, in that it allowed for the celebration of regular annual anniversary masses for the repose of their souls. Hence, when planning his university, Elphinstone was concerned not only to include in its layout and organization a chapel which would provide its religious services, but that its worship should be dignified, meaningful and would serve its whole community as their focal point. That this was his intention may also be inferred from the date he caused to be inscribed on the western front of the chapel to commemorate when the masons began to build it, namely 2 April, which was precisely the day and month when Solomon began to build the Temple in Jerusalem for the glory of God, the symbolism of which would certainly not have escaped him, since we now know that he was much drawn to this particular date within its accompanying text in the Old Testament.[5] In addition to the recruitment of his masters and students, then, he recognized that he would need to select and appoint a group of professional vicars choral and choir boys skilled in Gregorian chant and polyphonic music, who would be incorporated and beneficed as a separate body within the university's constitution. They would also be required to live nearby within the College Bounds, and their task would be to sing the Divine Office at various set times throughout each day, while the masters and students of the college would join them for evening prayers, and for mass on Sundays, festivals and other holy days. The following account is an attempt to show how and why, from the very beginning, he gave so much thought and care, not only to the design of the chapel itself and its interior fittings, but especially to its liturgical organization and content, within the structure of the university he was about to create.

Notes

[1] Fuller details of Elphinstone's diocesan problems in 1488, and how he resolved them, are provided in Macfarlane, 1995, 200–89.

[2] J. Durkan and J. Kirk, *The University of Glasgow 1451–1577,* Glasgow, 1977, 31, 128–29.

[3] Macfarlane, 1995, 308–26.

[4] Vatican Archives, *Registra Supplicationum,* 1000, fol. 82ᵛ; *Fasti,* 4; Eeles, 1956, 140–41.

[5] See Chapter 5, and G. P. Edwards, 'William Elphinstone, his College Chapel and the Second of April', *AUR,* LI, 1985, 1–17.

CHAPTER TWO

THE DIVINE OFFICE AND THE MASS

By Leslie Macfarlane

The Daily Services in Chapel: their Nature and Content

When we come to examine the daily services which were celebrated in chapel by the prebendary chaplains (vicars choral) and their choir boys, and in part, by the academic community from the time when corporate life in the college first began in 1505,[1] we notice that they followed the pattern of worship already well established in the other collegiate churches, cathedrals and monasteries throughout Scotland and the western church itself, namely the celebration of the Divine Office (the Liturgy of the Hours), and that of the mass.[2] Two essential service books were required in order to perform these Offices: the breviary and the missal. The breviary contained all the hymns, antiphons, psalms, prayers and responses, readings from scripture and the lives of saints, designed to be appropriate for each of the seven Offices of Matins and Lauds, Prime, Terce, Sext, None, Vespers and Compline, which were sung at set times by the prebendary chaplains and choir boys throughout the day, echoing as they did the prayer of the Psalmist: 'Seven times a day have I praised you, O God'.[3] The missal, on the other hand, contained the Office of the mass which, whether sung or said, was fitted into this rhythm between the morning Offices of each day, and consisted of the Introit, Kyrie, Gloria, Epistle, Gospel, the recitation of the Creed, the Eucharistic Prayer, Communion and the Concluding Rite. The content of both the Divine Office and the mass also varied according to the day and the season; whether, for instance, it was a feast or saint's day, or a ferial (an ordinary non-feast day), and whether it took place within the Advent, Christmas, Lent, Easter or Pentecost cycle of the church's year. Such a formal structure of worship may at first sight appear to have been rigid and repetitive, if not too complex. But quite apart from the added beauty and dignity brought to these Offices by their choral content, which will be discussed more fully later,[4] it has to be remembered that they were designed to be comprehensive in adoration, praise, thanksgiving and petition, in that they drew deeply and widely on texts from both the Old and New Testaments and the lives of the saints, and were thus seen to be a fitting and timeless part of that long tradition of daily public worship central to the church's life from its earliest years onwards. Even so, as far as university colleges were concerned, such a structure had to keep, and was meant to keep, a proper balance between the amount of time which should be spent in chapel every day by the academic community, and that required for their studies; it was for this reason that from the very beginning of corporate life at King's, the prebendary chaplains and choir boys were endowed as a separate body from the masters and students in order that they should carry the main burden of the Offices, while the latter joined them for evening prayers, and at other times, in addition, on Sundays, feast days, and holy days of obligation. With this said, it must be added that the college's regulations also laid down that the prebendary chaplains and choir boys were themselves to be ensured a sufficient amount of time in their daily timetable for choir practice and further studies in Latin and scriptural literature, in order to enhance their performance of these Offices, and to advance their own education. We can see more clearly how each community accomplished this balance when we look at their respective daily timetables spelt out for them in the college's Foundation Charters of 1505 and 1514, as promulgated by the university's third chancellor, Bishop Gavin Dunbar in 1529.[5]

THE DAILY TIMETABLE

As far as the prebendary chaplains and choir boys were concerned, on every weekday morning, unless it were a major feast day or holy day of obligation, they walked up from their nearby manses which had been built for them on the east side of College Bounds immediately south of the Powis Brig,[6] in order to be in their allotted stalls in chapel by 6 a.m., when they sang Matins and Lauds. On three mornings a week they returned to chapel after an interval for breakfast, when the chaplains were joined by those ordained students of theology and those doctors and masters of the college who were already priests, so that each of them could say mass at the existing five altars in the chapel (increased to six c. 1536) as prescribed for them by the weekly timetable. These low unsung masses were either votive or anniversary masses for the souls of benefactors or alumni, the choir boys acting as their servers. Time had to be arranged during this early morning period, however, for mass to be sung by the cantor and choir boys, and celebrated by one of the prebendary chaplains in commemoration of the Blessed Virgin Mary on those weekdays when it was also being sung in St Machar's Cathedral, the celebrant on these occasions also having been nominated on a weekly rota basis. All these masses had to be finished by 9 a.m., however, since every day the chaplains and choir boys were required to begin singing the solemn high mass of the day, which had to be finished by 10 a.m., after which all weekday mornings were left free for the chaplains and choir boys to pursue their music practice or literary studies until dinner at 12 noon. Every afternoon the chaplains and choir boys returned to chapel to sing Vespers at the unusually early hour of 2 p.m. in the winter and 3 p.m. in the summer, possibly to take advantage of the light before it began to fail in the winter, but which in any case had to be finished by 4 p.m.; and at 6 p.m. they returned for the last service of the day, when they were joined by the whole resident academic community for Compline, which always included evening prayers and a sung salutation to the Blessed Virgin, the *Salve Regina*, with its antiphon and collect, and then the *Angelus* and a final benediction, processing in pairs out of the chapel to the organ playing the antiphon *Sub tuam protectionem* with its collect *Gratiam tuam*, when they all went across to the Great Hall for supper.

On Sundays, however, and at the major feast days in the church's calendar like Christmas, Easter and Pentecost, holy days of obligation like the Ascension, Corpus Christi and the Assumption, national saints' days like those of St Andrew and St Margaret, or that of St Machar for the diocese of Aberdeen, a fuller liturgical programme obtained, when the chaplains and choir boys sang all the canonical hours throughout the day, and in which the academic community participated more fully than on weekdays. This meant that, having sung Matins and Lauds, at which the academic community was required to be present, the chaplains and choir boys returned to the chapel after breakfast to sing the lesser canonical hours of Prime and Terce; to be followed by a reading of the Martyrology before the celebration of sung high mass, when they were again joined by the whole academic community, fully robed, at which one of the doctors, masters or theology students preached, two others were deacons, with one or more of the liberal arts students acting as servers. The lesser hours of Sext and None were then completed on their own by the chaplains and choir boys before dinner. They were joined by the academic community in the afternoon or early evening for Vespers and Compline, with the blessing and the salutations to the Blessed Virgin with their proper antiphons and collects completing their festal worship of the day before they proceeded to supper.[7]

The Ministers, their Duties and Stipends

Such a detailed programme of worship for every day of the year clearly meant that everybody in the college had to be aware of what duties and responsibilities in chapel were expected of them, and these were outlined in the Foundation Charters of 1505 and 1514. In the first place, all of the eight prebendary chaplains had to be priests and had to be skilled in Gregorian chant and polyphonic music, with measures and descant, and to be examined in their competence before being admitted to their office by senior members of the university. One of them had to be an organist. The choir boys, poor youths or boys, had to be capable and taught in at least Gregorian chant, and were probably domiciled in the cantor's manse. Of the chaplains, the principal, the cantor, was to govern the choir, maintain a song school, draw up the weekly table of those who were to celebrate at the altar, keep all the song books and descants under his care, and note any late arrivals or absentees from divine services. His salary of twenty merks,[8] plus one merk for his surplice, black furred hood and almuce,[9] made a total of £14 per year, which in addition to his free lodgings, reflected the importance of his responsibilities. The sacrist, too, had onerous if somewhat different duties. He was responsible for keeping the college clock in good order and ringing the chapel bells at the times specified for each of the services throughout the day, for arranging the order of processions entering and leaving the chapel on Sundays and festivals, for vesting the altars, ensuring that celebrants had access to the vessels, books and bread and wine required for their particular service, and wore the vestments proper to it, as also for the heating and lighting of the chapel, and its cleanliness at all times. For these manifold tasks in addition to his choral duties, he was also paid twenty merks per year, plus one merk for his surplice, hood and almuce, as well as having free lodgings, and was given an additional twenty shillings yearly to cover his cleaning expenses. He was also required to ensure that the altar cloths, albs[10] and other similar white linen used in the chapel were washed four times a year, for which he was allowed 6*s*. 8*d*. per year 'to distribute to the honest matron or young woman who washed them'.[11] The remaining six chaplains who formed the main bulk of the choir, singing the Hours and acting as deacons and subdeacons when required of them, were each paid sixteen merks per year (£10 13*s*. 4*d*.) plus 6*s*. 8*d*. for their surplice and hood, making a total of £11 and their free lodgings. The organist among them was expected to be familiar with all the chants, and required to play at the accustomed hours on ferial and feast days, for which he received an extra two merks in addition to his stipend of sixteen, and half a merk for his surplice and hood, making a total of £12 6*s*. 8*d*. and free lodgings. The choir boys were each to be given four merks (£2 13*s*. 4*d*.) a year[12] and free lodgings, one of them being designated to ring the bells at those times when the sacrist was occupied on other duties, for which he was to be given two extra merks per year. When in choir, all chaplains were to speak in Latin and be fined if late or absent from services without due reason.

From the above, we recognize that Bishop Elphinstone required a high level of choir discipline, musical knowledge and skills of his prebendary chaplains. It is clear, however, that he took this into account when setting the level of their annual stipends, which were higher than those of many other vicars choral in Scotland at this time, and which had to be distributed to them by the procurator of the university at four set regular intervals throughout the year.[13] Most important of all, like the academic staff, their office was open to life tenure. Much was expected of them, but much, too, was on offer to them: the opportunity to develop their considerable abilities within a stable career governed by a strong sense of community and purpose.

Bishop Elphinstone's Liturgical Reforms and their Consolidation

Such, then, were the basic regulations provided for the guidance of the chaplains and choir boys who sang the Divine Office in King's College Chapel every day. If, however, we compare them with the constitutions of 1506 which Bishop Elphinstone drafted for the twenty vicars choral and eleven choirboys at St Machar's Cathedral,[14] and those which he had already drawn up in 1491 for the sixteen choristers at St Nicholas parish church in the royal burgh of Aberdeen,[15] we begin to realize that they were part of a planned programme of liturgical reform which the bishop intended to introduce throughout his whole diocese. At first sight, we may well be inclined to ask why a busy bishop, already besieged with the cares attached to securing the financial viability of his newly founded university, as well as the constraints imposed upon his time by having to spend several months of each year in Edinburgh on state business, should concern himself with matters he could surely have left to the prebendary canons of his cathedral chapter. But in fact there were a number of compelling reasons for him to give serious thought to the public worship of God when he entered his diocese in 1488.

In the first place, the Offices being sung by the vicars choral throughout his diocese at this time followed no uniform Use, being Scottish variants either of the Sarum (Salisbury) or Roman rite going back to the thirteenth century. In practice this meant that the Order of the Saints to be found in their breviaries and missals, was already crowded with details not only of the lives of those saints who had been universally acclaimed in the western church from the earliest centuries onwards, but also with the Offices of a considerable number of early English saints, into which there had been room to insert the Offices of only a few nationally representative saints like Andrew, Ninian, Columba, Kentigern, Margaret and, for the diocese of Aberdeen, Machar; a situation which sometimes made it difficult to know which Office of the day had priority. Added to this was the effect which the Wars of Independence had had on the Scottish clergy throughout the fifteenth century, given that patriotic works like Walter Bower's *Scotichronicon* and John Barbour's *Bruce*, which attempted to instil into the hearts of their readers a pride in their country's past, and even to re-forge its identity as a nation, were now being widely read by them. This in turn had stimulated a number of their bishops to search back into the lives and missionary endeavours of their own local early British, Celtic or Pictish saints, to encourage pilgrimages to their shrines, and to call for their recognition in the liturgy.[16] A further problem for Elphinstone lay in the fact that his extensive travels abroad on church and state affairs had enabled him to participate in, and become familiar with a number of religious feasts then being incorporated into both the Sarum and Roman rite, like the Holy Name of Jesus, the Iconia, the Five Wounds, the Crown of Thorns and the Compassion of the Blessed Virgin, some of which, although they gave eloquent expression to the devotional piety of the age with its emphasis on the suffering humanity of Christ, had not yet been integrated into his own diocesan service books.[17] Moreover, it must have occurred to Elphinstone that because most Scottish service books were imported from abroad, and since 1450 were now being printed, the Scottish market would soon be flooded with cheap printed editions of breviaries and missals of the Sarum and Roman rites which would thus perpetuate an unsatisfactory and unresolved situation, as far as the Scottish Church was concerned, of an unreformed Scottish liturgy. Clearly, in order to resolve the situation, what was urgently required was the construction of a Scottish Use acceptable to all its bishops, which could be sung in all the cathedrals, collegiate and parish churches throughout the land; a Use based on the calendar of the western church, with its annual cycle of major seasons and feasts, but one which would eliminate most of the old Anglo-Saxon saints of the Sarum rite, and substitute in their place the new feasts of the church together with those Offices which would allow each Scottish diocese to celebrate the feast days of its own local saints.

The undertaking of such a task at this time, however, could hardly have been more unpropitious. For although all Scottish bishops were by now aware of the liturgical deficiencies of their service books, they were simply baulked by the difficulties which such a co-operative interdiocesan venture would entail. The truth was that by the end of the fifteenth century, the structure of the Scottish Church had so evolved as to make it almost impossible for its bishops to speak with one voice on any administrative issue at all. For as far back as 1192, Celestine III's bull *Cum Universi* had not only declared the Scottish Church once and for all time independent of the province of York, but had also decreed that each of its dioceses was to be a special daughter of the Holy See, and subject directly to its jurisdiction alone.[18] This had meant that thereafter all Scottish bishops had acted independently of each other, taking their own spiritual appeals directly to Rome, and taking it in turns to preside over provincial synods, even though they acknowledged St Andrews to be the country's senior see. In 1472, however, Sixtus IV had raised St Andrews to primatial and metropolitan status, which had the advantage of removing Candida Casa from the jurisdiction of the province of York, and the dioceses of Orkney and the Isles from the Norwegian province of Trondheim, thereby placing all thirteen Scottish sees under the jurisdiction of the Archbishop of St Andrews, and providing the Scottish Church with an ecclesiastical unity for the first time in its history.[19] Such a move, however, robbed the dioceses of their right to have their spiritual appeals heard first in Rome, which by tradition they clearly preferred. This situation could only have been aggravated in 1492, when Innocent VIII raised the diocese of Glasgow into a metropolitan archbishopric and province of its own, thus freeing it from the jurisdiction of the Archbishop of St Andrews, and placing under its own jurisdiction the suffragan sees of Dunkeld, Dunblane, Candida Casa and Lismore.[20] Fragmented and rival jurisdictions of this nature were hardly likely to produce the kind of interdiocesan co-operation required for a reformed, printed national breviary.

Even so, it was at this very time that two circumstances combined to bring such a venture into being. The first was that between 1494 and 1504, while Bishop Elphinstone was engaged on completing the new choir he was planning for St Machar's Cathedral, he encouraged a small team of his clergy to search out and gather together the legendaries, local Offices and lives of the early patron saints of the parishes in his diocese as a first step in the compilation of a reformed Aberdeen Martyrology, Breviary and Missal.[21] The second and vital dynamic, which widened the whole scope of this liturgical exercise into a national programme, and partially accomplished its purpose, was the firm practical support given to it by James IV. His reasons for doing so, it is true, were more political than liturgical, in that he saw the establishment of a national breviary throughout the Scottish Church as the ecclesiastical counterpart of his own secular programme for the political hegemony of his country, which by this time he was well on the way to achieving. Moreover, he was then on excellent terms with the papacy, both Innocent VIII and Alexander VI having shown him marks of their especial favour with their gifts to him of a Golden Rose and a silver-gilt sceptre, to which by 1507 Julius II had added a splendid sword of state,[22] so that James could well afford to look benevolently at any scheme which brought a sense of unity to the Scottish Church and the nation.

Now it so happened that the king, as he perambulated the country dispensing justice, had by now become acutely aware that one of the most serious weaknesses in the dispensation of that justice was the total lack of printed statutes of the realm, acts of parliament, and other legal text books required as works of reference by those of his legal officers responsible for administering the laws of the land. Accordingly, after taking advice from his council, he instructed Bishop Elphinstone, as Keeper of the Privy Seal, to establish the country's first printing press in Edinburgh in 1507, and to set up the patent by which two Edinburgh burgesses, Walter Chepman and Andrew Myllar would provide the press, be given the sole right to print such legal texts as were required, and to sell them at prices to be advised by the crown. At the same time, the king gave the two printers the sole right to print those breviaries, missals and martyrologies then being compiled as the Scottish Use by Bishop Elphinstone and others, and that from then on, printed liturgical books of the Sarum rite were to be forbidden entry into the country, and if found, escheated and their importers punished.[23] Supported by this statute, the bishop was then able to widen the co-operation he had already obtained from some of his fellow bishops by sending out his team to the remaining dioceses to collect the hymns, antiphons, collects and legendaries of their local saints, to insert them also into his Aberdeen Breviary, and thus to transform it into one 'efter our awin Scottis use'. It is unlikely that he would have been able to obtain the co-operation of all Scottish bishops without this royal command. But in the event, after three years, thanks to the hard work put into the venture by the printers and the bishop's liturgical team, the first part of this enlarged Aberdeen Breviary, the *pars hyemalis*, was run off the Southgait Press in Edinburgh on 13 February 1510, and the second and final section, the *pars aestivalis*, on 4 June of the same year. It was Scotland's, and indeed, Europe's first national breviary.

When we come to compare the printed version of this Aberdeen Breviary with those then in use in Scotland at this time, the first noticeable difference is to be seen in the removal of many of the Offices of the English saints from their Calendars, Litanies and Propers of the Saints, and their replacement in the Aberdeen Breviary by those of some eighty-one early Scottish saints drawn from right across the country, including those Northumbrian saints with Scottish missionary connections. At the same time, the Offices of a number of the remaining English saints have been down graded in festal rank, and some of their Scottish counterparts, including the patron saints of all the Scottish cathedrals, have been upgraded to become principal major feasts in their place. At first sight this looks like a retaliative liturgical exercise undertaken by its compilers in answer to the damage inflicted upon the Scottish Church and its religious orders by the English during the Wars of Independence, and as a witness of the consequent Anglophobia still latent in the nation. But this would be to misunderstand the purpose of the national breviary. For the past twenty years Bishop Elphinstone had been Scotland's chief negotiator conducting peace treaties with Richard III and Henry VII of England, as a result of which a perpetual peace between the two nations had been signed in 1502, ratified and confirmed by Pope Alexander VI on 28 May 1503, and James IV had married Henry VII's daughter Margaret Tudor on 8 August 1503.[24] This was the very time for all those Scots who daily sang the Divine Office in their cathedrals, colleges and parishes, and indeed for all Scottish priests throughout the land, to draw a line under the negative patriotism of the past two centuries, and to reflect more positively on the lives of those early saints who had laid the foundations of the nation's differing traditions and Christian culture. Again, by satisfying diocesan as well as national needs, it was hoped that a unifying liturgy 'efter our awin Scottis use', would help to heal the more recent rival jurisdictions which had afflicted the Scottish Church. That was the true purpose behind the publication of the Aberdeen Breviary in 1510.

Just how widely this first edition of the breviary was distributed and used throughout the Scottish Church we now have no means of knowing, given the destruction of so many printed liturgical service books in Scotland at and shortly after the Reformation in 1560. There is evidence that it was in use in the diocese of Moray before that event, and it is inconceivable that Bishop Elphinstone would not have ordered its use by the prebendary chaplains at King's College Chapel, the vicars choral at St Machar's Cathedral, the parish church of St Nicholas in Aberdeen and other collegiate churches in the diocese shortly after 1510; and it would appear to have continued in use throughout the diocese thereafter until 1560. Added attractions for its purchase by individual parish priests might also have been its comparative cheapness and its being 'efter our awin Scottis use'. But the fact that it was never reprinted by Chepman and Myllar, or went into a second edition, even to correct its typographical errors, requires an explanation. Certainly, the shock of the king's death with that of most of his nobility, including the young Archbishop of St Andrews at Flodden on 9 September 1513, brought temporary paralysis to the Scottish Church and nation, while the death on 25 October 1514 of the driving force behind the Aberdeen Breviary, Bishop Elphinstone, must have added further uncertainty as to its future. At a more fundamental level, however, there were a number of reasons why this breviary never had a second edition. First, when we come to examine the sources from which the Offices of its numerous early Scottish saints were constructed, we discover that they were not taken from the earliest original medieval sources on which they should have been based, and which were still available to the compilers of the hymns, collects and legendaries to be found in the Breviary, but rather from the Offices of service books then currently in use, a number of which had long required serious revision, especially in the legends of the saints.[25] Such a major revision would doubtless have required a much longer time than we must suppose the compilers felt they had at their disposal to carry out, but the lack of it lost them the opportunity to produce a properly reformed breviary in 1510, and this must have weakened its durability from the outset. Again, a revised printed edition of the Sarum Breviary had already appeared in Rouen by 1497, and it is more than likely that some of these were already circulating in Scotland before their import was forbidden in 1507; indeed, by 1510 Chepman and Myllar were complaining to the Privy Council that Edinburgh merchants were infringing their patent by continuing to import them.[26] But undoubtedly, the most serious obstacle to the wider dissemination of the Aberdeen Breviary throughout the country was the Scottish clergy's continued use of the Roman Breviary. Unlike the Sarum rite, its import was not forbidden under the 1507 patent, which therefore allowed for its free availability in Scotland throughout this period; but more importantly, by the end of the fifteenth century the papacy had realized that the Divine Office of whatever rite was in need of a thorough revision, and Clement VII had ordered Cardinal Quiñones to prepare a new edition. By excising the historical lessons and restoring much of its scriptural content, the

Quiñones Breviary of 1533 went some way to overcome the imbalance and shortcomings of most of the breviaries then in use.[27] Accordingly, it became popular in Scotland before itself being finally taken over by the standard Roman Breviary of 1568, by which time the revision of the Aberdeen Breviary was no longer required or possible. Of all these future events, of course, Bishop Elphinstone could have had no inkling in 1495, when he first began to plan the content of the liturgy to be sung in his college chapel and throughout his diocese. He recognized the need for its reform, and by 1510 he had produced a national breviary and martyrology, which latter, incidentally, was never printed. With all its faults, his breviary was a considerable achievement, although it is unlikely that he himself saw it other than a first step in the right direction.

The election of Elphinstone's successor as Bishop of Aberdeen could hardly have come at a worse moment for King's College. Both the Scottish Church and the nation were virtually leaderless in 1514. James V was an infant, St Andrews still lacked its primate following the death of its young archbishop at Flodden, and neither John Stewart, Duke of Albany, called to be governor of the kingdom, nor Pope Leo X, who had only recently been elected to his office, could have had any clear understanding of the needs of the diocese or of its young university. As a result, the see was vacant for nearly two years while three nominees contested the succession; a situation which was especially perilous for King's College, given that in the absence of a new chancellor, the £10,000 which Bishop Elphinstone had bequeathed in his will, partially for the needs of the university, had not yet been released,[28] and the second Foundation Charter which the latter had drafted by August 1514 to increase its membership, extend its privileges and strengthen its faculties, had not yet been ratified. In the event, Alexander Gordon was provided to the see on 6 June 1516, but suffering from chronic ill health, he died on 30 June 1518, leaving the university even more exposed as Bishop Elphinstone had earlier foreseen, 'to ravening wolves who might invade the college and its flock'.[29]

Fortunately, Gordon's successor, Gavin Dunbar, who was consecrated in St Machar's Cathedral on 20 February 1519, proved to be the very man required to redeem the critical situation into which the university and the diocese had fallen.[30] As Lord Clerk Register of the kingdom he was already one of its most experienced administrators, and he quickly set himself the task of completing Elphinstone's unfinished programmes. Within a few days of his consecration, he toured the college and discussed with the principal and senior masters its most urgent problems. Elphinstone's bequest of £10,000 was unfrozen, and immediately put to use completing the external manses and those parts of the college buildings still unfinished in 1514. He then set in motion the process of obtaining royal and papal confirmation and ratification of all the university's foundation charters, in order to safeguard its constitution, endowments and privileges, which he finally obtained in 1529. But beyond all this rescue work, vital though it was for the college's survival, lay his resolve to carry through and consolidate those liturgical reforms which Bishop Elphinstone had already begun to introduce throughout his diocese. By now a more meaningful Divine Office with its own Scottish Use was being sung by an increased number of highly qualified, life tenured vicars choral in St Machar's Cathedral and in the newly completed choirs of King's College Chapel and St Nicholas parish church. There remained, however, the huge task of completing the cruciform structure of the cathedral, which involved re-modelling its south transept and extending the choir eastwards beyond the central crossing to accommodate the twenty vicars choral already in office, but which choir, in fact, Bishop Dunbar was unable to complete before his death in 1532. During his episcopate, however, he not only consolidated most of Elphinstone's liturgical programmes, but added some of his own. He reconstructed the south transept and furnished it in order to accommodate the extra number of vicars choral until the enlarged choir at the east end would be ready. For the same reason, he built or extended the Chaplains' Court, the residence of the vicars choral near the cathedral's east end. As for the cathedral's interior, we know from its 1549 inventory that he presented to the vicars choral a beautiful vellum epistolary and silver plated gospel book for use in the choir at high mass;[31] and early in his episcopate, between 1519 and 1521, he ordered the construction of the nave's unique heraldic ceiling, a triple row of the shields of the emperor and kings of Europe, the pope, archbishops, bishops and abbots of Scotland, and those of the Scottish king with his nobility, with the shields of the two burghs of Aberdeen and its university terminating the three rows at the west end: an emblematic reconstruction of western Christendom as seen through Scottish eyes at the time.[32] Given, however, that all these shields were orientated towards the focal point of the cathedral's public worship, the Eucharist on the high altar, it would seem that their overall designer, Alexander Galloway, who had already designed a number of sacrament houses throughout the diocese, intended their orientation to have in addition a sacramental dimension, which was meant to be read liturgically, giving added point to the words of the psalm which reverberated throughout the cathedral each time they were sung by the vicars choral in their Divine Office:

> The princes of the peoples are assembled
> With the people of Abraham's God.
> The rulers of the earth belong to God
> To God who reigns over all.[33]

In spite of the deep political uncertainty and unrest of the times, Bishop Dunbar may now justly be seen as the university's second founder. He had restored its financial stability, maintained its academic excellence, and with a number of generous gifts had beautified its chapel and brought added meaning and dignity to those liturgical programmes which its founder had introduced both in the chapel and throughout the diocese. It was left to Bishop William Stewart who succeeded Gavin Dunbar, to confirm them with the publication of his constitutions of 1540, a statement in itself of his readiness both to uphold and to bring further order to them.[34]

THE CHAPEL'S INTERIOR LAYOUT BEFORE 1560

> O Lord, I love the house where you dwell,
> The place where your glory abides.[35]

In addition to the liturgical, constitutional and political evidence which informs us about the university of Aberdeen during its early years, a wealth of contemporary evidence also exists to enable us to recreate the interior of its beautiful chapel at this time. In the first place we have a detailed Inventory of its furnishings and moveable possessions as they were being listed for the college's statutory annual inspection in 1542 by its rector, James Strachan, and four canons of St Machar's Cathedral: a compilation in itself which provides us with an invaluable description of the chapel's six altars with their retables and frontals, with its gold, silver and brass sacred vessels and ornaments with the names of their donors, together with the vestments worn by all those taking part in its services throughout the liturgical year, the choir books they used on these occasions, and with a brief description of the founder's tomb placed centrally before the high altar at the foot of the sanctuary.[36] If we add to this information Hector Boece's own description of the building as he witnessed its construction between 1497 and 1505, and then that of his own participation in its services between 1505 and 1522 when he published his book on the lives of the Bishops of Aberdeen,[37] we are able to bring to life a close picture of divine worship as it existed at King's College during the whole of its pre-Reformation period, and to reflect on the purpose behind its formal structure.

To begin with, we have to remember that the construction and layout of the chapel differed fundamentally from that of a parish church, in that its sanctuary and choir were separated from its nave by a rood screen, which enabled its prebendary chaplains and choir boys to sing the Divine Office in choir throughout the day, to be joined in their own stalls by the college's internal masters and scholars at set times for mass and evening prayers, without the presence of the public. The nave, however, was reserved for those officials of the university, for postgraduate students in law and medicine, and those other external students who lived in manses or lodgings outwith the college and who, on account of their duties or visits to local courts or hospitals, could not be bound to the timetable which governed the attendance in chapel of the internal students. This enables us to see that from the beginning the founder foresaw and planned the liturgical needs of all those university students including married students, for whom stalls were not available in choir, but whom he firmly intended to belong to the academic community by being able, in addition to their studies, to take part in the chapel services when possible. The chapel, thus, was intended for the exclusive use of its university members, and not for the parishioners of Old Aberdeen, the founder having already arranged for their worship by building the parish church of St Mary of the Snows for them nearby, in the western area of College Bounds by 1503, some two years before the official opening of King's College Chapel itself.[38]

With this in mind, we can now visualize how the chapel looked during its early years, and how and why its worship was conducted in the manner it was. In the first place, from the details supplied by the 1542 Inventory, from Bishop Elphinstone's own purchases supplied by Andrew Halyburton, who was the Conservator of the Scottish Staple in Flanders, and from a number of generous donors to the chapel at this time, it is clear that its overall appearance was richly decorous, its individual furnishings and movable possessions showing the same strong Flemish and French influences on their quality and design as did the chapel's structure itself: reminiscent in fact, of Bishop Kennedy's chapel at St Salvator's in St Andrews, after which Bishop Elphinstone had probably modelled his own.[39] It is also clear from the twenty-six candlesticks listed in the Inventory which were placed strategically around the choir and sanctuary, that the chapel could be well illumined when required, especially during the long dark winter mornings and early evenings, when Matins, Lauds and Vespers had to be sung, thus showing that the founder had also reckoned on the country's latitude when planning the chapel's interior. Given the absence of any listing of charcoal burners or other forms of heating in the Inventory, however, it may well be that the founder had to rely only on his provision of the thick serge cassocks and copes to be worn by the participants in these services, to counter the chapel's distinct chill during these hours.

To turn to the chapel's six altars. As will be seen in the accompanying plan (Fig. 2.1), the high altar was centred on the sanctuary and dominated the building's eastern apse. It stood free and was curtained on each side by a rich fabric described in the Inventory as being a mixture of silk and soft wool interwoven with the arms of James IV and Bishop Elphinstone, not only to provide the chapel's focal point, but also as if to underline the cooperation required of both to found the university itself. The altar was dedicated to St Mary in the Nativity,[40] and was backed by a retable (a wooden altar piece or reredos), probably in the form of a long, low, fixed triptych, its central panel probably portraying the familiar Christmas Nativity scene at Bethlehem with the two outer panels as portraits of the two chief donors of the chapel, the king and the bishop, kneeling on either side of the central scene.[41] Of the three interchangeable frontals to the altar, the best, reserved for feast days, was embroidered with scenes from the Virgin's life, the second with figures of the apostles Peter, Andrew and John, while the third was for daily use. A brass candelabra, suspended above the altar, provided extra light during the services. During Lent, when all the statues in the chapel were covered, a large white linen curtain could be drawn right across the sanctuary between the choir and the high altar.

Of the two altars positioned at the foot of the sanctuary, that of the Blessed Sacrament or Eucharist was situated close to the chapel's northern wall, and west of its eastern apse, as shown in the plan (Fig. 2.1). As prescribed by Canon Law, it was built on a north–south axis in order that those celebrating at it should face east when doing so. It was also positioned so as to allow those intending to proceed to the high altar sufficient room to pass between it and the founder's tomb, and to mount the sanctuary steps without hazard. The sacrament house itself, designed by Alexander Galloway, was pyramidal in form, and was either set into the chapel's northern wall close by and just above the altar, or, more likely, given the strong influence of Continental Eucharistic customs on the Scottish Church at this time, was housed on the altar itself.[42] Opposite this altar on the south side of the sanctuary was the altar dedicated to St Catherine and St Barbara,[43] erected by Arthur Boece on the instructions of his brother Hector, who had died in 1536 and had been buried only two or three yards due west from it at the foot of the sanctuary; and fittingly, as the university's first principal, next to the tomb of its founder and his patron, Bishop

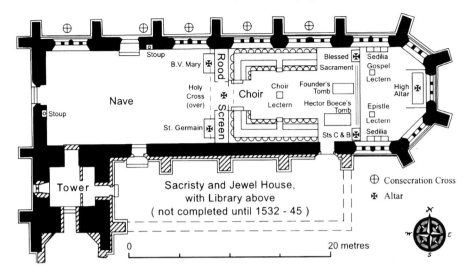

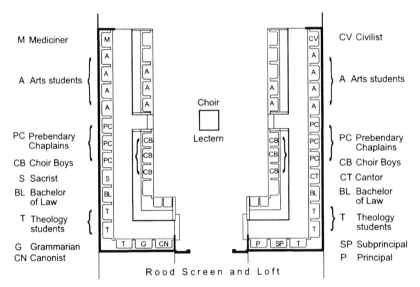

Seating for Civil Law Prebendary of St. Nicholas, Aberdeen,
not provided for in 1514 Constitution
After G. Hay and W. Kelly

Fig. 2.1.   (Above) Plan of King's College Chapel in its pre-Reformation period;
(Below) seating arrangements in 1514

Elphinstone. This altar, like that of the Blessed Sacrament opposite, was close to the chapel wall and was also curtained only on the side nearest to the middle of the sanctuary, the altar itself being backed by an altar piece depicting the two saints on either side of the Virgin Mary, probably in the form of a triptych, in addition to which its front panel displayed the saltire arms of Hector Boece.

Balancing off these three altars on the sanctuary were three in the nave of the chapel, if we include the one on the west side of the rood screen gallery and over its central doorway, all of them being donated by Bishop Elphinstone. The first of these altars, the one to the north of the rood door, was dedicated to the Virgin Mary, to whom he had a particular devotion throughout his life. It had a beautiful altar piece in sculptured wood in keeping with the rood screen itself, which would have depicted a scene or scenes from the Virgin's life. The altar also had two statues similarly richly carved to match the screen, one of the Virgin and the other of the patron saint of Glasgow, St Kentigern; perhaps to remind himself and others of the place of his birth, childhood and young manhood, just as he had reminded himself and others of both saints whose figures he had included in his seal when he was consecrated Bishop of Aberdeen in 1488. Two of its three interchangeable front panels were of embroidered silk depicting both saints surrounded by flowers. The altar to the south of the rood screen's doorway was dedicated to St Germain (Germanus), a saint after whom a hospital in Tranent in East Lothian had been named. The hospital had once belonged to the moribund Bethlehemite Order but Elphinstone had persuaded Alexander VI to transfer its annual revenues to the diocese of Aberdeen as an endowment in 1494 in order to initiate the university's financial viability.[44] This altar had a sculptured wooden retable which also harmonized with, and backed on to, the rood screen, in addition to which it had two statues, one of the Saviour being scourged, and the other of St Christopher. Given that its main frontal in embroidered silk depicted the figure of Our Lady of Pity or Compassion, a fifteenth-century devotion popular in Scotland at this time, it would appear that Elphinstone wished to remind those who worshipped at this altar not only of the suffering endured for them by the Saviour and St Christopher, but to link it in this way with St Germain's hospital and the wider suffering of the age. The third altar in the nave was that of the Holy Cross on the rood gallery itself, placed directly below and west of the rood with its statues of the Virgin and St John on either side, at which mass could be said or the Eucharist venerated on regular occasions for the graduate students below. The furnishings of this altar, together with its appropriate vestments and a missal were donated as a set by William Elphinstone, the rector of Clatt and a kinsman of the bishop.

As for the vestments worn at these six altars, the 1542 Inventory lists in some detail the sets of copes, chasubles, dalmatics and tunics which were available for priests and deacons when celebrating or assisting at mass throughout the year.[45] They were mostly of watered silk, their distinctive colours and embroidered motifs or features being chosen according to the order of the day in the liturgical calendar: possibly white and gold for solemn festivals such as at Christmas and Easter; red for martyrs' feast days; blue or white for the feasts of the Virgin; purple for Advent and Lent; black or purple for requiem masses, and green for ordinary Sundays of the year and non-festive days, as was later to become the norm. And finally, given the high level of musical competence at the chapel throughout this period, and in keeping with its proper sense of the order of its worship, it is not surprising to discover the impressive list of service books noted as being kept in chapel in 1542, consisting of psalters, breviaries, antiphoners, responses and processionals, which were available for the prebendary priests and choir boys when singing the Divine Office every day; in addition to which there was a book of music for the organist and a vocabulary for the cantor, together with a number of missals, epistolaries and evangelaries, some of them beautifully illuminated, which were used by the priests, assisted by their deacons and subdeacons, when singing the high mass of the day.[46]

With these additional details, then, we now have a clearer idea of how the chapel would have looked during high mass on any Sunday during this period. Each internal member of the college would have been in his allotted stall: the doctors and masters in their black serge cassocks,[47] over which each wore a white surplice, cope and almuce; the theology and law students similarly in cassocks, surplices and copes, with short black furred hoods; the liberal arts students in their cassocks, surplices and round hoods; the prebendary chaplains in their cassocks, surplices, copes and distinctive black furred hoods, the cantor and sacrist alone among them wearing in addition their almuces, while the choir boys were dressed like the liberal arts students though without hoods, and possibly, like the prebendary chaplains, distinguished by a different coloured cassock; in the nave, appropriately robed, any additional post graduate students in canon or civil law, or medicine without stalls in the choir, whose professional duties did not require them to be absent elsewhere; and finally the ministers at the high altar in their vestments coloured according to the order of the day, with the music of the mass having been chosen by the cantor for that particular Sunday (Fig. 2.1). All such worship was ornate and highly organized, a not uncommon sight in fact, to be found in any collegiate church or university chapel throughout Europe before the Reformation. Theirs was an ordered, self contained and privileged world, and as yet seemingly unaware of the trials, storms and near shipwreck which shortly lay ahead for many of them. But of one thing we may be certain. Such public worship was for them full of meaning, and far from being empty ceremony, was central to their whole Christian belief, as we shall now see.

The Reformation in Scotland in 1560 was the result of the complex interplay of deeply held political, dynastic and religious convictions which have been widely discussed ever since, but which would be inappropriate to examine in detail here except in as far that they affected Aberdeen and student life and worship at King's College Chapel.[48] In August of that year a well attended parliament, sitting in Edinburgh, passed an act which approved of the Scots Confession of Faith: a Confession which had been strongly influenced by the spread of Lutheran and Calvinist beliefs introduced into the country in the reign of James V, and which had already condemned a number of long-held Catholic practices and beliefs such as the practice of intercessary prayers to the Virgin and the saints, belief in purgatory, in the apostolic authority of the papacy to bind and loose, in auricular confession, and especially, in the real presence of Christ in the Eucharist. The act, however, took the Confession a logical stage further by abrogating the authority of the papacy throughout the land and abolishing the celebration of the mass. At the time it was by no means certain that the Lords of Congregation who had supported the Confession would be able to command the backing of the majority of the community of the realm to carry through such a radical programme of religious reform. Indeed, the return of Queen Mary from France in 1561 could only have intensified the ideological dilemma then facing a number of Protestant leaders of the Government, namely, that of remaining loyal to a Catholic sovereign while being determined to effect their own political and religious ends.[49] Certainly, long before then, most Scots whether Protestant or Catholic, had recognized that the late medieval Scottish Church was in urgent need of pastoral and spiritual reform.[50] The conflict, however, lay in the means by which the church should be reformed: whether from within, through the series of national councils proposed and organized by John Hamilton, the Archbishop of St Andrews, between 1549 and 1559, aided by the issue of his *Catechism* in 1552, as well as through the Council of Trent which had been setting out such reforms since 1545;[51] or outwith the auspices of the church by political revolution and a newly formed system of church government legitimized through acts of parliament; a dilemma, in fact, which was only solved when Mary was forced to abdicate the throne in 1567 and Scotland was committed to the Protestant cause.[52]

From the beginning, the conservative north-east of the country, the royal burgh of Aberdeen and King's College had shown little enthusiasm for the fundamental changes which the reformers deemed to be required of them. William Gordon, the Bishop of Aberdeen since 1546, was aware of the spread of heresy as he saw it, and seconded a master of theology from his cathedral, John Watson, to refute it by preaching throughout the diocese,[53] as well as absenting himself from the Reformation Parliament in 1560 and supporting Queen Mary in the civil war which followed her return from France; and these actions, together with the Catholic presence of the powerful Earl of Huntly nearby, may have given the area a sense of reassurance that it would only be temporarily affected by such radical ideas. But in the event, Bishop Gordon lacked the spiritual leadership and personal example to provide a convincing challenge to the reformers' alternative form of church government, in consequence of which the cathedral was vandalized by a raiding party from Angus and the Mearns in December 1559, falling into further disrepair when its roof was stripped of its lead, its bells removed from the tower, and much of its artistic heritage destroyed.[54] More in keeping with the reformers' convictions and purpose, the Divine Office and the mass were no longer allowed to be celebrated in the cathedral, its canons and vicars choral were pensioned off, and the building was re-established as the parish church of Old Aberdeen in place of the Snow Kirk. The reformed church, however, was not yet sufficiently established to supply a fully alternative ministry throughout the country, and it was not until 1569 that a reformed minister was appointed to the newly created parish church of St Machar. Even so, Bishop Gordon could not be dislodged from his office, and he died unmolested in his palace in Old Aberdeen in 1577. As for the merchant community of the royal burgh, it was at first reluctant to become embroiled in religious change. A close oligarchy of prominent local families, they were loyal to the crown, had established good relations with their nearby bishops in the past, and were proud of their newly enlarged parish church of St Nicholas. But understandably they were more concerned with their commercial activities and burgh affairs, and until the reformed church was able to stabilize itself and they were able to identify themselves with the newly formed kirk session of St Nicholas and to establish a more workable political relationship with the local lairds, they preferred to keep their heads down.[55]

So it was that the firmest resistance to the Reformation in Aberdeen came not from its bishop, nor from the merchants of the royal burgh, but from the principal and senior masters of King's College, and we have to ask ourselves why this was so. In order to justify and consolidate their political and ecclesial position in the country, both the government and the General Assembly of the reformed church had realized by 1561 that it was essential that the three universities conformed to the doctrinal, humanist and administrative reforms laid down in the Confession of Faith and the First Book of Discipline, if necessary by force. Doctrinally, as they saw the situation, the fundamental reason why the papacy could not reform its fiscal and pastoral system of government, and the abuses which had arisen from it, was that its traditional claim to possess universal jurisdiction over the whole of Christian Europe on the grounds of the primacy afforded to its office, had no basis in fact, neither had its claim that the nature of the church required a sacrificing, hierarchically ordained ministry, supposedly ruled over by the successors of Peter. As they saw it, too, it was also clear from the First Book of Discipline that Renaissance humanists among the reformers had already exposed the poverty of late medieval scholasticism, with its barbarous Latin, its out of date philosophical realism and its unreformed biblical scholarship. It was therefore necessary to eradicate from the courses then being offered in the three Scottish universities, especially in their faculties of the liberal arts and theology, those writings of earlier theologians and canon lawyers which reflected these erroneous concepts, and to substitute in their place those which had been purified and approved by biblical scholars and Renaissance humanists of the reformed church. Only in this way could they provide a new foundation from which ministers of the reformed church in Scotland would be able to preach the word of God to their parishioners based on the sacred scriptures alone.[56]

On 15 January 1561 the subprincipal of King's College, Alexander Anderson, its canonist John Leslie and other clerics, were summoned to Edinburgh by the Convention of Estates to subscribe to the Confession of Faith and account for the university's failure to reform itself on the lines laid down by the First Book of Discipline. They refused to subscribe to the Confession, and in their ensuing debate with John Knox and other Protestants ministers, they firmly upheld the university's refusal to accept the curriculum reforms required of them.[57] They argued that from the foundation of the college in 1505, its liberal arts courses had been based on all that was best in Renaissance humanism at the University of Paris. Far, then, from being lectured in barbarous Latin on the out of date works of medieval schoolmen, their first-year students had been introduced to texts written in the purest styles of classical literature and history given by their own outstanding teachers and humanists, Hector Boece, William Hay and John Vaus, and later in Greek by Theophilus Stewart, while the studies in their later years included modern nominalist commentaries on Aristotelian logic, ethics and metaphysics as the text books of their teachers would confirm.[58] This being so, they saw little advantage in replacing their own programme of studies for one based on similar lines in the First Book of Discipline, and they would not do so. Their own courses in the liberal arts were, they asserted, both Christian and humanist, neo-Platonic and neo-classical, and their purpose, when joined to the daily community worship in chapel, had been so designed to lead the students to love God and serve their fellow men.

Anderson and his colleagues, however, made no headway in their discussion on the structure of the church and the primacy of papal jurisdiction, or on the mass and the sacraments. Each side claimed the legitimacy and truth of their assertions, and according to Leslie, nothing was concluded and their audience was left confused. Given, however, that these arguments were central to the whole Reform movement still raging throughout Europe, and were to affect the eventual fate of public worship in King's College, it would seem essential to look at them a little more closely in order to understand their importance to those involved in them at this time. On the matter of the structure of the church and the primacy of papal jurisdiction, Anderson as a licentiate in theology, would probably have followed the Church's centuries-old traditional teaching, based on Matthew 16.18–19, as well as the letter of St Clement to the Corinthians, the works of St Irenaeus and the early Fathers, and the statements of medieval popes.[59] Knox, in his reply, ridiculed such claims, and would have countered them with arguments drawn from the writings of Calvin, opposing an hierarchical order for the church and replacing it with the authority given, rather, to the four offices of Christian ministry (pastors, doctors, elders, deacons); probably adding, as well, Luther's concept of the priesthood of the laity and the primacy belonging to Scripture alone. Their debate on the mass and the sacraments was no less confrontational and unresolved. As Knox understood the Eucharistic service, for example, the bread and wine offered to their congregations were simply the visible signs which represented the body and blood of Christ as a memorial of his once and for all propitiatory sacrifice and did not in any way constitute their conversion into his real presence. To interpret the service otherwise, as one in which the elements required adoration, was blasphemous. In this sense, therefore, anniversary masses offered by priests for the repose of the souls of the faithful were based on a false premiss. The orthodox Catholic view of the mass, presumably presented by Anderson as the theologian, would have insisted that far from being blasphemous, it was the ultimate act of worship. It was not only a memorial of Christ's passion, death and resurrection, implicit in his words spoken at the Last Supper,[60] but also that at the consecration, the elements of bread and wine truly became the sacramental presence of his body and blood, the inner reality of the risen and glorified Christ, a created act of God, a symbol, a sign, bringing into being something which was not there before; and to those present, a pledge of God's love for them. This being so, anniversary masses simply called upon Christ as the Redeemer, to look with mercy on the souls of the faithful departed and to intercede for them with the Father. Thus, as they stood, both views were irreconcilable, and small wonder that nothing was concluded. Eight fraught years were to pass before they were.

In the year following this bruising encounter, Queen Mary took King's College under her protection, which for a short while brought it a well needed breathing space, exempting it from a fresh tax which had been imposed upon the clergy in 1561, besides lessening the pressures on it to reform its teaching courses. In 1565, according to Knox, the Queen ordered Bishop Gordon to forbid the celebration of the Divine Office and the mass in King's College Chapel, from which we may infer that both were still continuing to be celebrated there however irregularly, in defiance of the law.[61] But this fragile situation could not withstand the political turmoil which engulfed the country during these years, and following Queen Mary's abdication in favour of her infant son, and upon the regency's passing to the Earl of Moray, her Protestant half-brother, in 1567, events moved swiftly to bring it to an end.

On 29 June 1569 Anderson, now principal of the university, and two of his regents in arts, were summoned by a special commission ordered by the Earl of Moray to subscribe to the Confession of Faith and to ensure that King's College carried out the reforms required of it. They appeared the next day and steadfastly refused to do so. Accordingly they were deprived of their posts 'as persons dangerous and unmeet to have the care of the instruction of the youth', and the college and its property ordered to be handed over to the provost of Aberdeen for safe-keeping until persons of sound doctrine were appointed to replace them.[62] By no means were all the remaining teaching staff dismissed, however. The mediciner, canonist, civilist, grammarian and sacrist were each allowed to continue in office, although clearly the sacrist would no longer be able to pursue all of his former duties in chapel: an indication in itself that in order to make a radical break with the existing order at King's, it was first necessary to reform the faculties of the liberal arts and theology, and to recreate the whole structure of daily worship in the chapel. We lack the records to know exactly what happened to the remaining seven prebendary chaplains of the choir and their choir boys, who would have become redundant by these reforms. Presumably, like the vicars choral at St Machar's Cathedral and those at the parish church of St Nicholas in Aberdeen, those who subscribed to the Confession would have been allowed to keep a proportion of their stipend and to seek employment elsewhere either in keeping with their musical accomplishments, or as tutors to families among the reformed burgesses and local lairds. Those who refused to subscribe would have been excommunicated and outlawed, and either went abroad, or found employment as tutors in the households of the minor nobility in the north-east who still practised the old faith, even if covertly; we cannot tell. But as for King's College Chapel itself, after 1569 it was no longer possible to practise the public worship which had been offered there since 1505. The Divine Office was no longer sung, the mass no longer celebrated. A new era had begun.

Notes

[1] *Fasti*, 53–64; Eeles, 1956, 174–83, 190–91, 200–03, 217–33, 244–55.

[2] See D. B. Forrester's article 'Worship' in *Dictionary of Scottish Church History and Theology*, ed. N. M. de S. Cameron, Edinburgh, 1993, 894–97; and D. B. Forrester and D. M. Murray (eds), *Studies in the History of Worship in Scotland,* Edinburgh, 1984.

[3] Psalm 118 (119), v. 164: '*Septies in die laudem dixi tibi…*'.

[4] See Chapter 3.

[5] *Fasti*, 53–64, 80–108; Eeles, 1956, 154–259.

[6] The manses of the prebendary chaplains and choir boys were built where the present University Road joins College Bounds, the present 48 College Bounds being on the site of the cantor's manse, the sacrist's next door at 46, for which see the map of Old Aberdeen in James Gordon, *Abredoniae utrius descriptio, A description of both touns of Aberdeen,* ed. C. Innes, Spalding Club, Edinburgh, 1842; and Macfarlane, 1995, 339.

[7] The times and arrangements for all these services were laid down in the college's foundation charters of 1505 and 1514, for which see Eeles, 1956, 154–265 and *Fasti*, 53–64, 80–108.

[8] The Scots merk, like the English mark, was originally valued at 13s. 4d. By 1506, however, its value against the English pound had fallen to four Scots merks for £1 sterling. These Anglo-Scottish rates have been compiled by J. M. Gilbert in 'The Usual Money of Scotland and Exchange Rates against Foreign Coin', in *Coinage in Medieval Scotland (1100–1600),* ed. D. M. Metcalf, British Archaeological Reports 45, Oxford, 1977.

[9] A surplice is a white, wide-sleeved linen garment worn over the cassock. The almuce was originally a hooded fur scarf, worn for warmth around the neck and shoulders by cathedral canons and vicars choral when in choir during the winter months. In the later Middle Ages it also appears to have become a mark of dignity of office. The regulations at King's College in 1505, for example, suggest that it was worn in choir only by the doctors and masters of the academic community, and by the cantor and sacrist alone among the prebendary chaplains. J. F. Niermyer, *Mediae Latinitatis Lexikon Minus,* Leiden, 1984, 35; *The Oxford Dictionary of the Christian Church,* ed. F. L. Cross, Oxford, 1997.

[10] An alb is a long white, wide-sleeved linen garment, corded at the waist, worn by priests at liturgical functions.

[11] *Registrum Episcopatus Aberdonensis,* ed. Cosmo Innes, Edinburgh, 1845, II, 102–06, especially at 105, which outlines the duties of the sacrist at St Machar's Cathedral, on which those of the sacrist at King's College were modelled, for which see Eeles, 1956, 216–23, especially at 220–21.

[12] Five merks each for four choir boys in 1505, but reduced to four merks for six choir boys in 1514, Eeles, 1956, 224–27.

[13] Eeles, 1956, 222–23.

[14] *Registrum Episcopatus Aberdonensis,* ed. Cosmo Innes, Edinburgh, 1845, II, 92–106.

[15] *Cartularium Ecclesiae Sancti Nicholai Aberdonensis,* ed. J. Cooper, Aberdeen, 1888, I, 255–60; Aberdeen, 1892, II, 226–38, especially 231–33; Macfarlane, 1995, 269–71.

[16] D. McRoberts, 'The Scottish Church and Nationalism in the fifteenth century', *Innes Review,* XIX, 1968, 3–14.

[17] R. W. Pfaff, *New Liturgical Feasts in later Medieval England,* Oxford, 1970.

[18] R. Somerville, *Scotia Pontificia,* Oxford, 1982, 3–10.

[19] Leslie J. Macfarlane, 'The Primacy of the Scottish Church 1472–1521', *Innes Review,* XX, 1969, 111–29.

[20] Leslie J. Macfarlane, 'The Elevation of the Diocese of Glasgow into an Archibishopric in 1492', *Innes Review,* XLIII, 1992, 99–118.

[21] The team was most likely drawn from Duncan Scherar, the procurator of St Machar's Cathedral, Alexander Galloway, and four of the bishop's own kinsmen, William, Alexander, Adam and Robert Elphinstone, with the work being co-ordinated by Archibald Lindsay, the precentor of the Cathedral, for which see Macfarlane, 1995, 240–43.

[22] Charles Burns, *Golden Rose and Blessed Sword: Papal gifts to Scottish Monarchs,* Glasgow, 1970.

[23] *Registrum Secreti Sigilli Regum Scotorum, 1488–1529,* ed. M. Livingstone, Edinburgh, 1908, I, no. 1546.

[24] T. Rymer, *Foedera,* XII, London, 1712, 787–804; Macfarlane, 1995, 426.

[25] For which see J. D. Galbraith, *The Sources of the Aberdeen Breviary,* Aberdeen University M Litt Thesis, 1970, and Macfarlane, 1995, 231–46. These legends formed the basis of the historical readings to be found in each Office.

[26] R. Dickson and J. P. Edmond, *Annals of Scottish Printing from 1507 to the beginning of the Seventeenth Century,* Cambridge, 1890, 84–85.

[27] D. McRoberts, 'Some sixteenth-century Scottish Breviaries', *Innes Review,* III, 1952, 33–48; I. A. Muirhead, 'A Quignonez Breviary', *Innes Review,* XIV, 1963, 74–75.

[28] Boece, 107, 114, 120, 122.

[29] *Fasti*, 63; Eeles, 1956, 182–83.

[30] For details of his life and career see E. John Powell, 'Bishop Gavin Dunbar: Second Founder of the University of Aberdeen', *AUR,* LVI, 1995, 151–61.

[31] For these gifts see Aberdeen University Library MSS 22 and 250, as listed in M. R. James, *A Catalogue of the Medieval Manuscripts in the University Library Aberdeen,* Cambridge 1932, 108 and 85–86. For a complete printed edition of the Epistolary, see *Epistolare in Usum Ecclesiae Cathedralis Aberdonensis,* ed. B. McEwen, Aberdeen, 1924.

[32] David McRoberts, 'The Heraldic Ceiling of St Machar's Cathedral, Aberdeen', *Friends of St Machar's Cathedral Occasional Papers,* No. 2, Aberdeen, 1981; and W. D. Geddes and P. Duguid, *Lacunar basilicae Sancti Macarii Aberdonensis. The heraldic ceiling of the cathedral church of St Machar, Old Aberdeen,* Aberdeen, 1888.

[33] Psalm 46 (47).10.

[34] *Registrum Episcopatus Aberdonensis,* ed. Cosmo Innes, Edinburgh, 1845, II, 110–21; Eeles, 1956, 68, 99, 131.

[35] Psalm 25 (26).8.

[36] This is AUL, Sh. 23d 1. Its Latin text with an English translation and detailed commentary is in Eeles, 1956, 4–69.

[37] Boece, 93–97.

[38] Fuller details of the construction of the parish boundaries of Old Aberdeen in order to accommodate its own parish church and to separate its function from that of King's College Chapel, are supplied in Macfarlane, 1995, 314–16.

[39] For which see R. G. Cant, *The College of St Salvator,* Edinburgh, 1950, and the same author, *The University of St Andrews: A Short History,* 3rd edn, St Andrews, 1992, 26–33.

[40] Eeles, 1956, 83, 36, infers from this title *Sancta Maria in Nativitate,* that the altar was dedicated to the birthday of the Blessed Virgin, 8 September, but this would have been a most unusual dedication at this time, and the phrase was and is normally translated to refer to the birthday of her Son, 25 December. On the altar was a 'large table made by pictorial art with great skill'.

[41] The probability has been argued that the late fifteenth- or early sixteenth-century portrait of Bishop Elphinstone, which the University of Aberdeen has always owned, may once have formed the right-hand, southern, panel of this altar piece, since the left-hand edge of the original wood bears clear evidence of hinge marks, which would also fit in with the kneeling prayerful pose, design and size of the original triptych; for which see Macfarlane, 1995, 334–35, 462 and 467, note 45; Lorne Campbell, 'Scottish Patrons and Netherlandish Painters in the Fifteenth and early Sixteenth Centuries' in *Scotland and the Low Countries 1124–1994,* ed. G. G. Simpson, Edinburgh, 1995, 89–103. However, Lorne Campbell points out (below p. 102) that there is no specific evidence to indicate that the portrait panel came from King's Chapel. It could equally have come from the cathedral or a private chapel.

[42] The position of the sacrament house in relation to its altar is also discussed by Eeles, 1956, 60–65, but is so vaguely described in the 1542 inventory as to prevent any definite conclusion. Alexander Galloway, rector of Kinkell, and Rector of the University (*c.* 1480–1552) designed and donated surviving sacrament houses at Kinkell and Dyce. Kelly, 1949, 28–30.

[43] It would appear that Hector Boece had a particular devotion to these two saints. St Catherine of Alexandria was the patron saint of clerical students, for which see the *Bibliotheca Sanctorum,* Rome, 1963, III, cols 954–78; for St Barbara, *Bibliotheca Sanctorum,* Rome, 1962, II, cols 751–76.

[44] The negotiations effecting this transfer are discussed in full in Macfarlane, 1995, 309–11.

[45] A cope is a long, semi-circular embroidered silk cloak or cape worn by ecclesiastics in choir and in processions; a chasuble is a sleeveless oval mantle worn over the alb, coloured according to the liturgical season or the feast day; a dalmatic is a short, coloured, open-sided tunic worn by deacons over all other vestments. Eeles, 1956, 10–13, 32–35, 52–55.

[46] Eeles, 1956, 17–20, 66–68.

[47] A cassock is a close-fitting, full length, sleeved, buttoned through dress, coloured according to the rank or office of the wearer.

[48] The literature on the Scottish Reformation is vast. A useful bibliography is supplied by J. Kirk in *Records of the Scottish Church History Society,* 23, 1987, 113–55. Among recent studies see especially I. B. Cowan, *The Scottish Reformation,* London, 1982; J. Kirk, *Patterns of Reform: Continuity and Change in the Reformation Kirk,* Edinburgh, 1989; J. Wormald, *Court, Kirk and Community: Scotland 1470–1625,* London, 1981; *Essays on the Scottish Reformation 1513–1625,* ed. D. McRoberts, Glasgow, 1962; Alister E. McGrath, *Reformation Thought: An Introduction,* 2nd edn, Oxford, 1993.

[49] R. A. Mason, 'Covenant and Commonweal: the Language of Politics in Reformation Scotland', in *Church, Politics and Society: Scotland 1408–1929*, ed. Norman Macdougall, Edinburgh, 1983, 97–126.

[50] Leslie J. Macfarlane, 'Was the Scottish Church reformable by 1513?' in *Church, Politics and Society: Scotland 1408–1929*, ed. Norman Macdougall, Edinburgh, 1983, 23–43.

[51] Thomas Winning, 'Church Councils in Sixteenth-Century Scotland', in *Essays on the Scottish Reformation 1513–1625*, ed. David McRoberts, Glasgow, 1962, 332–58.

[52] Maurice Taylor, 'The Conflicting Doctrines of the Scottish Reformation', in *Essays on the Scottish Reformation 1513–1625*, ed. David McRoberts, Glasgow, 1962, 245–73.

[53] Gilbert Hill OFM, 'The Sermons of John Watson, Canon of Aberdeen', *Innes Review*, XV, 1964, 3–34.

[54] David Stevenson, *St Machar's Cathedral and the Reformation*, Aberdeen, 1981, 8, 14–15; David McRoberts, 'Material Destruction caused by the Scottish Reformation', *Innes Review*, X, 1959, 126–72; see below note 2, p. 189.

[55] Allan White OP, *Religion, Politics and Society in Aberdeen 1543–1593*, PhD Thesis, University of Edinburgh, 1985; B. McLennan, 'The Reformation and the burgh of Aberdeen', *Northern Scotland*, 2, 1974–77, 119–44.

[56] For the manner in which the new foundation of studies of the reformed Church was introduced into the University of St Andrews, see Ronald G. Cant, *The University of St Andrews: A Short History*, 3rd edn, St Andrews, 1992, 51–67; into Glasgow, see John Durkan and James Kirk, *The University of Glasgow 1451–1577*, Glasgow, 1977, 225–346; and eventually in Aberdeen, David Stevenson, *King's College, Aberdeen, 1560–1641: From Protestant Reformation to Covenanting Revolution*, Aberdeen, 1990, 20–40, 149–66.

[57] The full debate has not survived, but a number of points raised during it appear in *John Knox's History of the Reformation in Scotland*, ed. W. C. Dickinson, Edinburgh, 1949, I, 352–54, and *The Historie of Scotland written first in Latin by Jhone Leslie*, ed. E. G. Cody and W. Murison, Edinburgh, 1895, II, 449–50; see also Stevenson, 1990, 9–10.

[58] J. Durkan and A. Ross, *Early Scottish Libraries*, Glasgow, 1961, 67–69, 77–78, 113–14, 150–51; for details of the whole of the courses in the liberal arts during this period, see Macfarlane, 1995, 362–72; for the humanist movement at Paris during this time, see *French Humanism 1470–1600*, ed. W. L. Gundersheimer, London, 1969, 65–89, 163–80.

[59] In Matthew 16.18–19, Christ gives Peter the keys of the kingdom with the powers to bind and to loose. These texts and a number of other related documents were normally included in the commentaries of theologians and canonists lecturing on the *Sentences* of Peter Lombard to Theology students in the medieval universities, for which see Macfarlane, 1995, 373–76; but see also K. Schatz, *Papal Primacy from its Origins to the Present*, Collegeville, Minnesota, 1996, and H. Denzinger, *Enchiridion Symbolorum et Definitionum*, Friburg, 1913, 20, 23, 39, 46, 67, 72.

[60] Matthew 26.26–28; Mark 14.22–24; Luke 22.17–20; and at the synagogue at Capharnaum, John 6.52–60.

[61] *John Knox's History of the Reformation in Scotland*, vol. 2, ed. W. C. Dickinson, Edinburgh, 1949, 141.

[62] Stevenson, 1990, 17.

CHAPTER THREE

MUSIC AND CEREMONIAL, *c.* 1500–1560

By John Harper

The basic design and layout of the chapel of King's College, Old Aberdeen, are quite distinct from those of the nearby cathedral of St Machar or the parish church of St Nicholas. The simple rectangular building divided by a galleried screen lacks the aisles, ambulatories, transepts, additional chapels, or even architecturally distinct nave. This is evidently not a space for substantial ceremonial or great processions. The dominant physical feature of the eastern half of the chapel is the carved stalls. Here the college assembled on three sides: the focus here is not, as in a parish church, the eastern altar, but the central lectern with the liturgical books. The elaboration of the liturgy is to be found in this space, dominated by word and song rather than by ceremony and ritual movement.

The provision of stalls and presbytery is typical of both monastic and cathedral churches: it is the restricted space east of the stalls which is untypical (Fig. 2.1). For an original college of thirty-six members, of whom about half were in holy orders, the modest presbytery offers restricted space for ritual at the high altar. Furthermore, that space was shared in due course with two other smaller altars as well as the founder's tomb. Parallels are to be found in the chapels of the English educational colleges, in the household chapels (especially the royal household chapels), and in chantry colleges, some of which occupied the eastern end of parish churches.[1] Of those conceived in the later fifteenth century or later, many have dimensions in their eastern half comparable with King's College, Old Aberdeen: a width of just under thirty feet, and a length of sixty to seventy-five feet. What do vary are the extent and configuration of the portion of these chapels west of the screen. At King's the western part of the chapel was originally almost half the length of the whole building. Furthermore, there are doors in both the north and west walls which have adjacent water stoops; these doors offered access to those living outside the confines of the college quadrangle.

Bishop Elphinstone established a pattern of worship in his college chapel which included three elements: the individual recitation of the daily mass by each priest at one of four (later five) lesser altars; the collegiate pattern of daily mass and Office; additional devotions in honour of the Blessed Virgin Mary. In an educational foundation this extensive pattern was achieved by separating two distinct groups: the academics (tutors and students), and the choral body of prebendaries and boys. Implicit in this division is a distinction of both duties and musical skills.

While the individual masses celebrated by each priest with a single assistant (boy or student) were spoken, all the other services in the chapel would have been almost entirely sung: '*dicentes*' in the pre-Reformation Church normally meant singing not saying. The singing was dominated by plainsong (*cantus Gregorianus*). The greater part of this singing consisted of recitation of prayers, readings, psalms and canticles on a single note with simple melodic decoration to mark points of punctuation. Such straightforward singing was a basic skill to be expected of any priest or ordinand, whether alone (in the prayers and readings), or collectively (in psalms and canticles). It was a practice learnt young and used daily. It did not require musical notation: the conventions were known and applied readily to any written text.

The remainder of the chant was written down in notation (though many knew great portions of it by heart). This included the repertory of the Ordinary chants of the mass (Kyrie, Gloria in excelsis, Credo, Sanctus, Agnus Dei) which varied according to the season or the rank of the day, and the far larger corpus of antiphons for psalms and canticles at the Office services (several thousands in number over the year, but often following standard formulaic patterns), and the antiphons at the Introit, Offertory and Communion in the mass (over five hundred in a year, and more elaborate musically). The remaining chants were especially elaborate, and included special sections for skilled singers (Gradual, Alleluia or Tract at mass, the Responds at Matins). Additionally there were the metrical texts of hymns in the Office, and Sequences at the mass with more syllabic chants. The ability to sing the chant was a minimum requirement of the choir boys at King's, but this extended by implication to the rest of the college.[2]

At St Machar's Cathedral, Bishop Elphinstone also set competence in singing plainsong as the minimum musical requirement for the twenty vicars choral who formed the core of the singing body there.[3] At his college he required significantly more of the eight choral priests (*prebendarii*). Ideally they were not only to be skilled in chant but also in singing polyphony. These skills included both the ability to sing written-down polyphonic music (pricksong) and also different kinds of improvised polyphony (descant, faburden, figuration).[4] Elphinstone, perhaps with a note of resigned realism, set a minimum of skills in singing the chant and certain aspects of improvised polyphony (faburden and figuration).[5] Even with these more limited musical requirements it is clear that Elphinstone had higher musical expectations of his singing priests in his new college than in his cathedral.

The most skilled and senior of the prebendaries was the Cantor. He had charge of all the music and ceremonial in the chapel (as did a precentor in a cathedral) and of instructing the boys in music (generally deputed to a lay instructor or master of the choristers by this time in English choral foundations). His charge as music teacher includes both the choir boys and also students with bursaries (*alios bursarios*), indicating that Elphinstone wished to raise the standards of singing among the students as well as the choral foundation.[6] It also shows that the acquisition of musical skills was an ongoing process among the boys and students: clearly they did not have all the skills or know all the repertory, and their participation in the service music was most likely selective. However, the four (later six) choir boys had at least to have the ability to sing the chant.[7] Their original place in the chapel is perhaps indicated by the four small stalls facing east in the front row (Fig. 3.1), though the Foundation Charter of 1514 states that they were to sit in front of the prebendaries, facing north and south.

One other musical requirement is specified in the foundation statutes: the appointment of an organist from among the prebendaries.[8] At this time the abilities to play the organ and to sing polyphony were more closely related since both required improvisation on plainsong. Evidence from English choral foundations establishes that boy choristers were all taught to sing improvised polyphony and a smaller number also learned to play the organ.[9] When these boy choristers became clerks or priests, as many did, they already possessed the skills needed in choral foundations. Thus it is not surprising that Elphinstone specified a priest-organist rather than a layman.

The need to have adequate time for learning conflicted with the demands of sustaining the sung celebration of the daily mass and Office. Therefore, the statutes are selective in their requirements. There was no need for any priest to attend the sung services so long as he fulfilled the general obligation to say the mass and Office daily, the first of which could be achieved at a simple 'low' mass, the second by private recitation from the Breviary at any convenient time. Recognizing that there was a risk that those committed to academic duties might not place attendance at the choral services as a high priority, Elphinstone suggested that all priests should be available to celebrate mass three times each week.[10]

On working days (Monday to Saturday, excluding feast days) the choir boys and prebendaries attended the chapel daily to sing Matins (i.e. Matins and Lauds), mass of the day, and Vespers (i.e. Vespers and Compline). On Sundays and feast days (i.e. non-working days) the whole college attended these services; additionally, the boys and prebendaries sang the little Offices (Prime, Terce, Sext and None). All these services took place in the eastern half of the chapel.[11]

On working days the boys alone with the Cantor sang Lady Mass, celebrated by one of the prebendaries.[12] This most likely was celebrated in the western part of the chapel at the Lady altar. This may seem demanding for the children, but in fact the chant for the Lady Mass was the same from one day of the week to the next; there were only four main cycles of chants for the Lady Mass during the year, according to the season. No doubt the college boys sang the chants from memory: they would not have needed stalls or desks at the Lady altar. They may perhaps have elaborated the chant with improvised polyphony: together with the Cantor this would have been possible, and the increase in numbers of boys in 1514 would have made it more practical, even if some of the boys were assisting as servers at the altar. Lady Mass sung by boys (or by a Lady Chapel choir) in cathedrals and monasteries was often attended by a lay public, for whom the Blessed Virgin Mary provided a particular devotional focus at this period, and this may have been the case at Old Aberdeen — not only in the cathedral but also in the college.

Only one form of service invariably involved the whole college on a daily basis throughout the year. This was the singing of three antiphons in honour of the Blessed Virgin Mary, each with an accompanying collect, versicle and response, at six o'clock in the evening, before dinner. Again this is typical of comparable foundations at the time, though not always was the whole community required to be present elsewhere, nor were the antiphons necessarily sung in church or chapel. At King's College, Bishop Elphinstone intended the antiphons to the Blessed Virgin Mary to be sung in the chapel, for they required the use of the organ. Furthermore, the foundation statutes stated that the antiphons were to be sung 'solemnly' (*solemniter*).[13]

Solemn observance of the liturgy is used to distinguish the daily singing of the Marian antiphons and also to mark the celebration of the mass on Sundays and feast days.[14] Such solemnity was marked by the dress of those present, the vestments used in the sanctuary, the numbers of candles lit, and the elaborateness of the ceremonial. It was also reflected in the music of both the mass and other services on Sundays and feast days. There were special solemn tones of the chant to be used in some items. More especially solemnity was achieved by the use of polyphony, whether sung or played on the organ.

The daily antiphons of the Blessed Virgin Mary were sung by all present, and therefore to plainsong melodies (*cantu*). According to the statutes the musical solemnity of the ceremony was bestowed by the use of the organ. The organ at this time was not used to accompany singing during services, but rather to play passages of chant decorated polyphonically in alternation (*alternatim*) with the singers. On Sundays and feast days the musical solemnity may have been achieved by choral polyphony or by use of the organ.

It is possible to establish from the Aberdeen Breviary which feasts were observed in the college, and which texts were sung at the Office. However, there is neither surviving chant nor polyphony. The evidence of books of chant surviving from other Scottish foundations suggests that most of the repertory coincided with that used in secular churches in England and Wales (the so-called Sarum or Salisbury Use), if with minor variants.[15] The small quantity of sixteenth-century Latin polyphony found in extant Scottish sources suggests that native works were comparable in style to those by contemporary English composers, but the manuscripts also contain some music from the Continent.[16] The extent of improvised polyphony is by its nature impossible to measure, though its nature can be deduced from surviving instruction manuals.

On Sundays and feast days the solemnity of the music was almost certainly concentrated on specific items. Evidence from British sources of the period suggests that polyphony was used for the last of the responds and the Te deum at Matins, for the Ordinary of the mass, for the Magnificat at Vespers, and at the Office hymn at Matins, Lauds, Vespers and Compline. Contemporary English and Continental keyboard sources include a substantial number of settings of Office hymns. In these hymns the organ played one verse and the singers sang the next to chant (or perhaps polyphony) in alternation. The organ may also have been used at the Offertory in the mass. In the absence of sources for polyphony associated specifically with King's College, how much polyphony was sung, how much of it was improvised, and how much was composed remains a matter of conjecture.[17] The amount of polyphony sung or played, and the extent of its stylistic and technical complexity, will almost certainly have varied from one feast to another, and from one season to another. It was most often prevalent and elaborate at the greatest feasts: Christmas, Easter, Pentecost, Corpus Christi, All Saints and specific saints. At King's such celebrations may also have included the feasts of the Assumption of the Blessed Virgin Mary (the chapel was dedicated to St Mary) and St Andrew.[18] On other Sundays and feast days any polyphonic provision may have been more modest.

Solemnity was marked not only by the elaborateness of the music, but by the location of the singers in the chapel. On ordinary working days all those present stood in their place in the stalls for both Office and mass (unless they had duties at the altar in the mass). On Sundays and feast days designated singers stood at the lectern in the middle of the choir stalls, from which they ruled the choir, and at mass the solo sections of the Gradual and Alleluia may have been sung from the gallery of the screen (the pulpitum). The ceremonial use of the pulpitum for singing certain chants on feast days is also reflected in the location of the organ: it is not simply a convenient place for an organ to be located, it also has ritual (and specifically festal) significance.

The archival evidence establishes that by 1500 organs were numerous in cathedrals, monasteries, colleges and many town parish churches throughout Britain; many had two or more organs, including one in the choir and one in the Lady Chapel. However, only three fragments of instruments[19] and two detailed contracts survive from the sixteenth century.[20] From the archival and physical information, it is possible to propose (albeit tentatively) that the organ on the pulpitum in King's College would have had one keyboard, a chromatic compass of forty-six notes, between five and seven stops, and pipes no longer than five feet in length.

The quality of surviving artefacts in the chapel may suggest that the original casework and sound of the organ may have been exquisite, but it was probably not physically large or forceful. Here, and in other comparable college and household chapels, the ambience is intimate; the acoustic effect close and immediate. This intimacy may have extended to the choral singing and especially the polyphony. Four (and later six) boys and eight priests (one of whom was organist) is not untypical of the size of a skilled choral body at the time (Fig. 3.1). At the sung mass some may have been in the sanctuary, and there may have been no more than one or two voices available for each part. Though the performance may have been physically intimate, we should not assume that it was gutless: again we can only speculate, and allow that then as now personal taste may have influenced the sound and style of each individual choir.

Frustrated as we may be that so little hard evidence remains of the repertory of the pre-Reformation chapel of King's College, Old Aberdeen, sufficient information can be gleaned from the dimensions, layout and furnishing of the chapel building, from the statutory requirements for the pattern of attendance and worship, and from the Aberdeen Breviary to enable us to suggest that what was taking place here was typical of a number of British colleges, chantries and household chapels of the period. Each had its own institutional and liturgical nuances, and must have been influenced in its detail by local practice and personnel as well as by the taste and personal experiences of its founder and senior staff. But ultimately we can recognize a remarkably consistent pattern of daily worship and devotional observances inflected by the distinctions of Sundays and feast days from ordinary working days, and by the liturgical seasons. In all these institutions it is the sound of the chant which we should remember as

Fig. 3.1.   King's College Chapel,
small seats for the choir boys

prevalent, adorned only rather occasionally on special days or at special moments by
the sound of vocal polyphony and of the organ. Such was almost certainly the practice
of the priests and boys of King's College in the years before 1560.

Notes

[1] As at Arundel, Fotheringhay, and Ludlow.

[2] The Cantor instructed the boys and other students (*alios bursarios*); discussed later. At a number of
English colleges the statutes specifically required all the fellows to be competent in plainsong.

[3] '. . . *in cantu Gregoriano ad minus periti et docti . . .*', *Registrum Episcopatus Aberdonensis*, 2 vols, ed.
C. Innes, Edinburgh, 1845, II, 92.

[4] '. . . *octo prebendarii in sacerdotio constituti in cantu Gregoriano rebus factis videlicet priksingin figuratione
faburdon cum mensuris et discantu periti et instructi . . .*', *Fasti*, 60.

[5] '. . . *in cantu Gregoriano rebus factis faburdon et figuratione ad minus bene instructi . . .*', *Fasti*, 60.

[6] '*Inter quos octo prebendarios primus erit cantor cujus officium erit in elevatione et depressione circa cantum cantores
regere et chorum gubernare ac ministros in tabula ordinare scolas per se tenere et in eidem hujusmodi quatuor pueros et
alios bursarios in cantu instruere et docere ad singulos in choris et scolis transgressores et errores circa cantum et
ceremonias punire corrigere et reformare*', *Fasti*, 61.

[7] '*In quo erunt etiam quatuor juvenes seu pueri pauperes abiles tantum in cantu Gregoriano ad minus instructi*',
Fasti, 60.

[8] '. . . *qui unum de predictis in ludo organorum peritum instituere teneatur*', *Fasti*, 62.

[9] Jane Flynn, 'The education of choristers in England during the sixteenth century', in ed. John
Morehen, *English Choral Practice 1400–1650*, Cambridge, 1995, 180–99.

[10] '*Et predicti omnes magistri presbyteri et prebendarii cum dispositi fuerint ter in hebdomeda dominicis presertim et aliis festivis diebus ad misses celebrandas se disponant et celebrent', Fasti, 61.*

[11] See above for more details.

[12] '*. . . missam in honore et commemoratione beate Marie virginis diebus congruentibus per dictum cantorem et quatuor juvenes cantari volumus et per unum de sex minoribus prebendariis exequi et celebrari', Fasti, 61.*

[13] '*. . . precipimus et obnixe exhortando rogamus quolibet die hora sexta post meridiem post vesperas ante cenam salve regina cum antiphona et collecta necnon angelus ad virginem sub tuam protectionem et collecta gratiam tuam etc. alternatis vicibus cum duodecim magne campane per intervalla pulsibus ad quartam partem hore circa sextam solempniter cum organis et cantu per dictos omnes et singulos magistros doctores regentes prebendarios juvenes et studentes cantare precipimus et devote', Fasti, 63.*

[14] '*. . . dominicis et festivis matutinis vesperis et completerio una cum missa solempniter celebrata . . .', Fasti, 61.*

[15] Isobel Woods, '"Our Awin Scottis Use": Chant usage in medieval Scotland', *Journal of the Royal Musical Association*, 112/1, 1986–87, 21–37.

[16] The outstanding Scottish composer of the earlier sixteenth century was Robert Carver (1487–1566), and a significant number of his compositions survives (edited in *Musica Scotica*, 1, Glasgow, 1996). He was an Augustinian canon of Scone Abbey, much involved in the royal household chapel at Stirling, and very likely known to the bishops of Aberdeen of his time. See James D. Ross, *Musick Fyne: Robert Carver and the Art of Music in Sixteenth-century Scotland*, Edinburgh, 1993; also the studies of Scottish church music before 1603 by Isobel Woods Preece (see note 15), (edited posthumously), *Musica Scotica*, Glasgow, forthcoming.

[17] Most of the English liturgical organ music is edited in *Early English Church Music*, vols 6 and 10, and in *Musica Britannica*, vols 1 and 66.

[18] Special commemorations with '*apparatu et pompa*' are specified on the days following these feasts in the foundation statutes, *Fasti*, 62–63.

[19] The much restored case at Old Radnor, Powys, and two soundboards from Wetheringsett and Wingfield, Suffolk, on temporary loan to the Royal College of Music, London.

[20] All Hallows by the Tower, London (1519–21) and Holy Trinity, Coventry (1526). On the sixteenth-century organ in England see Stephen Bicknell, *The History of the English Organ*, Cambridge, 1996, 11–59; and John Harper, *Sacred Pipes and Voices*, Oxford, forthcoming.

CHAPTER FOUR

THE MEDIEVAL BUILDING

By RICHARD FAWCETT

THE DATING EVIDENCE

Bishop William Elphinstone's plans for his new *studium generale* received the approval of Pope Alexander VI on 9 February 1495,[1] and the initial funding for his college was evidently in place by the following year. Preparations for building the chapel, which was to be dedicated to the Trinity and the Blessed Virgin Mary in her Nativity, may have been in progress in 1497–98 if Elphinstone's purchase of gunpowder, carts and wheelbarrows through the agency of Andrew Halyburton, Conservator of Scottish Privileges in the Netherlands, can be taken as an indication.[2] The site is said to have been inherently unstable because of swampiness, and extensive groundworks, involving the construction of a timber raft, were necessary before building could begin, according to Gordon of Rothemay writing in 1659;[3] even this did not prevent some settlement. It may have been the dampness of the site which led to the lower walls being built of a hard red sandstone of unknown provenance, whereas the rest of the masonry was of cream-coloured stone thought to be from Covesea on the Moray Firth.[4]

An inscription on the west front, to the left of the doorway arch, dates the commencement of building operations to 2 April 1500, though the significance of this date may have been more allegorical than real (Fig. 5.1).[5] Since the inscription is cut back into coursed masonry rather than incised on a monolithic tablet, its provision was presumably something of an afterthought. It has been pointed out that there are analogies between the date of foundation of the chapel as given in the inscription and the date that had come to be associated with Solomon's Temple, suggesting that Elphinstone had decided to emphasize a link between the foundation of his own chapel and that of the first House of God.[6]

Work must have been well advanced by 1504, since the arms of James, Duke of Ross and Archbishop of St Andrews, who died in that year, are above the north doorway. 1504 is also the date above the arms of James IV on a heraldic tablet on the northern of the two buttresses on the west side of the tower, which is almost at the height of the wall head of the main body of the chapel. The other arms of members of the royal family displayed along the west front are those of the king's illegitimate son, Alexander, who succeeded the Duke of Ross as Archbishop of St Andrews, and of Queen Margaret Tudor, whom the king had married in 1503 (Figs 10.1–10.4). The former is on the southern of the tower buttresses and the latter is on the northern

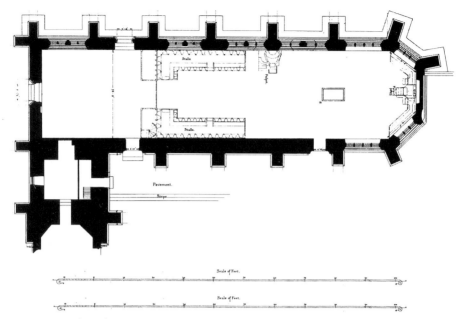

Fig. 4.1.   Plan of King's College Chapel, by J. C. Watt, 1885 (Copyright: University of Aberdeen)

buttress of the west front.[7] It must be assumed that work on the masonry of the chapel itself was substantially complete by 1506, since a contract for the lead-work of the roof was drawn up on 21 October with John Burwel or Burnel, Sergeant Plumber to Henry VII of England.[8] The chapel was ready for dedication in 1509,[9] by which date collegiate life had probably been active for a number of years.

It is possible that non-essential features, including perhaps even the crown steeple, were only finished once completion of the main brunt of work allowed a little breathing space, as discussed in Chapter 8. Nevertheless, the crown steeple must certainly have been nearing completion by 1522, since it is specifically referred to in Boece's account of the lives of Aberdeen's bishops, which was published in that year.[10] The range which used to run along much of the south side of the chapel, and which contained the sacristy, library and jewel house, was probably among the last parts to be completed because the arms of Bishop William Stewart (1532–45) were placed on it (Fig. 4.6).

A DESCRIPTION OF THE CHAPEL

The chapel is an aisle-less rectangle of six bays with a three-sided eastern apse (Fig. 4.1). Off the south side of its western bay is the tower, which is slightly longer on its north–south than its east–west axis. The demolished two-storeyed range, which housed the sacristy, treasury and library, extended along four bays of the south

Fig. 4.2.   The west doorway

flank and abutted the east side of the tower. The bay divisions and angles along the
west and north sides of the chapel and round the apse are marked by buttresses. There
are two main entrances into the chapel: a processional doorway at the centre of the
west front and a doorway in the second bay from the west on the north side. The
latter was presumably intended as the usual entrance into the nave. It is possible that
the west doorway was in fact a secondary insertion, since it is not fully coursed in with
the adjacent masonry and its bases have a slightly unresolved relationship with the
plinth course,[11] though at least some of these inconsistencies may result from
inaccurate renewal of masonry at a number of phases (Fig. 4.2). Both of these
doorways have three-centred arches with continuous mouldings rising from simple
bases. There were also two doorways into the sacristy range, one from the nave,
opposite the north doorway, and the other from the choir, through the second bay
from the east; since the demolition of the range these have been modified to form
external doorways.

The walls rise from a simple chamfered plinth course (Figs 4.3, 4.4, 4.5). Running
below the windows around the west and north sides and around the apse is a
continuous string course, which is generally higher below the nave windows than
below those of the choir. This string course steps down below the east light of the
window in what was the western bay of the choir, and then steps up again beneath
the two central lights of the next window to the east. The latter was possibly done

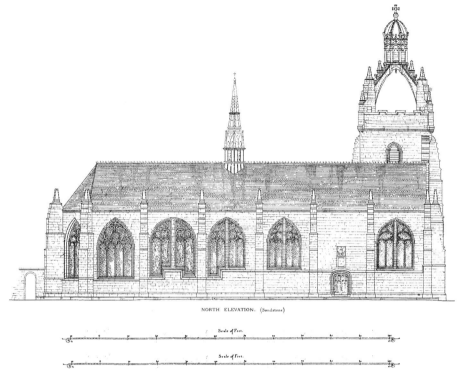

NORTH ELEVATION. (Sandstone)

Fig. 4.3.   The north elevation of King's College Chapel, by J. C. Watt, 1885 (Copyright: University of Aberdeen)

with the intention of having some liturgical feature such as a sacrament house or altar internally at this point, though in the event the choir stalls were to extend beyond here in their eventual arrangement and there is now no sign of any internal feature associated with this upward stepping.[12] The buttresses have multiple in-takes towards the wall-head and are capped by rather stumpy pinnacles; since the demolition of the fire-damaged sacristy range, buttresses have also been added along the south side of the chapel and the east side of the tower.

There are four-light windows in the west front and in all but one of the north flank bays, the exception being the bay with the nave doorway, which has no window (Fig. 4.3). There is also a four-light window in the easternmost straight bay on the south side, the only bay which was clear of the sacristy range (Fig. 4.4). Along the rest of the south flank, above the site of the sacristy, are irregularly spaced untraceried windows of two or three arched and cusped lights, punctuated by projecting sections of masonry; those to the choir are flat-headed, while those to the bays which originally formed the nave are very slightly arched. In the three faces of the apse, the windows are of three lights and have modern tracery, though that in the east face represents an attempt at authentic restoration on the basis of surviving evidence.[13] The main window arches throughout the chapel are varyingly pointed. The arch of

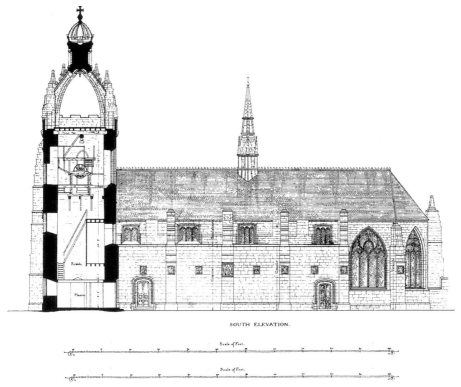

SOUTH ELEVATION.

Fig. 4.4.   The south elevation of King's College Chapel, by J. C. Watt, 1885 (Copyright: University of Aberdeen)

the window in the west front is almost semi-circular, while the window in the fifth bay from the west on the north is only slightly pointed. A notable feature of the windows in the west front and along the north flank is the massive central pier-like mullion which rises unbroken from the sill to the arch apex. This feature is absent from the windows around the apse (Fig. 16.8). However, all of the windows without a heavy central mullion, together with the easternmost windows on the north and south flanks which do have one, contain tracery which is entirely of the restorations of 1891 and 1931 on the evidence of early views of the chapel and of measured elevations dating from 1884.[14] On this basis, therefore, the only windows in which we can assume with reasonable certainty that the tracery perpetuates what was first built are that in the west front and those in the first, third, fourth and fifth bays of the north flank. The first three of these survived because their upper parts continued to light the library which was housed in the nave between about 1772 and 1870, while the fourth and fifth windows of the north flank were apparently preserved by being walled up. The medieval tracery is largely composed of tiered groupings of cusped mouchettes above rounded light heads; in the west window the light heads are uncusped.

WEST ELEVATION.

Scale of Feet.

Fig. 4.5.   The west elevation of
King's College Chapel, by J. C. Watt,
1885 (Copyright: University of
Aberdeen)

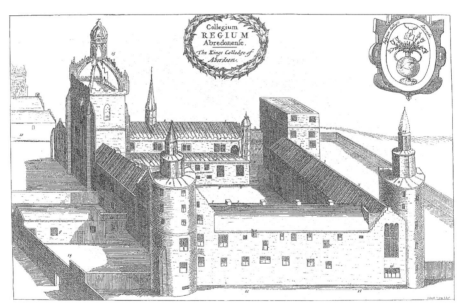

Fig. 4.6.   James Gordon's view of King's College, *c.* 1660 (Copyright: University of
Aberdeen)

The roof, which is now slated but was originally leaded, overhangs the cavetto wall-head cornice. This cornice is simply moulded except above the site of the sacristy range, where it has foliage decoration. Gordon of Rothemay shows a crenellated parapet, but little original evidence now remains of this unless a moulding at the north-east angle of the tower was meant to tie in with it (Fig. 4.6). The hexagonal lead-sheathed flèche, with simple pinnacles at the angles, is set on the roof apex over the fourth bay from the west, a little to the east of the original location of the choir screen; it was completely rebuilt in the seventeenth century.[15]

The south-west tower rises a single storey above the main body of the chapel and its oblong rather than square plan is particularly evident on the west side, where the buttresses are asymmetrically set in relation to its east–west axis (Fig. 4.5). It is possible that the final plan of the tower was the result of modifications introduced while work was in progress, and the part beyond the south buttress is off-set relative to the rest of the west front. It is significant that the internal space is square despite the overall oblong plan. Nevertheless, it must be remembered that towers of oblong plan were by no means unusual in Scotland, as may be seen at Stirling Holy Rude Church or Dysart Church in Fife, while buttresses might often be set well back from the angle they abutted, as is evident in the choir of Bothwell Collegiate Church in Lanarkshire for example or the nave of Dunglass Collegiate Church in East Lothian.

Surmounting the tower is a crown steeple with four flyers rising from diagonally set buttress-like pinnacles which slightly oversail the angles of the tower wall head. The pinnacles were originally pierced at their base by openings which were required because a pyramidal roof reduced access around the top of the tower to a wall-head walkway (Col. Pl. I).[16] The four flyers have arched soffits, while their straight angled upper faces are decorated with cusped cresting and an intermediate decorative pinnacle. The flyers support a central octagonal lantern-like drum with a blind arch on each of its faces and miniature columns at the angles, and this drum is capped by an open-arched imperial crown with an orb and cross finial. It is now difficult to be certain how much of this crown steeple is of the original build and how much dates from George Thomson's rebuilding of 1634, and this will be discussed further below.[17]

Internally the chapel is divided into two unequal parts by a timber choir screen. Ever since the 1873 re-ordering, the nave has been reduced to an ante-chapel of two bays, with the rest given over to a larger collegiate choir than was first intended. In the original arrangement, the screen was set one bay further east, thus leaving space for a nave of three bays, and the window in the fourth bay from the west is slightly displaced to the east to allow the screen to be located in that position. On the west side of the screen were altars dedicated to the Virgin and St Germain, to the north and south of the central doorway into the choir. Above the screen was the rood loft, with the altar of the Holy Cross at its centre, and there was a doorway from the upper floor of the sacristy range on to that loft which is now blocked. Within the eastern part of the chapel the choir stalls initially occupied much of the two west bays, while the presbytery area around the high altar was beyond the doorway into the sacristy. The position of the high altar was emphasized by a foliate corbel on each side, immediately before the turning of the apse. The chapel is covered by a timber wagon ceiling of flattened three-centred cross-section, which has been restored on more than one occasion but is still essentially authentic (Figs 16.8, 16.10).[18] Decorating the surface of the boards which formed the ceiling is a pattern of ribs set out in reflection of the configuration of stone quadripartite vaulting. At the intersections of the ribs are bosses from which sprigs of carved foliage radiate, and there are similar sprigs near the bases of the transverse ribs.

THE ARCHITECTURAL BACKGROUND TO THE DESIGN

No great work of architecture is produced in an artistic vacuum, and if we are to develop an understanding of a building such as King's College Chapel, we have to try to come to an appreciation of the range of ideas which may have stimulated those responsible for the design. This can be very difficult in later medieval Scotland, when it seems that patrons and craftsmen were looking directly to a much wider range of sources of inspiration than had their predecessors, and there can be no certainties. Nevertheless, knowing something of the architectural climate at the time the chapel was built, as well as of the cosmopolitan outlook of Bishop William Elphinstone himself, we can at least speculate on how the design of the chapel may have come to take the form that it did.

The plan.   The plan of King's College Chapel, with its six largely undifferentiated aisle-less bays terminating in a three-sided apse, was well-suited to the ecclesiastical needs of a collegiate community. The eastern apse is the feature which most obviously illustrates how Scottish architectural patrons in the later middle ages were choosing to look beyond England for their inspiration. It is true that, in the years around the marriage of James IV to Margaret Tudor in 1503, there was some renewal of interest in what was happening south of the Border, especially in works in which the king had an involvement, and we shall have to consider this further in looking at King's College's crown steeple. It is also true that a number of English buildings from the earlier fourteenth century onwards were being built with polygonal eastern apses, as at Lichfield Cathedral, Coventry St Michael or Madley Church in Herefordshire. Nevertheless, in England eastern terminations of this kind were very far from typical, and on balance it seems likely that it was a European rather than an English model which ultimately underlay what we see at Aberdeen.

Aisle-less apsidal churches are to be found throughout mainland Europe, though the idea was exploited earlier and more widely in France than elsewhere, and it was perhaps in France that chapels of this type were always most common. This is not the place to give detailed consideration to the historical development of this type of plan, but it can be said that in France it was evidently deemed to represent a particularly appropriate solution to the needs of what might be described as 'single purpose chapels' like those required by both ecclesiastical and secular lords. A relatively early example, albeit with a rounded rather than a polygonal apse, is the bishop's chapel at Noyon Cathedral, dating from about 1180–83, and a particularly fine illustration of

Fig. 4.7.   Vincennes Castle Chapel from the north (Photo: author)

the other episcopal examples is that at Reims, of the years around 1200. On a grander scale the type was to be deemed especially suitable for royal chapels, the best known example being the Sainte Chapelle in Paris of about 1242 to 1248,[19] though royal chapels of this plan were to be built over a long period, as demonstrated at Vincennes, where the castle chapel started in the late fourteenth century was eventually completed in the sixteenth (Fig. 4.7). In many of the French seigneurial chapels the principal space was at first-floor level, where it could be reached directly from the lord's lodging, with a less imposing place of worship for the household on the lower floor. The main chapel was certainly elevated in this way at many of the episcopal chapels, as well as at the Sainte Chapelle. But at Vincennes the floor was raised only a little above the external ground level, and this also seems to have been so in a number of cases where the plan type was adopted for a Lady Chapel attached to a major church, as at St Germain des Prés in Paris of about 1245 or at St Germer de Fly, which was begun around 1259.

We do not know as much as might be wished about university chapels in France, since these might be expected to have offered more accessible potential prototypes for King's College. But one example known through illustrations is the destroyed chapel attached to Cluny College in Paris, which was begun in 1269.[20] This apsed aisle-less structure appears to have had its main space at ground level, and in the overall proportions (if not necessarily the scale) as well as the relative proportions of windows to walls and buttresses we see a building which has clear similarities with King's College Chapel.

Attention has been concentrated on French examples of the plan type since, as has been said, it was probably in that country that some of the different ways in which the plan could be used had their origin and early development. It should also be remembered, however, that the plan was adopted for a variety of purposes in other countries. Since we shall be considering the possibility of links with the Netherlands for certain aspects of the design of King's College Chapel, it is worth pointing out here that there are many smaller parish churches which were rebuilt either wholly or partly to this plan in the later middle ages across that area, and especially within what is now Holland.[21]

On this evidence it may be thought inherently likely that Elphinstone's choice of plan for his new chapel was conditioned by what he had become familiar with in mainland Europe, and it must be recalled that, in addition to having been himself a student at Paris and Orleans, he had been an ambassador in France, the Netherlands and the Holy Roman Empire, and may have personally observed some of the buildings referred to above. However, it must also be recollected here that, by the time he was starting work on his chapel, Scotland itself already had a number of churches with this type of plan.[22] Under the abbacy of Colin (1460–91), the choir of the Cluniac abbey of Crossraguel, for example, had been rebuilt to this form, while the new collegiate choir of Seton church had been set out on this pattern by the first Lord Seton before his death in about 1478, though the simple clarity of the plan there was eventually compromised when Lady Janet Seton began to add transepts after the death of her lord at Flodden.

Several other Scottish examples could be cited, but the most important for our purposes is the collegiate chapel of St Salvator at St Andrews which, on present evidence, may be the earliest polygonally apsed chapel in Scotland, having been started by Bishop James Kennedy in 1450. There can be little doubt that European — and especially French — influences were a major consideration behind many aspects of Kennedy's planning of his St Andrews college. It has been pointed out that its constitution owes much to that of the university of Paris, as well as to those of Oxford and Prague,[23] and it is also worth noting that the exquisite college mace was cast by the goldsmith of the French dauphin, Jean Mayelle.[24] St Salvator's Chapel is therefore a leading contender for being the vehicle by which this type of plan was introduced into Scotland, both on grounds of its early date and of its founder's francophile sympathies.

A comparison of the plans shows the Aberdeen chapel to be slightly wider than St Salvator's (8.76m and 8.55m respectively) and significantly longer, with an internal length of 37.2m as opposed to the 32.7m of St Salvator's Chapel, even though the latter is of seven rather than six bays (Fig. 4.8). There are also differences resulting from the individual relationship of each of the chapels with the rest of their college buildings. Thus, at St Andrews the south flank of the chapel faced on to the street, with the rest of the college to the north, whereas at Aberdeen it was the west front which faced on to the street with the main body of the college to the south. Nevertheless, allowing for these differences, the overall plans are strikingly similar, and in each case there is a bell tower at the south-western corner, which is so

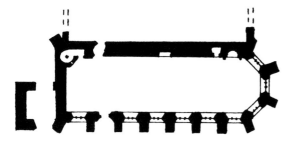

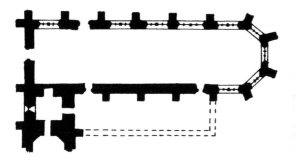

Fig. 4.8.   Plans to the same scale of St Salvator's College Chapel at St Andrews (top) and King's College Chapel (bottom) (Drawing: author)

positioned that it contributes to the street front of the chapel; thus at St Andrews it adjoins the west front and acts as an extension of the south flank, while at Aberdeen it adjoins the south flank and provides a continuation of the west front. There may have been further similarities in the relationship of the sacristy block to the chapel in each case. At Aberdeen, as we have seen, it ran along the south flank, on the side towards the main quadrangle, and had doors into it from both choir and nave. At St Andrews it was also on the side towards the quadrangle, and the way in which the two doorways on the north side of the chapel there open away from the chapel itself may indicate that the range was similarly planned to run along the greater part of the chapel's length.

On this evidence there is a good case for thinking that Elphinstone's immediate source for the plan of his college was St Salvator's Chapel, though in our ignorance of the chapels at most other Scottish colleges, it must be conceded that there could have been other intermediaries as well. Thus in this aspect at least Elphinstone was probably directly influenced by Scottish prototypes, even if what he encountered in Europe had predisposed him in favour of the type. But when we move on to look at other aspects of the design of his college we become increasingly aware of the wide range of ideas which may have conditioned the end result.

The window tracery.   The tracery of those four windows in the west front and north flank which appears to be largely authentic has patterns of tiered mouchettes arranged symmetrically on each side of a continuous central mullion (Fig. 4.9). In most cases

Fig. 4.9. Diagrammatic sketches of window tracery at King's College Aberdeen. 1–3, north flank; 4, west front. Not to scale (Drawing: author)

Fig. 4.10. Diagrammatic sketches of window tracery. 1, St Monans Church; 2, Stirling Church; 3, Linlithgow Church. Not to scale (Drawing: author)

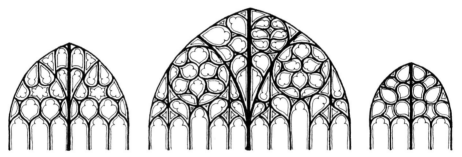

Fig. 4.11. Diagrammatic sketches of window tracery. 1, Liège St Jacques, clerestory; 2, 's-Hertogenbosch Cathedral, south transept; 3, Utrecht Cathedral, Doomprosten Chapel. Not to scale (Drawing: author)

the mouchettes are round-headed or only very slightly pointed, and thus reflect the rounded heads of the lights, the main exceptions being in the western window of the north flank, where the heads of the mouchettes are pointed. Putting aside consideration of the central unbroken mullion for the moment, the closest Scottish analogy for the majority of the Aberdeen windows is in the south choir flank at the church of St Monans in Fife, where the windows probably date from around the time of the establishment of the Dominican friary in 1471 rather than from the original building of the church in 1362–70. For the western window of the north flank at Aberdeen, which has two inward-pointing mouchettes above the light heads and vertically set axial mouchettes at the apex, there are analogies with windows in the choirs of the burgh churches of Linlithgow and Stirling, the former probably dating from between about 1497 and 1532 and the latter from between 1507 and 1542.[25] On this basis, the windows accord well enough with a date in the years around 1500 (Fig. 4.10).

At none of those other churches, however, is there what is the most distinctive feature of Aberdeen's windows, the massive central mullion in all of the windows in which the original tracery design is thought to survive. These vary in thickness, that in the fifth bay from the west on the north being especially broad, while in the west front window the shorter side mullions are almost as broad as that in the centre, with image corbels on all three. Mullions running the full height of a window, from sill to window arch are to be found elsewhere in a variety of contexts. In English Perpendicular architecture they are common as symmetrically set pairs on each side of the central axis of the window. In some cases, as in the Beauchamp Chapel at Warwick St Mary, of 1441–52, they can be almost as massive as at Aberdeen, though they are usually less so and their apparent mass is generally modulated by mouldings. Axial mullions are very much rarer in England, though there are examples in the flanks of the Beauchamp Chapel, where there is a distinction between the part of the mullion which supports the sub-arches of the window and the part which continues up through the tracery field to the arch apex, suggesting that a different effect was being cultivated than at Aberdeen. Nevertheless, some isolated examples of a continuous central mullion without such differentiation are to be found in England, as in the choir clerestory of Christchurch Priory, possibly of between 1502 and 1530, or, on a much more robust scale, in the west window of Wymondham Priory, started around 1445. But, as with apsidal plans, they are so exceptional in England that it is unlikely that any could have provided the germ of the idea for Aberdeen.

If enough of a search were carried out it would almost certainly be possible to find examples of axial mullions throughout most parts of western Europe. In France, for example, they are to be seen in the great windows of the north transepts at the cathedrals of Tours and Troyes, both dating from the earlier fourteenth century. But the area in which they are almost certainly found in the greatest numbers is the Netherlands, and it is also there that they are most commonly found in combination with rather freely disposed groupings of mouchettes comparable with those at Aberdeen. The largest single number of cases is to be seen in the clerestories and transepts of the church of Liège St Jacques, where the axial mullion is a particular leitmotif of that highly enriched church (Fig. 4.11).[26] However, most of what is seen there was the work of Arnold van Mulken between 1513 and 1533, and is therefore later than the examples at Aberdeen.

Further examples which might be cited are in the transepts of 's-Hertogenbosch Cathedral, which were under construction between about 1445 and 1517, and the north transept of Brussels Notre-Dame-du-Sablon, where the transepts were probably reached in the middle decades of the fifteenth century. Although all of these were conceived on a very much grander scale than the Aberdeen windows, and the central mullions tend to be treated more decoratively, sometimes with a pinnacle in front of the main tracery field, the groupings of mouchettes in the south transept at 's-Hertogenbosch do show some distant kinship with those at Aberdeen. Care has to be taken in making comparisons, since much of the detail now seen at 's-Hertogenbosch dates from a restoration started in 1886, though the reinstated tracery was based on the evidence of early views. However, since the tracery at 's-Hertogenbosch was probably only put in place between 1505 and 1517,[27] it is unlikely to have been a specific source for Aberdeen so much as an indicator of the range of ideas current in one of the areas that may have been particularly influential on Elphinstone.

The same is also true of a window at Utrecht Cathedral which has tracery with comparable forms, though in this case both the scale and the date are rather closer to the work in King's College Chapel (Fig. 4.11). The window in question is in the south wall of the Domproostenkapel on the east side of the south transept, a chapel known to have been remodelled for Dean Simon van der Sluys in about 1497.[28] Elphinstone certainly passed through the Netherlands in 1495 in the course of an embassy to the Emperor Maximilian when he was charged with discussing the possibility of a marriage between the emperor's daughter, Margaret, and James IV. At that time he stayed in Bruges during Holy Week, when he carried out some of the duties of the Bishop of Tournai, before moving on to meet the emperor at Worms.[29] Whilst he is unlikely to have passed through Utrecht itself on that journey, and the Domproostenkapel may not even have been designed by then, it is certainly a possibility that the memory of related recent buildings he had seen in the Netherlands were fresh in his mind when work started on King's College Chapel. Indeed, since his plans for the college were probably beginning to take shape as early as 1495, it could even be that members of his entourage — including perhaps a mason? — were specifically charged with noting details of buildings they observed in the course of their travels.

The wagon ceiling.   What we see in the windows at King's College Chapel is tracery which was almost certainly designed by a Scottish mason whose approach to the problem before him was firmly conditioned by current Scottish tastes, but who was also being required to respond to fashions in continental Europe by a patron of markedly European outlook. The result is a fascinating hybrid. We may see something of the same admixture of ideas in the timber wagon ceiling which covers the chapel, and again we are made conscious of the presence behind the project of a patron with a keen concern to ensure that what was created for him was an adequate reflection of his role as an international statesman and prelate.

At St Salvator's Chapel in St Andrews, which as suggested above may have been the model for the plan of King's Chapel, a stone vault had been built for Bishop Kennedy as the covering of the internal space. Since this was removed in 1773 we cannot be entirely certain of its form, though it is very likely that it was a pointed barrel vault. It cannot be ruled out that Elphinstone initially also intended to place a stone vault over his chapel, though it is perhaps significant that his buttresses are more widely spaced and less deep than those at St Andrews, suggesting that a stone vault is not quite so likely to have been the original intention, and it would certainly be hard to imagine a more appropriate covering than the timber wagon ceiling we now see.

Scotland had a long history of constructing timber wagon ceilings. The cathedral of the bishops who saw themselves as leaders of the Scottish Church, at St Andrews, which was started soon after 1160, was relatively unusual in having high stone vaults over the eastern arm as well as over the lower spaces of the aisles, though even there the nave was timber covered. But in the nation's second most important cathedral, at Glasgow, where much of what we now see was built between the 1230s and the end of the thirteenth century, only the lower spaces of crypt, aisles and eastern chapels were vaulted. Over the high spaces of Glasgow it was pointed wagon ceilings that were built. That over the eastern limb was given a delicately cusped profile and an overall net-like pattern of ribs within the basic matrix of parallel transverse ribs, while views drawn before its replacement show that the later ceiling over the nave was simply subdivided by transverse ribs reflecting the bay rhythm. Elsewhere, Elgin Cathedral's eastern limb evidently had a steeply pointed wagon ceiling over the choir on the indications of the masonry of the east gable; the surviving evidence probably relates to the rebuilding after the fire of 1390, but it may well have been of that profile since the rebuilding and extension carried out after the fire of 1270.

In considering the visual impact of such ceilings it is perhaps worth noting that, when both masonry and timberwork were limewashed and decorated with appropriate colouring, the differences between a stone vault and a timber ceiling may not have been immediately evident to the less observant. Indeed, on some occasions timber ceilings closely imitated the form of quadripartite stone vaults; this was common in England and it appears to have been the case in the aisles of the nave started at Dunkeld Cathedral in 1406. At King's College Chapel the pattern of the ribs also reflected the rib configuration seen in stone vaulting, though there were no lateral arched severies to complete the illusion.

In aisle-less churches timber wagon ceilings enjoyed a renewed vogue in the later middle ages, though the limited surviving evidence may indicate that a more depressed three-centred profile, like that of King's College, had come to be preferred over the more steeply pointed profiles favoured earlier. This was certainly the case over the small collegiate aisle added to Guthrie Church, where the college was founded in about 1479. There the structural framework of the roof still survives in place, while the painted boards of the ceiling itself are now in the Museum of Scotland. That ceiling had a decorative application of transverse ribs, with longitudinal ribs at ridge and mid-height, though it seems certain that some at least of those ribs were added in 1881. At Foulis Easter, another collegiate foundation, which was rebuilt in 1452–53, the evidence for the profile of the ceiling on the boards of a crucifixion painting from above the rood screen suggests that it had a ceiling of similar profile to the one at Guthrie.[30] The King's College ceiling is also similar to Guthrie in its general profile, but differs in its pattern of ribs which combines ridge, diagonal and transverse ribs.

The most precise parallel for the King's College ceiling was over the chancel of another of the churches in which Bishop Elphinstone took a close interest, the parish church of St Nicholas in New Aberdeen (Fig. 4.12). The fruits of that parish had been appropriated to the prebend of the bishops of Aberdeen in their cathedral chapter since at least 1256, with the consequence that the bishops were technically responsible for the fabric of the eastern parts of the church.[31] Plans to rebuild the chancel may have been taking shape as early as 1442, but it was only some decades later that work

INTERIOR
OF
EAST CHURCH.

Fig. 4.12.   Aberdeen, St
Nicholas, ceiling of the East Kirk
before 1835 (*Book of Bon Accord*)

began. By 1495 the wright John Fendour had contracted for its ceiling, and the new chancel was sufficiently complete for Bishop Elphinstone to dedicate it in 1498, even if work was still under way on the ceiling in 1510 and 1517 on the evidence of inscriptions on the cornice.[32] The ceiling of St Nicholas' Kirk was destroyed when the chancel as a whole was rebuilt in 1835, but a view of it published in 1839 shows it to have been strikingly similar to that of King's College Chapel in nearly all respects,[33] and there must be a good case for believing that the same wright was responsible for the design and construction of both. The widely sprigged foliate bosses set at the rib intersections of the two ceilings are a particularly notable feature, and they were also to be reflected in the splendid heraldic ceiling placed over the nave of Aberdeen Cathedral at the behest of Elphinstone's successor in the see, Gavin Dunbar (1518–32). It is arguable on the evidence of these bosses that John Fendour may have been responsible for the cathedral ceiling as well, and we certainly know that he worked on the cathedral's central tower for Elphinstone from 1511. Though there is a local tradition that one James Winter was the wright for the ceiling over the cathedral nave, it may be that the latter name was a corruption of Fendour.[34]

  The use of these bosses at King's College could be a further illustration of the architectural impact of Elphinstone's Netherlandish travels. Timber ceilings were an especially common form of church covering in the Low Countries, where a shortage of building stone encouraged the use of more readily available materials, and comparable sprigged bosses were used as early as around 1402 in the timber vault constructed by Jean de Valenciennes over the main hall of the town hall in Bruges (Fig. 4.13). It is possible that it was the bosses of this prestigious ceiling which provided Elphinstone with the idea for the bosses at King's College although similar, if rather less riotously sprigged bosses are also to be seen in the ribbed wagon ceilings of a number of churches in Bruges. For our purposes a particularly interesting group of these bosses is to be seen on the late fifteenth-century wagon ceilings over the choir aisles of the church of St Giles in that city, since the Scottish artisans resident there were housed in that quarter and they had a chapel dedicated to St Andrew in the church (Fig. 4.14).[35] These ceilings have been heavily restored, but it is likely that what we now see still reflects the intentions of the medieval carpenter.[36]

On this basis there is a good case for arguing that at least some of the characteristics of the Aberdeen ceilings were drawn from Netherlandish prototypes. Nevertheless, it must be said that most of the wagon ceilings in the Low Countries, including those in Bruges St Giles, have a considerably steeper profile of two-centred form than those we see at Aberdeen. Even more importantly, there appear to be few close Netherlandish parallels for the diagonal arrangement of ribs of King's Chapel, with the refectory ceiling at the the the Bijloke Abbey in Ghent of about 1325–30 offering one rare parallel.[37] The Aberdeen rib pattern, like the flatter three-centred profile itself, thus must surely be a largely Scottish feature. On the evidence remaining to us, it is one possibility that the inspiration for the rib pattern — if not the profile — at King's College might have been a particularly Scottish type of stone vaulting rather than other timber ceilings. Later medieval Scotland witnessed a marked revival of interest in the construction of pointed barrel vaults over both churches and secular buildings, a revival which has no real counterparts elsewhere.[38] From the start, a number of the more ambitious examples of these vaults were decorated with an essentially cosmetic application of ribs, sometimes set out as a series of parallel transverse ribs, but in other cases on a diagonal arrangement aping that of quadripartite vaulting. Early examples of the latter type were being built by the last quarter of the fourteenth century, over the upper hall at the royal castle of Dundonald and over the chancel aisles of the burgh church of St Giles in Edinburgh. Diagonally ribbed barrel vaults continued to be built throughout the later middle ages, amongst the finest of the later examples being the choir vault at the collegiate church of Seton, where the new eastern extension started before the death of the first Lord Seton in about 1478 was completed by the second Lord Seton before his death in 1508.[39] It is possible that the vault over St Salvator's Chapel in St Andrews itself was of this type, since the small barrel vault over the south porch there also has a quadripartite pattern of ribs; if so, this could presumably have been a further factor in Elphinstone's choice of design.

Since so few Scottish wagon ceilings have survived, it must be conceded that it would be unsafe to be too dogmatic in identifying the architectural stimuli which underlay the design of that at King's College. But there can be little doubt that there was more than one idea behind the end result, some of native origin and some which further suggest that Elphinstone had taken ideas from what he had seen in the course of his European travels. The evidence also suggests that craftsmen were not reluctant

Fig. 4.13.   Bruges Town Hall, ceiling boss in main hall (Photo: author)

Fig. 4.14.   Bruges, St Giles, choir chapel ceiling (Photo: author)

NORTH ELEVATION

Fig. 4.15. Edinburgh St Giles, from the north, showing the crown steeple and church before restoration (*Registrum . . . Sancti Egidii*)

to consider solutions that had been developed for materials other than those in which they were themselves working, an attitude which perhaps partly underlay the design of the chapel's crown steeple.

The crown steeple.   The crown steeple is King's College's most distinctive feature, with its drum and imperial crown carried with what seems like effortless ease by four arched flyers (Figs 4.5, 16.1). Crown steeples have become relatively common currency since they were adopted as a favoured feature by the more Scottish-inspired Gothic revival architects of the later nineteenth and earlier twentieth centuries, but to the age which first produced them they must have seemed the very acme of architectural virtuosity. Significantly, in view of the technical difficulties inherent in their construction, a number of those which were evidently planned probably never left the tracing house, while both of the two surviving Scottish crown steeples had to be extensively rebuilt as early as the seventeenth century and we cannot be entirely certain that their original forms were replicated. The other of the two surviving examples is on the central tower of Edinburgh's burgh church of St Giles, which has eight flyers rather than the four of Aberdeen (Fig. 4.15). It was for a number of the greatest of the burgh churches that other crown steeples were conceived, and the example over the west tower at Linlithgow St Michael, with four flyers, survived until it was dismantled in about 1821. Others were planned for the west tower of Dundee St Mary and probably for the central tower of Haddington St Mary, both of which were apparently to have had eight flyers as at Edinburgh, though there is no firm structural or documentary evidence that either of these was built.[40]

None of the other crown steeples is as relatively securely dated as that at Aberdeen, though most of them were probably designed in the years around 1500. At Linlithgow and Dundee the chief pointer to their probable date of conception is the gift of bells, which are unlikely to have been donated long before the main body of the towers was structurally near enough completion for their hanging to be in prospect. At Linlithgow we know that the bell named Blessed Mary was cast in 1490, and by 1497 thoughts were moving eastwards to the reconstruction of the chancel,[41] while at Dundee a bell was given in 1495.[42]

Scotland's crown steeples are the nation's finest contribution to a late Gothic love of the ostentatious demonstration of the apparent ability of stone to soar in defiance of gravity. It has to be said that the spirit which engendered them is not widely reflected in other aspects of Scottish late Gothic architecture, in which a more solidly based approach was generally preferred, but across much of Britain and Europe such virtuoso display was widely valued. In trying to understand some of the various strands of thought which culminated in the construction of crown steeples, a fascination with the elaborately combined and superimposed canopies known as tabernacles must be seen as an essential pre-requisite. In the Neville Screen, constructed as a backdrop for the high altar of Durham Cathedral in the 1370s, the multi-tiered polygonal tabernacles which seem to be only tenuously connected to the supporting buttress-like piers by mini-flyers, demonstrate in fully fledged form the daring effects which were being so increasingly cultivated.[43] Over the next century and a half this same approach is to be seen reflected in stonework on the more lavishly designed tombs, in timber work over the choir stalls of many cathedrals and abbeys, as well as in paintings, stained glass, seals and many other media across Europe.

It is tempting to suspect that some of these fantasies were first worked out for two-dimensional designs, and were essentially the solutions of draughtsmen in whose media the calls of gravity held diminished sway. It is worth noting that a number of English monumental brasses show tabernacles rising from arches which, in silhouette at least, look rather like what we see in the later crown steeples. Examples which may be cited are the memorial of Sir Reginald Braybrook at Cobham in Kent, of 1405, and that of Prior Thomas Nelond of Lewes at Cowfold in Sussex, of 1433.[44]

Moving on to three-dimensional designs, such a daring approach to design carried a limited risk when executed on a small scale, and it was particularly appropriate for metalwork designed for especially sacred uses, in which there was a wish to evoke the anticipated architectural splendours of the heavenly Jerusalem. Such uses included reliquaries for the earthly remains of saints, or monstrances for the display of the consecrated host. Reliquaries are rare survivals in Britain, but if we consider a number of continental examples it can be seen how designs comparable to what we see in the crown steeples could emerge. The 'Three Towers Reliquary' of about 1370 in the cathedral treasury at Aachen, for example, has upward tapering superstructures in which each stage, more slender than that which carries it, is supported by flyers as well as by miniature buttress-like piers, very much in the same spirit as the tabernacles of the Neville Screen. Moving on to a silver-gilt image of St Anne made in 1472 by the Bavarian goldsmith Hans Grieff and now in the Cluny Museum in Paris, we see how the vertical supports for the canopy could be reduced,[45] while in an early sixteenth-century reliquary at the church of Mailley (Haute-Saône) an elaborate hexagonal lantern stage is carried purely by lateral supports.[46] These examples are, of course, offered as illustrations of the range of possibilities inherent in the use of such materials rather than as a chronologically sequential development, and it would be over-simplistic to see such a sequence as precisely reflecting the way in which the idea of the crown steeple may have emerged.

Nevertheless, parallels are also to be found in work produced in other media. On a larger scale, the use of timber particularly lent itself to soaring and minimally supported superstructures, as may be seen in the bishop's throne at Exeter Catheral, of 1313–16, in the fifteenth-century enclosure around the font at Trunch in Norfolk, or in a number of smaller font covers, including that at Frieston in Lincolnshire. On a far more technically demanding scale, the possibilities of cantilevering elaborate superstructures inwards and upwards by means of lateral timbers may have encouraged masons to speculate on the structural, as well as the decorative potential of their own medium more fully. At Ely Cathedral, for example, the octagon within the widened crossing, which was created after the collapse of the central tower in 1322, involved a complex system of supporting a timber lantern stage by cantilevers, a solution which could only have been achieved with wood at that time.[47] Since the lower structural timbers of Ely were then masked in a timber cladding intended to look like stone vaulting, it may be questioned how widely this engineering solution can have been known, though the technical premises were to be further — if generally less audaciously — exploited in hammer-beam roofs in both England and Scotland.

None of the designs considered briefly above could have afforded prototypes for the Aberdeen crown steeple; works of this kind were, however, part of the development of a late Gothic decorative and structural repertoire which was to be ultimately of inspiration to stone masons as well as to workers in the more tractable materials of metal and timber. We also know that stone masons themselves had been attempting to extend the possibilities of their own medium over many years in a way which must have predisposed them to developing ever more ambitious cappings for the tower heads of their buildings, where the play of light through complex fretworks of solid and void could be especially eye-catching.

The earlier stages in this process may be seen in towers designed in several countries, of which examples in France, the Netherlands and England provide the most useful illustrations for our present purposes. At Notre Dame-de-l'Épine near Châlons-sur-Marne the two western towers have highly complex openwork spires rising from octagonal bases, the skeletal spires and the pinnacles around the bases being inter-connected by miniature flyers. Of the two spires there, the southern is the more elaborate, but probably reflects the original design as completed in 1459, the northern one having been rebuilt after partial destruction in 1798. A similar approach to design, with flyers reaching across to an octagonal superstructure capped by a spire, is seen in the additions made to the north tower of Chartres Cathedral in 1506. Elsewhere in France it became common to have octagonal lantern stages flanked at the diagonal faces by multi-tiered pinnacles, with flyers interconnecting the elements, as in the central tower of Rouen St Ouen of 1440, the south-west Tour de Beurre of Rouen Cathedral started in 1482 or the west towers of Toul Cathedral completed in 1496.

Amongst the most ambitious schemes for extravagantly heightened and enriched towers with polygonal superstructures connected to angle pinnacles by flyers were a number planned in the Netherlands. The finest extant examples are those on the tower of Brussels Town Hall, which was completed in 1455, and on the north-west tower of Antwerp Cathedral, where the octagonal stage was started in 1501. Amongst the grandest designs of all were a number that either never left the drawing board or that were left incomplete; indeed, some of the most delightful architectural drawings that have ever been produced are for these towers. They include a proposal of about 1468 for the west tower of Breda, a design by Rombout II Keldermans of around 1519 for the west tower of Mechelen St Rombout, and another by the same mason of about 1530 for the west tower of Zierikzee.[48] Stone could hardly be persuaded to do more than is expected of it in these designs.

By comparison with such essays in the art of the barely possible, most of the comparable English designs appear more staid. Amongst the earlier buildings to show an interest in light polygonal superstructures was the superstructure added to the west tower of Ely Cathedral at an unknown date in the later fourteenth century, where a simple octagonal lantern stage was flanked by octagonal turrets at its diagonal faces, with connecting intermediate flyers and arched walkways. Around the same time a spire was added to Patrington Church in the East Riding of Yorkshire where a spire rose from an octagonal cage, which was in turn connected to the angle pinnacles by small flyers. Perhaps the finest development of this particular idea was the spire on the west tower at Coventry St Michael, which was begun in 1432. But in England experiments of this kind were not limited to church towers, and a number of market crosses of varying scale show developments on the same idea. Some of the most ambitious were designed with an arcaded polygonal main structure surmounted by ogee-arched flyers carrying a lantern stage. The best illustration of the type is the market cross at Chichester, built in 1501, and in this we come even closer in spirit to the Scottish crown steeples.

In those market crosses, however, there was still a continuous pier from ground level up to the lantern stage so that, although it seems clear in the Chichester market cross that the lantern was meant to look as if supported chiefly by the flyers, there was still an unbroken vertical line between ground and lantern. Nevertheless, this unbroken vertical line is clearly close to the conceptual breaking point which was to result in crown steeples, and on present evidence it does seem that it was at an English church that the vertical connection between substructure and superstructure was first cut, leaving only flyers to support the latter. In fact this step had probably already

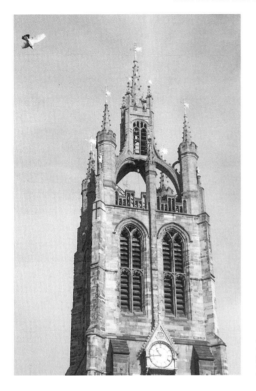

Fig. 4.16. Newcastle Cathedral, crown steeple (Crown Copyright: courtesy of Historic Scotland)

been taken not long before the Chichester market cross was built. The two medieval examples of crown steeples on church towers known to have been built in England are at Newcastle St Nicholas (now the cathedral) and at London St Mary le Bow (destroyed in 1666) (Fig. 4.16). The dates of neither of these examples is known with certainty, but that at Newcastle is thought to have been built under the patronage of Robert Rhodes, who died in 1474, and whose arms are on the tower vault; it was partly rebuilt in 1608 and further restored in the nineteenth century, but is thought to be still essentially as built. The crown steeple at St Mary le Bow is said to have been complete in 1512, though it is not known how long before then work may have been finished.

Insufficient is known of the St Mary le Bow steeple to make valid comparisons with that at Aberdeen, but comparison between Newcastle and Aberdeen reveals differences of approach. Most obviously, at the former the lantern is square and the upper faces of the supporting flyers are extended up the angles of the lantern in an ogee curve, resulting in a markedly graceful effect. Also, at Newcastle the flyers spring directly from the octagonal pinnacles which develop directly out of the diagonally set corner buttresses, thus creating four continuous lines from the ground to the apex of the steeple. By contrast, at Aberdeen the tower buttresses stop below the wall-head string course and the flyers spring slightly abruptly from the buttress-like pinnacles at parapet level, meaning that there is a less clearly expressed structural inter-relationship between tower and crown steeple. Despite this, however, the differences between Newcastle and Aberdeen are probably what one would expect from masons responding to the same idea but working out their particular solutions within the architectural vocabulary with which they were most familiar.

On present evidence therefore, and despite the differences, it seems inherently likely that Newcastle's crown steeple was the prototype for the Scottish examples, and we must remember that Elphinstone may have passed through the city on at least some of his embassies to the English court. There is no reason to imagine that Elphinstone would have been in any way opposed to the adoption of English architectural ideas at a time when Anglo-Scottish relations were probably closer than they had been for many decades, particularly since we know that he employed an English plumber in the roofing of the chapel. If it is objected that the idea of the crown steeple was taken up with greater enthusiasm in Scotland than in England and that it therefore could be an idea of native origin, it must be countered that, except for a small number of church furnishings,[49] there is little to suggest that Scotland had chosen to play a great part in the earlier experiments which led to the development of such delightful superstructures. It is hard to think that the idea could have been born fully formed without a greater indigenous pre-history.

All things considered, it thus seems that King's College's crown steeple should be understood as a Scottish response to those experiments to push the use of stone close to its structural limits. These experiments were in the air throughout much of Europe in the decades around 1500, but this response in particular took its immediate lead from a final significant development in northern England. Nevertheless, in trying to understand King's College's crown steeple, we must bear in mind that it was almost certainly the last part to be completed; and what we now see was at least partly modified in the course of the repairs of 1634 by George Thomson. William Kelly, for example, argued that the crown steeple would originally have been 'more Gothic and . . . more graceful' before those repairs.[50]

In the absence of views of the tower as first built there can be no certainties, though the overall similarity of the main structure of the crown steeple to an imperial crown certainly corresponds with Boece's description of an 'imperialis diadematis' in his history of Aberdeen's bishops published in 1522. Beyond this, clear parallels of a number of the details of the crown steeple with the fountain in the inner close at Linlithgow Palace support the idea that the basic design is likely to be essentially of the earlier sixteenth century (Fig. 4.17). Despite being heavily restored in 1930, we know from early views of the Linlithgow fountain that the imperial crown which caps it was always similar to that at Aberdeen, while the cusped cresting around the basins and beneath the flyers of the fountain shows marked likenesses with the cresting on the Aberdeen flyers. The fountain was probably only completed in about 1538.[51] Further parallels may be pointed out with the decorative crowns which once served as finials to the conical roofs of James V's tower at Holyrood, which was probably built between 1528 and 1532 (Fig. 4.18).[52] Taken together, such parallels may well support a view that the top crown of the Aberdeen steeple was only installed during the years of James V's personal rule from 1528 to 1542. This would certainly be

Fig. 4.17. Linlithgow Palace, fountain (Crown Copyright: courtesy of Historic Scotland)

Fig. 4.18. The Palace of Holyrood c. 1649, showing the crown finials on James V's tower (James Gordon of Rothemay)

PALATIVM REGIVM EDINENSE,
quod & Cænobium S. Crucis.
The royal palace of holy rood-hous. by J.G.

consistent with that monarch's known concern for the heraldic expression of his kingship, and it must also be remembered that it was James V who, in 1539, was to have the Scottish crown remodelled in the form it still takes, at a time when it seems that the iconography of the imperial crown had assumed a heightened significance.[53]

However, the drum of Aberdeen's crown steeple has several features which must represent modifications made during the repairs of 1634, chief amongst which are the Tuscan columns at the angles of the drum. Taking account of all this, we can probably conclude that while the basic design is sixteenth century, some of the details were adapted to later tastes in the partial rebuilding of 1634. The restoration is discussed further in Chapter 16.

CONCLUSION

If this brief study of King's College Chapel has established nothing else, it is hoped it has confirmed that it is a complex building in which architectural ideas from a variety of sources were taken and blended into a coherent and satisfying whole. Behind it was one of the great architectural patrons of late medieval Scotland, amongst whose other projects were the central tower and choir of Aberdeen Cathedral and the chancel of Aberdeen St Nicholas, and who also planned to build a bridge over the Dee. But there can be little doubt that King's College was Elphinstone's most favoured project, and that he took a close personal interest in all aspects of its design. Indeed, we can almost certainly assume that nothing was done which did not have his approval and that the ideas reflected in its masonry and woodwork were to a significant extent a consequence of his own interventions.

The master mason who designed the chapel and supervised its construction was evidently a Scottish craftsman since so much of his vocabulary is what we would expect to see in a major Scottish building of this period. This is particularly clear in the mouldings which frame doorways and windows, in the detailed treatment of buttresses and pinnacles, and in the basic approach to tracery design. It is unfortunate that Elphinstone's other projects have been destroyed so that we are unable to determine if he employed this same mason elsewhere; however, from the little we know about St Nicholas' Church, there is a clear possibility that the wright John Fendour who was engaged on the ceiling there was also involved at King's College. There is thus some reason for assuming that Elphinstone might choose to rely on craftsmen who were well used to meeting the specific requirements of so demanding a patron. Taking this possibility a little further, Kelly suggested that one of the master masons who worked on the chapel could have been a member of the Gray family, since there is a reference to the appointment of one John Gray to the work on St Nicholas' Church in New Aberdeen in 1484, while in the same year an Alexander Gray appears to have been involved in the work on St Giles' Church in Edinburgh.[54] It is certainly attractive to speculate that one mason could have been at work on two of Elphinstone's Aberdeen projects, while another mason of the same family was working on one of Scotland's other crown steeples, though this can be no more than a possibility in our present state of knowledge.

If, as has been suggested above, there were ultimately French precedents for the plan, Netherlandish prototypes for aspects of both the window tracery and wagon ceiling, and French, Netherlandish and English inspiration behind the crown steeple, the synthesis of these disparate elements into a relatively seamless whole was no mean achievement, whoever was the mason responsible. The late middle ages was a period when, as a result of commercial, political and cultural links, Scotland was probably more directly open to a wider variety of external influences than at any time before, and the architectural evidence of this contact had been evident from at least the late fourteenth century. But there are few Scottish buildings in which the European outlook and intellectual interests of a patron are so fully manifest as at King's College Chapel.

APPENDIX

THE PROPORTIONS AND SOLOMON'S TEMPLE

By JANE GEDDES

To a casual visitor, the façades of King's College Chapel appear disturbingly irregular, their composition almost haphazard. However, behind and within, it can be shown that there was a clear geometric and theological plan which, in some areas, had to be altered for functional or structural reasons.

Most of south front, originally hidden within the sacristy and library, is faced with eighteenth-century granite. The sides and angles of the apse, all different, are considerably rebuilt due to subsidence. On the north side, no bays are exactly equal in length although they average just below 6.1m. No windows on the north side are exactly alike or evenly spaced. Some of these discrepancies are due to the internal arrangements: the position of altars, rood screen, the north door. The west door, perhaps a slightly later insertion, is not in the centre of the west front[55] and the tower, originally intended to be 7.14m square, was extended southwards to 8.26m possibly to provide stability for the bells.[56]

Inside, however, the underlying harmony and logic becomes apparent. The proportion of the building is simple: the body of the chapel, up to the wall head, consists of four cubes just about 8.65m on each side.[57] The nave, before the rood was moved westwards, was two cubes; the seating of the choir stalls (excluding the rood) made one cube. Each cube defines a major feature. The first extends from the west wall to west jamb of the south door; the second goes from the south door to the upper rood door; the third from the rood door to the west jamb of the south-east door; and the fourth from the south-east door to the cord of the apse (Fig. 4.1).[58]

It is clear that even if the detailed measurements are irregular, the size of Bishop Elphinstone's chapel carried a particular message: it was be be larger in significant dimensions than St Salvator's at St Andrews and the nave of St Machar's Cathedral. King's Chapel is 37.2m long; St Salvator's 32.7m long internally. King's is 8.76m wide, St Salvator's 8.55m. King's Chapel bays are approximately 6.1m long; St Machar's are 5.18m long.[59]

Obviously Elphinstone's primary consideration in deciding on the size of the chapel was its practical function, hence the irregularity of the north wall. However, it is possible that he had one other consideration in mind, apart from exceeding comparable establishments. Many medieval churches took their dimensions, in one form or another, from the description of Solomon's Temple in the Old Testament (1 Kings 6).[60] The oblique reference to the building of the Temple, implied by the dedication inscription, suggests that Elphinstone saw his chapel

Fig. 4.19.   The Temple of Solomon, from the *Biblia Sacra* annotated by Nicholas of Lyra, AUL, Inc 180 (Copyright: University of Aberdeen)

and university as an embodiment of the Temple's holiness and Solomon's wisdom. The symbolism on his tomb also indicates an interest in the Temple.[61]

In view of these references, it is worth exploring the possibility that Elphinstone was interested in applying the dimensions of the Temple to his own chapel. In 1512, Elphinstone gave to the university his own copy of the *Biblia Sacra* complete with Nicholas of Lyra's notes and illustrations, printed in 1498.[62] It has an illustration of 1 Kings 6.2–10, which shows a thoroughly medieval stone structure with a lower timber building abutting it (Fig. 4.19).[63] Edwards asks cautiously 'Is it perhaps not too fanciful to see in this drawing a germ of inspiration for the design of King's College Chapel, against the south wall of which once abutted a building which accommodated Sacristy, Jewel House and Library, on two floors but still low enough to leave room for the clerestory windows?'.[64] Even though the south range was not completed until after Elphinstone's death, the position of the walled up rood door high on the south wall of the chapel, shows it was part of the original plan; and the chapel originally had a parapet like the Lyra illustration. James Gordon's college view of 1660 makes the comparison particularly clear, showing the windows, string courses and parapets. (Figs 4.6, 4.19).

According to 1 Kings 6.2–3, the width of Solomon's Temple was 20 cubits and the total length was 70 cubits. A cubit was the length of a forearm, about 1ft 6ins long. Using cubits at King's would produce an unnecessarily large building and the unit of measurement is likely to have been the Scots foot. However, no simple unit of measurement has emerged at the chapel. Using the Scots foot, the basic cube within the building is just under 29ft,[65] the external bay length is just under 20ft. However, perhaps as a distant echo of Solomon's three score cubits' length for the great chamber, and 20 cubits for the Holy of Holies, the east wall of King's rood to the east wall of the apse is 64ft, and the sanctuary from the bottom step to the east wall is 20ft 6ins.

Although the measurements themselves fail to produce particularly striking evidence, the proportions are clearly calculated to carry a theological message. Unfortunately the integrity of this vision was destroyed when the choir stalls were moved. At the Temple, the proportion of width to length was 1:3.5. Externally the chapel's ratio of width to length is almost 1:3.5.[66]

Internally, the ratio of the interior width to the length, from the west door to the steps marking the sanctuary is 1.3.5.[67] At the Temple, the Holy of Holies occupied 20 cubits within the great chamber which was 60 cubits long (1:3). At King's the same ratio applies to the sanctuary (from the altar steps eastward) within the choir enclosed by the east face of the rood screen (1:3).[68] Within the Temple, Solomon clad the walls and ceiling with carved wood (1 Kings 6.15–18), as Elphinstone sheathed his presbytery with wooden stalls and ceiling.

From this evidence, it is clear that the irregularities of the exterior, in particular the uneven six-bay system, provided a structural skeleton for a much more significant sacred space within, which led symbolically through the external porch of the Temple, into the great chamber and finally, swathed in the finest wood carving, into the Holy of Holies. Bishop Elphinstone's clue about Solomon's Temple in the inscription is manifest in his building. He even chose to be buried not, as was usual, in the cathedral, but at the steps to his own Holy of Holies.

Notes

[1] Vatican Archives, *Registra Supplicationum*, 1000, fols 8^vi–82^v. For fuller discussion of the foundation see Ian B. Cowan and David E. Easson, *Medieval religious houses: Scotland*, London and New York, 2nd edn, 1976, 231–32; and Macfarlane, 1995, 290–308.

[2] *The Ledger of Andrew Halyburton 1492–1503*, ed. Cosmo Innes, Edinburgh, 1867, 183–84.

[3] James Gordon, *Abredoniae utriusque descriptio. A description of both towns of Aberdeen*, ed. Cosmo Innes, Spalding Club, Aberdeen, 1842.

[4] Kelly, 1949, 49–50 and 54–55. Dr Kelly's various papers on the architecture of the college are invaluable and highly perceptive sources of information, and many of his views are accepted in this paper.

[5] The inscription reads: '*Per serenissimum, illustrissimum ac invictissimum J 4 R / Quarto nonas aprilis anno millesimo quingentesimo / hoc insigne collegium latomi inceperunt aedificare*'. See Chapter 5.

[6] G. Patrick Edwards, 'William Elphinstone and his college chapel and the second of April', *AUR*, 51, 1985, 1–17. See also pp. 61–63 & 66–73.

[7] P. J. Anderson, 'Notes on heraldic representations at King's College, Old Aberdeen, *PSAS*, 23, 1888–89, 82.

[8] *Fasti*, lvii.

[9] Macfarlane, 1995, 327.

[10] Boece, 95.

[11] In support of this possibility, Eeles (1956, 83) also points out that, while the north doorway has what appear to be incised consecration crosses, the west doorway has none, suggesting that it was only inserted after the chapel had been consecrated and that the north doorway must have been regarded as the main entrance at the time of the consecration.

[12] See Chapter 6.

[13] See Chapter 16.

[14] Measured drawings of 1884 by James C. Watt, AUL, A5/1–6. Some of his drawings, together with others, were also used to illustrate Macpherson, 1889.

[15] See pp. 181–82.

[16] See pp. 179–80.

[17] See pp. 175–79.

[18] The most significant change to the ceiling — albeit one which may be symptomatic of greater changes — appears to have been towards the west end of the south side. Billings evidently shows that where the roof abutted the tower it was carried on internally exposed corbels, since it could not be extended over the wall head at this point, and the main cornice was raised up over the corbels. (Robert

William Billings, *The baronial and ecclesiastical antiquities of Scotland*, Edinburgh, 1845–52, vol. 1.) see Fig. 16.10, below. Photographs dating from later that century, however, show a continuous cornice.

[19] I. Hacker-Stück, 'La Sainte-Chapelle de Paris et les chapelles palatines du moyen âge en France', *Cahiers archéologiques*, 13, 1962, 217–57.

[20] P. Anger, *Le collège de Cluny*, Paris, 1916; a view of 1824 by Pernot is reproduced in Robert Branner, *St Louis and the court style in Gothic architecture*, London, 1965, pl. 80.

[21] See Gé Verheul, *De oude Dorpskerken* (2 vols), Bussum, 1982–83.

[22] For fuller discussion of the author's views on the revived use of apses in Scotland see Richard Fawcett, *Scottish architecture from the accession of the Stewarts to the Reformation, 1371–1560*, Edinburgh, 1994, 102–03, 159–66 and 198–211.

[23] Ronald Cant, *The college of St Salvator*, Edinburgh and London, 1950, 4.

[24] Godfrey Evans, 'The mace of St Salvator's College', in *Medieval art and architecture in the diocese of St Andrews*, British Archaeological Association Transactions for 1986, ed. John Higgitt, Leeds, 1994, 197–212.

[25] See Richard Fawcett, 'Scottish medieval window tracery', in *Studies in Scottish antiquity*, ed. David J. Breeze, Edinburgh, 1984, 180–81 and 174–75.

[26] This was pointed out by William Geddes in 'Old Aberdeen', *Transactions of the Aberdeen Philosophical Society*, 1, 1884, 18.

[27] C. Peeters, *De Sint Janskathedraal te 's-Hertogenbosch* (De Monumenten van Geschiedenis en Kunst), The Hague, 1985, 13, 76, 104–05, 390–99.

[28] E. J. Haslinghuis and C. J. A. Peeters, *De Dom van Utrecht* (De Nederlandse Monumenten van Geschiedenis en Kunst), The Hague, 1965, 265–66.

[29] Macfarlane, 1995, 232.

[30] M. R. Apted and W. Norman Robertson, 'Late fifteenth-century church paintings from Guthrie and Foulis Easter', *PSAS*, 95, 1961–62, 262–79.

[31] Ian B. Cowan, *The parishes of Medieval Scotland*, Scottish Record Society, Edinburgh, 1967, 2.

[32] William Kelly, 'Carved oak from St Nicholas' Church, Aberdeen', *PSAS*, 68, 1933–34, 355–66.

[33] J. Robertson, *The book of Bon-Accord*, Aberdeen, 1839.

[34] W. D. Geddes, *Lacunar basilicae Sancti Macarii Aberdonensis*, New Spalding Club, Aberdeen, 1888.

[35] *Souvenirs Britanniques à Bruges*, Exhibition Catalogue, Bruges, 1966, 11–13. A fuller study of Scottish links with Bruges, 'Medieval Scottish associations with Bruges', by Dr Alexander Stevenson, is to be published in the festschrift for Dr Grant Simpson. I am grateful to Dr Stevenson for letting me see a draft of his paper, and for discussing his views with me.

[36] A. Duclos, *Bruges, histoire et souvenirs*, Bruges, 1913, 335–36; Luc Devliegher, 'De opkomst van de Kerkelijke Gotische Bouwkunst in West-Vlaanderen gedurende de XIIe eew', *Bulletin van de Koninklijke Commissie voor monumenten en landschappen*, 5, 1954, 201–03.

[37] Marjan Buyle, Thomas Coomans, Jan Esther, Luc Francis Genicot, *Architecture Gothique en Belgique*, Tielt, 1997, 123–25. There may also have been a similar ceiling over the Dominican church in Ghent, which was destroyed in 1870.

[38] For a slightly fuller discussion of the author's views on pointed barrel vaults see R. Fawcett, *The Architectural History of Scotland, 1371–1560*, Edinburgh, 1994, 33–35.

[39] Richard Maitland, *History of the House of Seytoun*, ed. John Fullarton, Maitland Club, Edinburgh, 1829. (The numbering of the lords Seton is here modified to take account of accepted current practice.)

[40] Kelly, 1949, 34–42. For an historical analysis of the Scottish Imperial Crown, see R. A. Mason, 'This Realm of Scotland is an Empire?', in *Church, Chronicle and Learning in Medieval and Early Renaissance Scotland*, ed. B. Crawford, Edinburgh, 1999, ch. 4.

[41] *Liber Cartarum Prioratus Sancti Andree*, ed. Thomas Thomson, Bannatyne Club, Edinburgh, 1841, xxxviii, no. 47.

[42] *Registrum episcopatus Brechinensis*, Patrick Chalmers and Cosmo Innes (eds), Bannatyne Club, Aberdeen, 1856, vol. 2, 316.

[43] Christopher Wilson, 'The Neville Screen', *Medieval art and architecture at Durham Cathedral*, British Archaeological Association Transactions for 1977, Nicola Coldstream and Peter Draper (eds), Leeds, 1980, 90–104.

[44] Muriel Clayton, *Catalogue of rubbings of brasses and incised slabs* (Victoria and Albert Museum), London, 1968, pls 14 and 59.

[45] Alain Erlande-Brandenburg *et al.*, *Musée national du Moyen Age, Thermes de Cluny, guide to the collections*, Paris, 1993, 105.

[46] *Les trésors des églises de France* (Musée des Arts Décoratifs, Paris), 2nd edn, Paris, 1965, pl. 172.

[47] See the analytical diagrams in Cecil A. Hewett, *English cathedral and monastic carpentry*, Chichester, 1985, 114–22.

[48] R. Meischke, 'Het architectonische ontwerp in de Nederlanden gedurende de late middeleeuwen en de zesiende eeuw', in ibid., *De gothische bouwtraditie*, Amersfoort, 1988, 127–207.

[49] The most ambitious surviving example of Scottish tabernacle work is the tomb of Bishop James Kennedy in his chapel of St Salvator at St Andrews. But it is likely that a similar approach was to be found in other church furnishings. The retable of St Katherine's altar in St Machar's Cathedral (destroyed in 1642), for example, appears to have had two levels of canopies (Orem, 1791, 103); David Stevenson, *St Machar's Cathedral and the Reformation: 1560–1690* (Friends of St Machar's Cathedral Occasional Papers no. 7), Aberdeen, 1981, 12; I am grateful to Richard Emerson for reminding me of this reference.

[50] Kelly, 1949, 46. And see pp. 175–79 in this volume.

[51] The lead pipe to the fountain was found to be inscribed with the date 1538 when excavated in 1894. See T. M.Halliday, 'Donations to the Museum', *PSAS*, LXVI, 1931–32, 22; and *The Buildings of Scotland, Lothian*, ed. Colin McWilliam, Harmondsworth, 1978, 297.

[52] John Dunbar, 'The palace of Holyroodhouse during the first half of the sixteenth century', *Archaeological Journal*, 120, 1964, 242–54. The crowns are shown in the view by Gordon of Rothemay of around 1649.

[53] Charles J.Burnett, 'Outward signs of Majesty', in *Stewart Style 1513–42*, ed. Janet Hadley, Phantassie, 1996, 289–302; particularly the section on the remaking of the crown, 293–94.

[54] Kelly, 1949, 45, 43.

[55] It is 3.3m from the north butttress, and 3.66m from the south buttress.

[56] Measured at the top.

[57] The internal height to the wall head is 9.05m, according to J. C. Watt's measurements. All the other measurements are by the author, using a steel metric tape.

[58] Squares from the interior of the west wall to the cord of the apse, 865cm: 865cm; 876cm; 802cm.

[59] Kelly, 1949, 53. Measurements from Kelly.

[60] The relationship is spelled out in William Durandus, *Rationale Divinorum Officiorum*, written in the thirteenth century: '*Ab utroque, scilicet a tabernaculo et a templo, nostra materialis ecclesia formam sumpsit*'. Aberdeen University has a printed edition (AUL, Inc 12) from 1484 but it is not known when this was acquired. On the Temple proportions and churches: E. Battisti, 'Il significo simbolico della Capella Sistine', *Commentari*, VIII, 1957, 96–104; E. Battisti, *Roma apocolittica e Re Salomone*, Turin, 1960. I would like to thank Ian Campbell for his advice in this section.

[61] See Chapters 5 and 9.

[62] AUL, Inc. 180.

[63] I Kings 6.5, 'And against the wall of the house he built chambers round about'.

[64] G. P. Edwards, 'William Elphinstone, his College Chapel, and the Second of April', *AUR*, LI, 1985, 7–9.

[65] Between 28ft 4ins and 28ft 8ins.

[66] 11.5m width: 39.3m length = 1:3.4. This ratio was observed by Aonghus Mackechnie, 'James VI's architects and their architecture', in *The Reign of James VI*, Julian Goodare and Michael Lynch (eds), East Linton, 2000, 163–64, note 4.

[67] Width at west end 8.65m: length from west wall to foot of sanctuary steps 30.94m = 1: 3.57. The sanctuary steps obviously marked an essential point in the sacred geometry of the building. They were removed in 1824 but replaced in 1889–91 (see Chapter 16). Their present location must be reasonably accurate because they were situated just east of Bishop Elphinstone's grave (see Chapter 9).

[68] Bottom of steps to east wall 6.25m: east face of rood to east wall 19.50m = 1.3.1.

CHAPTER FIVE

THE DEDICATION INSCRIPTION

By JOHN HIGGITT

As you approach the west front of King's College Chapel you are confronted by a modest display of royal heraldry. The three coats of arms set into the three buttresses are those of James IV, Margaret Tudor, his queen, and Archbishop Alexander Stewart of St Andrews, his illegitimate son.[1] Above these, surmounting the bell-tower, is the chapel's most salient feature, an open-work spire in the form of an imperial crown that has been seen as 'an expression of James IV's imperial pretensions'.[2] Below these and closer to the viewer, the king's name is prominently displayed in the opening of a three-line inscription in Latin carved on the wall just to the left of the top of the west door (Fig. 5.1). The inscription may be transcribed as follows:[3]

> *Per : serenissimu(m) Illustrissimu(m) : ac inuictissimu(m) I(acobum) 4 (= quartum) Regem*
> *Quarto : nonas : aprilis : anno : millesimo : et quingentesimo :*
> *hoc : insigne : collegium : latomi : inceperunt : edificare*

of which the following is a literal English translation:

> 'Through [By the grace of ? Through the agency of ?] the most serene, most illustrious and most victorious James IV King
> On the fourth day before the nones of April [2 April] in the one-thousand-and-five-hundredth year [1500]
> This eminent college the masons began to build'

The inscription is ostensibly a record of the date at which building work started on the chapel. It cannot, however, have been a contemporary record, since it was carved several courses up the west front, just below the window, and is clearly later than the courses of sandstone masonry into which it was fitted.[4] Although apparently an afterthought the inscription is well placed, at around a metre above eye-level, to catch the eye of anyone approaching the door. (The bottoms of the minims of the lowest line of lettering are 2.78m above the present ground level.) The lettering was left in relief, with the background cut back from around the letters, rather than incised into the stone. The broad raised strips of the letter strokes are bolder and more legible than incised lettering, particularly close-packed Gothic minuscule, would be; and, at least in good weather, their form is emphasized by shadow. Lettering in relief was rare through most of the middle ages but there seems to have been something of a fashion for this style of lettering in later medieval Scotland.[5]

Legibility is now heightened by the regilding of 1979 and it is likely that colour was used to pick out the inscription when it was first carved. The repairs ordered by the Royal Visitation of 1623 included the instruction that 'the dettoun [a phrase or motto,

Fig. 5.1.   The inscription on the west front of the chapel

i.e. the inscription] besyd the said window [should be] cullorit with oyle culloris'. As this is included in a list of 'ruingis and decayit pairtis' that were to be 'helpit and mendit', it was presumably meant to renew an earlier layer of colouring that was by then looking shabby. The wording implies that more than one colour was used. Medieval sculpture and architectural detail was of course frequently painted.[6]

The condition of the inscription is remarkably good, considering its exposed position, and it remains fully legible. The stone to the right of the last word of the inscription is new and so it is possible that there has been a short loss at the end, but the text seems to be complete as it stands. A comparison of the inscription in its present condition with older photographs shows some loss of detail. There would also appear to have been some recutting since they were taken. The vertical letter strokes now look narrower in proportion to the spaces separating them than they do in earlier photographs.[7]

The inscription is cut into three masonry courses of differing heights. The minims (shorter vertical strokes) in lines 1, 2 and 3 are respectively 12, 12 and 11cm in height. In the top line the background has been cut back to an even distance above and below the minims, giving a more or less even edge to the horizontal 'raised' bands of stone that run parallel to the line of lettering. Ascending and descending strokes cut into these bands. In the lower two lines the bands clear the ascenders but are cut into by descenders. The secondary and somewhat *ad hoc* character of the inscription can be seen in the way that the letter-cutter has made the inscription fit in with the masonry joints. Line 2 starts and ends hard up against vertical joints. The left edges of lines 1 and 3 are lined up with line 2, more or less. Line 3 also finishes up against a joint.

The top line, which pays tribute to the king, is distinguished from lines 2 and 3. The letters of line 1 are, as we have seen, a little taller and are perceptibly broader in their proportions and less compressed in layout. The lettering of all three lines is a well executed formal Gothic minuscule (or *textualis quadrata*, or *textura*, and traditionally known as 'black letter' in Britain) with lozenge-like terminations to most verticals. Lines 1 and 2 (but not line 3) of the inscription open with somewhat enlarged initials in the form of capitals, a further indication, along with the bolder lettering of line 1, that the inscription was conceived of as falling into two sections: (1) the opening line concerning the king; (2) lines 2 and 3, which relate to the building. A foliate capital I serves as the initial of '*Illustrissimu(m)*' and for the king's name, 'I(acobum)'. An R of capital form is used to stand for 'R(egem)' and within words, perhaps to achieve a slightly more monumental effect, in line 1 and at the end of line 3. The abbreviated form used for James's name at the end of line 1 (I 4 R) saves space but it also makes his name stand out more prominently. Final -um is abbreviated three times in line 1 and a bar over the final 'u' marks the suspension.

Punctuation consists of a sinuous, S-like stop, except after the first word of the inscription, which is marked off by a symbol like a modern colon. The S-like stop developed out of a medieval punctuation symbol marking an intermediate pause, the *punctus elevatus*.[8] In the more compressed lines 2 and 3 these sinuous stops are used as word-separators. The somewhat more elaborate example in line 1 acts as a mark of punctuation half-way through the king's title. The noticeable gap in line 1 between 'ac' and 'inuictissimu(m)' has no obvious explanation.

Gothic minuscule was the normal script for inscriptions in Scotland in the later middle ages.[9] It is interesting, however, that the date (ANNO D(OMI)NI 1504) in the heraldic panel with the arms of James IV higher up the west front is instead inscribed in an early sixteenth-century type of non-classical capital that is embellished with 'bites' into the top and bottom of verticals and with knob-like protuberances (Fig. 10.2).[10] It is therefore unlikely that the same designer was responsible both for the principal inscription in Gothic minuscule and for the heraldic panels. This conclusion is confirmed by comparing the Arabic numeral 4 of the date in James IV's heraldic panel and that used at the end of the first line of the main inscription. The 4 in the heraldic panel of 1504 resembles an inverted version of the Scottish National Party logo, whereas that in the 'I 4 R' below is much like the modern numeral with its horizontal cross-bar. In England Arabic numerals had occasionally been used in inscriptions from around the middle of the fifteenth century but Roman numerals continued to be the norm well into the sixteenth. In Scotland examples from the second half of the fifteenth century have been noted in the former collegiate church at Corstorphine (1457?) and in the tomb inscription of the first Earl of Huntly in Elgin Cathedral (giving the date of his death, 1470), although it has been suggested that the inscription could be later than this date. The 'inverted SNP logo' form of 4 was the normal form in England and Scotland (and also in Germany) in the fifteenth and early sixteenth centuries. It was still the form used in 1524 on the sacrament house given to the church at Kinkell (Aberdeenshire) by its rector, Alexander Galloway, Official of the diocese of Aberdeen and more than once Rector of the University. In Italy, however, the 'modern' form of 4 with a horizontal cross-bar had been the norm throughout the fifteenth century. The 4 in 'I 4 R' in the King's College Chapel inscription could therefore be an early, if modest, reflection of Italian Renaissance script or inscriptions, although it appears surrounded by Gothic lettering.[11] This italianate numeral was of course more or less contemporary with the earliest impact of Italian humanist hands in Scotland, in particular in the script of James IV's illegitimate son, Alexander Stewart.[12]

The text of the inscription is in Latin, which was the normal language for monumental inscriptions in Scotland at this time, although, as we shall see, Scots was also used on occasion. The text, which is transcribed and translated at the beginning of this paper, falls into two sections:

(1)   *Per serenissimum Illustrissimum ac inuictissimum Iacobum quartum Regem*
(2)   (i) *Quarto nonas aprilis* (ii) *anno millesimo et quingentesimo*
       (i) *hoc insigne collegium* (ii) *latomi inceperunt edificare*

We have noticed that each of these two sections opens with a capital letter and that Section 1 is written in larger and bolder lettering. Section 2 is composed of two lines of nearly equal length (of nineteen and twenty syllables respectively). These two lines are each in their turn made up of two balanced half lines.

The division into two sections that is indicated by the layout and the lettering reflects a division in the content. Section 1 refers to the king's involvement in, or at least sanctioning of, the event described in Section 2. The three superlatives used to describe James IV are conventional epithets which echo contemporary documents.[13] Section 2 purports to record the exact date according to the Roman calendar and the Christian era (equivalent to 2 April 1500) on which the masons began to build the college. The word '*collegium*' could refer to the whole complex but may refer more particularly to the building on which the inscription is carved, the chapel or collegiate church. Such a restriction of meaning appears in Elphinstone's charters for King's College ('*ecclesiam collegiatam seu collegium*'; '*in choro dicti collegii*').[14] The second line of Section 2 inverts the natural word order, apparently in order to throw the stress onto the religious foundation ('*hoc insigne collegium*') rather than onto the subject of the sentence, the '*latomi*'.

The ostensible purpose of the inscription is to record the date of the start of building work at the college and to show or imply royal patronage. The inscription says nothing about the dedication of the church in the name of St Mary in the Nativity, which seems to have taken place in 1509;[15] nor does it mention the founder, Bishop William Elphinstone. (Both may of course have been celebrated in one or more, now lost, inscriptions elsewhere in the chapel.) How unusual were the contents of the King's College inscription? A full assessment of its significance is very difficult in the regrettable absence of modern published corpora of Scottish and English medieval inscriptions of the sort that have been in progress for some time in a number of Continental countries.[16] Medieval inscriptions are far from uniform in their contents but nevertheless most belong to a number of common types and many make use of more or less standardized formulae. Two well established classes of inscriptions relating to church buildings are those recording liturgical ceremonies marking the beginning and, in theory, the completion of building work: the blessing and laying of the first stone and the dedication of the church. The inscriptions commemorating the laying of the first stone of Bisham Abbey (Berkshire) in 1333 and the dedication in 1241 of the church at Ashbourne (Derbyshire) are comparatively well-known English examples because they were inscribed onto brass plaques and have therefore been noticed by those concerned with monumental brasses.[17] Formal dedication inscriptions seem to have given way to inscriptions recording patronage in later medieval Britain but inscriptions marking first stones continue to be carved, perhaps because of the opportunity they afforded for involving and commemorating the patron. The inscription on the first stone laid in 1503 at Henry VII's Chapel at Westminster Abbey was more or less contemporary with the King's College inscription but recorded royal involvement, that of Henry, who was James's father-in-law, in a more direct way, although with only one superlative: '*Illustrissimus Henricus septimus rex Angliae et Franciae, et dominus Hiberniae, posuit hanc petram . . .* (The most illustrious Henry VII, King of England and France and Lord of Ireland, laid this stone . . .)'.[18]

The King's College inscription does not, however, commemorate the laying of the first stone. Instead it gives the reader the date at which the building work began, without reference to the first stone. This did not necessarily make it unique, as two inscriptions from England show. One, on a stone found in the eighteenth century at Woodham Walter (Essex) but now apparently lost, dated the start of work to August 1450 and to the twenty-eighth year of the reign Henry VI ('. . . *fuit hoc opus incept(um)*'). The other, which was carved below the west window of the church tower at Mayfield (Staffordshire), gave the year in which building began and named the patron: '*Hoc op(us) i(n)cept(um) p(er) Thoma(m) Rolleston a(nn)o d(omi)ni 1515*'. The general import of these two inscriptions is similar to the second part of the Aberdeen inscription and all three use the verb *incipere*.[19] Further work in Britain and on the Continent would no doubt uncover more examples.

Few architectural inscriptions of the late middle ages survive in Scotland but four surviving examples from the fifteenth century show both originality and some sophistication. A somewhat cryptic sequence of letters carved in relief on shields along the cornice of the north wall of Roslin collegiate church has been interpreted as stating that William Sinclair founded the college in 1450.[20] An inscription in raised lettering from the precinct walls of Paisley Abbey named Abbot George Shaw as the instigator, in 1485, of 'thus nobil fundacioun' in six lines of Scots verse.[21] Some years earlier the master mason John Morow had recorded his direction of the work at Melrose Abbey in two verse inscriptions inside the south transept, again both in Scots, one incised and the other in relief.[22]

There were then a number of precedents on ambitious Scottish buildings for the bold epigraphic statement carved by the west door of King's College Chapel; and, as we have seen, it was not the only ecclesiastical inscription to record the date of the start of building work. It is clearly an expression of pride in the new institution and its chapel, '*hoc insigne collegium*' (this eminent college); but is it possible to be more precise about the purpose of this inscription? On the face of it the inscription, like the heraldry on the buttresses and the architectural symbolism of the crown, was a visible tribute to the illustrious royal patron of what soon came to be known as the King's College.[23] This has, however, been dismissed as a superficial reading by Patrick Edwards in his thought-provoking study of the text of this inscription.[24] In a scholarly *tour-de-force* he demonstrated that the date, 2 April, on which the masons began their work *could* have been intended as an allusion to the date on which work began on Solomon's Temple, even if this cannot be proved. Unfortunately the Vulgate (II Paralipomenon (II Chronicles) 3.2) gives the date simply as '*mense secundo*' (in the second month). Against this difficulty Edwards was able to show that Jerome, in his

Liber Quaestionum Hebraicarum in Genesim, gave the date as the second day of the second month and that elsewhere he stated that the 'second month' was the equivalent of April. Edwards's argument that Elphinstone could have associated 2 April with the Temple of Solomon is greatly strengthened by another, more recent, source for a dating to the second day of the second month, in a surviving book which Elphinstone is known to have owned, a copy of Nicholas of Lyra's *Postillae* on the Old Testament. For Edwards therefore a truer and profounder interpretation of the inscription links the college and chapel with their Old Testament archetype, the Temple of Solomon.[25]

The possible verbal echoes of Vulgate accounts of the building of the Temple that Edwards sees in the inscription are intriguing if not conclusive. The word *latomus*, for example, is used of the masons working on the Temple (III Kings (I Kings) 5.15; I Paralipomenon (I Chronicles) 22.2, 22.15) but it was also a word in current use for masons in the later middle ages.[26] Nevertheless it is true that the inscription resembles two of the biblical passages in linking a king, a dating by year and month, and the start of building work. We can in addition compare the use of *aedificare* (to build), not itself an unusual word, in '*latomi inceperunt edificare*' of the King's College inscription with these passages: '. . . *aedificari coepit domus Domino*', '*Et coepit Salomon aedificare domum Domini . . . Coepit autem aedificare . . .*' (III Kings (I Kings) 6.1; II Paralipomenon (II Chronicles) 3.1–2). There would have been nothing very strange about recalling what were seen as Old Testament foreshadowings of the Christian church in this way. Bethel and the Temple in Jerusalem were both recalled in the liturgy for the dedication of a church and in many inscriptions derived from that liturgy.[27]

Whilst the inscription might simply have been a literal record of the date on which the masons started work, it is tempting to look for a symbolic significance in the choice of date. 2 April would not, however, appear to have been a day of any special ecclesiastical significance in late medieval Aberdeen. The Aberdeen Breviary lists the feast of St Mary of Egypt on 2 April and in 1500 it would have been a Thursday in Lent. The choice of 2 April for the commencement of work, whether or not work actually started on that day, *could* have been a deliberate allusion to the Temple. How likely is it, on the other hand, that Elphinstone, or one of his circle, would have devised an inscription that implied a comparison between his chapel and the Temple of Jerusalem without signalling the parallel in a more obvious way?

If, however, we do accept the hypothesis that the author of the inscription text intended a reference to the Temple, we should consider the possibility that he may equally have wished to invoke the memory of Solomon. Solomon was of course the Old Testament ideal of a wise, just and divinely sanctioned king. Solomonic imagery was therefore an important source of royal symbolism. In England in the time of Henry III and Edward, for example, references to Solomon are made in wall-paintings in the Palace of Westminster, in royal seals, in the Coronation Chair, in the coronation order and elsewhere.[28] In a Scottish context we have the admonitions for kings added in the fifteenth century by Walter Bower to Fordun's *Scotichronicon*, which include three references to Solomon, two quotations from books of the Bible attributed to Solomon and the famous story of the Judgement of Solomon.[29] We would not in fact need to choose between an ecclesiological and a royal reading, when both meanings would have been latent in an allusion to Solomon's building of the Temple. The implied comparison between the Scottish royal patron and King Solomon would, however, have needed to be pointed out to most, perhaps all, readers in order for it to have had any effect.

If we cannot prove (or disprove) that the author of the inscription intended a highly erudite reference to the start of work on Solomon's Temple, we should not forget that what is now an isolated inscription would have fitted into a wider symbolic context in the chapel and the college and that it could have been supplemented orally and visually in various ways. Jane Geddes has, for example, shown how the proportions of the chapel may have been intended, in a similarly veiled manner, to echo those of the Temple.[30] If these references were intended, we should perhaps imagine Elphinstone, or members of the college, providing an oral translation of the inscription and a commentary on the symbolism encoded into the inscription, building and its furnishings. It is not unlikely that the inscription was first cut to play a part in some ceremonial occasion, perhaps during one of James IV's several visits to Aberdeen, into which it would not have been difficult to work an allusion to the Temple and to the Old Testament king renowned both as its builder and as a wise and magnificent ruler.[31] Edwards's allegorical interpretation of the wording of the inscription is very attractive but, if accepted, it should be broadened to take account of its implications for the Christian ideal of kingship. Taken more literally the inscription is an effectively worded and carefully laid out epigraphic tribute to the king and an expression of pride in the new foundation and of surprising reticence on the part of the bishop who founded it.

Notes

I am very grateful to my colleague Allan Hood for his advice on the structure of the text of the King's College inscription and to Jane Geddes, who in addition to editing this volume has very kindly provided me with the measurements of the inscription.

[1] P. J. Anderson, 'Note on Heraldic Representations at King's College, Old Aberdeen', *PSAS,* XXIII, 1889, 80–86; and Chapter 10.

[2] Macfarlane, 1995, 330; R. Fawcett, 'The Architecture of King's College Chapel and Greyfriars' Church, Aberdeen', *AUR,* LIII, 1989, 102.

[3] Abbreviations are expanded in brackets and ':' is used to indicate punctuation marks of any form.

[4] See p. 35.

[5] J. Higgitt, 'The Inscriptions', in O. Owen and B. Smith, 'Kebister, Shetland: an armorial stone, and archdeacon's teind barn?', *Post-Medieval Archaeology,* 22, 1988, 10–11; K. A. Steer and J. W. M. Bannerman, *Late Medieval Monumental Sculpture in the West Highlands,* Edinburgh, 1977, 93; R. Brown, *The History of Paisley from the Roman Period down to 1884,* 2 vols, Paisley, 1886, vol. 1, 52–53; J. Malden, *The Abbey and Monastery of Paisley,* Renfrew District Council, Paisley, 1993, 20–21 and pl. on p. 20.

[6] *Fasti,* 282; Kelly, 1949, 70.

[7] R. Walker and A. M. Munro, *Handbook to City and University, University of Aberdeen Quatercentenary Celebrations, September 1906,* Aberdeen, 1906, 77; Kelly, 1949, fig. 19.

[8] M. B. Parkes, *Pause and Effect: an Introduction to the History of Punctuation in the West,* Aldershot, 1992, pl. 22; S. Badham, J. Blair and R. Emmerson, *Specimens of Lettering from English Monumental Brasses,* London, 1976, nos 129–30, 132–33, 200–01.

[9] Higgitt, 1988, 10–11.

[10] Anderson, 1889, pl. I; N. Gray, *A History of Lettering: Creative Experiment and Letter Identity,* Oxford, 1986, 148–50.

[11] G. F. Hill, *The Development of Arabic Numerals in Europe exhibited in sixty-four tables*, Oxford, 1915, tables XVII–XXI, XXIII–XXIX, LXI–LXII, for Corstorphine, Elgin and Kinkell see tables XIX and XVII; Kelly, 1949, 19–33.

[12] G. G. Simpson, *Scottish Handwriting 1150–1650*, Edinburgh, 1973, 21–23, fig. 7.

[13] G. P. Edwards, 'William Elphinstone, his College Chapel, and the Second of April', *AUR*, LI, 1985, 11 and in note 39 on p. 16.

[14] Eeles, 1956, 156–57, 234–35.

[15] Macfarlane, 1995, 327, 334.

[16] For example *Die deutschen Inschriften* and the *Corpus des inscriptions de la France médiévale*. See the convenient listing of corpora in R. Favreau, *Épigraphie médiévale*, Turnhout, 1997, 10–23 and the bibliographical surveys in *Literaturbericht zur mittelalterlichen und neuzeitlichen Epigraphik, 1976–1984*, ed. W. Koch, Munich, 1987 and *Literaturbericht zur mittelalterlichen und neuzeitlichen Epigraphik, 1985–1991*, Munich, 1994 = *Monumenta Germaniae Historica, Hilfsmittel*, 11 and 14.

[17] E.g. M. Clayton, *Catalogue of Brasses and Incised Slabs*, Victoria and Albert Museum, London, 1968, pl. 63.1, Bisham; *The Earliest English Brasses: Patronage, Style and Workshops 1270–1350*, ed. J. Coales, Monumental Brass Society, London, 1987, fig. 3, Ashbourne; S. Pegge, *A Sylloge of the Remaining Authentic Inscriptions relative to the Erection of our English Churches*, London, 1787, 26, 57–58, 93–94; J. Harvey, *English Medieval Architects: a Biographical Dictionary down to 1550*, new edn, Gloucester, 1984, 305; R. Favreau, *Études d'épigraphie médiévale*, 2 vols, Limoges, 1995, 182–84, 274–75, 378–84; R. Favreau, *Épigraphie médiévale*, Turnhout, 1997, 214–17; J. Higgitt, 'The Dedication Inscription at Jarrow and its Context', *Antiquaries Journal*, LIX, 1979, 343–74; *Le Pontifical romain au moyen-âge*, ed. M. Andrieu, tome III, *Le pontifical de Guillaume Durand*, Città del Vaticano 1940, 451–78, for examples of the services for the laying of the first stone and of the dedication of a church.

[18] The wording of this inscription was recorded by Holinshed: *The History of the King's Works*, ed. H. M. Colvin, vol. III, *1485–1660, Part 1*, London, 1975, 211.

[19] Pegge, 1787, 59–60, 78, and plates opposite pp. 59 and 78; N. Pevsner, *Staffordshire, The Buildings of England*, Harmondsworth, 1974, 204.

[20] B. E. Crawford, 'Earl William Sinclair and the Building of Roslin Collegiate Church', in *Medieval Art and Architecture in the Diocese of St Andrews*, British Archaeological Association Conference Transactions, ed. J. Higgitt, Leeds, 1994, 101.

[21] R. Brown, *The History of Paisley from the Roman Period down to 1884*, 2 vols, Paisley, 1886, vol. I, 52–53; J. Malden, *The Abbey and Monastery of Paisley*, Renfrew District Council, Paisley, 1993, 20–21 and pl. on p. 20.

[22] *Roxburghshire*, 2 vols, Royal Commission on the Ancient Monuments of Scotland, Edinburgh, 1956, vol. II, 279–80, 290–91, figs 359, 390.

[23] Macfarlane, 1995, 330.

[24] Edwards, 1985, 11.

[25] Edwards, 1985, 11–12. Valerie Summers has pointed out (pers. comm.) that Sunday 2 April 1441 was the date on which Henry VI laid the first stone for King's College, Cambridge. It is interesting that this relates to work on the college rather than on the chapel, which was not begun until five years later, in 1446. See *Royal Commission on Historical Monuments England, City of Cambridge*, 2 vols, London, 1959, II, 98–99. The shared date suggests the possibility that someone wished to associate the two royal academic foundations.

[26] *Dictionary of Medieval Latin from British Sources*, ed. R. E. Latham, London, 1975–, *s.v. latomus*.

[27] Edwards, 1985, 12, 16–17; R. Favreau, *Études d'épigraphie médiévale*, 2 vols, Limoges, 1995, 274–75, 378–84.

[28] F. Wormald, 'The Throne of Solomon and St. Edward's Chair', in *Francis Wormald: Collected Writing*, J. J. G. Alexander, T. J. Brown and J. Gibbs (eds), vol. II, Studies in English and Continental Art of the Later Middle Ages, London, 1988, 61–69; P. Binski, *Westminster Abbey and the Plantagenets: Kingship and the Representation of Power 1200–1400*, New Haven and London, 1995, 61–62, 84, 130, 134, 138–39.

[29] *Scotichronicon by Walter Bower*, 9 vols, ed. D. E. R. Watt, 1987–98, vol. 2, 1989, 280–83, 286–87, 424–25.

[30] See pp. 61–63.

[31] James visited Aberdeen in 1492, 1495, 1497, 1500, 1501, 1504, 1509 and 1510. Macfarlane, 1995, 272, 289, n 227.

CHAPTER SIX

THE CHOIR STALLS AND ROOD SCREEN

By SALLYANNE SIMPSON

The oak choir stalls, canopies and screen in King's College Chapel are the finest remaining example of early sixteenth-century woodwork anywhere in Scotland, in both their richness and completeness (Fig. 6.1). They were probably installed between 1506 when lead was put on the roof and 1509 when the chapel was dedicated.[1] This chapter examines their construction and design, followed by an analysis of their sources, both Netherlandish and Scottish.[2]

DESCRIPTION OF THE CHOIR STALLS

A choir stall is an individual seat within the choir of the church. Each stall is divided from the next by a side panel with arm rest. The seat or misericord is hinged at the back and folds up to provide a resting ledge for the long periods of standing involved in a medieval service. At King's, the side panels and seat backs support a horizontal band of carving which is deeply carved with foliage, at shoulder height. The stalls at King's are divided into two groups: upper stalls with canopies and lower stalls, or *subsellia*, without canopies. Above the carved ribbon of the upper stalls are the back linings. At King's these are formed of plain panelling which is a modern replacement. Above the linings is a carved design of running vine leaf and grape motifs. Above this is the curved hood of the canopy. At the front of the hood hang the intricately carved, open-work tracery panels of the canopy. The stall ends are carved with blind tracery. The eight lower stall ends once terminated in poppy heads, probably cut off at the Reformation.[3] The four upper stall ends continue above stall height with an open-work design linking them to the canopy. One is of oak leaves and acorns, one of vine leaves and grapes and the last two are both of thistles.

There are fifty-two stalls, twenty-six on either side of the aisle. Each side has fifteen upper stalls, twelve running parallel to the aisle and three forming returns at the west end. The eleven lower stalls are arranged with two small return stalls and the remaining nine in two groups divided by a passage, five to the east and four to the west (Fig. 2.1).

Kelly suggested that, because Bishop Elphinstone's foundation charter of 1505 only included thirty-six college members, only thirty-four stalls were initially planned (with an organist and organ blower in the loft); twenty upper stalls with canopies and fourteen *subsellia*.[4] However, by 1514 Elphinstone's second charter had increased the college members to forty-two. This charter gives details of their seating within the

Fig. 6.1.   The stalls, from the east

choir from which Fig. 2.1 has been prepared.[5] Therefore Kelly proposed five more stalls on each side were ordered, making thirty stalls, and twenty-two *subsellia*, fifty-two places in all, as at present. It seems likely that by the consecration of 1509 the full fifty-two stalls were planned or in place. The proposal that the stalls developed in two closely–dated sequences may account for certain features in the architecture of the chapel, and variations in the design of the stalls.[6]

The vagaries of the string course on the exterior north wall suggest there may have been an early change of plan concerning the stalls and their canopies (Fig. 4.3). Twenty upper stalls could be contained within the length of the third bay (from the east) (Fig. 2.1). The string course below this window drops down at the eastern lancet. It is possible that, at the outset, only fourteen stalls for dignitaries were intended to

Fig. 6.2, a–g.   The misericord panels (Copyright: University of Aberdeen)

have canopies which backed against the high string course, while the remaining six stalls were lower, explaining the drop in the string course.

The horizontal carved band which runs along the top of the stalls is decorated with vine leaves and grapes above the upper stalls and oak leaves and acorns above the lower stalls. The frieze diminished appropriately to allow a comfortable back support. The backs of the upper stalls are plain whereas the lower stall backs are decorated with linen-fold panels. Misericord ledges are often decorated with amusing, secular, or even irreverent images due to their inconspicuous location on the under side of the seat. However five of the seven carvings which remain at King's match the stalls with vine leaf, grape and thistle motifs. The other designs are a crown and the sacred initials 'IHS' (*Jesus* or *In Hoc Signo*). The misericords at King's are unusual in having no supporters (smaller designs on either side of the principal carving), following the European rather than the English tradition (Fig. 6.2, a–g).

The stall ends and canopies are decorated with flamboyant tracery designs. Each of the twelve stall ends contains a different design. The thirty canopy panels each contain three sub-panels, forming a continuous flat screen; ninety designs in total of which very few are exact repeats. This represents a diversity unmatched by the remains of contemporary stalls in Scotland. The three sub-panels consist of a lower, roughly square panel with an ogival arch of vine leaves defining its lower edge and two upper rectangular panels divided by a buttress (Fig. 6.3).

The buttress divisions between the canopy panels are made from applied stiles with crocketted pinnacles.[7] On the edge of the upper stall ends there are pedestals to hold figures with a crocketted pinnacle above forming a niche.

At the west end of the stalls, a splendidly elaborate doorway leads into the nave. Open-work panels of flamboyant mouchettes are topped by panels of fleurs-de-lis (Fig. 6.4). Above, is the broad platform for the organ, altar, choristers and preacher. It was reached from the nave by a spiral staircase inside the screen. There was also direct access from the sacristy through a door in the south wall. A wooden ambo, for preaching in the nave, projected from the gallery, and there were statues of the Saviour and the apostles 'on the front of the rood loft'.[8] Above the platform, in the

Fig. 6.3. The canopies, by J. C. Watt, 1885 (Copyright: University of Aberdeen)

centre, was the great rood or crucifix surmounted by a coved canopy attached to the rood beam, which traversed the nave at wall-plate level. On either side of the rood were two lower coved canopies supported on a delicate open screen (Fig. 6.5). On the west side of the screen, two altars fronted the present areas of blank panelling.[9]

The thistle and rose on the stalls are one of the few reminders on the interior of the chapel of its royal patron. The thistle appears boldly on the end panels of the west stalls, on a canopy and more discretely on a misericord where the rose is also found. In 1502 Sir Thomas Galbraith decorated the ratification of the marriage of James IV and Margaret Tudor with her rose and daisy entwined with his thistle. The first written reference to the thistle as a Scottish emblem comes in a poem of 1503 by William Dunbar entitled 'The Thistle and the Rose' in reference to the king's marriage. The *Book of Hours* commissioned by James as a wedding gift is filled with thistles and daisies or marguerites.[10]

HISTORICAL RECORD

The first recorded description of the choir stalls comes from Boece in 1521, where he describes 'fine carved work, seats for the use of the priests, and benches for the boys, made with wonderful art', all donated by Bishop Elphinstone.[11] The stalls must therefore have been commissioned and constructed some time between the start of

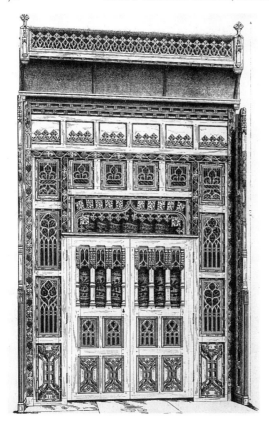

Fig. 6.4.   The screen door from the
east, by J. C. Watt, 1885 (Copyright:
University of Aberdeen)

work on the chapel in 1500 and the consecration in 1509. It is unlikely that they were
installed before the roof was leaded in 1506. In the Inventory of 1542 there is no
description of the stalls.[12] Orem mentions in 1725 '. . . in this chapel there is a middle
wall of timber, and above it an excellent loft with a pulpit on the left side thereof
where the priest preached; . . . and in the east end . . . yet there are stalls and seats
remaining for the prebends and masters of the college'.[13] Douglas, in 1780, provides
the only contemporary description of the lost back panels: 'the stalls and back linings
on the side walls are wainscot, and richly ornamented with most accurate carved
work.'[14] However by the early nineteenth century, these panels had deteriorated so
badly that they were replaced with plain new wood.[15]

   Little happened to the woodwork in the seventeenth and eighteenth centuries,
apart from the gradual accretion of graffiti,[16] but new demands were made on the
fabric after services resumed 1823. As student numbers increased, it became necessary
to enlarge the area available for worship. In 1870 the library was removed from the
nave, and in 1873 the ancient screen and stalls were shifted one bay westwards to
enlarge the choir, leaving the upper door to the rood loft blocked in the middle of an
empty wall. The open screen and canopies above the gallery were taken down and

Fig. 6.5.   Choir screen, 1890s, with upper screen installed (Copyright: University of Aberdeen)

the ambo temporarily lost.[17] The deliberate removal of the screen and canopies was perhaps the most drastic alteration to the woodwork since the early reformers had taken down all the images on the rood. It brought Macpherson, the chapel historian, to the point of outrage, that such destruction could have taken place as late as the 1870s. The episode is poorly documented but Macpherson found out that Dean Stanley was personally responsible. 'No one but Mr Matheson, then of the Board of Works, knew or respected what he [Stanley] contemplated til the result was accomplished. His judgement alone as an architect dictated the lowering of the canopies, the mutilation of the gallery and the burying of the ambo in the vault below the [Scottish] parliament house'.[18] In 1891 Macpherson made an heroic effort to reconstruct what was lost, begging the Principal to find an illustration of the old east end of the library and retrieving fragments of the screen from Edinburgh where the Office of Works had taken them for 'safekeeping'.[19] Eventually a slight sketch from 1845 was found, which showed the great beam across the roof.[20] Bishop Pococke had recorded in 1760 'a fine Covered Screen and Gallery, with a pulpit in it'.[21] It was clear from the disparaging 1782 description by Douglas that book shelves had simply been put up in front of the old screen, leaving the rood loft as access to the upper tier of books.[22] Andrew Kerr, architect from the Office of Works, was exploring around the old book cases at the east end of the library and found the dismantled uprights, seven per side, which supported the canopies. They had grooves in them for slotting in tracery panels. The canopy over the central space, housing statues of the Crucifixion, the Virgin and St John was supported by the great rood beam.[23] Principal Geddes reminded Macpherson how sensitive his congregation was to doctrine and liturgy: although it was agreed to restore the screen and canopies, the word 'rood' was not to be mentioned in any account.[24] Eventually Macpherson's careful archaeological reasoning led to Rowand Anderson's designs for restoring the loft canopies, but at the same time, installing an unhistorically-large organ on top of the screen.[25]

The organ, installed as part of the 1891 campaign, was made by Norman Bros. of Norwich.[26] This organ was becoming excessively expensive to repair by 1959 and was replaced in 1960 with a new one made by Harrison and Harrison of Norwich.[27] At this stage, the lofty arcade and canopy, resurrected so painstakingly by Macpherson in the 1890s was once more removed and the canopies lowered to their present illogical position, resting on the upper edge of the rood.[28] Once again, the second removal of the arcade is poorly documented, with only two hints that dry rot may have been the problem.[29]

ANALYSIS OF THE CARVINGS

The carving falls into three broad categories: foliage or plant forms, tracery and linen-fold. Foliage, in the form of running vine scrolls decorate the stalls while large foliage panels form the west returns of the upper stalls. Flamboyant tracery, in exuberant variety, decorates the stall ends and the canopies.

Two different techniques for carving mouldings can be observed on the woodwork. They are found on the edgings, plant stems and the tracery outlines. These are defined as Group 1 and Group 2 in the following discussion.

Group 1.   Group 1 is distinguished by its use of rounded, plasticine-like mouldings (Figs 3.1, 6.6). These can be seen along the edge of the horizontal band around the top of the stalls (Fig. 3.1). The running stems of the vines and oak leaves are carved in a similar way. The same moulding runs down the curved edge of the stall divisions and outlines the arm-rest motif. This technique can also be seen in seven of the twelve stall ends. The four upper stall ends all display these bold, rounded profiles. The open-work panels of thistles, oak leaves and acorns and vine leaves and grapes which link these stall ends to the canopy have a similar robust handling (Fig. 6.6a). The three lower stall ends of Group 1 profile are also of a slightly different design to those of the other group. One has a rose window motif and the other two consist of twin pointed arch designs (Figs 6.6b–c).

Amongst the canopy panels several of the upper sub-panels can be seen to have the same rounded treatment, appearing heavier than those of the second technical grouping. These Group 1 canopy panels are mostly located above the western stalls. They include the fleur-de-lis also found on the rood door (Fig. 6.4, 6.6d, upper right). One of the lower panels may also belong to this group (Fig. 6.6e).

Group 2.   Group 2 is distinguished by its use of sharply cut, angled mouldings (Fig. 6.7a–e). These can be seen on five of the eight lower stall ends, all of which have a

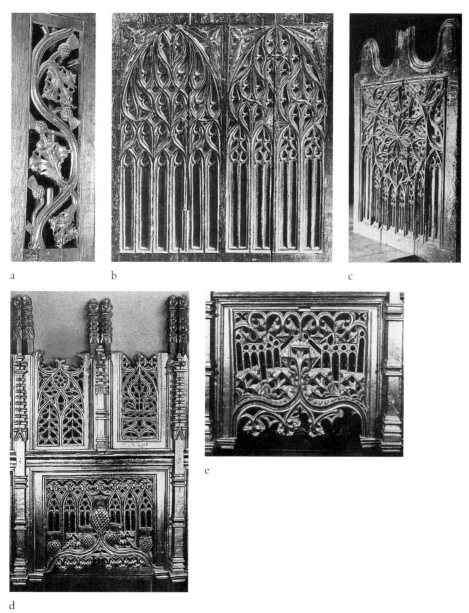

a b c

d e

Fig. 6.6. Group 1 carvings (Copyright: University of Aberdeen)

similar design; two pointed arches flanked by vertical strips of geometric patterning (Fig. 6.7a).

Additionally, Group 2 includes the majority of the canopy panels. The angled profiles of this group give a crisper effect to the open-work canopy panels, making

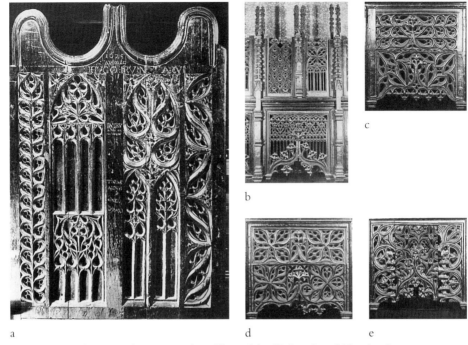

Fig. 6.7.   Group 2 carvings (Copyright: University of Aberdeen)

them more delicate in appearance. Of the larger, lower canopy panels, twenty-eight appear to be Group 2. These can be sub-divided into two types by panel design.

Design 1.   Design 1 is characterized by a single large ogival arch, cusped with vine leaves, which reaches to approximately three-quarters of the height of the panel (Fig. 6.7b). A row of arched tracery fills the rest of the panel. Design 1 is the larger group comprising eighteen of the panels. Three of the these panels are repaired using part of another panel. This indicates that there were originally more panels of this design.

Design 2.   Design 2, comprising nine of the panels, is characterized by two vine leaf, cusped, ogival arches each occupying half the height of the panel (Fig. 6.3d). In four of the panels, the resultant rectangular areas are filled with tracery designs. In the remaining five panels, four square tracery motifs decorate the corners. This leaves two final panels. The first is a repaired composite, comprising fragments from panels which do not appear to conform to either Design 1 or Design 2, although it may still belong to Group 2 (Fig. 6.7e). The second panel is an adaptation of Design 1 which features rather flaccid thistle heads in place of the vine leaf motifs. It is possible that this panel may be a nineteenth-century restoration and therefore does not belong to either Group 1 or Group 2 (Fig. 6.6d).

In conclusion, the technique and composition of the stalls and canopies at King's can be classified in several ways (Fig. 6.8). Two different approaches to technique can

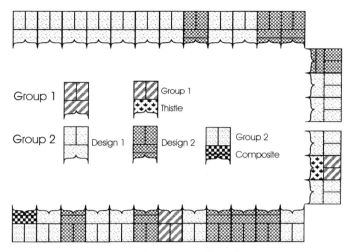

Fig. 6.8.   Layout of panels

be identified. Group 1 is characterized by rounded mouldings whereas Group 2 has angled mouldings. Group 1 includes the stall carvings, seven of the stall ends, several upper canopy panels and one lower canopy panel. Group 2 includes the remaining five stall ends, twenty-eight of the lower canopy panels and the remaining upper canopy panels. The twenty-eight Group 2 lower canopy panels can be further divided by design. Design 1 contains a single ogival arch and open-work tracery. Design 2 contains two ogival arches and tracery designs. There is a unique lower canopy panel with thistle head motifs which may be a restoration replacement.

ANALYSIS OF STYLE

The rich use of flamboyant tracery gives the stalls and screen a distinctly Netherlandish appearance.[30] This influence is also apparent in the ceiling, window tracery and Bishop Elphinstone's portrait and tomb.[31] Before assigning a source for the style of the stalls and screen, it is necessary to explore and compare woodwork from the Low Countries and Scotland around 1500. Fig. 6.9 provides a summary of the features under discussion.

Netherlandish style.   One of the problems of defining a 'Netherlandish Style' is the lack of extant examples. Many choir stalls in the Low Countries have been destroyed, particularly during the Napoleonic era.[32] The examples cited span a period from the mid-fifteenth century to the early sixteenth century. They are Netherlandish and, as all remain *in situ*, have a secure provenance. Their style can be characterized by several features. Blind fenestrated tracery occurs on stall ends and back linings. Common elements in the carvings include ogival arches with vine leaves, figures and crocketted pinnacles. Linen-fold decoration occurs on desk fronts and screen doors. These

	Blind Tracery	Open Tracery	Linen fold	Ogival Arch	Vine Leaf	Crocketted Pinnacles	Figures
Bolsward	●		●	●	●	●	●
Breda	●			●	●	●	●
's-Hertogenbosch	●			●	●	●	●
Haarlem	●	●	●		●		●
King's College	●	●	●	●	●	●	
Carlisle		●	●		●		
Dunblane		●		●	●	●	●
Foulis Easter		●	●			●	
Jarrow	●			●	●		●
Lincluden							●
St Andrews							
"Beaton Panels"	●	●			●		●
Aberdeen, Trinity Hall	●	●	●	●	●		
Aberdeen, St Nicholas		●		●	●	●	
Dumfriesshire	●			●			
Stirling	●			●	●		

Fig. 6.9.   Table of features

examples of stalls do not feature much open-work. This was however extensively used on other objects like altarpieces.[33]

At St Martinuskerk, Bolsward (*c.* 1500) there are linen-fold panels framed by running vine scrolls on the desk fronts while the back linings are decorated with panels of ogival arches cusped with vine leaves and surmounted by lancet tracery. At St Bavokerk, Haarlem (1512) there are linen-fold panels on the bottom of the screen doors, blind tracery on the stall ends and openwork panels of flamboyant tracery.[34] At Onze Lieve Vrouwenkerk, Breda (*c.* 1475) and St Johns, 's-Hertogenbosch (*c.* 1427–75) (Fig. 6.10) there are panels particularly like King's Design 1. An ogival arch decorated with leaves pushes its way through dense spandrels of flamboyant tracery (Figs 6.7b, 6.10).[35]

A significant feature about these Netherlandish examples is that they are almost all likely to be earlier than the King's woodwork. Flamboyant geometric designs reached the peak of Gothic intensity by the mid-fifteenth century, for instance in architecture like the town halls of Brussels and Louvain, finished in 1455 and 1463 respectively, or church furniture like the tabernacle of 1450 in St Peter's Louvain. By the late fifteenth century, naturalism and classical motifs were superceding abstract tracery. Examples of this radical shift in style can be seen on the renaissance stalls of Onze Lieve Vrouwekerk, Dortrecht, made in 1538–42.[36]

Scottish style.   As with the Low Countries, the paucity of extant examples is a major problem in assessing the nature of Scottish ecclesiastical woodwork at the turn of the

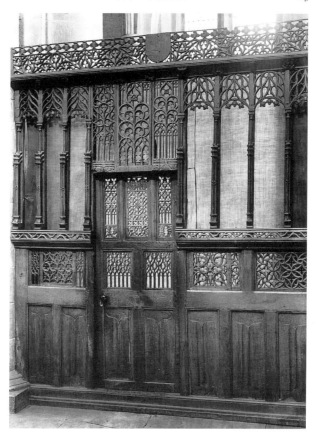

Fig. 6.10.
's-Hertogenbosch, St John's
Church, stall end

Fig. 6.11.   Carlisle Cathedral, St Catherine's Chapel
(Copyright: Batsford)

sixteenth century. Fawcett laments that the few remaining stalls in Scotland provide 'an inadequate basis on which to generalize about stall design in Scotland'.[37] The examples compared in the table all appear to be roughly contemporary, either late fifteenth century or very early sixteenth century.

The only other choir seating which survives in a fairly complete state are the sixteen stalls at Dunblane Cathedral, six of which retain their canopies. These canopied stalls bear the arms of Bishop James Chisholm (1487–1526). With their fleshy, naturalistic foliage, they are already beginning to show signs of the Renaissance and must date from the end of Chisholm's tenure. Although the canopies are not especially like King's, the remaining misericords include foliate motifs like the thistle and vine.[38]

At Holy Trinity, St Andrews there are two choir stalls, bereft of backings and canopies.[39] As at King's, these stalls have a carved ribbon decorated with floral motifs running along the top, at shoulder height. The stalls bear the arms of King James IV and Gavin Dunbar, archdeacon of St Andrews from 1503 to 1518, and were presumably carved before the king's death in 1513. Although Dunbar went on to become chancellor of Aberdeen University and a great patron of art and architecture there, his stalls at Holy Trinity do not provide a close comparison with Bishop Elphinstone's at King's.

The rood screen doors at Foulis Easter, although much coarser and simpler than those at King's, have the same approach to design.[40] The lowest panels of the doors are solid linen-fold, and below the arcade are four open-work flamboyant tracery panels. Of slightly later date, probably 1520–40, are the Beaton Panels.[41] These are of very high quality craftsmanship. They are surrounded by frames of running vine scroll and have fragments of inventive flamboyant tracery attached to the base of some panels. They include fleshy and florid depictions of the thistle and rose. Caldwell argues that, in spite of some continental features, they are most likely to be made in Scotland. There are further, unprovenanced, panels of rather simple flamboyant tracery from Dumfriesshire and Stirling.[42]

Three more Scottish examples, from St Nicholas', Aberdeen are discussed below (pp. 89–92), in connection with the provenance of the King's stalls.

Two northern English examples are also worth mentioning as they illustrate designs current at the time. The screen and door on the west side of St Catherine's Chapel, erected at Carlisle Cathedral between 1465 and 1500 have linen-fold panels at their base while the upper parts are filled with virtuoso open-work tracery as wildly exuberant and individual as the canopy panels at King's. The door has two panels of open fleur-de-lis similar to those on the King's doorway (Figs 6.11, 6.4).[43] At St Paul's, Jarrow, the stall ends are filled with varieties of blind tracery and still retain their poppy head finials.[44]

These Scottish and north English examples appear to have many features in common with the Netherlandish style already described. They frequently include flamboyant tracery, ogival arches and vine leaf decoration. Linen-fold work and crocketted pinnacles are also found. Where characteristic features are missing it may be due to the incomplete nature of the remaining fragments. For example at Holy Trinity, St Andrews, only two stalls remain, without stall ends, back linings or canopies. It is therefore impossible to say whether the St Andrews' carvings originally included any of the features listed. Additionally open-work tracery occurs in the Scottish examples but in only one of the Netherlandish examples given, at Haarlem. This example just post-dates King's and the style of the open-work tracery is moving towards renaissance types of foliage designs.

A QUESTION OF ORIGIN

Even though documentary evidence and surviving examples are scanty, three possible origins for the King's stalls need to be explored. First, they could have been made in the Low Countries and shipped complete to Aberdeen. This was suggested by Principal Geddes.[45] Second, a Flemish craftsman could have come over and made them in Aberdeen and third, they could be a local Aberdonian product.

Fig. 6.12. Desk-end from St Machar's Cathedral, shown as the bottom left tracery panel in the view of King's College Chapel by R. W. Billings (Copyright: University of Aberdeen)

For a long time, works of art and other high-quality finished goods had been imported from the Low Countries into Scotland. In particular Melrose Abbey imported choir stalls from Bruges as early as 1441.[46] Many other church furnishings were commissioned including paintings, sculpture, altarpieces and arras fabrics. The painted altar panels for Holy Trinity Church, Edinburgh were made by Hugo van der Goes *c.* 1478–79.[47] Robert Ballantyne, abbot of Holyrood purchased vestments for his abbey in Bruges in 1494; James Brown, dean of Aberdeen, bought a book of hours in the Netherlands in 1498; and around 1508 two 'tabernacles' commissioned in Flanders were set up in Pluscarden Abbey.[48] The ledger of Andrew Halyburton, 'Conservator of the Privileges of the Scotch Nation in the Netherlands', testifies to a flourishing trade, whereby Bishop Elphinstone even bought wheelbarrows for building the chapel from abroad.[49] At St Machar's Cathedral, there was a magnificent golden altar retable, destroyed in 1642. From Orem's slight description, it was apparently of the elaborate type produced on the Continent.[50] Since Bishop Elphinstone built the new cathedral choir, he may also have provided the retable.[51]

He visited Bruges in 1495, he chose to wear episcopal vestments in the Flemish style and his portrait was made in the Flemish style.[52]

If the King's choir stalls were purchased complete from the Low Countries, one would expect to find closer similarities with continental work and, more significantly, by the early sixteenth century one would expect more evidence of renaissance detailing, like naturalistic, organic foliage, classical mouldings and perhaps balusters.

There is a large quantity of contemporary evidence for the second possibility, that Flemish craftsmen were employed in Aberdeen, because they were working all over Britain in the late fifteenth century. Their skills had been widely sought after for a long time. King James I (1406–37) 'brocht oute of Ingland and Flanderis ingenious men of sindry craftis to instruct his pepill in vertewis occupacioun'.[53] The painter Meynnart Wewyck visited James IV in 1502. Andrew Halyburton, who supplied Elphinstone with so many of his basic materials for the chapel, was related by marriage to three great Netherlandish painters and consequently was asked by James IV to send over a suitable court painter from the Low Countries. 'Piers the painter' worked in Scotland from 1505 to 1508.[54] Craftsmen with the surnames 'Flemyng' and 'Flemisman' were employed at Holyrood in 1531–32 and Falkland in 1538–39 respectively.[55]

Documentary evidence outwith Scotland sheds some light on how complex items of church furnishing were created and assembled. The remarkable accounts from St George's Chapel, Windsor between 1477 and 1484 provide a unique insight into the production of woodwork, in this case the stalls of the Knights of the Garter.[56] These stalls also have a general Flemish appearance, but no direct parallel with surviving examples. The head carver William Berkeley spent considerable time in London supervising the carving of canopies. These were made by Robert Ellis and John Filles.[57] At least seven of Berkeley's team were English but two Flemings, Dirike Vangrove and Giles van Castell, were employed to produce figure sculpture for the rood. Each section of the stalls including spandrels, poppy-heads, 'baberies' (misericords), 'trails and crests' and finials is specified and paid for at different times. A 'dead store' presumably of finished parts waiting to be assembled, is also mentioned in the accounts.

This division of labour is further documented in contracts for Netherlandish altarpieces.[58] Specialized *metselarijsnijders* were responsible for the tracery and evidence shows that they used stencils to repeat their designs accurately.[59] If the design was not copied by stencil, it could have been transferred by one of the many *patroons* (design drawings) mentioned in contracts for the altarpieces.[60] It was not unusual for one workshop or artist to provide the pattern for another to execute.[61] Moreover, some elements of altarpieces, particularly the tracery frieze around the base, were prefabricated by the yard and were on sale as independent strips on the open market.[62]

There are no accounts for the stalls in Henry VII's Chapel, Westminster, but these must have been made around 1512. They also show a certain flamboyant Flemish exuberance, now modified by renaissance naturalism. Their carvers are not known, but a team of joiners with Flemish surnames (Duche, Vanclyffe, Vanshanhale and de Freseland) were working nearby at the Savoy Hospital.[63] Meanwhile a 'Ducheman Smyth' produced the distinctly English-looking bronze screen for Henry VII's tomb at Westminster in 1505–06.[64] So, at least in England, there is evidence of

Netherlandish craftsmen working alongside English carvers and producing designs which look exotic and somewhat foreign but not exactly like work in the Low Countries. Equally, a 'Ducheman' could produce an openwork screen in Westminster with a decidedly English appearance, reflecting the desire of the patron. The movement of skilled craftsmen worked in both directions: surnames recorded in the Antwerp Guild of Sculptors between 1495 and 1520 include some which appear to be Scottish.[65] It remains to be seen whether a Netherlandish craftsman was directly involved at King's or whether Scotsmen could have made the woodwork on their own.

The third possible origin for the King's stalls is local, and Aberdeen is able to provide evidence for a thriving woodwork craft both before and around 1500.[66] Bishop Spens (1459–80) provided new seating for the choir in St Machar's Cathedral. According to Boece , he 'removed the ancient seats (stalls as they are called) in the choir . . . He put in their places new ones of rare art and beauty, along with a throne of equal artistic beauty for the use of the bishop'.[67] Boece implies that Spens only withdrew to his diocese in Aberdeen at the end of his widely travelled career, during the 1470s, eventually becoming a generous patron of his cathedral to secure his eternal welfare. Between 1449 and the 1460s he was a frequent visitor to the Low Countries and northern France. It may be due to designs brought to Aberdeen in his time that the King's Chapel ceiling and stalls appear to reflect fashion in the Low Countries from earlier in the fifteenth century.

Early in the nineteenth century, new pews were being installed in the cathedral and fragments of old woodwork were rescued by the carpenter who happened to be working in the chapel at the same time. He brought from the cathedral a fine traceried door and a desk-end from the choir stalls (Fig. 6.13). This was incorporated by Kelly into the modern replica seats on the north side of the presbytery. Its design is like that of Group 2, with angled mouldings on the tracery.[68] If it formed part of Spens' choir stalls, then the conclusion must be that this type of design remained part of the Aberdeen stock in trade for about twenty-five years and was reused at King's, or else it was part of a special, but undocumented commission for the cathedral by Bishop Elphinstone around 1500. There was a further link between Spens and the woodwork at King's, but the location of both items is no longer known. Spens had some carved wooden panels made between 1471 and 1480. These included his own coat of arms and the royal arms of Scotland: the lion rampant in a shield, and a circlet on top. The royal arms, carved in oak, were also found at King's, below the eaves valance at the east end of the chapel.[69]

The most important joiner working in Aberdeen around 1500 was John Fendour. He was engaged to make the 'ruff and tymmir of the queyr' for the old East Kirk of St Nicholas in 1495.[70] The ceiling, dated by inscription to 1510–15, was remarkably similar to the one in King's, sharing both the sprigged bosses and a valance of vine leaves (Figs 4.12, 6.1).[71] Fendour was commissioned to 'big, oupmak and finally end and complet the xxxiiij stallis in thar queyr, with the spiris and the chanslar dur'. The burgh expected this job to be completed between December 1507 and Michaelmas 1508.[72] This implies that Fendour was working with a considerable team of trained

Fig. 6.13.   Fragments from Aberdeen, St Nicholas, East Kirk, in the Museum of Scotland
(Photo: © The Trustees of the National Museums of Scotland 1999)

Fig. 6.14.   Panels from Aberdeen, St Nicholas, East Kirk, now in St Mary's undercroft
(Crown Copyright: Royal Commission on the Ancient and Historical Monuments of
Scotland)

men. In 1511 he was commissioned on behalf of Bishop Elphinstone to make 'the tymmer werk of the grat stepile of the Cathedrall Kirk of Aberdoun'.[73]

John Fendour's work at St Nicholas' only survives in fragments. Tracery panels, vine-leaf cresting and five stiles from a door are in the Museum of Scotland in Edinburgh; some panels have been incorporated into two desks in St Mary's Chapel, the undercroft of St Nicholas';[74] and some are made into the chair of the Deacon Convenor for the Aberdeen Incorporated Trades at Trinity Hall. Aberdeen Trades have owned the Deacon Convenor's Chair since the 1570s, gifted by Matthew Guild who seems to have obtained fragments of the choir furnishings when they were removed at the Reformation.[75]

The Edinburgh fragments form a continuous screen of four canopy panels (Fig. 6.13). They follow the same formula as Design 1 at King's, although the ogival arches reach the full height of the panel and the fenestrated design is simpler. The design is repeated on all four panels without variation. They are also of a heavier, more restrained execution than the lively, lacy panels at King's. There are no upper panels in the St Nicholas' fragments. The St Nicholas' panels are separated by figure niches instead of the buttresses at King's although something similar can be seen at King's on the front edge of the upright at the ends of the upper stalls which link the stalls with the canopy (Fig. 6.12) The stiles have fewer mouldings than those at King's but they follow the same formula, being topped by a trefoil gablet and crockets. The vine-leaf cresting is simpler than most of the crests and valences of the King's ceiling and screen door, but it follows a very similar pattern to the crest below the coving on the screen west door (east side). Most telling of all are the seven panels which now form the desk front at St Mary's Chapel (Fig. 6.14). They are identical in size (28 x 69cm) and design to those at the base of the King's screen, to the right and left of the door (Fig. 6.4).[76]

The Trinity Hall pieces are equally striking (Fig. 6.15). Two extremely fine panels of flamboyant tracery are fitted into the back of the Deacon Convenor's chair. They have the same quivering energy as the finest King's canopy panels, and the mouldings are sharply edged like Group 2.[77] The two panels on the front of the chair are of elaborate blind tracery, with rounded mouldings like Group 1. Both the front and back panels of the chair are 19cm wide, exactly the same width as the top panels of the King's canopies on the north and south sides.[78]

Further evidence of Aberdeen craftsmanship are the two panels of Bishop Elphinstone's arms, now in the chapel, and the elaborate arms of James V (1514–42) reputedly from the Mint Building in Exchequer Row, Aberdeen. The latter are framed by vine scrolls like those on the stalls.[79]

Without doubt, the same craftsmen worked on the St Nicholas' furnishings and those at King's. However, both these extensive projects were underway at the same time: St Nicholas's 1507–08, and King's 1506–09. John Fendour must have had to draft in a considerable team to keep up with his patrons and this clearly accounts for the variable quality of the work. In particular, the rood screen appears to be somewhat coarser than the finest canopies on the north and south sides. Possibly separate elements of the woodwork may have originated from different sources or at different times. The Windsor accounts showed that a large team of craftsmen was organized by

Fig. 6.15.   Aberdeen, Trinity Hall,
Deacon Convenor's chair (Copyright:
The Incorporated Trades of Aberdeen)

William Berkeley who subcontracted the complicated canopy work to men in London while the seating was made on site.[80]

If the stalls and canopies were planned and commissioned around 1500 when building work began, they could not have been installed until the roof went on in 1506. The intricacy of the carving, however, would mean that the commission would have taken quite some time to complete. It is possible that work began on the carving of the canopy panels fairly early on and that these were accumulated in a store, like the 'dead store' mentioned at Windsor. Without the surrounding framework they would have occupied fairly little space. As each one is individual it would also have been possible to work on them between other jobs. If, as Kelly suggested, it was originally planned to provide only thirty-four stalls with twenty canopies, this may explain the discrepancy in design between the lower canopy panels of Design 1 and Design 2. The eighteen panels of Design 1 may represent the panels carved for the originally intended twenty canopy panels. Once these were complete, work may have begun on constructing and carving the thirty-four stalls. However, as Elphinstone's revised charter of 1514 suggests, it was quickly realized that additional stalls were required. If this occurred during the making of the stalls, it would have been simple to provide a further ten stalls consistent in design and execution with the originals and install them without any change being apparent. Then, before the canopy was assembled, a further ten canopy panels were commissioned. The nine surviving Design 2 panels may represent this later commission, which could account for their different composition. The upper panels attributed to Group 1 may also have been completed at this time. Such adjustments and additions would be easier to organize locally than abroad.

Finally, with respect to John Fendour, there remains the question of his own origin. Was he Scottish or was he a Flemish immigrant? Kelly speculated that the name 'Fendour' which also appears variously as Findour, Fyndour, Fendeur, Findon and possibly Winter, was originally of French origin. He went on to assert that John Fendour was a French-speaking Fleming.[81] There is no clear answer to this question, but it is apparent that if Fendour was working on the roof at St Nicholas' in 1495 and also on its ceiling in 1515, then he was resident in Aberdeen for quite some time. His reputation in Aberdeen during this busy period was so high that he was simultaneously employed by James IV at Falkland Palace between 1501 and 1504, procuring and assembling large amounts of timber, mainly for roofing.[82] The specific requirements of his Falkland Palace work clearly involved a lot of negotiation with timber suppliers in the Highlands, a job more suited to a local man than a French-speaking foreigner. His long term commitments in the North-East make it unlikely that he was part of a team of travelling foreign craftsmen but rather that he was settled in Scotland. Surviving woodwork elsewhere in Scotland shows that native products existed. The prevalence of the 'Flemish style' was such a prominent feature of Scottish design at the time, that it had been absorbed into the Scottish idiom.[83] Important architectural features like the King's window tracery and ceiling, together with Bishop Elphinstone's Netherlandish-looking portrait are discussed elsewhere.[84] Clearly John Fendour was organizing a considerable team of skilled men for his commissions all around Aberdeen, and these artisans would have assembled in a relatively short period around 1500. Fendour must have summoned them from all over the country and perhaps a few came from abroad. Contracts for Netherlandish altarpieces have shown that craftsmen and workshops exchanged templates for designs, at their patron's request which could also account for the rich variety of Flemish-looking tracery at King's.

The patron provides a final strand of circumstantial evidence. Bishop Elphinstone was troubled by the practical aspects of his new venture. Despite having papal and royal approval, he struggled to ensure its financial security. During the years of founding and building the university Elphinstone experienced severe financial strain on his resources.[85] He worked hard to draw in money from various parishes within his diocese and traded goods such as salmon, trout and wool with his Flemish agent in order to acquire building equipment. In 1500, the year of the chapel's foundation, he was already nearly seventy years old. With the restrictions of time and money which he faced it would have seemed the obvious choice to look to the best local craftsmen rather than abroad. The account of Elphinstone's monument in Chapter 24 illustrates precisely the problems of commissioning a complex work of art in another country.

Notes

[1] See pp. 35–36.

[2] This chapter derives from an unpublished dissertation, *Bishop Elphinstone's Choir Stalls in King's College, Aberdeen*, by Sallyanne Sweet (now Simpson) for the Master of Arts degree in History of Art, Aberdeen University, 1996. The section on the restoration of the rood screen (pp. 78–80) is by Jane Geddes.

[3] Eeles, 1956, 80.

[4] Kelly, 1949, 55; Macfarlane, 1995, 347; Eeles, 1956, 78–79, 159–81.

[5] Eeles, 1956, 199, 221, 227–29.

[6] The stall variations are discussed on pp. 92–93.

[7] A stile is a long thin post of wood.

[8] Eeles, 1956, 39. This arrangement is found on the pulpitum at St Pierre, Louvain, 1490, illustrated in Macpherson, 1889, pl. LVIII.

[9] See p. 19. Eeles, 1956, 72–74; Macpherson, 1889, pl. LVII.

[10] Vienna, Österreichische Nationalbibliothek, Codex Vindobonensis 1897, fol. 24ᵛ. Facsimile with a commentary by F. Unterkircher, *Das Gebetbuch Jakobs IV von Schottland un seiner Gemahlin Margaret Tudor*, Codices Selecti 85, Graz, 1987.

[11] Boece, 94.

[12] Eeles, 1956, 4–46.

[13] Orem, 1791, 173.

[14] F. Douglas, *A General Description of the East Coast of Scotland, from Edinburgh to Cullen, including a brief account of the Universities of St Andrews and Aberdeen*, Paisley, 1782, reprinted Aberdeen, 1826, 154.

[15] Macpherson (1889, 16) says 'When I first remember the chapel the framework of the panels was dark like the carved oak, but the panels were modern and light wainscot. They were stained dark at a comparatively recent date. I think I have been told that the original panels were carved with Gothic tracery, but were too much decayed to be repaired in 1823'.

[16] See p. 163, n. 22.

[17] Macpherson, 1889, 13; AUL, MS 201, King's College Chapel Improvement Scheme. Minute Book, 1889–93: report on the fabric by Rowand Anderson, 19 July 1889. 'G', 'The Ambo in King's College Chapel', *Scottish Notes and Queries*, April 1889, II, no. 11, 161–62. Eeles, 1956, pl. 1, shows the screen between 1873 and 1891. The screen was lifted again in 1890. A new damp-proof floor was being laid over the whole chapel so, while the stalls were raised, they were also treated for rot at the base. Ecclesiological Notes, *Transactions of the Ecclesiological Society*, Aberdeen, 5th year, 1890 (1891), 63.

[18] AUL, MS U 618, letter from Professor Norman Macpherson to the Principal, William Geddes, 31 May 1889.

[19] 'The ambo in King's College Chapel' by 'G'. *Scottish Notes and Queries*, II, no. 11, April 1889, Aberdeen, 161, and illustration opposite.

[20] AUL, MS U 618, letters from Professor Norman Macpherson to the Principal, William Geddes, 6, 8, 10 January 1889. By 15 January, Macpherson had been able to sketch his own idea of the reconstruction, on which pls LVII and LXIII in Macpherson 1889 were based.

[21] R. Pococke, *Tours in Scotland, 1747, 1750, 1760*, ed. D. W. Kemp, Scottish History Society: Publications I.1, Edinburgh, 1887, 207.

[22] 'Above the books, on the east end, is some very curious carved work on the boards which divide the library form the chapel, to humour which the cross gallery has ancient rails; but in my opinion they neither look well, nor at all correspond with the modern ones'. Douglas, 1826, 154–55.

[23] Macpherson, 1889, 34.

[24] AUL, MS U 618, Macpherson to Geddes, 8 March 1889, 'I have acted largely on your hints as to not obtruding the word Rood and struck it out very often, but I cannot bring myself to strike it out altogether'.

[25] AUL, MS U 201, King's College Chapel Improvement scheme, Minute Book 1889–93, Rowand Anderson's Report on the Fabric, 19 July 1889.

[26] AUL, MS U 662. Aberdeen University Court, Edilis Committee, 1890–96, 10 June 1895. The organ was hydraulically operated.

[27] Aberdeen University, Estates Office file, 92/92, King's College Organ, December 1953–September 1992. Letters 20 February 1959, 17 May 1960. The chapel committee expressed its appreciation of the installation of the organ to the Senatus on 3 February 1960. University of Aberdeen, *Minutes of the Senatus Academicus*, XXII, 1960, Aberdeen, 62.

[28] The rearrangement of the woodwork around the new organ was organized by the architect Ian G. Lindsay of Edinburgh and carried out by Messrs R. and J. Reid. Correspondence between Lindsay and the University mentions a problem with dry rot and the need to re-install the ambo (which never happened). Aberdeen University, Estates Office file, 92/92, King's College Organ, December 1953–September 1992. Letters 25 January 1961, 12 February 1962, 14 May 1962.

[29] The Edilis papers for the late 1950s and early 1960s were destroyed by a flood in the basement of Elphinstone Hall. Dry rot in the wooden ceiling of the chapel is mentioned in the oral record of J. Kelman. AUL, Tape recording, Interview No. 23(i), 3 April 1985. 'The dry rot reinstatement work will be taking place . . . and we should like if the replacement of the ambo could take place at the same time', University Estates to Ian Lindsay, architect, 12 February 1962. 'Come prepared with a scheme for the replacement of the ambo', University Estates to Ian Lindsay, architect, 14 May 1962. Aberdeen University, Estates Office file, 92/92, King's College Organ, December 1953–September 1992.

[30] This has been noted by William Kelly, 'Carved oak from St Nicholas' Church, Aberdeen', *PSAS*, LXVIII, 1933–34, 364; 1949, 57; Macfarlane, 1995, 333; R. Fawcett, 'The architecture of King's College Chapel and Greyfriars' Church, Aberdeen', *AUR*, 53, 1989, 113.

[31] See pp. 45–51, 98–107, 115–29.

[32] C. Tracy, *English Gothic Choir-Stalls, 1400–1540*, Woodbridge, 1990, 47.

[33] L. F. Jacobs, *Early Netherlandish Carved Altarpieces, 1380–1550*, Cambridge, 1998.

[34] J. S. Witsen Elias, *De Nederlandsche Koorbanken en tijdens Gothiek en Renaissance*, Amsterdam, 1946, 43–36.

[35] Witsen Elias, 1946, 22–24, 17–22.

[36] Witsen Elias, 1946, 113–24, 130, pl. 16.

[37] Fawcett, 1989, 110.

[38] J. Hutchison Cockburn, 'The Ochiltree Stalls and other medieval carvings in Dunblane Cathedral', *Journal of the Society of Friends of Dunblane Cathedral*, VIII, 1958–61, pt III, 102–03, pt IV, 142–45.

[39] W. E. K. Rankin, *The Parish Church of the Holy Trinity, St Andrews*, London, 1955, 39.

[40] The church was founded in 1453 and the decoration continued through the century. A. B. Dalgetty, *History of the Church of Foulis Easter*, Dundee, 1933; M. R. Apted and W. N. Robertson, 'Late fifteenth-century church paintings from Guthrie and Foulis Easter', *PSAS*, XCV, 1961–62, 273–75.

[41] Now in the Royal Museum of Scotland. D. Caldwell, 'The Beaton Panels — Scottish carvings of the 1520s or 1530s', *Medieval Art and Architecture in the Diocese of St Andrews*, British Archaeological Society Conference Transactions, ed. John Higgitt, Leeds, 1994, 174–84.

[42] J. S. Richardson, 'Unrecorded Scottish wood carvings', *PSAS*, LX, May 1925–26, 384–408.

[43] Billings recorded that, before its removal in 1839, a door panel was carved with the initials Prior Thomas Gondibour, 1465–c. 1500. Billings shows the panels before restoration and reassembly: R. W. Billings, *Illustrations of geometric tracery from the panelling belonging to Carlisle Cathedral*, London, 1842, 4, pl. 1. Gondibour is recorded as Prior in 1465 in Cumbria Record Office D/Wyb/2/167, and had been succeeded by Prior Simon Senhouse by 5 March 1500, R. M. le F. Senhouse, 'Senhouse of Seascale Hall, in Cumberland', *Transactions of the Cumberland and Westmorland Antiquarian and Archaeological Society*, OS, 1893, XII, 254. I would like to thank Canon David Weston for these dates. A. Vallance, *Greater English Church Screens*, London, 1947, 37.

[44] J. C. Cox and A. Harvey, *English Church Furniture*, London, 1907, 270.

[45] W. Geddes, 'Local aspects of the Fine Arts', *Aberdeen Philosophical Society*, 11 November 1873, 19–21.

[46] M. O. Delepierre, 'Documents from the records of West Flanders relative to the carved stalls of Melrose Abbey', *Archaeologia*, 31, 1846, 346–49.

[47] C. Thompson and L. Campbell, *Hugo van der Goes and the Trinity Panels in Edinburgh*, Edinburgh, 1974.

[48] A detailed account of these artistic connections is in L. Campbell, 'Scottish patrons and Netherlandish painters in the fifteenth and sixteenth centuries', *Scotland and the Low Countries 1124–1994*, ed. G. Simpson, University of Aberdeen, The Mackie Monographs, 3, East Linton, 1996, 89–97; and D. McRoberts, 'Dean Brown's Book of Hours', *Innes Review*, XIX, 1968, 144–67.

[49] *The Ledger of Andrew Halyburton*, ed. Cosmo Innes, Edinburgh, 1867, 183–84.

[50] Orem, 1791, 132–33; J. S. Richardson, 'Fragments of altar retables of late medieval date in Scotland', *PSAS*, 12 March 1928, LXII, 1927–28, 200–01; Macfarlane, 1995, 334, 396. Richardson and Macfarlane assume the retable was of a type made in Brussels or Antwerp. However, Orem refers to 'three crowns uppermost and other kinds of crowns beneath, well carved, with golden knaps'. Delicate tracery crowns (*Aufsatz* or *Auszug*) on top of the carved panels are a particular feature of German altarpieces, not found in Netherlandish work. Jacobs, 1998, 126.

[51] Macfarlane, 1995, 334, 396.

[52] Macfarlane, 1995, 232. See Chapter 7.

[53] *The Chronicles of Scotland, compiled by Hector Boece, translated into Scots by John Bellenden, 1531*, ed. W. Seton, R. W. Chambers *et al.*, Scottish Text Society, 3rd ser., 10, 15, Edinburgh, 1938–41, II, 393.

[54] L. Campbell, 'Scottish patrons and Netherlandish painters in the fifteenth and sixteenth centuries', *Scotland and the Low Countries 1124–1994*, ed. G. Simpson, University of Aberdeen, The Mackie Monographs, 3, East Linton, 1996, 89–97.

[55] *Accounts of the Masters of Works*, ed. H. M.Paton, Edinburgh, 1957, 176, 256.

[56] W. H. St John Hope, *Windsor Castle, an architectural history*, London, 1913, II, 398–406, 429–43.

[57] St John Hope, 1913, II, 378.

[58] Jacobs, 1998, 210–19.

[59] Jacobs, 1998, 210, 225. On the St Dymphna altarpiece at Geel one of the stencils used for creating much of the arcading was itself inserted in the retable. R. H. Marijnissen and M. Sawko-Michalski, 'De twee gotische retabels van Geel: een onderzoek van materiël feiten', *Institute Royal de Patrimoine Artistique Bulletin*, 3, 1960, 157.

[60] Jacobs, 1998, 171–73.

[61] The patrons of the St Anne altar at St Pierre Louvain provided Jan van Kessele and Jan Petercels with a *patroon* from Antwerp; the St Arnold's confraternity and brewers' guild of Louvain commissioned Jan Petercels to make an altarpiece designed by Mathys Keldermans. Jacobs, 1998, 222.

[62] Jacobs, 1998, 229.

[63] *The History of the King's Works*, ed. H. M. C. Colvin, III, London, 1975, 218.

[64] Colvin, 1975, 218.

[65] Richardson, 1927–28, 203. Thomaes Adam, Jan Wraghe, Gillessone, Matheus Boentyn.

[66] W. Kelly, 'Carved Oak from St Nicholas' Church, Aberdeen', *PSAS*, LXVIII, 1933–34, 355–65. D. McRoberts, *The Heraldic Ceiling of St. Machar's Cathedral, Aberdeen*, Friends of St Machar's Cathedral, Occasional Papers, No. 2, Aberdeen, 1981.

[67] Boece, 53.

[68] Macpherson, 1889, 27, pl. LXVII; R. W. Billings, *The Baronial and Ecclesiastical Antiquities of Scotland*, Edinburgh, 1845–52, I, 1; AUL, MS U 1494/A7/32.

[69] W. Kelly, 'Four Scottish ecclesiastical carved oak panels, *c.* 1500–25', *PSAS*, LXIV, 1930, 336–38. Kelly saw these panels in a private sale in Aberdeen. In this article he mis-identifies the heraldry, corrected in W. Kelly, 'A correction', *PSAS*, LXVIII, 1934, 366. The wooden arms at King's, which he observes in W. Kelly, 'Carved oak from St Nicholas' Church, Aberdeen', *PSAS*, LXVIII, 1934, 365, has disappeared since that date. It is shown *in situ* in the frontispiece to *Hectoris Boetii Murthlacensium et Aberdonensium episcoporum vitae*, ed. J. Moir, New Spalding Club, 1894, Aberdeen. The wooden royal arms belonging to Bishop Spens must be post 1471 when an act was passed to remove the double tressure around the design, and this example accordingly omits the tressure across the top. The lost arms at King's, like most other examples, ignore the ruling and retain the double tressure. C. J. Burnett, 'The Act of 1471 and its effect on the Royal Arms of Scotland', *PSAS*, CV, 1972–74, 312–15.

[70] *Extracts from the Council Register of the Burgh of Aberdeen, 1398–1570*, ed. J. Stuart, Spalding Club, Aberdeen, 1844, I, 56.

[71] See p. 50.

[72] *Extracts from the Council Register of the Burgh of Aberdeen, 1398–1570*, ed. J. Stuart, Spalding Club, Aberdeen, 1844, I, 1844, 77–78.

[73] *Records of the Sheriff Court of Aberdeenshire*, ed. D. Littlejohn, New Spalding Club, Aberdeen, 1904, I, 102. The heraldic ceiling at St Machar's was put up around 1520 and, according to Orem, the wright was James Winter of Angus; Orem, 1791, 42. Kelly considered that 'Winter' might be a misunderstnding of 'Findour' or 'Fendour'; Kelly, 1934, 360.

[74] For the provenance of the fragments in Edinburgh and St Mary's Chapel, Kelly, 1934, 355–58, 363.

[75] D. Learmont, 'The Trinity Hall Chairs', *Furniture History*, 1978, 14, pp. 1–2. C. Graham, *Ceremonial and Commemorative Chairs*, Victoria and Albert Museum, 1994.

[76] Kelly, 1934, 363. The same pattern repeats on smaller panels: the two desk ends at St Mary's are 22 x 63cm, while the four panels at the base of the King's doors are 23 x 45cm. Kelly identified as John Fendour's 'trade-mark' a small four-petalled flower framing many of the panels at King's and St Mary's. It is also found on the King's ambo, on the upper stall end panels, and on the St Nicholas' fragments in Edinburgh. It does not appear on any of the panels of the Trinity Hall Chair.

[77] They may be compared with the reticulated canopy panel in Fig. 6.3 (top left) and the stall end (middle passage, north side, facing east, Eeles, 1956, pl. 14).

[78] On the west side, the individual canopy panels are 27cm wide. The complete height of the Aberdeen canopies (without the finials) is 115cm; the back panels of the Dean Convenor's chair are 99cm high.

[79] For Elphinstone's arms, see Chapter 10; James V's arms are in Marischal Museum, ABDUA: 36842. They include the symbol of the Aberdeen moneyer William Rolland.

[80] Chapter 17, about Bishop Forbes' stall explores such workshop practice in Aberdeen in the early seventeenth century.

[81] Kelly, 1934, 360–64.

[82] *Accounts of the Lord High Treasurer of Scotland*, ed. J. B. Paul, Edinburgh, 1904, II, 1500–04, 89, 273, 275. He had to obtain timber from Glenlion, some was carried down the Water of Tay, some brought 'furth of the Hieland', some obtained from Duncan Campbell in the Highlands. The name 'Fendour' is not unique in Scotland at this period: Symon Fendor lived in Gullane, East Lothian betwen 1502 and 1507: *The Exchequer Rolls of Scotland*, ed. G. Burnett, Edinburgh, 1889, XII, 1502–07, 697.

[83] R. Fawcett, 'Late Gothic architecture in Scotland: Considerations on the influence of the Low Countries', *PSAS*, CXII, 1982, 477–96.

[84] See pp. 45–51, 98–107.

[85] Macfarlane, 1995, 316–17.

CHAPTER SEVEN

THE PORTRAIT OF BISHOP ELPHINSTONE

By LORNE CAMPBELL

with a technical report by JOHN DICK

The portrait of William Elphinstone, Bishop of Aberdeen, now in the Marischal Museum (No. ABDUA:30005), was painted in about 1500 (Col. Pl. II). Precisely when, precisely where and precisely why are questions impossible to answer with confidence.

John Dick has established that the panel and the applied frame are oak and that the frame is original (see below). The painted surface is reasonably well preserved; some alterations were made during the course of execution (Fig. 7.1). The bishop's right eye has been moved. Both the landscape and the architecture are painted over a red underlayer. The painter's first intention seems to have been to place the bishop in front of a crimson background, perhaps curtains, but there was a change of plan. There is nothing particularly unusual about the changes, or indeed about the construction of the panel and its frame, the pigments used or the painting and gilding techniques. By Netherlandish standards, neither the carpentry nor the painting is especially sophisticated.

The left side of the frame has recesses for hinges and the remains of old fixings for hinges are visible in the X-radiograph (Fig. 7.1). The reverse of the panel has not been very neatly planed and it bears no traces of paint or preparation for paint. Because of the hinge marks, and because of its composition, the portrait must be the right wing of a small diptych or triptych. The unpainted reverse, however, would have looked unsightly if the diptych or triptych had been closed and the picture was perhaps part of a structure with fixed wings.

The saints on the orphreys of the cope are apostles (Col. Pl. II). At this time, the artists of northern Europe had not yet assigned standard attributes to the lesser apostles, who, consequently, are difficult to identify. The saint carrying the spear is probably Thomas; the saint with the carpenter's square could be Matthew or Jude (or indeed Thomas);[1] below him is Saint James Major, carrying a scallop shell. On the crosier, the central saint is John the Evangelist, holding a chalice; the other two saints do not have identifying attributes. The reasons for this choice of saints are not obvious. Neither the mitre nor the cope correspond to objects described in the inventories of St Machar's Cathedral or King's College Chapel. Claims that the landscape shows the estuary of the River Don have not been substantiated.[2]

The picture resembles in some respects the *Saint Clement and a Donor* in the National Gallery, London, which was painted in about 1490 by a rather incompetent

Fig. 7.1. X-radiograph of Bishop Elphinstone's portrait (Copyright: University of Aberdeen)

follower of Simon Marmion.[3] The stylistic similarities, however, are not so strong as to suggest any direct connection between the two paintings.

The first possible reference to the Aberdeen portrait is in the 'Procuration Accompts King's College Aberdeen by Mr George Gordon, Professor of Oriental Languages [*sic*, he was in fact Professor of Hebrew] from Michaelmas 1746 to Michaelmas 1747'. Under 'Section 2. Money Rent. Art. 3rd. Discharge of Money' is the entry

> By John Alexander, Painter his Receipt in part payment of a Copy of Bishop Elphinstons Picture   £50–08–00.[4]

In the accounts for the following year, 'Procuration Accompts. Dr John Chalmers, Principal of King's College, Michaelmas 1747 to Michaelmas 1748', is the entry

> To Mr Alexander, Painter, in part payment of a copy of Bishop Elphinstone's picture, Nine Guineas, he having received four guineas before as in last Accompt   £113.8.0.[5]

The accounts were kept in pounds Scots. Thirteen guineas (£13 13*s*. sterling) were equivalent to £163 16*s*. Scots.

A picture considered to be the original and a copy — probably Alexander's — were mentioned in the 'Description of Old Aberdeen' written in 1771.

The hall [*sc.* of King's College] is ornamented with some tolerable portraits.
Over the chimney, bishops Elphinston and Dunbar, copied from originals in the
principal's lodge.[6]

The version by John Alexander, which is signed *JAlexr pinxit AD 1747* (JA being
in monogram), is preserved at King's College (Fig. 7.2). John Alexander (1686–
c. 1766) was a descendant of George Jamesone and the father of Cosmo Alexander
(1724–72), also a painter.[7] John Alexander's version is a free and enlarged copy of the
original; it was not necessarily made directly from the original and might derive from
another version. In Alexander's painting, the composition is extended on all four
sides, a curtain is slung across the background, a cross hangs from the bishop's morse
and a tree appears above and to our right of the coat of arms.

If the original was recognized in 1746–47 for what it is and if Alexander's copy was
made directly from it, then the original was available in Aberdeen at that time. The
fact that a copy was commissioned for King's College may imply that the original was
not then in the possession of the university. By 1771, what was believed to be the
original was in the Principal's Lodge at King's College. The Principal was then John
Chalmers (1712–1800), who became Principal in 1746[8] and who in 1747–48 had
authorized the second payment for Alexander's copy. It is not clear from the text of
1771 whether the 'originals' of Bishops Elphinstone and Dunbar belonged to
Chalmers or to the college. The portrait of Dunbar, who died in 1532, has been lost,
though a copy survives; the portrait of Elphinstone is believed to be the picture now
in the Marischal Museum, the original from which derive all the versions now
known.[9]

Other copies or possible versions are mentioned in various sources. In 1633 Charles
I made his entry into Edinburgh and at the Salt Tron saw a representation of Parnassus
populated by 'ancient worthies of Scotland' including Bishop Elphinstone.[10] The
'ancient worthies', all literary men, were probably represented in painted portraits
which would have been lost when 'an fatal neglect' brought about within a few years
the destruction of all the 'pageants' made for Charles's entry.[11] It is possible that the
representation of Bishop Elphinstone manufactured for the pageant at the Salt Tron
was based on the Aberdeen portrait; it is conceivable that the version of the portrait
now in Lord Elphinstone's collection (Fig. 7.3) was made in or about 1633 or that it
was copied from a seventeenth-century version. In 1633 the title was held by
Alexander, fourth Lord Elphinstone (1552–1638). His son Alexander, afterwards fifth
Lord Elphinstone (1577–1648), was certainly in Edinburgh in June 1633 when
Charles I made his entry and might have taken the opportunity to acquire a picture of
his illustrious relative.[12]

A free copy by David Steuart Erskine, eleventh Earl of Buchan (1742–1829), was
made 'from the Original by a French Painter in King's College Aberde[en]' and must
have been among the 'drawings, most of which were by my own hand' which the
Earl supplied to John Pinkerton for his *Iconographia Scotica*, published in 1797.[13] The
stipple engraving of Elphinstone made after Buchan's drawing and published by
Pinkerton was 'From an Original Painting in the University of Aberdeen'.[14] Lord
Buchan's version is known from a tracing made by the Earl himself and bequeathed

Fig. 7.2. Copy of Bishop
Elphinstone's portrait, by John
Alexander, King's College
(Copyright: University of
Aberdeen)

Fig. 7.3. Copy of Bishop
Elphinstone's portrait in Lord
Elphinstone's collection

by William Findlay Watson (1810–81) to the National Galleries of Scotland.[15] Buchan's copy would appear to have been a free and inaccurate version of the original.

Another version, made in 1849 by James Giles (1801–70), may be based on both the original and on John Alexander's copy.[16] Other nineteenth- and twentieth-century copies are similar to Alexander's version;[17] but in 1923 John Bulloch Souter (1890–1972) carefully reproduced the original in a painting now in the Marischal Museum.[18]

The original and all the known copies have always been recognized as portraits of William Elphinstone. The original may have been described in 1746–47 as 'Bishop Elphinstons Picture'; many of the copies, including Lord Elphinstone's, bear inscriptions identifying the sitter. In the original, the coat of arms of the Elphinstone family is surmounted by a bishop's mitre; below the shield are what should be three golden fish in fret and a scroll with the motto '*Non Confundar*', taken from Psalm 31 verse 1: *Non confundar in aeternum*, Let me never be put to shame.

William Elphinstone was born in about 1431, became Bishop of Ross in 1481 but was never consecrated and was transferred to Aberdeen in 1483. He was finally consecrated Bishop of Aberdeen in 1488, when he was about fifty-seven.[19] In the portrait, presumably painted after his consecration, he looks younger than fifty-seven; but it would be a mistake to conclude that the picture cannot have been taken from life. The X-radiograph (Fig. 7.1) shows that the painter had some difficulty in placing Elphinstone's right eye, which would be hard to explain if he had been working from an image by another artist.

It would be incautious to assume that the portrait was necessarily painted for King's College or that it has always been in the possession of the university. The theory has been put forward that it is the right wing of a triptych painted for the high altar of King's College Chapel.[20] In 1542, however, there was on the principal altar *una tabula magna, arte pictoria miro ingenio confecta*.[21] A small triptych would hardly have been described in that way and a portrait of the founder would surely have been mentioned. The portrait might have been made for Elphinstone's private use or for St Machar's Cathedral; it need not necessarily have been painted after the foundation of King's College in 1495.

Towards the end of the eighteenth century, Lord Buchan attributed the original to a 'French Painter'. Lord Elphinstone's copy used to have attached to its frame a plate inscribed WILLIAM OF BRUGES.[22] It is just conceivable that this mysterious attribution to an otherwise unknown Flemish painter derives from some ancient tradition associated with the original.

Elphinstone made a visit, probably brief, to Bruges in 1495,[23] when he was about sixty-four: he might have sat then to a Bruges painter. Memling had died in the previous year but other eminent painters, notably Gerard David, were available. It seems unlikely that Elphinstone, with all the painters of Bruges at his disposal, would have chosen the relatively incompetent provincial who executed the Aberdeen portrait.[24] It is surely more likely that it was painted in Scotland, by an immigrant Netherlander or by a Scot who had received some instruction in Netherlandish techniques.[25] It could have been painted in Aberdeen, where at least one competent portrait-painter was at work.

Alexander Reid of Pitfoddels, who was Provost of Aberdeen in 1492–93 and who died early in 1507, was the subject of a portrait which in 1640 was hanging in the Session House of the church of St Nicholas. It was good enough and life-like enough to have been noticed by, and to have offended, 'some capitanes and gentilmen of the regiment of sojeris lying in this town'. They considered it as 'smelling somequhat of poperie' and the Kirk Session ordained that it should be 'tein doun and not . . . set up again'.[26] It has not been seen or heard of since 1640.

Elswhere I have suggested that the Bruges artist Willem Wallinc, who became a master of the Bruges guild in 1506, might have worked in Scotland and that he might have been the painter 'William Wallanch' who was employed between 1505 and 1516 by George Brown, Bishop of Dunkeld. No reference to Willem Wallinc has been found in the Bruges records between October 1506 and the summer of 1516; thereafter he was regularly mentioned until his death in 1553.[27] George Brown knew William Elphinstone, whom he must often have encountered on official business. Indeed he gave a cope to King's College Chapel.[28] His close relative James Brown was Dean of Aberdeen from the mid-1480s until his death in 1505 and was therefore in constant contact with Elphinstone. James Brown owned a prayer-book commissioned in 1498, when he passed the summer and autumn in the Low Countries.[29] It is possible that Bishop Brown's painter William Wallanch might have painted Bishop Elphinstone's portrait; that William Wallanch was the Bruges artist Willem Wallinc; that he was known as 'William of Bruges'; and that his name was remembered in connection with the portrait of Elphinstone. The label WILLIAM OF BRUGES once on Lord Elphinstone's copy of the Aberdeen portrait would then provide a vital link in a chain of tenuous conjectures. If the Aberdeen portrait is the work of the emigrant Fleming Willem Wallinc or Wallanch, William of Bruges, it would have been painted in about 1510, when Elphinstone was about eighty. The portrait would consequently be a likeness flatteringly, indeed miraculously, rejuvenated.

It is the almost total destruction of paintings produced in Scotland at this period, together with a sad lack of relevant documentation, that makes it impossible to decide whether the *Elphinstone* was painted in the Low Countries, by a minor artist, or in Scotland, by an artist trained in Netherlandish traditions and techniques. The second alternative is perhaps the more plausible.

TECHNICAL REPORT ON THE PORTRAIT OF BISHOP WILLIAM ELPHINSTONE

By JOHN DICK

This technical examination of the portrait provides information on the way in which the panel and frame were constructed and the various stages in which it was painted. Although it has been suggested that the original painting has been cut down because it is narrower than the copy by John Alexander, evidence that the frame is original refutes this.[30] Earlier descriptions of the portrait mention in 1903 that 'it hangs in shreds from the panel on which it was painted';[31] and in 1925 that it is '. . . painted on a wooden panel, now cracked down the middle; the colours have faded, all save the gold which had been used freely in the work; and in many places the paint has come away from the panel in flakes leaving the bare wood exposed', and goes on to state that 'To restore the picture was, of course, impossible. No one would have dreamed of such vandalism. . .'.[32]

Technical analysis confirms that both in construction and in the application of paint, the portrait could have been produced either in the Netherlands, or by a painter trained in the Netherlandish way.

SUPPORT

Wood 75.8 x 47.6cm — including frame
        70.0 x 42.0 cm — painted surface

Painted on a panel comprising two vertical planks of oak 23.3cm; 24.3cm wide 1.5cm thick and smoothed on the reverse. The join is a tapered tongue and groove which is open and loose along its length.[33]

A 14cm split runs from the top edge in the left hand plank. A hole at top centre of the panel is the location of an old hanging fixture. Woodworm damage occurs, in particular, along the line of the join.

There is no decoration on the reverse of the panel as is often to be found on a triptych wing.

FRAME

The frame, also made of oak, is 1.5cm thick by 3cm wide and is fixed to the unpainted margin of the panel by dowels which are visible on the face of the frame.[34]

The profile of the frame is a bevel, ogee and flat on top and sides and a plain bevel and flat on the bottom (Fig. 7.4). The top corner joints are mitres while those at the bottom are half-lap (Fig. 7.5). A mortise and tenon element of the joints which would normally be combined with these is lacking and this, taken with the evidence of a more recently planed outer edge, suggests a later reduction in the width of the frame.[35] This is somewhat contradicted by the existence of hinge recesses on the left-hand side but these could have been recut after the frame had been reduced in width. The remains of the probably original fixings of the hinges appear clearly in the X-radiograph (Fig. 7.1).

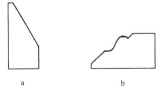

a   b

Fig. 7.4.   Bishop Elphinstone's portrait, drawing of frame section profiles

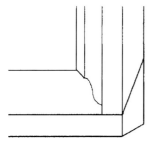

Fig. 7.5   Bishop Elphinstone's portrait, drawing of frame corner joint

The frame is finished with a thick black layer with gilded decorations at the corners. The gilding shows the typical cracking of an oil mordant. There are numerous losses from the painted layer and trickles of black paint on the recently smooth-planed outer edges of the frame suggest that the frame has been at least partly touched up at a relatively recent date. A paint sample cross-section from the frame indicates an earlier existing decoration.

Evidence for the originality of the frame is cumulative rather than conclusive. During construction, frame and panel would have been prepared as a unit, causing a build up of preparation material at the junction of the front edge of the frame and panel. Although cracked, this accumulation is still visible. The panel under the frame is unpainted; and the dowel rods penetrate the whole structure.

PAINT LAYER

The paint layer is cracked throughout. Much of this cracking is raised and there are many restored losses, some of them severe, notably at top centre, top right corner and at bottom centre. A number of smaller losses affect the face. The losses have not been filled but retouched directly on to the surface of the support and can be recognized by their being lower in level than the surrounding paint layer. These can all be seen on an old photograph taken before restoration.[36] There is an area of severely raised cleavage of the paint layer at the bottom left corner which is very insecure. The remaining original paint surface is in good condition. Notable features of the handling are: the simulation of the fur trim around the edge of the cope by scoring into the soft paint, possibly with the end of the brush; the incising of the lines of the window and the use of glazing colours over gold leaf in the bishop's cope.

X-RADIOGRAPH

The X-radiograph reveals the extent of the losses from the paint layer with few alterations in the composition apart from indecision around the sitter's right eye and indications of a change in the landscape seen through the window (Fig. 7.1). Otherwise it tends to confirm the techniques of a sixteenth-century Netherlandish painting: these include the carefully planned composition with relatively few alterations, the incision of the architectural shape of the window and the thinness of the flesh paint with highlights carefully and sparingly emphasized. Also to be seen are the old fixings for the hinges and the dowels fixing the frame to the panel.

PAINT SAMPLE CROSS-SECTIONS

The paint cross-sections also show the layer structure, palette and technique typical of a sixteenth-century Netherlandish painting.

A notable feature of cross-section samples taken from the landscape and from the background behind the sitter is the presence of an organic red underlayer (Col. Pls IIIa, IIIb). This suggests a previously existing background such as a crimson drapery. The cross-sections also confirm that the dark band along the bottom of the painting is a later addition (Col. Pl. IIIc).

The sample taken from the frame shows a complicated layer structure and suggests that it originally was decorated in red and gold (Col. Pl. IIId). Further sampling would be necessary to confirm the extent of this decoration.

Sample 1 — Landscape background where land and sea meet, upper left.
Layer 1. Deep blue particles, in pale blue matrix.
   2. Organic red.
   3. White priming.
   4. Ground.

Sample 2 — Dark background to left of window.
Layer 1. Varnish.
   2. Fine ground black particles.
   3. Organic red.
   4. White priming.
   5. Ground.

Sample 3 — Dark band along bottom edge.
Layer 1. Fine black particles.
   2. Pale green and white particles.
   3. Fine, black, discontinuous black particles.
   4. Ground.

Sample 4 — Frame, upper left edge.
Layer 1. Discoloured varnish.
   2. Gold.
   3. Fine red and yellow particles.
   4. Yellow particles.
   5. Organic red particles.
   6. Yellow particles with a few red.
   7. Organic red.
   8. Coarse white particles.
   9. Ground.

Notes

[1] In the Grimani Breviary, for example, it is Saint Jude who holds a carpenter's square (Venice, Biblioteca Marciana, MS Lat. IX, 67 (7351), fol. 786: reproduced in G. E. Ferrari, M. Salmi and G. L. Mellini, *The Grimani Breviary*, London, 1972, pl. 101); in the Hours of Catherine of Cleves (New York, The Pierpont Morgan Library, M. 917, p. 231) and in a print by Jérôme Wierix (Alvin 679), it is Saint Matthew who holds this emblem (J. Plummer, *The Hours of Catherine of Cleves*, London, 1966, pl. 113; M. Mauquoy-Hendrickx, *Les Estampes des Wierix*, Brussels, 1978–83, vol. II, pl. 125 (877)).

[2] Macfarlane, 1995, 334.

[3] L. Campbell, *National Gallery Catalogues, The Fifteenth-Century Netherlandish Schools*, London, 1998, 310–15.

[4] AUL, MS K 57/25. This reference was kindly sent by Jane B. Pirie, Senior Curatorial Assistant.

[5] AUL, MS K 57/26, 'Casual Money Rent', 6: reference kindly sent by Leslie Macfarlane.

[6] In Orem, 1791, 40. This copy was possibly made in an attempt to improve the decoration of the hall. Orem, writing in 1724, notes 'There are also in the said common hall about twenty-one pictures of several persons, hanging about the walls thereof, many of which are much defaced. Only the picture of Queen Mary of Scotland and that of Mr. George Buchanan remain yet clear'. Orem, 1791, 182–83.

[7] J. Holloway, *Patrons and Painters, Art in Scotland 1650–1760*, exhibition catalogue, Scottish National Portrait Gallery, Edinburgh, 1989, 85–103, 140–41.

[8] H. Scott, *Fasti Ecclesiae Scoticanae*, new edn, VII, Edinburgh, 1928, 367.

[9] H. A., 'The Portrait of Bishop Elphinstone', *AUR*, XIII, 1925–26, 133–37, 135.

[10] E. McGrath, 'Local Heroes: the Scottish Humanist Parnassus for Charles I' in *England and the Continental Renaissance, Essays in Honour of J. B. Trapp*, Woodbridge, 1990, 257–70.

[11] McGrath, 1990, 270.

[12] He attended meetings of the Privy Council at Holyrood on 13 June 1633: see *The Register of the Privy Council of Scotland*, ed. Hume Brown, 2nd ser., V, Edinburgh, 1904, 114–15. For the Lords Elphinstone and their collections of portraits, see W. Fraser, *The Elphinstone Family Book of the Lords Elphinstone of Balmerino and Coupar*, 2 vols, Edinburgh, 1897.

[13] D. Turner, *The Literary Correspondence of John Pinkerton, Esq.*, 2 vols, London, 1830, I, 271 note.

[14] J. Pinkerton, *Iconographia Scotica*, London, 1797, 92. The engraving is by Harding.

[15] Scottish National Portrait Gallery, PG 1619: see H. Smailes, *The Concise Catalogue of the Scottish National Portrait Gallery*, Edinburgh, 1990, 100. For Watson and his collection, see K. Andrews, *Drawings from the Bequest of W. F. Watson 1881–1981*, exhibition catalogue, National Gallery of Scotland, Edinburgh, 1981.

[16] Giles's copy is now in the SRC Office at King's College; another version is at Fyvie Castle. A coloured lithograph corresponding to Giles's painting was published in *Fasti* (1854), frontispiece, from 'a careful drawing by Mr. Giles'.

[17] For example the copy lent by Sir James Dalrymple-Horn-Elphinstone to the Aberdeen *Archaeological Exhibition* of 1859 (*Catalogue of Historical Portraits*, 3, No. 2) and later in the possession of his granddaughter Esther Winifred (1877–1960), wife of Thomas Alexander Headlam, Piper's Hey, Evershot (Dorset). Other old copies were, in the nineteenth century, at Tulliallan Castle in the collection of the Elphinstones, Barons Keith of Stonehaven Marischal, and, in *c.* 1930, at Frome St Quintin (Dorset) in the collection of the widow of Major-General Douglas Keith Elphinstone Hall (1869–1929), whose grandfather was Captain Alexander Francis Elphinstone, RN (1789–1865), of Livonia House near Sidmouth (Devon). Photographs of Mrs Headlam's and Mrs Hall's copies are in Aberdeen University Library, MS 2119.

[18] H. A., 1925–26.

[19] Macfarlane, 1995, 192.

[20] Macfarlane, 1995, 334–35.

[21] Eeles, 1956, 14.

[22] J. Caw, *Scottish Portraits*, 2 vols, Edinburgh and London, 1903, vol. I, pl. V. R. Brydall, *Art in Scotland, Its Origins and Progress*, Edinburgh and London, 1889, 33, suggested that the Aberdeen portrait was 'possibly the work of a Flemish artist'.

[23] Macfarlane, 1995, 232.

[24] For the lesser painters active at Bruges, see D. De Vos, 'Enkele minder bekende anonieme Brugse schilders uit het einde van de 15de en het begin van de 16de eeuw', *Bulletin des Musées royaux des beaux-arts de Belgique*, XXXVIII–XL, 1989–91, Nos 1–3, *Miscellanea Henri Pauwels*, 187–203.

[25] For Scottish artists being trained in the Netherlands, see L. Campbell, 'Scottish Patrons and Netherlandish Painters in the Fifteenth and Sixteenth Centuries' in *Scotland and the Low Countries 1124–1994*, ed. G. G. Simpson, The Mackie Monographs, 3, Phantassie, 1996, 96–97.

[26] A. M. Munro, *Memorials of the Aldermen, Provosts, and Lord Provosts of Aberdeen, 1272–1895*, Aberdeen, 1897, 69.

[27] Campbell, 1996, 89–103. Wallinc is discussed on pp. 95–96, with the relevant citations.

[28] Eeles, 1956, 33.

[29] D. McRoberts, 'Dean Brown's Book of Hours', *Innes Review*, XIX, 1968, 144–67 (the manuscript is in the National Library of Scotland, MS 10270).

[30] H. A., 'The Portrait of Bishop Elphinstone', *AUR*, XIII, 1925–26, 133–37.

[31] J. Caw, *Scottish Portraits*, 2 vols, Edinburgh and London, 1903, I, 15.

[32] H. A., 1925–26, 133–37.

[33] Helene Verougstraete-Marcq and Roger Van Schoute, *Cadres et supports dans la peinture flamande aux 15e et 16e siecles*, Heure-le-romain, 1989, 38, fig. 7/8. Other panel paintings with this type of join are those in the church at Foulis Easter and the portrait of Sir Duncan Campbell by an unknown artist dated 1619 in the Scottish National Portait Gallery.

[34] Verougstraete-Marcq and van Schoute, 1989, 50, fig. 14/2.

[35] Verougstraete-Marcq and van Schoute, 1989, 39–48.

[36] The restoration was carried out by H. R. H. Woolford, of the National Galleries of Scotland, some time after 1930. The plate glass negatives are in the possession of the author.

CHAPTER EIGHT

THE BELLS

By JANE GEDDES

Bells were an integral part of Bishop Elphinstone's liturgical plan, their use being described in the Foundation Charter of 1505. Boece wrote in 1521 that the tower 'contains thirteen bells, pleasing the ear with sweet and holy melody. All these were the gift of Bishop William'.[1] Strachan wrote in 1631 that the King's bells might call the very stones to prayer by the sweetness of their melody.[2] John Forbes, Professor of Divinity, writing in 1634 just after the crown had blown off the tower, said 'the steeple hath within it an musicall harmonie of costlie and pleasant bells'.[3]

Major bell ringing sessions took place three times a day. The day began at five a.m. when the sacrist began ringing for fifteen minutes, then for half that time and then another fifteen minutes. The clock would then strike at the sixth hour ready for Matins to begin. There was a similar performance at the ninth hour, before noon for the sung mass; and before evensong, at the second hour in winter and the third hour in summer. The bell was also rung to announce the opening of the college gates: at five a.m. in winter, four a.m. in summer, and the hour of nine when the college closed. Every day while the Sanctus was sung until the elevation of the Host the bell was rung '*tinniendo aut tonando*'. In addition the sacrist was to toll or chime the bell for any celebration in the college.[4]

The Inventory of 1542 describes the twelve bells in the tower:

> Item five great bells, Trinity, Maria, Michael, Gabriel, Raphael. Five small bells for marking the middles of the hours, with as many iron clappers. Two bells for daily use. Bells in the church: Three small bells of which one at the principal altar, one at the altar of St Germain and the third at the altar of the Blessed Virgin, for use there in things sacred.[5]

The inscriptions on the bells are added to the Inventory in a seventeenth- or eighteenth-century hand: Trinity, 'May this bell be blessed by the sacred Trinity'; Maria, 'Holy Mary, lovingly protect those whom I summon'; Michael, 'Behold, I bring you tidings of joy which shall be to all people, [made] by me George Waghevens 1519'; Gabriel, 'I am called Gabriel; sing to the Lord a new song, sing with all your skill to him with a joyful noise, [made] by me George Waghevens, in the year of our lord 1519'; Raphael, 'Sing to the Lord a new song, sing with all your skill to him with a joyful noise, [made] by me George Waghevens, in the year of our Lord 1519'.[6] Orem adds that the mighty Trinity was 5 feet 5 inches (1.65m) and according to Parson Gordon the two large bells were of greater weight than any in

Scotland. By his time, in 1661, there were only ten bells left in the tower.[7] Eeles and Clouston calculate that Trinity weighed about 48cwt.[8]

The dispersal of this great treasure was gradual and sad. A French founder Monsieur Gelly proposed in 1700 to recast the bells. His conditions required the college to break down the bells and deliver the scrap metal to him. He would produce five or six good bells for the chapel and keep the rest of the bronze as payment. As a trial, it was resolved to break the two bells hanging next to the eight-hour bell and cast them into one. The Principal decided, 'If this works we may proceed piecemeal to break down the rest'.[9] One of Gelly's bells survives in the tower, cast in 1702 with his name on the inscription. This was presumably cast from the two original bells which Gelly managed to remove. The new bells were tested for sound with the help of Alexander Coupar, possibly the former Master of the Music School; and they were were hung in 1702 by Alexander Scot, an Aberdeen skipper, and his crew.[10] The 'swords [battens]' of the bells were renewed in the 1760s; the cumbersome process of lifting, inserting and hanging aanother bell is chronicled in payments made in 1768.[11] Douglas records in 1782 that there were still five bells in the tower, the largest being three feet ten inches (1.17m) across the mouth.[12] Then, between 1797 and 1800, four bells weighing 5566lbs went for scrap.[13] In 1823, to raise money for the new west block, the remaining old bells were sold. The doorway into the tower had to be broken down in order to get the huge objects out.[14]

By an extraordinary quirk of fate, one of the original small bells has survived. John Mowat, who was the successor to Albert Gelly in the Old Aberdeen Foundry was a Master of the Guild of Hammermen. He made many bells for the locality between 1733 and 1765, including the Old Aberdeen Town House and Town Crier's bell[15] and 'bought the musick bells of King's College'.[16] These might have included the 72lbs of bell metal sold for scrap in 1736.[17] Mowat was approached in the same year by Patrick Copland, the minister of Tough church, Aberdeenshire, who wanted a new bell for his steeple. His parishioners had been reluctant to contribute towards the costs until Copland offered a free service of bell ringing at the funeral of every subscriber and their descendants. Eventually Mowat agreed to sell the old King's bell in return for the old Tough bell and 'all the bad money in the box' as part payment. The bell arrived at Tough on 4 April 1736 and the eligible subscribers carefully wrote down their names and all their descendants living in that year. By 23 April the minister was aware that the situation could get out of hand as a result of his generous offer. 'If there was no regulation made concerning the ringing of the bell at funerals, the friends of such contributors, as should happen to die, would soon render the same useless by ringing it excessively every day betwixt their contributing relation's death and their internment, as had been the practice some time past.' Copland decided that the bell should only be rung once by a kirk officer upon notification of a death, and the officer alone was to toll at the funeral itself 'otherwise he would be accountable to the session for what damage should be done to the bell'. Ironically the bell was already cracked when it was examined in 1957,[18] perhaps due to excessive ringing at funerals. Repaired in 1998, it was returned to King's Chapel in 1999, being replaced

Fig. 8.1.   William Culverden's bell   Fig. 8.2.   Detail of William Culverden's rebus
                                                       on the King's Chapel bell

at Tough by a nineteenth-century bell from the college tower,[19] a fitting exchange after the 1736 deal.

The Tough bell is identified by the shield and rebus of William Culverden, a major London founder who was working between 1497 and 1522 (Figs 8.1 and 8.2).[20] The shield shows a bell with the word 'Foñd' for founder. Around it are the words 'In dño cõ fido', coming from Psalm 11, 'In the Lord put I my trust; how say ye to my soul, Flee as a bird to your mountain'. This bird is depicted at the bottom of the shield with the letters 'dê' above it. The bird is therefore a pigeon or culver, with 'den' above, and the letter W for William is on the other side of the shield.[21] The fleur-de-lis cross stamp was already old when Culverden used it, appearing on bells cast in London by Robert Burford in 1418.[22] Thirty-three bells by Culverden survive, mainly in the Home Counties.[23] They range in diameter from 14 to 45 inches, with the majority between 20 and 30 inches. The Tough bell is 19 inches. William Culverden's will of 1522 survives.[24] His house, sheds and garden were in Houndsditch and he was brought up in Westminster Abbey. He sold all his bell moulds and implements to another founder, Thomas Lawrence.

The three lighter bells in the heavy chime of five at King's were cast by George Waghevens.[25] The Waghevens were a dynasty of bell-founders working in Mechelen and exporting their wares all over Europe during the sixteenth century. George also made the common bell at St John's, Perth in 1520 (now lost), while his brother Peter made the preaching bell called John the Baptist in 1506, still surviving in St John's and one of the finest medieval bells in Scotland.[26]

According to Walters, the inscription on the greatest college bell, Trinitas was commonly found on bells from the Nottingham foundry while Maria's inscription came from the Exeter foundry.[27] According to Clouston, even though these inscriptions are found in the provinces, it is quite likely that they were made in London, the greatest centre for bell founding in England and more strategically sited for delivery by sea to Aberdeen.[28]

The installation of these bells was a major technical challenge and may have some implications for the dating of the tower. Although Culverden's earliest recorded bell was made in 1497, one must assume that the bronze founder had achieved an international reputation before it was decided to buy a bell from London. Culverden's small bell could have been carried into the tower at any date after about 1508 but his peak production was around 1520, so perhaps the whole peal arrived at about the same time, under the auspices of Bishop Dunbar. We do not know when the two largest bells were made, but even the three Waghevens bells of 1519 would have been difficult to install if the tower was complete at that date. They would have been too wide to fit through the door or the louvres and most likely came through the roof. This implies that either the newly leaded roof of the tower was removed in 1519, or else it was not complete. If the huge size of the bells (up to 1.65m diameter) was only appreciated around 1519, this may explain the change of plan whereby the originally square tower was extended some 2.24m to the south, producing its asymmetrical elevation. A glance at the plan of the tower (Fig. 4.1) shows that the southern extension does not increase the hanging space within the belfry but would provide additional stability when the bells were in motion.

It is traditionally assumed that Bishop Elphinstone completed the chapel around 1506, or else in time for the 1509 dedication. Boece says firmly that Elphinstone covered the college church, the towers and almost all the other houses with lead,[29] but this does not rule out a later date for the completion of the crown tower itself. Elphinstone's priority was to get the essential core of the university complete before he died: this meant the chapel and basic accommodation (the towers mentioned by Boece were for housing students at the south corners of the quad). Boece mentions that Elphinstone failed to complete the exterior manses and it is not known how many details remained unfinished at his death.[30] Boece was, through loyalty, inclined to give Elphinstone the credit for buildings which were actually completed later. According to Orem, 'Principal Boece would not allow Dunbar to place his name and armorial coat upon the south work'[31] even though it was Dunbar who built the wing, financed by Elphinstone's money. Boece does the same thing with the bells, saying they were the gift of Elphinstone, but some at least were not actually made until 1519, five years after the bishop's death. Therefore, although Boece says Elphinstone built the tower with its crown of arches, it could have been modified and completed by Dunbar, commissioning the small bells from London and the large ones from Mechelen, and perhaps Exeter and Nottingham.

The last bell, though not strictly related to the chapel and intended for purely secular use, is the dreaded Clatter Vengeance. It originally hung in the Timber Muses, the little turret added to the east end of the chapel in 1657–58. With two different ringing modes, it was intended to summon students to morning prayers and lectures, and to 'discipline'.[32] It is inscribed

.IOHANNES.BVRGERHVYS.ME.FECIT.ANNO.1660.COLLEGIUM
.REGIUM.ABERDONENSIS.

The Burgherhuys dynasty ran a foundry in Middelburg, Holland, producing bells for Scotland from 1609–79. Ten bells by Jan Burgerhuys have been identified in Scotland.[33] Clatter Vengeance still survives, silent and immobile in the university conference centre.

The original peel of bells added a magnificent aural dimension to life in the chapel and around the quad. Even though only one medieval bell survives, its return to the chapel, made possible by a generous benefactor, serves as a fitting tribute to the Quincentenary.

Notes

[1] Boece, 95.

[2] Quoted in Macpherson, 1889, 4: from A. Strachan, *Panegyricus Inauguralis*, Aberdeen, 1631, *'quae vel lapides dulcissima melodia ad sacra vocarent'*.

[3] *Fasti*, 305, Representation to the King.

[4] Eeles, 1956, 69, 90, 177, 217–19; *tinniendo* may mean the frequent ringing of a small bell and *tonando* the slower tolling of a large bell.

[5] Eeles, 1956, 45–46.

[6] *'Trinitate sacra fiat haec campana beata'*; Maria, *'Protege precor pia quos convoco sancta maria;* Michael, *'Ecce anuntio vobis gaudium quod erit omni populo per me Georgium Waghevens MDXIX'*, Gabriel, *'Vocor Gabriel cantate domino canticum novum bene psallite ei in vociferatione per me Georgium Waghevens anno dni MDXIX'*; 'Raphael [. . ..] *Cantate domino canticum novum bene psallite ei in vociferatione per me Georgium Waghevens anno dni MDXIX'*. Eeles, 1956, 5–6; Orem, 1791, 169. I would like to thank Morton Gauld for the translation.

[7] James Gordon, *Abredoniae utriusque descriptio. A description of both touns of Aberdeen*, Spalding Club, Edinburgh, 1842, 23.

[8] F. C. Eeles and R. W. M. Clouston, 'The church and other bells of Aberdeenshire, part III', *PSAS*, XCIV, 1960–61, 287.

[9] *Fasti*, 438.

[10] AUL, MS K 39, pp. 15, 33, 36; K 56/1, pp. 18, 19; K 56/2, p. 13; *Fasti*, 438; *Records of Old Aberdeen*, ed. A. M. Munro, New Spalding Club, 2 vols, Aberdeen, 1899, 1909, I, 170, 238; II, 239. I am grateful to Colin McLaren for this and the following reference.

[11] AUL, MS K 257/20/1/7; K 257/20/2/3; K 257/20/3/6; K 257/20/8/13; K 257/20/9/9.

[12] F. Douglas, *A General Description of the East Coast of Scotland, from Edinburgh to Cullen, including a brief account of the Universities of St Andrews and Aberdeen*, Paisley, 1782, 189–91.

[13] Eeles and Clouston, 1960–61, 286, 288–89.

[14] Macpherson, 1889, 6, records that this was part of the 1823 refurbishment campaign.

[15] Eeles and Clouston, 1960–61, 294–95.

[16] SRO, CH2/356/3, Tough Kirk Session Accounts. I would like to thank Ranald Clouston for telling me the story of Tough bell and for suggesting its return to King's.

[17] Eeles and Clouston, 1960–61, 289.

[18] F. C. Eeles and R. W. M. Clouston, 'The church and other bells of Aberdeenshire', *PSAS*, XCI, 1957–58, 107–08.

[19] The old bell was repaired by Soundweld of Lode, Ely and installed by Hayward Mills Associates of Radford. The college bell was cast by Mears and Stainbank of London in 1869. Eeles and Clouston, 1960–61, 286.

[20] G. P. Elphick, *Sussex Bells and Belfries*, London, 1970, 62; C. Deedes and H. B. Walters, *The Church Bells of Essex*, 1909, 42–43.

[21] J. J. Raven, *Church Bells of Suffolk*, London, 1890, 37–39.

[22] Eeles and Clouston, 1957–58, 107–08.

[23] H. B. Walters, 'London Church Bells and Bell-Founders', *Transactions of St Paul's Ecclesiological Society*, VI, 1907, 109; and additional bells listed in correspondence from R. W. M. Clouston who also provided their sizes. Elphick, 1970, 62, 119, 122; C. Deedes and H. B. Walters, *The Church Bells of Essex*, Aberdeen,

1909, 42–43; T. M. N. Owen, *Church Bells of Huntingdonshire*, London, 1899, 14–15; J. J. Raven, *Church Bells of Suffolk*, 1890, 37–39; J. J. Raven, *Church Bells of Cambridgeshire*, Cambridge, 1881, 2nd edn, 42–48.

[24] Raven, 1881, 43–46.

[25] M. and K. van Bets-Decoster, *De Mechelse klokkengeiters*, Mechelen, 1998.

[26] The quality of their work was often exceptional. Peter Wagheven's preaching bell at Perth 'is without question one of the finest pre-Reformation European bells in existence'; R. W. M. Clouston, 'The Bells of Perthshire: St John's Kirk, Perth', *PSAS*, CXXIV, 1994, 527–29, 537–38.

[27] H. B. Walters, *The Church Bells of England*, London, 1912, 325.

[28] Clouston, pers. comm.

[29] Boece, 96.

[30] Macfarlane, 1995, 337–38.

[31] Orem, 1791, 175.

[32] Macpherson, 1889, 6.

[33] Eeles and Clouston, 1960–61, 286, 292.

CHAPTER NINE

BISHOP ELPHINSTONE'S TOMB

By IAN CAMPBELL

Only a few stone fragments survive from the original tomb of William Elphinstone, but these, combined with documentary evidence, suggest that the tomb ranked among the most splendid in Scotland, rivalling royal tombs in its ambition, and emulating one of the most influential Renaissance papal tombs. The present article explores both the form and the content and attempts a reconstruction and an explanation of its meaning.

THE EVIDENCE

The physical remains are incorporated into the modern Founder's Memorial, dedicated in 1931, on the site of the original tomb, centrally placed at the foot of the sanctuary.[1] They comprise a base, composed of several pieces, and a monolithic lid, of a dark blue-grey fossil limestone, identifiable as Tournai Black or touchstone, from quarries now in Belgium, a stone popular for monuments from the early middle ages (Figs 9.1, 6.1).[2] It is likely that the stone imported from Flanders into Scotland for tombs such as those of William Scheves, Archbishop of St Andrews (d. 1497), and the

Fig. 9.1.   Top and base of original tomb incorporated in the modern Founder's Memorial

second son of James III, James, Duke of Ross and Archbishop of St Andrews (d. 1504) was the same touchstone.[3] The base mouldings correspond broadly to the Attic type, the most common form of Roman column base, i.e. principally a broad concave moulding sandwiched between two half-round convex members. The lid has mouldings which do not correspond as a whole to any known ancient architectural detail, but the two mouldings, which combine a concave and a convex curve above and below the central convex half-round moulding, are essentially classical cyma rectas. Very similar mouldings already appear on the transitional Gothic-Renaissance tomb of Mary of Burgundy, erected in the church of Our Lady in Bruges around 1500.[4]

The earliest reference to Elphinstone's tomb is the description of his funeral in Boece's *Life*, published in 1522, which says that his body was buried (*humatum*) in front of the high altar. During the ceremony Elphinstone's crozier broke and part fell into the grave (*fossa*), establishing that the body was interred.[5] This is confirmed by Boece's account of the first visit to the chapel by Bishop Gavin Dunbar in 1518, who was dismayed to find the grave covered by carpets.[6]

According to Boece, Dunbar resolved immediately to complete Elphinstone's various building projects, and he was almost certainly responsible for the erection of the elaborate tomb, described by James Strachan and Alexander Galloway in the 1542 Inventory:

> The sepulchre of the Lord Founder, in the upper part of which is his effigy in bishop's vestments, with two angels carrying two candlesticks at the head and two beadsmen carrying the epitaph graven in brass at the feet; below, on the south side are the three theological Virtues and Contemplation; on the north side are the four cardinal Virtues distinguished by their emblems; on the east and west sides the arms of the Founder carried by angels.[7]

The next piece of documentary evidence is in James Gordon of Rothemay's 1662 description of Aberdeen where we read:

> In this church [King's College Chapel], Wm. Elphinstone lyes buryed, his tombe stone of black towtch stone; the upper part upheld of old by thretteine statues of brasse; his statua of brasse lying betwix the two stons; all these robbed and sold long ago.[8]

The fact that he is writing after the tomb's destruction, which has been attributed to the Covenanters who sacked St Machar's Cathedral in 1639–40, means his testimony has to be treated with caution, but he certainly seems to be relying on some detailed memory whether his own or another's.

William Orem, writing in 1724–25, says that Elphinstone was 'interred on the first step to the high altar in the said college chapel, under a double black marble stone, anno 1514 . . .'.[9] Orem also says that the chapel 'was spoiled of all its rich ornaments in the beginning of the Reformation'.[10] However, included with Orem's text is another description of Old Aberdeen dated 1771, which states that 'Before the high altar was the tomb of Bishop Elphinston, the founder, lately stripped of its canopy and ornaments for fear of accidents and reduced to a plain blue marble slab'.[11] Given the trustworthiness of Orem in general, one can only assume that this description comes from a much earlier source, apparently predating Gordon's. It is of interest in suggesting that the tomb was dismantled with care rather than being vandalised. However, at some stage Elphinstone's physical remains were also removed because exacvations in 1891 revealed traces of earlier disturbance under his tomb, and no bones.[12]

A final piece of documentary evidence was proposed by John Durkan in the form of a contract dated 5 January 1529, between a Parisian tomb maker, Pierre Prisié, and a priest, Robert 'Alphinseton' (i.e. Elphinstone) for two brass strips each $4\frac{1}{2}$ feet (c. 1.46m) long and 8 inches (c. 21cm) wide, engraved with four coats of arms and an inscription, to be ready for Candlemas (2 February).[13] There is no proof that the commission is linked with William Elphinstone's tomb, but Robert Elphinstone, his kinsman, was archdeacon of Aberdeen, and 1529 is the date when Dunbar finally succeeded in promulgating Elphinstone's second constitution for the college.[14] What time could be more appropriate to inaugurate the Founder's tomb?

THE RECONSTRUCTION

Eeles ignored the testimony of Gordon of Rothemay and assumed that, because the Inventory specifies only the material of the epitaph (brass), that the effigy was of stone, probably 'fine sandstone, certainly richly coloured and gilt'.[15] This seems very unlikely given the use of the higher quality imported touchstone to support it. Eeles also ignored the fact that the tomb appears in the section of the Inventory headed *Vasa ennea* (Bronze vessels), which appears strange at first but is consistent with the classicizing character of the first part of the document, which he proposes was begun in collaboration with Boece.[16] The 1549 *Inventarium Jocalium* (Inventory of precious objects/jewels) of St Machar's Cathedral, compiled by Alexander Galloway (on whom see more below) similarly puts the tomb of Bishop Gavin Dunbar, with its bronze effigy, among the *Vasa ennea*.[17] Thus both tombs are treated as if they were ancient Roman cinerary urns. Another parallel is that the King's Inventory goes out of its way to specify that the epitaph was of *aes* (brass), making a distinction between it and the '*aenus*' (bronze) of the rest of the monument, while in the St Machar's Inventory, Dunbar's effigy is specified to be *ex ere*, in contrast to the four candelabra in the preceding entry which are *ennee* and the chandelier in the next entry which is *enneum*.[18] The terms 'brass' and 'bronze' were used virtually interchangeably until recent times, but if Elphinstone's epitaph was related to the inscriptions cast in Paris, while, as I believe, the effigy and other sculptures were cast in Flanders and imported with the touchstone, there may have been some difference in appearance.[19] There are some difficulties with this suggestion, as we shall see.

The descriptions from the Inventory and Gordon appear to contradict each other, but the differences may be due to the gradual attrition of the monument over one hundred difficult years. According to the Inventory, the table was carried by twelve figures (counting two angels at each end), and the bishop lay on top with four more figures. According to Gordon, there were thirteen figures supporting the table and the bishop's effigy lay beneath the table. The lack of mention of figures on top of the

Fig. 9.2.   Tomb of Philibert of Savoy, St Nicholas de Tolentine, Brou, Burgundy. Begun 1512, completed by Conrad Meit, 1526–31 (Coll. Médiathèque du Patrimoine/© Caisse Nationale des Monuments Historiques et de Sites, Paris)

tomb suggests they had been removed at some earlier date, perhaps as early as 1569, when Catholic worship finally ceased in the chapel.[20]

It is hard to reconcile the twelve with the thirteen supporting figures. One possibility can be seen on the tomb of Philibert of Savoy, in his votive church of St Nicholas de Tolentine at Brou, Burgundy (Fig. 9.2) where the centre of the tomb is supported by non-figurative columns. On Elphinstone's tomb, the twelve figures holding up the rim might have been supplemented by one column in the middle. Alternatively, Gordon's description 'of old' may be imprecise: if we count the seven Virtues, plus Contemplation on the two long sides, and assume that pairs of angels supported the coats of arms at either end, we have twelve, leaving the effigy of Elphinstone to make thirteen. But the effigy should have been on top according to the Inventory, unless there was a second effigy or transi below. The transi was usually the effigy of a decaying cadaver, lying as if in an open tomb chest under the effigy of the deceased portrayed as in life, a motif enthusiastically employed in many fifteenth- and sixteenth-century tombs, especially in France and England.[21] However, a variant, best seen in the early sixteenth-century tombs of Philibert of Savoy and of his widow, Margaret of Austria, at Brou (Fig. 9.2) shows the transis as if asleep in less formal dress, rather than decayed.[22] While one would have expected the Inventory to refer to any second effigy, it does not provide a detailed description and this element could have been overlooked. Another possibility is that when the figures were removed from the

Fig. 9.3.   Axonometric reconstruction of Bishop Elphinstone's tomb (David Stronach and Ian Campbell)

top, the effigy was inserted below, human representations perhaps being acceptable whereas supernatural beings were not. This scenario can be paralleled at St Machar's Cathedral in August 1640 when Covenanters zealously but carefully removed the Arma Christi from each end of Bishop Dunbar's tomb but left his bronze effigy in tact.[23] However, in the same year, when the General Assembly met in Greyfriars' Kirk, Aberdeen, there was a debate about a newly installed loft on the front of which

> were the figures of Faith, Hope and Charity, and the Moral Vertwes, as they used to be painted emblem wyse: There stood Faithe leaning upon the Cross. This was as soon quarrelled at as espyed by severall ministers, commissioners of the Assemblye, who looked upon all that new frontispiece as savouring of superstitione, and would needs have Faith or her Crosse removed from ther. The magistratts durst not excuse it; and many others were silent least they should be suspected.[24]

That the Greyfriars' Virtues were allowed finally to remain whereas Elphinstone's have gone may reflect a distinction between tolerable painted and intolerable 'graven' images, or it may simply be that the metal figures had some value melted down.

The fact that Gordon describes Elphinstone's effigy as lying between the two stones implies that there were no walls to the tomb and that it was a table tomb rather than an altar tomb, with the statues of angels and Virtues supporting the lid as caryatids.[25] This would account for the survival of only the basement and the lid of the tomb. Had there been a stone tomb chest there seems no reason why its walls should not have survived. The 1771 reference to the tomb having a canopy is consonant with its being a table tomb.[26]

We are left to find homes for the two brass inscriptions, if they were indeed part of this monument. Their length is slightly less than the width of the top slab, while their width matches its height. However, the slab's projecting mouldings would prevent the fixing of the inscriptions on its ends vertically, and if they had been on top, there should be evidence of fixing holes at both ends, whereas we only have the two plugged holes at the west end. The dearth of holes also raises the question of how the figures (the angels, beadsmen and the effigy) were attached to the lid.

The most likely solution is the presence of another horizontal slab fixed on the present top by two plugs. Such additional slabs are not uncommon in contemporary tombs (Fig. 9.5).[27] If it were of metal it would have been melted down with the statues, or, if of stone, was probably broken up when the statues were removed. To accommodate the two Parisian inscriptions at either end, it must have been at least 1.46m wide and 21cm high. This allows us to posit a tentative reconstruction of the tomb in Fig. 9.3, before turning to precedents and parallels.

PRECEDENTS AND PARALLELS

A slightly earlier tomb with the effigy on the lid supported by free-standing statues was the late Burgundian tomb of Philippe Pot (d. 1493), originally in the abbey of Cîteaux, where eight *pleurants* act as pall bearers.[28] However, the seven Virtues on the tomb of a bishop inevitably recall the influential Renaissance tomb of Pope Sixtus IV (d. 1484), which was installed in Old St Peter's in 1493 by Antonio Pollaiuolo. It is bronze, and rather like an altar tomb with concave sides splayed out: Panofsky describes it as a 'truncated pyramid'.[29] On the flat rectangular top, the effigy of Sixtus lies surrounded by reliefs of the Virtues in rectangular panels, one at his head and three along each side. An eighth panel at Sixtus' feet contains the epitaph, and coats of arms occupy the four corners (Fig. 9.4). While the overall form of the tomb differs from Elphinstone's, the points of correspondence are several: the use of bronze, the recumbent effigy, the position of the epitaph and, if we accept that the Parisian brass strips were part of the tomb, the four corner coats of arms. There is also correspondence in the siting of both tombs, Sixtus' being placed in front of the altar in the choir chapel of the college of canons of St Peter's.[30] The magnificence of the tomb and its siting in front of what was effectively the second most important altar in the basilica ensured its prominence. Even after the building of the new St Peter's, it still attracted more attention than other monuments. It and that of Innocent VIII, also by Pollaiuolo are the only tombs named by William Kerr, later third Earl of Lothian, on his grand tour in 1624–25.[31]

The influence of Sixtus' tomb was quickly felt north of the Alps, on the tomb of Charles VIII of France (who would have seen it in Rome during his Italian expedition of 1494–95), erected soon after his death in 1498.[32] His tomb takes the form of an altar with the Virtues included among twelve personifications in circular relief panels on the walls of the tomb chest, while on the lid the king kneels in prayer surrounded

Fig. 9.4. Tomb of Pope Sixtus IV, St Peter's Rome. Antonio Pollaiolo, installed 1493 (Fratelli Alinari, Florence)

by four kneeling angels each bearing a shield. The base and lid of the tomb appear to have been in dark marble with mouldings close to those of the Elphinstone tomb. It stood in the abbey of St Denis until its destruction in 1798, and therefore would have been familiar to Scots visiting Paris.

Closer to Elphinstone's is that of Philibert of Savoy (d. 1504), which stood in the centre of the choir at Brou (Fig. 9.2). The French sculptors Jean Perréal and Michel Colombe were originally engaged to carve the tomb but no substantial work had been completed by 1512, and the commission passed to a Brabantine atelier, headed by Jan van Roome from Brussels.[33] It was finally completed between 1526 and 1531, by Conrat Meit, a German working in Mechelen in Flanders, seat of the court of Philibert's widow, Margaret of Austria, Regent of the Netherlands from 1508 until her death in 1530.[34] Apart from the analogous site of Philibert's tomb, it resembles Elphinstone's in having a touchstone base and lid with recumbent effigy, and the original contract with Colombe specified the Virtues among the ten statues within niches in the six outer piers supporting the lid.[35] The present statues, in transitional Gothic-Renaissance style, are now acknowledged to be Sibyls, and appear to be the

Fig. 9.5.   Tomb of King Frederick I of Denmark, Schleswig Cathedral, Germany.
Cornelis Floris, 1551–55 (Bildarchiv Foto Marburg)

work of the Brabantine atelier, while the two effigies of the deceased, in life and
death, and the six putti or cherubs on the lid are fully Renaissance, and are the work
of Meit.[36] The two pairs of putti standing to support the shields at the ends of the lid
correspond to the angels performing the same function on Elphinstone's tomb but
there they were below the lid and a closer parallel can be seen on the bronze reliefs in
the end panels of Torrigiani's altar tomb of Henry VII of England and Margaret of
York in Westminster Abbey, executed between 1512 and 1518. On the lid of the

latter are perched four more bronze putti each sharing the support of shields with one hand, while formerly holding banners and the sword of state with the other.[37] We recall that the angels on top of the Aberdeen tomb carried candles and the beadsmen the epitaph.

After Margaret of Austria's death, Mechelen rapidly declined, and by 1534 Meit had moved to Antwerp, where Cornelis Floris II (1514–75) designed the tomb of King Frederick I of Denmark, installed in Schleswig Cathedral in 1555.[38] It has six Ionic caryatid-like Virtues supporting the touchstone table top, on which rests a white marble bed supporting the recumbent effigy of the king. At the king's feet, a figure holds up the epitaph (Fig. 9.5). Two years later Hieronymus Cock published an engraving of a very similar table tomb designed by Floris, with biblical texts inscribed in the friezes of the base and the top.[39] The correspondences with our reconstruction of Elphinstone's tomb are very striking: the caryatid Virtues, the figure(s) holding the epitaph, the presence of inscriptions, etc. Given its earlier date, Elphinstone's tomb seems to be the missing link between Brou and Antwerp. Since no documented works by Floris date from before 1548, it seems possible that Meit may have already devised the type, and, since we know the King's chapel bells were cast in Mechelen, it is tempting to suggest that Elphinstone's tomb also was largely executed there, perhaps in Meit's workshop.[40]

These parallels demonstrate that Elphinstone's tomb was in the forefront of northern Renaissance tomb design, using features at this date reserved for sovereigns and their familes. Even allowing for the fact that he had been Chancellor of Scotland, the tomb appears to have been of unusual magnificence for a cleric. The explanation may lie in its programme, which suggests it not only served as a memorial, but also a more ambitious symbolic and didactic purpose.

THE PROGRAMME

The four cardinal or active Virtues (Justice, Fortitude, Prudence and Temperance) are taken over from pagan philosophy by the early Church Fathers, who add the three theological or contemplative Virtues (Faith, Hope and Charity) and these become the canonical set of seven, although there are others. They soon appear personified in early Christian art, identifiable by their individual attributes.[41] During the middle ages, the Virtues appear on tombs only of saints, testifying to the heroic virtue of the deceased, but, as we have seen, their use is extended on tombs during the Renaissance.[42] What distinguishes Elphinstone's tomb is the additional presence of Contemplation. According to the standard schema of Christian prayer in the middle ages, the four stages in ascending order were reading, meditation, prayer (i.e. petition) and contemplation, the ultimate goal, when the subject has direct knowledge and beholds the face of God.[43] Contemplation is not therefore a Virtue, i.e. a moral quality, but rather a state of mind.[44] Nor was it personified as such but regarded as the activity proper to the cherubim, the second highest order of angels. The most explicit biblical references to cherubim are in Exodus 25.17–22, where God tells Moses to make a pair of golden cherubs to stand on the Ark of the Covenant, which was later installed in the Holy of Holies in Solomon's Temple; and in Ezekiel, where they are the four monstrous creatures which surround Ezekiel's vision of God (Ezekiel 1.4–28 and 10.8–22). The connection between contemplation and cherubim derives from the latter's etymology, and was expounded in Dionysius the pseudo-Areopagite's, *Celestial Hierarchy*, written around A.D. 500.[45] His codification of the angelic orders was immensely influential in the western church, throughout the middle ages and beyond: Milton still speaks of the Cherub Contemplation in the seventeenth century.[46] 'Virtues' is also the name of the fifth order of angels, but more generally the cardinal Virtues are linked to all seven lower orders, while the theological Virtues pertain to the cherubim and seraphim.[47]

The Temple connection is significant since we know that the chapel's inscribed foundation date (2 April 1500) recalls Solomon's Temple, but what connects it with the Virtues?[48] One likely source is Gregory the Great, whose Homilies on Ezekiel, were required reading on the Temple. Commenting on Ezekiel 1.8, Gregory links the four faces of the cherubim to the cardinal Virtues and then discusses the merits of the active and contemplative lives.[49] Later, expatiating on Ezekiel 40.47, he brings all seven Virtues into his discussion of the dimensions of the Temple's inner court, and this is summarised in the *Glossa ordinaria*, the standard medieval bible commentary.[50] While many of these themes are touched on by others, the theologian who discusses them most comprehensively is the great Franciscan, St Bonaventure (c. 1217–74).[51] Bonaventure enjoyed a revival around the time of his canonization in 1482, and even the neo-platonist philosopher Pico della Mirandola's (1463–94) *On the Dignity of Man* has as many echoes of Bonaventure as of Dionysius when discussing contemplation.[52] The overall conception of Bonaventure's well known *Itinerarium mentis in Deum* is of a journey through the desert and into the Tabernacle, erected by Moses, according to God's instructions (Exodus 25–27), and on which Solomon's Temple was modelled.[53] In addition, in the fourth chapter, he says that our minds should be clothed with the theological Virtues as a prerequisite for achieving contemplation, and compares the nine orders of angels with nine levels of the mind. When our mind is illuminated by contemplation, it becomes like the House of God, a Temple of the Holy Spirit. In the sixth chapter, he equates the reader in a state of contemplation to the two cherubs on the Ark of the Covenant.[54]

An even more pertinent link between the Temple and Contemplation is a sermon of Bonaventure for Candlemas, the Feast of the Purification of the Virgin (2 February). His text is part of the Epistle or first reading for the Mass, Malachi 3.1–4, where God takes his throne on the Ark of the Covenant in the Temple, and purifies the sons of Levi as gold and silver are refined. Bonaventure tells us that all ministers of the Church must be so purified, and that Mary is their exemplar, filled with the cardinal Virtues (silver), and, and the theological Virtues (gold). He then moves on to one of Mary's titles, the Ark of the Covenant, made of gold, and refers to the two cherubim. Next he quotes the Song of Songs 3.9–10, to bring in another Old Testament type of Mary, the 'Throne of Solomon' or 'Seat of Wisdom', equating its silver legs (*columnae* in the Vulgate) with the cardinal Virtues and its gold seat back with the theological.[55] In order to be good servants of the glorious Virgin, we must

'Look and do/make following the exemplar', God's instructions to Moses for making the Ark of the Covenant (Exodus 25.40). This is accomplished by choosing the 'gold and the silver' leading neither a purely active nor contemplative life. First one must exercise the active Virtues, leading to contemplation, and then, after contemplation, must follow action.[56] The resonances with Elphinstone's tomb are clear: not only do we have contemplation linked to all the the Virtues but the latter are also compared to metal columns, as well as the two angels on top of the tomb (which I think we can safely assume were cherubs) referring to the Ark of the Covenant.[57] The tomb at the most obvious level is meant to remind the members of King's College, both masters and students, in their daily worship in a chapel associated with the Temple, that their founder embodied these Virtues and practised an exemplary life, both active and contemplative. We can be certain that they would also learn to recognize the references to Solomon's Throne and to the Ark of the Covenant, since it was the duty of the theology students to take it in turn to read aloud the Bible and the relevant passages from the *Glossa Ordinaria* with Nicholas of Lyra's additional commentary daily at dinner and supper to all students.[58] That the Blessed Virgin Mary, co-patron of the chapel, was equated with the Ark of the Covenant and Solomon's Throne would be known through one of the increasingly popular late medieval Marian Litanies, which would have been heard on Marian feasts.[59] Elphinstone in a sense is reposing on Mary herself, which leads us back to his own life and the key to the programme.[60]

THE ORIGIN OF THE PROGRAMME

Boece relates how, as a child, Elphinstone dreamed that the Blessed Virgin told him 'to apply himself wholly to Virtue' and to restoring her 'temples', and that at his death 'he passed to the Holy Virgin to whom he devoted himself in youth and whom he had served all his life, whom he had honoured, if the word may be forgiven, by building churches [*templa*], and whose aid with his last breath he had implored'.[61] The tomb thus appears to allude to Elphinstone's personal devotion to Mary, his emulation of her exemplary practice of Virtue(s) and his building of temples to her. So was he responsible for its programme? We know he owned the relevant parts of the Bible with the Glossa Ordinaria and Lyra's additions, since he gifted its three volumes to King's College in 1512.[62] His library also contained a small collection of works by Bonaventure; Marian devotional works and a treatise on the four [cardinal] Virtues, attributed to Seneca.[63] Nor can he have failed to see the tomb of Sixtus IV on his visit to Rome in 1494–95.[64]

However, as we have seen, the tomb was not begun before the episcopate of Gavin Dunbar, who is the most likely commissioner of the new tomb, but there is no reason to suppose he was involved with the details.[65] Hector Boece, as principal of the college, could be expected to have some input, but the most likely candidate for devising the programme and conceiving the overall design is Alexander Galloway, rector of Kinkell, who was elected rector of the college in 1516, 1521, 1530 and 1549.[66] He is described in contemporary sources as an 'architect' and seems to have designed some sacrament houses, including that in the chapel itself.[67] Galloway had his own Bible with the Glossa ordinaria and Nicholas of Lyra's commentary, and therefore would have been familiar with its reconstructions of the Ark of the Covenant.[68] He also owned Gregory the Great's complete works and so also had direct access to the *Homilies on Ezekiel*.[69] As for the works of Bonaventure, they were not yet all in print, but it is likely that most would have been available in manuscript at the Aberdeen friary of the Observant Franciscans, founded c. 1470.[70] Dunbar financed the rebuilding of their church around 1530, and Galloway both erected it and donated an altarpiece, and so one can assume relations were close.[71] Boece tells us that that Galloway was Elphinstone's 'chief and most faithful friend', who 'in Elphinstone's lifetime had above all others favoured the college and done much for its advantage'. Therefore Gavin Dunbar entrusted Galloway with finishing the projects initiated by Elphinstone, including completion of the college buildings.[72] No one was better placed or suited to design the tomb, and had Boece written his life of Elphinstone after its erection, he may even have been credited with it.

Conclusion

We can only speculate as to the exact form of Elphinstone's tomb and to the roles of Alexander Galloway and Conrad Meit, but there can be no doubt that we have lost a masterpiece, combining the subtlest theological symbolism with Renaissance artistic originality. While regretting it appears to have only survived intact a century, we have to be grateful that at least some indications of its appearance survive, given that in most cases we cannot even begin to guess the extent of losses of Scottish pre-Reformation ecclesiastical art.

Notes

[1] I would like to thank Eamon Duffy, Jane Geddes and Leslie Macfarlane for their invaluable support in supplying ideas, information and criticism. J. Thomas, 'The Elphinstone Monument at King's College Aberdeen', *AUR*, LIV, 1992, 322. The band of brass lettering between the slabs was added by William Kelly. W. D. Simpson, 'The Founder's Memorial', *AUR*, XVIII, 1931, 214.

[2] C. Cnudde, J.-J. Harotin, J.-Majot, *Stones and Marbles of Wallonia*, Brussels, 1988, 126. The base of Elphinstone's tomb is 2.29m long by 1.29m wide and 28cm high; the lid is 21cm high; and the upper surface (i.e. not including the projecting mouldings) is 2.5m by 1.6m. At the west end of the top surface are two plugged holes about 2cm diameter, that on the north side 9cm from the west edge and 24cm from the north edge; that on the south side 11cm from the west edge and 22cm from the south edge. I am indebted to Jane Geddes and Leslie Macfarlane for supplying these measurements.

[3] *The Ledger of Andrew Halyburton: Conservator of the privileges of the Scotch nation in the Netherlands 1492–1503*, ed. Cosmo Innes, Edinburgh, 1867, 7, 215.

[4] See G. von der Osten and H. Vey, *Paintings and Sculpture in Germany and the Netherlands 1500 to 1600*, Harmondsworth, 1969, 58; and Theodor Müller, *Sculpture in the Netherlands, Germany, France and Spain 1400 to 1500*, Harmondsworth, 1966, 160–61.

[5] Boece, 109.

[6] Boece, 121.

[7] Eeles, 1956, 32; the original Latin on p. 10 reads: '*Sepulchrum domini Fundatoris in cuius superiore parte imago ipsius in pontificalibus, cum duobus angelis portantibus duo candelabra ad caput, et duobus mercenariis epitaphium in ere insculptum ad pedes portantibus; inferius, ex australi parte tres virtutes theologice et Contemplatio; in boreali 4 virtutes cardinales suis signis distincte; in orientali et occidentali partibus, domini Fundatoris insignia ab angelis lata*'.

[8] J. Gordon, *Abredoniae utriusque descriptio: A description of both touns of Aberdeen by James Gordon; with a selection of the charters of the burgh*, Spalding Club, Edinburgh, 1842, 23.

[9] Orem, 1791, 175.

[10] Orem, 1791, 173.

[11] Orem, 1791, 41. In the first edition of Orem, 1782, 161, this passage is ascribed to G. and W. Paterson.

[12] W. Geddes, 'Note on the Restoration of King's College Chapel, 1891', *Transactions of the Aberdeen Ecclesiological Society*, II, 6th year, 1891 (1892), 65. One occasion for the disturbance might have been around 1740 when the floor of the chapel was 'pathmented' [paved], AUL, MS K 57/18, p. 6, K 257/5/4/26–8.

[13] J. Durkan, 'Early humanism and King's College', *AUR*, 163, 1980, 260. The original can be found published in J. Guiffrey, 'Artistes et tombiers parisiens du commencement de XVIe siècle', *Revue de l'art français*, 1896, 21–22, no. 58: '*5 janvier 1529: Marché entre Pierre Prisié, maître tombier à Paris, et Robert Alphinseton, prêtre, maître des arts pour la fourniture de deux lames de cuivre jaune, mesurant chacune 4 pieds et demi de long sur 8 pouces de large, où seront gravés les quatre écussons et l'inscription donnés au tombier; à livrier pour la Chandeleur, moyennant 9 liv. 10 s.t.*' The pied de roi was 32.484cm: see H. Doursther, *Dictionnaire universelle des poids et mesures anciens et modernes*, Brussels, 1840, s.v.

[14] Macfarlane, 1995, 348.

[15] Eeles, 1956, 51–52.

[16] Eeles, 1956, 47–48.

[17] *Registrum Episcopatus Aberdonensis*, 2 vols, Spalding Club, Edinburgh, 1845, II, 188: '*Item per eosdem ymago dicti domini episcopi [Dunbar] ex ere fuso cum epitaphio eiusdem*'.

[18] *Registrum*, II, 188.

[19] G. Savage, *A concise history of bronzes*, London, 1968, 12.

[20] See Chapter 14.

[21] K. Cohen, *Metamorphosis of a death symbol: The transi in the late Middle Ages and the Renaissance*, Berkeley and London, 1973.

[22] Cohen, 1973, 120–25 and E. Panofsky, *Tomb sculpture: Its changing aspects from ancient Egypt to Bernini*, London, 1992, 78–79.

[23] 'He [the Earl of Seaforth] caused ane mason to strike out Christis arms in hewn wark on each end of Bishop Dunbars tomb', J. Spalding, *Memorialls of the Trubles in Scotland and in Englnd, AD 1624–AD 1645*, Spalding Club, Aberdeen, 1850–51, I, 313–14.

[24] James Gordon, *History of Scots Affairs from MDCXXXVIII to MDCXLI*, ed. J. Robertson and G. Grub, Spalding Club, Aberdeen, 1841, III, 219.

[25] On table tombs, see Panofsky, 1992, 53–54.

[26] Orem, 1791, 41. Thomas, 1992, fig. 4, illustrates a model of an early design by Henry Wilson for his new memorial based on the inventory description, which also took the form of a table tomb.

[27] See the 1531 tomb in Swansea illustrated in F. H. Crossley, *English Church Monuments A.D. 1150–1550*, London, 1921, 123, which has a slab with plain vertical sides above a slab with mouldings very similar to Elphinstone's.

[28] Müller, 1966, 136–37, pl. 143.

[29] Panofsky, 1992, 87–88.

[30] P. Fehl, 'Monumenti e arte del lutto: le tombe dei papi e dei principi a S. Pietro: Un ciclo di conferenze di Philipp Fehl: III. Tombe dall'antica basilica di S. Pietro nella nuova chiesa' (unpublished notes of a lecture at the Austrian Historical Institute in Rome, 28 November 1996).

[31] National Library of Scotland, MS 5785, fol. 7^v: 'There are many monuments of brasse & marble as that of Sixtus Quartus and of Innocentius Octavus'.

[32] Panofsky, 1992, 75–76, fig. 325.

[33] M.-F. Poiret, *Le Monastère de Brou: le Chef d'oeuvre d'une fille d'empereur*, Paris, 1994, 67–75, 90–96.

[34] Poiret, 1994, 98–102; Panofsky, 1992, 78; Cohen, 1973, 123 ff. On Meit, see C. Lowenthal, *Conrat Meit*, unpub. Dissertation, New York University, 1976.

[35] Poiret, 1994, 73.

[36] Poiret, 1994, 94–96, 98. Another similarity with Aberdeen is that the church tower was originally topped by a stone crown imperial, but structural problems caused its removal in the mid-seventeenth century (Poiret, 1994, 86).

[37] Crossley, 1921, 107–08, illus. p. 111. Though the Henry VII tomb is in full blown Renaissance style, with Corinthian pilasters decorated with grotesques, the iconography is traditional with twelve paired saints in the garlanded roundels.

[38] A. Huysmans, 'De grafmonumenten van Cornelis Floris', *Revue belge d'archéologie et de l'histoire de l'art*, 56, 1987, 106–08, and 112–13. It should be noted that virtues had already served as caryatids on a series of Italian wall tombs, the earliest of which are for the Angevin royal family in Naples around 1330 by Tino di Camaino (Panofsky, 1992, 74–75).

[39] Huysmans, 1987, 99–100; Panofsky, 1992, 76 and fig. 332.

[40] On the bells, see Chapter 8. It may also be worth noting that Gavin Dunbar had a new Epistolary for St Machar's copied in Antwerp in 1527: see F. C. Eeles' 'Introduction' in *Epistolare in usum Ecclesiae Cathedralis Aberdoniensis*, ed. B. McEwen, Aberdeen University Studies no. 93, Edinburgh, 1924, xviii-xix.

[41] See A. E. M. Katzellenbogen, *Allegories of the Virtues and Vices in Mediaeval Art*, London, 1939; and *New Catholic Encyclopedia*, 17 vols, New York, 1967–74, vol. 13, 704–11.

[42] Panofsky, 1992, 62–63, 74–76; and Cohen, 1973, 142–46.

[43] See S. Tugwell, *Ways of imperfection: An exploration of Christian spirituality*, London, 1984, 93–124.

[44] Contemplation is counted as a Virtue in a work uncertainly ascribed St Bonaventure, but along with it and the seven standard Virtues are 22 others, many of which would not normally be regarded as such, including Fear and Joy: see *De gradibus virtutum* in St Bonaventure, *Opera omnia*, 10 vols, Quaracchi, 1882–1902, vol. 8, 653.

[45] Pseudo-Dionysius, *The complete works*, tr. by Colm Luibheid, New York, 1987, 162–63.

[46] John Milton, *Il Penseroso*, l. 54: see W. K. Leask, *Interamna Borealis*, Aberdeen, 1917, 281–83.

[47] E. G. Gardner, *Dante*, London, 1923, 194–95.

[48] See Chapter 5. G. Edwards, 'William Elphinstone, his college chapel, and the Second of April', *AUR*, Spring 1985, LI, 1, no. 173, 1–17.

[49] Gregory the Great, *Homiliarum in Ezechielem*, Bk 1, Hom. 4.7–9 in J.-P. Migne (ed.), *Patrologia Latina*, 221 vols, Paris, 1844–65, vol. 176, coll. 808–09.

[50] Gregory, *In Ezechielem*, Bk 2, Hom. 10.17–18 in ibid., colls 1067–69. On the *Glossa ordinaria* and the Temple, see H. Rosenau, *Vision of the Temple: The image of the Temple of Jerusalem in Judaism and Christianity*, London, 1979, 38–43.

[51] *New Catholic Encyclopedia*, vol. 3, 260.

[52] E. Cassirer, P. O. Kristeller and J. J. Randall (eds), *The Renaissance philosophy of Man*, Chicago, 1948, 227–31. Pico's complete works were in Scotland by at latest the mid-sixteenth century: see J. Durkan and A. Ross, *Early Scottish Libraries*, Glasgow, 1961, 98.

[53] Bonaventure, *Itinerarium mentis in Deum*, in *Opera omnia*, 10 vols, Quaracchi, 1882–1902, V, 295–313: for an English translation see Saint Bonaventura, *The Mind's Road to God*, tr. G. Boas, Indianapolis and New York, 1953. The references to the Tabernacle are *Itinerarium*, 3.1 and 5.1: *Opera*, 303 and 308; *Mind's Road*, 22 and 34. On the correspondence of Solomon's Temple to the Tabernacle, see Rosenau, 1979, 14.

[54] Bonaventure, *Itinerarium*, IV.3–7 and VI.4–6; *Opera*, V, 306–8 and 311–12; *Mind's Road*, 29–33 and 41–42.

[55] On Mary as Solomon's throne, see I. H. Forsyth, *The Throne of Wisdom: Wood sculptures of the Madonna in Romanesque France*, Princeton, 1972, 24–26.

[56] *De Purificatione B. Virginis Mariae: Sermo I* in Bonaventure, *Opera*, vol. 9, 638–40.

[57] Whether they were yet represented as *putti* is uncertain. They could well have been if the tomb was executed in the Meit workshop. However they appear as conventional northern Gothic long-haired adult angels in both reconstructions of the Ark of the Covenant in the woodcuts, which appear first in Anton Koberger's Bible printed in Nuremberg in 1481, with the *Glossa Ordinaria* and Nicholas of Lyra's *Postillae*, reprinted many times in various cities into the 1540s with the same woodcuts. For the transformation of cherubs in the Renaissance from awesome monsters to *putti*, see A. Nagel, *Cherubs: Angels of love*, London, 1994, 16–18. For the Koberger illustrations see Rosenau, 1979, 39–40.

[58] Edwards, 1985, 7; Eeles, 1956, 212.

[59] See 'The Litany of Loreto' in the *Catholic Encyclopedia*, 1998 electronic version at http:www.csn.net/advent/cathen/09287a.htm.

[60] The wall tomb of Cardinal Chiaves, erected by Isaia da Pisa in the mid-Quattrocento in the Lateran in Rome, seems to have incorporated similar ideas: the sarcophagus rested on the four cardinal virtues as caryatids, while the three theological virtues stood behind, i.e like the columns and back of Solomon's throne, with an Annunciation relief above: see M. Kühlenthal, 'Zwei Grabmäler des frühen Quattrocento in Rom: Kardinal Martinez de Chiaves und Papst Eugen IV', *Römisches Jahrbuch für Kunstgeschichte*, 16, 1976, 17–56.

[61] Boece, 59 and 112. The churches he built were the chapel itself and the parish church of Old Aberdeen, St Mary of the Snows: see E. Dennison and J. Stones, *Historic Aberdeen*, Edinburgh, 1997, 101–02.

[62] Edwards, 1985, 7.

[63] L. Macfarlane, 'William Elphinstone's Library Revisited', in *The Renaissance in Scotland: Studies in Literature, Religion, History and Culture*, ed. A. A. MacDonald, M. Lynch and I. B. Cowan, Leiden, 1994, 66–81, especially 78–81.

[64] Macfarlane, 1995, 291–92.

[65] Bishop Dunbar's own tomb (d. 1532), set into the south transept wall of St Machar's Cathedral, is a conservative gothic monument. Its main concession to the new classicism is the moulding of the plinth.

[66] Boece, 161. It is unlikely that the sculptor executing the tomb had any input into the overall programme: Meit had none either at Brou or in his other known tomb commission; Lowenthal, 1976, 21–22.

[67] Macfarlane, 1995, 335, 351; Kelly, 1949, 19–33. Some of the sacrament houses seem to contain Temple symbolism, which I hope to explore in another article.

[68] Durkan and Ross, 1961, 100.

[69] Durkan and Ross, 1961, 102.

[70] Macfarlane, 1995, 256–58.

[71] Kelly, 1949, 26–27, 31.

[72] Boece, 92, 122.

CHAPTER TEN

THE ORIGINAL ARMORIALS

By CHARLES J. BURNETT ESQ., ROSS HERALD OF ARMS

Aberdeenshire has a distinctive creative art tradition, which requires more detailed study, in which armorial display takes its place, providing us with examples which do not follow national norms, and are unique to the region. The great heraldic layout on the ceiling of St Machar's Cathedral, and the armorial table above the entrance to Huntly Castle are only two schemes which demonstrate the intellectual approach to heraldic art — one of the characteristics of the north-east.

King's College Chapel provides in microcosm a representative range of this regional heraldic art, rendered in a remarkable variety of media: stone, lead, glass, wood, and paint. The range is also chronological and provides evidence of changing artistic style from the medieval period through to the early twentieth century.

The various armorial achievements were listed and published 110 years ago,[1] but a reappraisal in this volume not only places the armory in context, but provides an opportunity to extend the list to include heraldic art added to the chapel since 1888 (in Chapter 21).

The earliest examples, carved *c.* 1504,[2] are four in number, and constitute a royal family group consisting of the arms of James IV, his queen, his younger brother,[3] and an illegitimate son. Such a familial combination is not found anywhere else in Scotland and indicates that whoever directed the carver wished to express particular appreciation of the sovereign and his lady alongside two members of his family closely connected with the Catholic Church. The director must have been Bishop William Elphinstone, whose own arms and those of Pope Alexander VI who granted the authority to establish the university surprisingly did not appear on the original exterior of the chapel. Indeed, another building under construction at the same time, directly linked with the King of Scots, the great hall of Edinburgh Castle, has no display of contemporary royal family heraldry.[4]

The four stone panels are situated on the west and north fronts, three on the former, and one on the latter. The arms of Margaret Tudor appear on the northern buttress to the left of the west door carved on a stone (106 x 84cm), now weathered but still with visible details (Fig. 10.1). A full-bottomed shield bears the impaled arms of Scotland and the quartered arms of France and England. Political sensitivities in Scotland were not so acute to omit the fleurs-de-lis of France. During the reign of the succeeding monarch, James V, England's claim to the throne of France was ignored in heraldic representations of the English royal arms on the ceiling of St Machar's Cathedral and over the fore entry to Linlithgow Palace.[5]

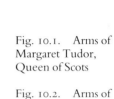

Fig. 10.1.   Arms of
Margaret Tudor,
Queen of Scots

Fig. 10.2.   Arms of
James IV, King of
Scots

Fig. 10.3.   Arms of
Alexander Stewart,
Archbishop of St
Andrews

Fig. 10.4.   Arms of
James Stewart, Duke
of Ross, Archbishop of
St Andrews

Margaret Tudor's shield is supported on the dexter side by a dragon and on the sinister by a greyhound. These beasts had been adopted by Margaret's father, Henry VII of England to proclaim his Welsh and Lancastrian ancestry.[6] The supporters are unusual in being reguardant, i.e. looking back over their shoulder, a feature which also occurs in the royal arms of James IV. Both beasts have tails which hang down between their legs, a common practice in Scottish heraldic art of the time, it was not until the seventeenth century that supporting animal tails curled upwards.[7]

Below the shield is a Scottish thistle flanked by what might be two English roses, the first time in Scotland this combination appears in carved stone. The combination had already appeared as painted decoration on one side of the marriage contract, dated 17 December 1502, of James IV and Margaret Tudor which had been executed by Sir Thomas Galbraith.[8] However the flowers have daisy-like heads and may represent marigolds. If so they echo the punning symbolism of Margaret's name which had aleady been employed as border decoration on a page in the *Vienna Book of Hours*, the wedding gift of James IV to his new bride.[9] Above the shield is a non-imperial royal crown, of alternate crosses and fleur-de-lis apparently containing a bonnet of estate without the usual ermine trim. The King's College Chapel panel is the only surviving example in Scotland of the full achievement of arms of Margaret Tudor of England.[10]

The central buttress on the west front bears the royal arms of Scotland carved on a large stone measuring 142 x 87cm (Fig. 10.2). This bears the date ANNO DNI 1504 at the top of the panel, making this version the earliest dated stone carved example in Scotland. Apart from this distinction, the design of the arms has unique elements. The panel is the earliest carved example of the full armorial achievement with shield, helmet, wreath, mantling, crown, crest, motto and supporters. Earlier versions do not have helmet, mantling and motto. Comments will be made on each element in turn.

The shield is straightforward and follows contemporary examples with sixteen alternate fleurs-de-lis on the double tressure.[11] The lion rampant fills the space inside the double tressure in the best traditions of heraldic art and the tail curves inwards as usual for the time. The helmet appears odd and rather too flat to contain a head but the carver may have been compensating for the fact the panel is set high on the wall and the arms are viewed from below. The enriched decorative trim to the helmet is indicative of high rank.

When he came to carve the mantling on either side of the helmet, the stone mason created an original solution. It takes the form of thistle leaves with terminating flowers. This apt form of mantling for a Scottish king is quite unlike anything seen before, or since, in the heraldic art of Scotland.[12] The mantling is held in place on top of the helmet with a twisted wreath. It is unusual to see this detail on carved royal arms of the period and indicates the heraldic knowledge of the carver, or the person who possibly prepared drawings for each of the four panels as a guide. Above the wreath is a non-imperial crown of alternate crosses and fleurs-de-lis enclosing a bonnet of estate on which rests the crest, a crowned demi-lion holding a sword in its right paw. Two years earlier the *Vienna Book of Hours* showed the lion crest also carrying a saltire flag.[13] Either this detail was unknown to the carver or he simply chose to use the crest associated with James III which would have been more familiar. Behind the crest is a scroll bearing the motto IN DE FENS. This, the shortened version of the original royal motto IN MY DEFENS GOD US DEFEND was adopted by James III, King of Scots *c.* 1471.[14] The unicorn supporters are gorged with open crowns, again of alternate fleurs-de-lis and crosses, and chained with links running between the forelegs, over the backs and terminating in a ring near the hind hooves. The supporter tails are couée as in the Margaret Tudor panel.

The most remarkable feature is the reguardant position of the two unicorns, as previously mentioned. This method of portraying the royal supporters is unique to north-east Scotland. Another example, dating from the reign of James V, can be seen in Marischal College Museum. It is a carved wooden panel bearing the full achievement of arms above a small shield carved with the initials of William Roland, the Master of the Aberdeen Mint.[15] As late as *c.* 1603 when the Mercat Cross at Fraserburgh in Aberdeenshire was carved the lion and unicorn supporters of the royal arms of Great Britain are also shown reguardant.

The final feature of the King's College Chapel panel is the clump of thistles at the bottom of the panel beneath the shield. This appropriate space filler was first used at

Paisley Abbey *c.* 1471 on a panel of the royal arms, now in the Place of Paisley. The plant badge is located in this position in the royal arms of the United Kingdom to this day.

The third panel on the south buttress of the chapel tower is much weathered (Fig. 10.3). This measures 114 x 91cm and is carved with a variant of the arms of Alexander Stuart, the natural son of James IV who was Archbishop of St Andrews from 1509 until his death at the battle of Flodden in 1513. Faintly visible below the shield are the letters AS. Two angels support a shield of the royal arms of Scotland. Alexander Steward did not difference the arms with a bordure compony, the normal mark of illegitimacy. Behind the shield is an archiepiscopal cross flanked by two vertical elements which become thicker towards the top of the panel. Corresponding curved lines on the dexter and sinister sides of the panel beside the angel supporters suggest the arms may have been set within an architectural setting of three arches. There are curious socket holes above the head of each angel which may have supported a band of stone carved with a motto.

There are two seal impressions from matrices used by Alexander Stewart as Archbishop of St Andrews.[16] Neither use angels as supporters which may have been intended by the carver to reinforce the ecclesiastical office of the owner of the arms.

The fourth royal panel is located above the north front door of the chapel (Fig. 10.4). Unfortunately this too is much weathered but bears the arms of James Stewart, second son of James III who, as Duke of Ross and Marquess of Ormonde was appointed Archbishop of St Andrews in 1498. He died in 1504.

Carved on the stone is a shield of the royal arms of Scotland, supported by two angels, surmounted by a princely coronet probably consisting of alternate crosses and fleurs-de-lis with an archiepiscopal cross behind the shield and appearing above the coronet. Behind the head of the cross there is a weathered scroll carved with illegible letters which may have described the owner of the arms. The seal used by the archbishop carried unicorn supporters and an elaborate legend describing all his royal titles.[17]

The four panels form a remarkable group not only for the royal association but as a coherent scheme of armorial decoration executed in the opening years of the sixteenth century far from the heraldic centre around the Court in Edinburgh. It may be significant that Marchmont Herald was a north-east man, William Cumming of Inverallochy, later Lyon King of Arms.[18] It is possible Bishop Elphinstone sought heraldic advice from him. The preservation of these important panels would be greatly assisted by tincturing.[19]

Although any original heraldic reference to the founder bishop is remarkably absent from the chapel, two of his armorials from elsewhere in the university have found an appropriate home here.

Inside the chapel, on the north wall, high above the choir stalls are two unpainted oak carvings bearing the arms of Bishop William Elphinstone. The larger panel, with a finely carved gothic canopy, once hung in the old college hall on the east side of the quadrangle and was removed to the chapel about 1823. It was placed in its present location after the Second World War (Fig. 10.5).[20]

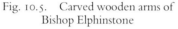

Fig. 10.5.   Carved wooden arms of   Fig. 10.6.   Carved wooden arms of
Bishop Elphinstone   Bishop Elphinstone

The panel dates from Bishop Elphinstone's lifetime and consists of the canopy above an upright oblong panel framed with a moulding decorated at top and sides with twenty-three square four-leaved flowers. Within the moulding a heater-shape shield, charged with a chevron between three boar heads erased, surmounted by a *mitra pretiosa* with the *infulae* resting on and then hanging down on either side of the shield. This compact arrangement is set amidst a riot of lily leaves and flowers which stem from a small bough-pot beneath the shield. The pot is decorated with three salmon fishes in fret.

King's College was dedicated to Saint Mary in the Nativity at the instigation of Bishop Elphinstone.[21] To the medieval mind, a suitable symbol for the Virgin was a pot of lilies and her connection with the Trinity is represented by the three interwoven fish. The latter were also important Christian symbols. For the personal arms of the Bishop to be surrounded by the Virgin's flowers neatly symbolized his spiritual attachment to the Mother of Our Lord. After Bishop Elphinstone's death the bough-pot of lilies were adopted as the arms of the City of Old Aberdeen and so appear on the heraldic ceiling of St Machar's Cathedral.[22]

Behind the bough-pot is a riband curving with lively grace on which is the Bishop's motto NON CONFVDAR. The words have been expanded and crushed to fit the available space on either side of the bough-pot. Dr William Kelly was convinced the panel had been carved by John Fendour who probably also carved the choir stalls in the chapel.[23]

The second panel of the Bishop's arms is smaller (Fig. 10.6). The carving quality is inferior to the first panel which was the obvious source of inspiration. Again we find the Bishop's arms on a shield, surmounted by a mitre with *infulae* elevated above the shield in a clumsy way. The shield has encircling lily plants stemming from a bough-pot with fretted fish. The carver has placed two intertwining stems on the dexter side but only one on the sinister side, as traditionally only three lily stems are normally shown.

At the base of the panel, behind the bough-pot, there is a motto riband but it is entirely blank. This is evidence that the carving was originally painted and the words of the motto rendered in colour.

The original purpose and location of the second panel is unknown.

Notes

[1] P. J. Anderson, 'Note on Heraldic Representations at King's College, Old Aberdeen', *PSAS*, XXIII, 1888–89, 80–86.

[2] Only the royal arms of James IV are dated, but all are contemporary.

[3] Suggested by Leslie J. Macfarlane in the revised second edition, *A Visitor's guide to King's College*, 1992, 10.

[4] Royal Commission on Ancient and Historical Monuments, *The City of Edinburgh*, Edinburgh, 1951, 21.

[5] C. J. Burnett, 'Development of the Royal Arms of Scotland', *Journal of the Heraldry Society of Scotland*, Vol. I, 1977, 9–19.

[6] H. Stanford London, *The Queen's Beasts*, London, 1953, 42, 46.

[7] C. J. Burnett, 'Development of the Royal Arms of Scotland', *Journal of the Heraldry Society of Scotland*, I, 1977, 19.

[8] The contract is held in the Public Record Office, London, E/39/81. For Galbraith's part in its decoration see *Accounts of the Lord High Treasurer of Scotland, 1500–1504*, T. Dickson and Sir T. Balfour Paul (eds), Edinburgh, 1877–1916, II, 350.

[9] Leslie J. Macfarlane, 'The Book of Hours of James IV and Margaret Tudor', The Innes Review, XI, 1960, 9; Vienna, Österreichische Nationalbibliothek, Codex Vindobonensis 1897. Facsimile of the *Vienna Book of Hours* with a commentary by F. Unterkircher, *Das Gebetbuch Jakobs IV von Schottland un seiner Gemahlin Margaret Tudor*, Codices Selecti 85, Graz, 1987.

[10] Painted versions of Margaret's Arms, without supporters, are found in the *Vienna Book of Hours*, fols 14v and 243v, and Scottish Armorials including Sir David Lindsay of the Mount's *Armorial*, 1542, ed. D. Laing, Edinburgh, 1878.

[11] The modern practice of only featuring eight or less fleurs-de-lis is to be deplored.

[12] For the use of the thistle see C. J. Burnett, 'The Thistle as a Symbol', in *Emblems of Scotland*, The Heraldry Society of Scotland, 1997, 45–52.

[13] *Vienna Book of Hours*, fol. 14[v].

[14] The motto appears on the Amiens medal, a gift from James III to a famous reliquary in Amiens Cathedral, which was destroyed in the French Revolution. E. Burns, *The Coinage of Scotland*, Edinburgh, 1887.

[15] See Sir T. Innes of Learney, *Scots Heraldry*, 2nd edn, Edinburgh, 1956, pl. XXXVIII. The panel in Marischal Museum is ABDUA:36842

[16] W. R. Macdonald, *Scottish Armorial Seals*, Edinburgh, 1904, Nos 2590, 2591, 329.

[17] Macdonald, 1904, No. 2584, 328.

[18] Sir F. J. Grant, *Court of the Lord Lyon*, Edinburgh, 1946, 3.

[19] In 1702 there is a Procuration Account 'To colouring of Kings armes and dyall, £12.0.0', AUL, MS K 56, 1700–02, Part 4, second section, articulus secundus.

[20] Kelly, 1949, 65.

[21] J. J. Carter and C. A. McLaren, *Crown and Gown 1495–1995*, Aberdeen, 1994, 13.

[22] W. D. Geddes and P. Duguid, *The Heraldic Ceiling of the Cathedral Church of St Machar, Old Aberdeen*, New Spalding Club, 1888, 28.

[23] Kelly, 1949, 57.

CHAPTER ELEVEN

BISHOP STEWART'S PULPIT

By Richard Emerson

The pulpit of Kings College Chapel, originally erected in the late 1530s at St Machar's Cathedral, Aberdeen, owes its survival to a characteristically Aberdonian quality: a fierce sense of the city's history.

That it is possible to write anything new about this remarkable survival, the only functioning pre-Reformation pulpit to remain in Scotland,[1] is due largely to the work of two of the north-east's most remarkable scholars, James Logan,[2] and William Kelly,[3] upon whose shoulders any succeeding historian must stand to see the past with any clarity.[4]

Reconstructed, moved and adapted on at least five occasions in the last five centuries, the pulpit's original form would be difficult to establish without the manuscript description and watercolour drawings which James Logan made between *c.* 1808 and 1815. At this time the pulpit stood in the session room or consistory court at St Machar's, a room originally fashioned out of the westernmost two bays of the north aisle of the cathedral by Bishop Stewart (1532–45).[5] This was reduced in length by one bay at some time before 1815 before being removed in 1824 when the north aisle was raised in height and re-roofed.[6]

Logan made two drawings of the pulpit, separated by date and by his ability to draw, which had improved in the interim by studying drawing in London. The earlier and larger, on paper watermarked 1808,[7] is a painstaking if, in its handling of perspective, naive record of the pulpit, and clearly shows an asymmetrical arrangement of the panelled well of the pulpit. This is confirmed by his second view, undated but included in his illustrated manuscript description of St Machar's of 1815.[8]

This markedly more proficient drawing departs from the earlier drawing only in showing the boards of the underside of the sounding board running from side to side rather than from front to back.[9] Clearly drawing at the table which appears in the foreground, Logan shows the light falling from the right, thus locating the pulpit against the west wall of the session room (Col. Pl. IIIe).[10]

The drawing accompanies a description of the pulpit:

In the session room is preserved the Cathedral pulpit made in the time of William Stewart who was Bhp from [blank]. It is of oak and in tolerable preservation.
Its form, a hexigon [*sic*] of unequal sides, so made to suit its original position by the south pillar in the transept and towards the west. Amongst the curious carving that ornamented it the crucifix was conspicuous in the centre panel, but as a piece of rank popish superstition it was chiselled out at the Reformation. Traces of the cross may yet be perceived.[11]

Just as the two drawings are the only visual record of the pulpit substantially in its original condition, if lacking its base, so this description provides us with three important facts: the plan of the pulpit well; the pulpit's position prior to 1793;[12] and some evidence of the original subject of the panel shown blank in the drawing. Details of this panel are discussed later.

In the two drawings, only five carved panels on each of the two lower tiers are in view: the lower tier is of rectangular panels containing lozenges of similar foliate ornament in a quincunx framed by foliate spandrels. Above this are, from left to right, two classical profile heads in bas-relief contained within roundels facing each other, with, above the roundel, but still within the rectangular panel, paired dolphins alternately affronted in the first panel and addorsed in the second. The third panel has a profile head in a roundel looking to the right with affronted dolphins above, whilst the fourth panel contains the arms and initials of Bishop James Stewart, establishing the donor of the pulpit. The fifth panel contains another profile head in a roundel, looking to the left with affronted dolphins above.

Fortunately, further drawings by Logan illustrate not only the bishop's arms from the second tier[13] but also the four panels with profile heads in roundels described above, together with two further classical profile heads contained within lozenges with foliate corner spandrels (Fig. 11.1).[14] Since these occur in the middle of the same sheet as the heads in roundels, it may be assumed they formed one of the two sides not visible in either of two frontal views of the pulpit. All these panels still survive as part of the pulpit.

Examination of the panels containing heads in lozenges, however, shows that they were originally almost square in shape, and that each has been lengthened by the addition of a piece of unrelated carving at the bottom. Comparison with the adjacent carvings of heads in roundels suggests, moreover, that the two sets of panels are unrelated to each other: in addition to the discrepancy in size, the heads in lozenges are bordered, along the inner frame of the lozenge, with an incised scalloped border, which both as a detail and a technique occurs nowhere else on the pulpit. The strips of carving which have been added, however, do relate to other panels on the pulpit, and are evidently taken from the top and bottom of a flat panel carved with a sinuous frond, terminating at the top in a flower and at the bottom with the cut end of the branch.[15] In his two general views Logan shows four similar panels on the third tier of carving. The centre, broadest, panel is similar but includes small human masks among the foliage, and foliate panels are found again on the two thin outermost panels of the fifth tier. All these survive on the present pulpit.

Bishop Stewart's arms appear for a second time on the left-hand side of the curving back of the pulpit, as can be discerned in the general views. Balancing the bishop's arms on the right side of the blank central panel — 'upon which traces of the cross may yet be perceived' are the royal arms, the subject also of a separate illustration by Logan.[16] Above all this and evidently once bracketed out from the back, is a hexagonal sounding board, its angles marked by crocketted pinnacles, between which runs a ribbon ornament matching that round the lip of the well, a pierced frieze of flamboyant tracery and openwork trefoil crocketted cresting.

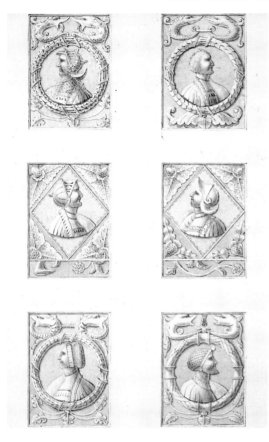

Fig. 11.1.   Watercolour detail of panels on Bishop Stewart's pulpit, by James Logan, 1815 (AUL, MS 2928, vol. III, fol. 14) (Copyright: University of Aberdeen)

If, thanks to Logan's description and illustrations, we have a clear picture of what the pulpit 'in tolerable preservation' looked like, about twenty years after its removal from its position at the south-west crossing pier, and a decade before it was unceremoniously dumped in the sexton's store at the foot of the south-west tower, several questions remain: why, given the bilaterally symmetrical hexagonal form of the sounding board, is the well of the pulpit an irregular hexagon in plan? Why are two of the panels from the second tier, the heads in lozenges, evidently cannibalized from something else, and if the strips which lengthen them come from the pulpit, where did this broad flat rectangular foliate panel, of which the top and bottom survive, come from?

The last question is perhaps the easiest to answer. As set up in the session room, the pulpit was raised about 18 inches from the floor on a stage, with steps on the right-hand side, thus showing incidentally that this side of the pulpit was open and therefore the lozenge-framed profile head panels must have been on the left-hand, invisible, return. However, before 1793 when it was in use as the cathedral pulpit, it must have been raised further above the ground, and the whole of this lower base, itself presumably ornamented, was removed on its transfer to the session room, a comparatively low space below the lean-to roof of the north aisle. The flat rectangular panel decorated with a flowering frond, and whose short dimension matches those of the first and second tiers, presumably came from this missing base, and may give us a clearer indication of the pulpit's original design.

Whilst Logan is undoubtedly accurate in stating that before 1793 the pulpit was set against the south-west crossing pier facing west,[17] this position is not ideal for a pulpit, since it faces not into the body of the church, but confronts the first cylindrical pier of the south nave arcade. It is tempting to suggest that this was not its intended original position and that, if not, it may have been adapted so as to throw the well of the pulpit northwards to give the minister and his congregation better lines of sight. The second proposition is incapable of proof, but it is worth considering in more detail whether the pulpit as first designed was intended to face westwards.

In the 1530s the east end of St Machar's Cathedral was incomplete. The choir begun by Bishop William Elphinstone (1483–1514) was unfinished and unroofed and the choir stalls and high altar would have been moved temporarily into the crossing under the central tower, whilst the east crossing arch would have been built up. This arrangement, however temporary it was intended to be, probably persisted until the end of the middle ages.[18] Certainly Bishop James Stewart's predecessor, Bishop Gavin Dunbar (1518–32), had recently completed the south transept and funds to continue work on the choir may have been exhausted. In any event, Bishop Stewart's building works at St Machar's were very limited and he can be credited only with the formation of the consistory court/session room and the timber pulpit under discussion.

The form of the pulpit, with its trefoil-shaped back, is clearly designed to fit one of the four crossing piers built by Bishop Alexander Kininmund II (1355–80), for the remaining piers of the nave are all cylindrical[19] and it seems likely that it was originally designed to be set up against the south-west crossing pier facing *north*, allowing a clear line of sight both into the nave and the crossing.

With its largely secular iconography, and given the pulpit's central role in reformed worship, it is not surprising that it survived the Reformation unscathed. Not until August 1640 did iconoclasts erase the 'arms of our Lord Jesus Christ' which, flanked by the royal arms and the arms of Bishop Stewart, still held pride of place on the back.[20]

The T-plan church of nave and transepts was equally well suited to presbyterian worship and by the 1680s the transepts had been colonized by lofts. The Marquis of Huntly had a loft in the north transept, and the crossing and south transept contained the College loft and the Merchants' loft.[21] Each could only have seen the pulpit had it faced north. On 9 May 1688, however, the central tower fell, destroying the lofts.[22] Damage to the nave was limited and the pulpit, if indeed it did face north across the western crossing arch, must have been salvageable, though the substitution of lozenge-framed heads for those in roundels on the left hand, or eastern side of the pulpit coupled with the damage to the openwork cresting on the same side, as shown by Logan, suggests that it was affected.

The immediate reaction to the collapse was to further reduce the length of the church, building up a wall between the surviving western crossing piers.[23] Following this, the pulpit could no longer face north and may have been repaired and repositioned to face west, a place it was to occupy for just over a hundred years, until 1793.

If its original position is a matter of surmise, the date of the pulpit is quite closely identifiable: the pulpit is intentionally self documenting: Bishop Stewart's arms both identify the donor, and, in retrospect, provide the date bracket 1532–45. The royal arms, balancing those of the bishop may help narrow the gap. During James V's reign, the iconography of the royal arms was consistently revised.[24] The simple treatment of the arms on the pulpit contrasts with elaborate treatment of the arms, with supporters, helm and crest, on the Beaton panels, which probably depends on the woodcut published on the title page of Hector Boece's *Scotorum Historiae* published in Paris 1526.[25] Nonetheless, the form of the shield on the pulpit appears to be unique. The closest parallel is with the sculptured panel now built into the wall at Abbey Strand but formerly on the gatehouse to the Palace of Holyrood. Charles Burnett dates this to about 1538[26] and proposes a date in the late 1530s rather than the early 1540s for the royal arms on the pulpit, possibly 1539.

The precise subject of the larger, central panel once flanked by the arms of the bishop and the king, and now lost, is not known. Logan in 1815 states that the traces of a cross which had been chiselled off were still visible and supposed that the subject had been a crucifix. This suggests that the evidence showed that the cross had been quite large. However, Spalding, writing at the time of its destruction in August 1640 states that [The Earl of Seaforth] 'at St Machar's ordained our blessed Lord Jesus Christ his arms to be hewn out of the forefront of the pulpit thereof'.[27] These accounts are reconcilable, as on the Beaton panels a large cross accompanies the symbols of the passion contained with a shield.[28] Kelly's suggestion that the shield might have been held by an angel reflects that treatment. However, given the absence of supporters on the royal arms, it seems unlikely that an angel 'supporter' would have figured on the central panel.

The mannerist shapes of the shields are perhaps the most up-to-date features of the pulpit's decoration, whilst the profile heads in roundels may be among the earliest surviving examples carved in timber, if the date in the late 1530s proposed above is accepted. Their appearance in the pulpit is virtually coeval with the use of timber profile heads in roundels on a massive scale on the ceiling of Stirling Castle, thought to have been begun in 1538[29] and parallels their earliest surviving use in stone, at Falkland Palace in 1537 and 1539.[30] However, like the Stirling heads, the roundels on the pulpit are likely to be the work of local craftsmen, working within a familiar repertoire. The origins of the use of renaissance roundels in this country almost certainly lies earlier, in the influx of foreign craftsmen from England, France, Italy and Germany, for example, during the reign of James IV.[31] The earliest known documented use of roundels is contained within the accounts of the Lord High Treasurer of Scotland[32] recording payments in 1512 and 1516 to Thomas Peebles, glazing wright, for '7 painted rounds with chaplets' (rosaries) at the Queen's oratory in the Abbey, and Thomas Peebles again for '1 painted round' in the 'north window of my Lord's chamber' at Holyrood.[33]

These 'rounds' are likely to have contained arms — those contained within rosaries may have included sacred arms — the Arms of Christ and the Holy Ghost or others. Surviving stained glass roundels containing arms are slightly later, for instance the arms of Mary of Guise in the Magdalene Chapel, Edinburgh *c.* 1543 but the form is found earlier as in the royal arms of Scotland, surrounded by a collar of thistles, in the Cartulary of Cambuskenneth Abbey *c.* 1535.[34]

The use of profile heads in roundels comparable to those on the pulpit is common in timberwork with uncertain provenance and dates but mostly associated with east and central Scotland and probably broadly contemporary with Bishop Stewart's pulpit. The closest parallels include fifteen panels with profile heads in roundels said to have been part of the wainscoting at Stirling Castle, now in the Smith Institute Stirling.[35] A similar panel, formerly in the possession of J. S. Richardson, is also said to have come from Stirling.[36] Less closely resembling the profile heads from Bishop Stewart's pulpit, but with a secure provenance are the two profile heads within roundels on the aumbry doors at Kinnairdy Castle, Banffshire, possibly from the 1530s.[37]

As Mgr David McRoberts has pointed out in discussion of the heraldic display which ceiled the cathedral of St Machar's above the pulpit in its original position, these fragmentary survivals attest to the near absolute destruction of our late medieval and early Renaissance culture.[38] Against a monochrome inheritance of ruins and fragments, Bishop Stewart's pulpit stands almost alone, not as a high point of achievement, but as something once typical. For, nearer at hand, the re-use on the pulpit of two panels of profile heads within lozenges shows that there were also similarly decorated furnishings at St Machar's. Even closer in composition, but with no provenance before 1696 is one of the four re-used profile heads incorporated in the Master of Hospital's chair at Trinity Hall, Aberdeen (Figs 11.2, 11.3). A panel forming the back of the chair has, like the pulpit, a profile head in a roundel above addorsed dolphins.[39]

The early re-use of this panel, with its companions, argues for a local provenance and, taken together with the re-used heads in lozenges on the pulpit, it provides a reminder of what has been lost from the Aberdeen school of woodcarving which flourished towards the middle of the sixteenth century, and of whose work Bishop Stewart's pulpit now provides the most complete example.

It is of course an art-historical fault to see stylistic change as more interesting than stylistic continuity and to see the Renaissance as ousting the Gothic, but in the 1530s both could and did co-exist. What Logan's drawings of the pulpit show conclusively is that whilst the decorative forms of the Renaissance were current in the 1530s, they remained, in this case literally, anchored within a late gothic framework. Thus, its details, especially in the treatment of the sounding board or tester, can be closely paralleled in the surviving fragments of the choir stalls from St Nicholas Church, Aberdeen, carved by John Fendour in 1507–08 and in the canopies of the choir stalls

Fig. 11.2. Roundels on the Master of Hospital's Chair, Trinity Hall, Aberdeen (Copyright: The Incorporated Trades of Aberdeen)

Fig. 11.3. Roundels on Bishop Stewart's pulpit

of King's College Chapel.[40] The flamboyant tracery frieze can also be compared with that on the lower parts of the Beaton panels, datable to the 1530s.

It is a curiosity that the only functioning pre-Reformation pulpit in this country should have received scant attention, and this is in part due to its history since 1844[41] when it was rescued from the sexton's store at St Machar's where it was 'lying in a disjointed and fragmentary condition'[42] and reconstructed for use at King's College Chapel. According to Norman Macpherson, writing in 1889,

Its whole framework was complete, and one or two panels which were in part wanting were restored from the fragments that remained. The canopy seems the most doubtful part of it, but I remember well that the old carpenter employed was quite confident that what remained of the old work demonstrated the accuracy of the restoration he was ordered to carry out. Unfortunately no part of the base remained, and the desk of Bishop Forbes's seat was used, being nearly a century later in style and quite incongruous.[43]

Fig. 11.4.   The pulpit today, after William Kelly's restoration of 1933

Comparing Logan's views of the pulpit with photographs of it as reconstructed taken in 1891, still associated with Bishop Forbes's desk but not longer resting upon it; in the same year, with Bishop Forbes's desk removed and finally as reconstructed to Kelly's design in 1933,[44] it is clear that the pulpit's form has been considerably and repeatedly altered. Macpherson was right to doubt the canopy, which even as renewed by Kelly bears only a nodding resemblance to the sounding board which Logan illustrates. Similarly the trefoil plan of the back has been reduced to a semi-circle, with Bishop Stewart's arms now in the central position on the upper tier of the back. The defaced central panel which formerly bore the Arma Christi was presumably discarded at the time of the restoration, and the panel of the royal arms was also omitted, either to achieve symmetry, or because it had already been lost. This panel was, miraculously, to resurface around 1964.[45]

The foliate panels which flank Bishop Stewart's arms are new, but the outermost slender panels on the uppermost tier are original. All the panels on the lower tier of the back are original and in their original positions. Following Kelly's reconstruction of the pulpit well, all the panels which Logan illustrates are present and in his order, with an additional new bas-relief panel of a bearded man on the door. The recovered panel of the royal arms has been attached to Kelly's new pulpit stairs (Fig. 11.4).

If the consequence of the pulpit's dislocation from its original context at St Machar's and its three reconstructions in the century between 1844 and 1933 leaves one with the uneasy feeling that the sum of the parts is greater than that of the whole, the story of its survival, in almost continuous use from the 1530s to the present day is a remarkable one. Moreover, if its value, in the context of this chapter, lies in the fact that the pulpit, like the chapel itself, vividly demonstrates the extraordinary *mélange* of cultural influences that informed clients, craftsmen and designers working in early sixteenth-century Scotland, then its continuing use in King's College Chapel could hardly be more appropriate. The closely related roundel designs found on the pulpit and the Master of Hospital's chair provide the second link between the chapel and town woodwork; the first being the choir stalls and the third being Bishop Forbes' desk.[46] Bishop Stewart's pulpit thus provides, in its near-complete condition, a reminder of what has been lost from the 'Aberdeen school' of woodcarving towards the middle of the sixteenth century.

Notes

[1] The other complete, but unusable, pre-Reformation pulpit is the ambo from the King's rood, now incongruously fixed high on the west wall of the chapel: see Chapter 6. The Beaton panels (National Museums of Scotland, H.KL 222), are, in my view, clearly the dismembered parts of some ecclesiastical furnishing, possibly a pulpit, though a domestic origin is argued by David H. Caldwell, 'The Beaton Panels — Scottish Carvings of the 1520s or 1530s', in *Medieval Art and Architecture in the Diocese of St Andrews*, ed. J. Higgitt, British Archaeological Association Conference Transactions for the year 1986, 1994, 174–84.

[2] James Logan (*c.* 1794–1872). For a biography of James Logan see *Logan's Collections*, ed. J. Cruickshank, Third Spalding Club, Aberdeen, 1941, xi-xxx.

[3] Kelly, 1949, 1–18.

[4] I also owe a considerable debt to the living: my friends and colleagues Charles Burnett, Richard Fawcett, Georgina Lee, and Aonghus MacKechnie, have each helped me enormously.

[5] The enlargement of the two westernmost aisle windows in the north wall of the cathedral is the only evidence remaining *in situ* of this room's existence. Logan recorded a substantial corbel carved with Bishop Stewart's arms which was built into the south wall of the session house, providing evidence for the time of its construction. Logan's drawing is illustrated in *Logan's Collections*, 125, fig. 64.

[6] J. H. Alexander, Walter R. H. Duncan, Peter J. Skipton, Grant G. Simpson, Judith A. Stones and Andrew Stewart Todd, *Restoration of St Machar's Cathedral*, Aberdeen, 1991, 3.

[7] AUL, MS 3598/5, No. 5 in a set of six drawings by Logan which were transferred to the Library from Haddo House in 1936. It bears manuscript notes in the margin by Kelly, who describes the drawing in *Logan's Collections*, 146.

[8] AUL, MS 2928, III, fol. 14[b], *Descriptio Cathedralis Abredonensis*; illustrated in colour by Kelly, *Logan's Collections*, pl. VII, 1815–25. Kelly, 141, explains the dates.

[9] I am grateful to Georgina Lee for this observation.

[10] I am grateful to Georgina Lee for this observation.

[11] AUL, MS 2928, III, fol. 15; reproduced in *Records of Old Aberdeen*, II, ed. A. M. Munro, New Spalding Club, Aberdeen, 1909, 308.

[12] The cathedral was reseated in this year, and the pulpit removed, James Rettie, *Aberdeen Fifty Years Ago*, Aberdeen, 1868, 115. Rettie notes that while the pulpit was in store in the south-west steeple 'loons who had free ish and entry . . . failed not occasionally to take a little from the carved work of the poopit'.

[13] AUL, MS 2928, III, fol. 2[v]; illustrated in *Logan's Collections*, 120, fig. 57 and described therein by Kelly, p. 161. Kelly mistakes the detailed drawing of Bishop Stewart's arms, for the upper panel bearing his arms. Logan is inaccurate in failing to record that the initial S for Stewart is reversed on the original panel.

[14] AUL, MS 2928, III, fol. 14[a], illustrated in *Logan's Collections*, 126, fig. 66.

[15] I am grateful to Georgina Lee for this observation.

[16] AUL, MS 2928, III, fol. 2ᵛ; illustrated in *Logan's Collections*, 120, fig. 56.

[17] This is confirmed by Rettie, 1868, 115.

[18] Ronald G. Cant, *The Building of St Machar's Cathedral, Aberdeen*, Friends of St Machar's Cathedral, Occasional Papers No. 4, Aberdeen, 1976, 7.

[19] See Kelly, 1941, 147, for his conjectural reconstruction of the pulpit immediately before 1793.

[20] J. Spalding, *Memorialls of the trubles in Scotland and in England, AD 1624–AD 1645*, Spalding Club, Aberdeen 1841, I, 313–14; and Orem, 1791, 132, who notes that our Blessed Lord Jesus's arms were 'probably the instruments of the passion on shields'.

[21] David Stevenson, *St Machar's Cathedral and the Reformation 1560–1690*, Friends of St Machar's Cathedral, Occasional Papers No. 7, Aberdeen, 1981, 14–15.

[22] For a description and analysis of this collapse, see Stevenson, 1981, 15–16.

[23] Stevenson, 1981, 16.

[24] C. J. Burnett, 'Outward Signs of Majesty 1535–1540', *Stewart Style 1513–1542, Essays on the Court of James V*, J. H. Williams, East Linton, 1996, 289–302.

[25] Caldwell, 1994, 177.

[26] Burnett, 1996, 296 and fig. 7, and in correspondence with the author, 27 January 1999.

[27] Spalding, *Memorialls*, 313–14; quoted by Kelly, *Logan's Collections*, 148.

[28] Charles Carter, 'The Arma Christi in Scotland', *PSAS*, XC, 1956, 122–25 and pls XI–XIII for examples from Elgin Cathedral, *c.* 1500, and the Beaton panels.

[29] The Royal Commission on the Ancient and Historical Monuments of Scotland, J. Dunbar, *The Stirling Heads*, Edinburgh, 1975.

[30] For a detailed discussion of roundels see A. MacKechnie, *Some French Influences on the Development of 16th-Century Court Architecture: In-House*, Historic Scotland Research Papers, Edinburgh, 1992, 3–4. Copy in National Monuments Record of Scotland.

[31] For survey of this period see: M. Glendinning, R. MacInnes, A. MacKechnie, *A History of Scottish Architecture*, Edinburgh, 1996, Chapter 1.

[32] *Accounts of the Lord High Treasurer of Scotland*, T. Dickson and Sir T. Balfour Paul (eds), 11 vols, Edinburgh, 1877–1916, IV, 1507–13, p. 375 and v, 1515–31, 95 and 96.

[33] I am grateful to Aonghus MacKechnie for these references.

[34] National Library of Scotland, Adv MS 34.1.2 fol. 1, illustrated Burnett, 1996, fig. 2.

[35] J. S. Richardson, 'Unrecorded Scottish Woodcarvings', *PSAS*, LX, 1928, 403 and fig. 18.

[36] Richardson, 1928, 403 and fig. 19. See also another panel from Stirling, p. 404 and fig. 20, and the cupboard in the National Museum of Scotland, which is associated with Queen Mary, H.KL 104. A very similar cupboard, described as French, is illustrated by V. Chinnery, *Oak Furniture, The British Tradition*, Antique Collectors Club, Woodbridge, 1979, 422.

[37] J. S. Richardson, 1928, 400 and fig. 17.

[38] D. McRoberts, *The Heraldic Ceiling of St Machar's Cathedral, Aberdeen*, Friends of St Machar's Cathedral, Occasional Papers, No. 2, Aberdeen, 1981, 1.

[39] D. Learmount, 'The Trinity Hall Chairs, Aberdeen', *Furniture History*, XIV, 1978, 2. This chair, belonging the the Aberdeen Incorporated Trades, is first referred to in 1696 as 'King William's Chair'. The four panels with roundels make up the sides and part of the back. The rest of the chair was assembled at a later date. I am grateful to Jane Geddes for drawing my attention to this chair.

[40] William Kelly, 'Carved Oak from St Nicholas Church, Aberdeen', *PSAS*, LXVIII, 1934, 355–66. See Chapter 6.

[41] W. H. Duncan in J. H. Alexander et al., *Restoration of St Machar's Cathedral*, Aberdeen, 1991, 3, gives 1844 for the transfer to King's College Chapel.

[42] W. D. Geddes, *Notes on the Restoration of King's College Chapel, Aberdeen*, Aberdeen, 1892, 24.

[43] Macpherson, 1889, 30.

[44] Eeles, 1956, figs 1–5. See also AUL, A5/39, A7/36, 38, 39, 40, 41, 42 and 47 for drawings associated with Kelly's reconstruction in 1933.

[45] Presented to the University, by John Wilson Runcie, senior, who had inherited the panel from his father, Thomas Milne Runcie, cabinet maker of 91 Holburn Street, Aberdeen; the panel was recognized as coming from the pulpit, as the Runcie family tradition had held, by Douglas Simpson.

[46] See Chapters 6 and 17.

CHAPTER TWELVE

THE VIRGIN OF THE APOCALYPSE, FROM THE CIRCLE OF ARNT BEELDESNIDER

By Norbert Jopek

An oak relief of the Virgin of the Apocalypse was bequeathed to the University of Aberdeen by Dr Douglas Strachan, the stained glass artist, in 1944, and is now displayed over the south-east door in the chapel.[1] It depicts the standing Virgin and the Child surrounded by angels and symbols of her virginity (Fig. 12.1). The Virgin, in an aureole of rays, stands on the crescent moon, her head slightly turned towards her son. Her gown is drawn across her body and held under her left hand, while her mantle is lifted on either side by two hovering angels clad in tunics. She presents the naked Christ Child, who holds a bullfinch, which is pecking the thumb of his right hand. An oval ribbon of clouds with four angels, three with musical instruments and one singing, encircle the Virgin who is being crowned by two hovering further angels. The four corners show the following scenes: the seated Moses before the burning bush (top left, Fig. 12.2); the prophet Ezekiel pointing towards the closed east gate of the temple (top right, Fig. 12.3); the Roman Emperor Augustus with the Tiburtine sibyl (bottom left, Fig. 12.4); and Gideon kneeling in full armour (bottom right, Fig. 12.5). The carved panel in its present condition is unfortunately in an incomplete state caused by the loss of its polychromy. The original painted surface would certainly have clarified and defined certain details.

The relief conveys a complex iconography which will be discussed before going on to the question of its probable place of origin, date and original context. The aureole around the Virgin and the crescent moon beneath her feet are references to the Revelation of St John 12.1–3, 'a woman that wore the sun for her mantle, with the moon under her feet and a crown of twelve stars about her head', while the surrounding angels on a ribbon of clouds indicate the heavenly nature of the *Regina caelorum* (Queen of Heaven).[2] The meaning of the bullfinch held by the Christ Child remains ambiguous: it may symbolize death, the Passion of Christ, or the Resurrection.[3] The Virgin is here shown as the Mother of God embodying the redemption of mankind through the Passion of her Son. This traditional iconographic formula is additionally extended by three scenes from the Old Testament and the *Vision of the Emperor Augustus*. The scenes of *Moses and the burning bush* (Exodus 3.2–5),[4] *Ezekiel points to the closed gate of the temple* (Ezekiel 44.1–2),[5] and *Gideon and the fleece* (Judges 6.36–40)[6] are seen as symbolic prefigurations of the Virginity of Mary.

Fig. 12.1.
The Virgin
of the
Apocalypse

These episodes were used in this context in the *Speculum Humanae Salvationis* (hereafter *Speculum*) by the Dominican Ludolph of Saxony in Strasbourg in about 1324 (Fig. 12.6), and in the *Defensorium inviolatae virginitatis Mariae* (hereafter *Defensorium*) by the Dominican Franz von Retz of about 1400 (Fig. 12.7). Both didactic treatises refer to the same prefigurations from the Old Testament as formulated in the the *Bible moralisée* and the *Biblia Pauperum* for the Annunciation and the Nativity but slightly alter the meaning with a greater emphasis on Virginity.[7] They are based on typological pictorial programmes which often employ several scenes and events from the Old Testament (type) in juxtaposition with one event of the New Testament (antitype) to show that the latter is the fulfilment of the Old Testament. This scheme also reflects that the History of the World is divided into three stages, the time before and after Moses (*ante legem* and *sub lege*) and the time after Christ (*sub gratia*). A famous example of this description of history is the series of the enamelled plaques of the Klosterneuburg pulpit by Nicholas of Verdun, completed in

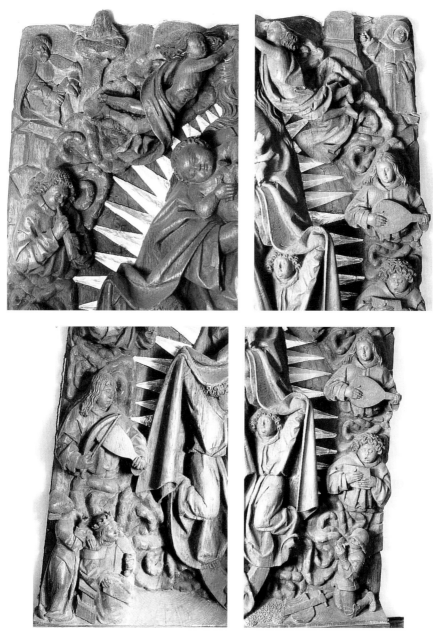

Figs 12.2–12.5.   12.2, Detail of Moses and the Burning Bush; 12.3, Detail of Ezekiel pointing to the closed gate of the Temple; 12.4, Detail of Emperor Augustus and the Tiburtine sibyl; 12.5, Detail of Gideon and the fleece

1181.[8] From the twelfth to the early sixteenth century such typological programmes appear in stained glass windows, illuminated manuscripts, paintings, wall-paintings and goldsmiths' works.[9] By the second half of the fifteenth century, typological picture cycles were further circulated throughout Europe by block-books and printed books.

Sculpted versions of the Apocalyptic Virgin surrounded by mariological attributes seem to emerge shortly after the the the dissemination of the *Defensorium*. Early prototypes of about 1420–30 only survive in the Baltic Sea area, for instance the Apocalyptic Virgin of Nystad, now in the Nationalmuseum in Helsinki, which was probably carved in Mecklenburg, where three other examples still exist,[10] but it seems highly likely that this type of image was widespread in other areas too.

It is now necessary to discuss each of the four scenes to understand their meaning in the typological context.

Depictions of the *Vision of the Emperor Augustus* of the Advent of Christ appeared first in Rome in about 1200.[11] They became popular in Northern Europe, when the theme entered the *Speculum* as a prefiguration of the Nativity of Christ. Illuminated manuscripts of the fourteenth century depict the Emperor and the Tiburtine Sibyl seated on a bench, and the bust of the Virgin with the Child in a roundel, often surrounded by sun-rays.[12] Later editions show Augustus seated, with the Sibyl standing next to his throne, but the *clipeus* is replaced in some Netherlandish block-books by the Apocalyptic Virgin[13] as is the case here. According to Hans Peter Hilger this combination was also common iconography in the Netherlands and the Lower Rhine as it can be seen in later examples, such as in a painting of the Nativity by Jan Joest on the high altar of the church of St Nicholas in Kalkar, completed in 1508/09, and as a three-dimensional example in the crowning superstructure of the altarpiece of the Seven Sorrows of Mary by Henrik Douvermann in the same church, dating from about 1518–22.[14]

The typological significance of *The Miracle of the Burning Bush* is adequately described by the verses beneath the illustration in the devotional book *The arte or crafte to lyue well and to dye well*, printed in London in 1505:

> Moyses sawe the busshe/ enflamed with fyre. /A voice also he herded but nothynge he perceyued./ Mary ye mayden as was her desyre./ without mannes sede the sone of god conceyued.[15]

The closest examples for this relief in iconographical terms is the scene with Moses in the first Latin edition of the *Speculum* (Fig. 12.6), printed in Utrecht in about 1468,[16] and the relevant scene of the *Defensorium* by Friedrich Walthern of Nördlingen of about 1470 in the Bayerische Staatsbibliothek, Munich which is probably based on a North German block-book of about 1450.[17]

The text in the *Speculum* which relates and explains the scene of *The closed gate of the Temple* reads '*Clausa porta significat beatam Virginem Mariam*' (The closed gate signifies the blessed Virgin Mary). Most of the examples of the *Speculum* depict only the gate of the temple without Zacharias, but according to Edgar Breitenbach some of the

Fig. 12.6.   The *Speculum Humanae*, Utrecht, 1468, showing Moses and the Burning Bush (Photo: Victoria and Albert Museum, Picture Library)

Fig. 12.7.   The *Defensorium immaculatae virginitatis*, showing Gideon and the Fleece (Photo: Victoria and Albert Museum, Picture Library)

Fig. 12.8.   Virgin and Child, Cleves, choir stalls
(Cologne, Rheinisches Bildarchiv)

manuscripts with a western European provenance show the prophet.[18] The
Defensorium generally shows Zacharias either kneeling or standing in front of the gate.

Gideon and the Fleece shows a kneeling knight praying to the Virgin and the Child.
The above mentioned Madonna in Helsinki of about 1420/30 also shows this
configuration. The present relief however additionally depicts a sword and a shield,
the latter posssibly being derived from the same scene in the *Defensorium* by Friedrich
Walthern of about 1470 which similarly depicts the kneeling Gideon in armour. The
fleece here lies in front of him and the clouds of rain on the ground look curiously
like a shield or *pavise* (Fig. 12.7).[19] It seems likely that the painter misunderstood the
illustration and therefore shows a shield in front of Gideon. The typological meaning
however is clearly stated: the dew on the fleece which fell from Heaven prefigures
the Immaculate Conception.

Certain iconographic features of the relief, for instance the combination of
Augustus and the Tiburtine Sibyl with the Apocalyptic Virgin suggest it originated in
the Lower Rhine or the Netherlands. Indeed, the type of wood — oak — was
prevalent in this region and above all the stylistic vocabulary indicates an origin in the

Lower Rhine area. The distinctive style of the central figure has its closest paralells with four statues of the Virgin and Child: in the church of St Nicholas in Xanten; in Geldern-Aengenesch chapel; one formerly in the Burckhardt collection, Cologne; and one of the choir stalls in the church of St Nicholas in Cleves (Fig. 12.8).[20] They show the same facial type with a relatively small mouth and long wavy hair, and the drapery of their mantles shows a similar pattern of angular and tubular folds. These three statues of the Virgin and Child have been dated to about 1480 and have been associated by Heribert Meurer and Ulrich Schäfer with the sculptor Arnt Beeldesnider who was active in Cleves from about 1460 until 1484, and in Zwolle from 1484 to 1492. Although closely related, the surrounding scenes and angels in the Aberdeen relief do not exhibit the same quality of carving seen in the figures ascribed to Arnt Beeldesnider. I would therefore suggest this relief was produced by a sculptor working in his circle, probably around 1480/90.

The size and the subject of this relief suggest it was originally displayed in the *corpus* of a side-altarpiece, probably with painted wings as was common in this region. Its presence in King's Chapel today is particularly appropriate. It serves as a reminder of the original Marian dedication, of Bishop Elphinstone's devotion to the Virgin and of the many other images of the Virgin which were donated to the chapel before the Reformation.[21]

Notes

[1] I would like to thank Jane Geddes who encouraged me to study this object, and Louise Bourdua for her assistance in Aberdeen, and my colleague Marjorie Trusted for her help. The donation by Douglas Strachan is noted in *Minutes of the University Court*, for 1944, XIV, Aberdeen, 1950, 523. It is also mentioned, with a Flemish attribution by 'T.D.', 'Two oak carvings in King's College Chapel', *AUR*, XXXI, 1944–46, 264. No further provenance is recorded. The relief consists of four planks of oak joined together. Height, 120cm; width (bottom) 120cm; width (top) 110cm; depth 11.5cm. The relief has completely been stripped of its polychromy, only traces of gesso survive. The re-gilding of the radiants appears to be of a more recent date. The crest of the crown, the left foot of the crowning angel on her left side, the toes of the Christ Child, and all the fingers of the right hand of the Tiburtine Sibyl are missing. The dorsum of the nose of the Virgin is a later addition.

[2] J. Fonrobert, Apocalyptic Virgin, in *Lexikon der Christlichen Ikonographie*, Freiburg, 1968, 1, cols 145–50.

[3] H. Friedmann, *The Symbolic Goldfinch: its history and significance in European Devotional Art*, Washington, 1946, 7–10.

[4] 'And here the Lord revealed himself through a flame that rose up from the midst of a bush; it seemed that the bush was alight, yet did not burn. Here is a great sight, said Moses, I must go up and see more of it, a bush that does not waste by burning. But now as he saw him coming up to look closer, the Lord called to him from the midst of the bush, Moses, Moses; and when he answered, I am here, at thy command, he was told, Do not come nearer; rather take the shoes from thy feet, thou art standing on holy ground.'

[5] 'Then he brought me back to the eastern gate of the outer precincts, that was fast shut. Shut this gate must ever be, the Lord told me, nor open its doors to give man entrance again, since the Lord of Israel, entered by it.'

[6] 'And Gideon asked for a sign from God: If thou meanest to fulfil thy promise, and make use of me to deliver Israel, let me have proof of it. This fleece shall lie on the threshing-floor; fall the dew on the fleece only, and let the ground be dry, I shall know thy promise holds good; I am to be the means of Israel's deliverance. And so it was; when he awoke next morning, he wrung it out, and filled a tankard with the dew. But he pleaded once again , Do not be angry with my if I put thee on one more test, still with the fleece for my proof. This time let the fleece remain dry, while the rest of the ground is wet with dew. And that night, God granted his prayer; dew lay all over the ground about it, and the fleece alone was dry.'

While consulting the Tiburtine Sibyl about his own deification, Augustus had a vision of the Virgin and Child who would eclipse all the Roman gods.

[7] J. von Schlosser, 'Zur Kenntnis der künstlerischen Überlieferung im späten Mittelalter', in *Jahrbuch der kunsthistorischen Sammlungen des Allerhöchsten Kaiserhauses*, 1902, XXIII, 279–313; and the entries for '*Defensorium*' by F. Zoepfl, in *Reallexikon zur deutschen Kunstgeschichte*, Munich, 1954, III, cols 1206–18; and by E. M. Vetter in *Lexikon der Christlichen Ikonographie*, Freiburg, 1968, I, cols 499–503. For the relation to the *Bible moralisée*, the *Speculum humanae salvationis*, and the *Biblia Pauperum*, G. Schmidt, *Die Armenbibeln des XIV. Jahrhunderts*, Köln/Graz, 1959, 101–04.

[8] For enamelled typological cycles in the twelfth century, see Nigel Morgan, 'The iconography of twelfth-century Mosan enamels', in *Rhein und Maas*, Cologne, 1973, II, 263–75. For the pulpit in Klosterneuburg, H. Buschhausen, *Der Verduner Altar*, Vienna, 1980.

[9] E. Sears, Typological cycles, in *The Dictionary of Art*, ed. J. Turner, Macmillan, London, 1996, XXXI, 498–501.

[10] J. von Bonsdorff, 'Art Transfer in the medieval Baltic Sea area', *Künstlerischer Austausch- Artistic Exchange*, ed. Thomas W. Gaethgens, Akten des XXVIII Internationalen Kongresses für Kunstgeschichte, Berlin, Berlin, 1993, II, 45, fig. 10 mentions the early example in the National Museum in Helsinki, and on p. 50 further figures in Kublank, Lindow, and in the Museum in Schwerin from Groß-Methling.

[11] See entry 'Augustus', in *Lexikon der christlichen Ikonographie*, Freiburg, 1968, I, col. 226.

[12] J. Lutz/ P. Perdrizet, *Speculum Humanae Salvationis*, Mulhouse/Leipzig, 1907, II, pl. 16.

[13] E. Breitenbach, *Speculum Humanae Salvationis: Eine typengeschichtliche Untersuchung*, Strasbourg, 1930, 128–29.

[14] H. P. Hilger, *Stadtpfarrkirche St Nicolai in Kalkar*, Kleve, 1990, 108, where the altarpiece of the Virgin for the St Janskerk in 's-Hertogenbosch by Adrian van Wesel of 1477 is also mentioned. However, according to Willy Halsema-Kubes, 'Der Altar Adrian van Wesels aus 's-Hertogenbosch-Rekonstruktion und kunstgeschichtliche Bedeutung', in *Flügelaltäre des späten Mittelalters*, H. Krohm and E. Oellermann (eds), Berlin, 1992, 154, the Virgin surmounting the altarpiece was not a Virgin of the Apocalypse, but more probably a figure of the Madonna who held a twig in her hand.

[15] M. W. Driver, 'The Image Redux: Pictures in Block-books and what becomes of them', in *Blockbücher des Mittelalters: Bilderfolgen als Lektüre* (exh. cat.), Mainz, Gutenberg Museum, 1991, 348.

[16] *Speculum Humanae Salvationis: Ein niederländisches Blockbuch*, ed. E. Kloss, Munich, 1925.

[17] *Defensorium Immaculatae Virginitatis*, ed. K. Pfister, Leipzig, 1925, 4.

[18] Breitenbach, 1930, 107.

[19] Breitenbach, 1930, 120, noticed similar misinterpretions of the dew in the *Speculum*. For this type of shield see J. Mann, *European arms and armour* (Wallace Collection Catalogues), London, 1962, I, cat. no. A.307, pl. 85.

[20] H. Meurer, *Das Klever Chorgestühl und Arnt Beeldesnider*, Düsseldorf, 1970, fig. 161 (Geldern-Aengenesch); fig. 162 (Kalkar, St Nicolai). U. Schäfer, *Kunst in Zeiten der Hochkonjunktur: Spätgotische Holzfiguren vom Niederrhein um 1500*, Münster, 1991, cat. no. 3 (Geldern-Aengenesch); cat. no. 25 (Kalkar, St Nicolai); cat. no. 62 (formerly Cologne, Burckhardt collection); he also provides the most recent discussion about Arnt Beeldesnider on pp. 7–32.

[21] As listed in the 1542 Inventory, Eeles, 1956, 30–46.

THE
POST-REFORMATION
CHAPEL

CHAPTER THIRTEEN

THE CHAPEL, THE COLLEGE AND THE UNIVERSITY, 1560–1945

By COLIN A. McLAREN

This chapter provides a chronological account of the various roles played by the chapel since the Reformation. Some aspects are dealt with in greater detail elsewhere, particularly in Chapters 14 and 16, concerning worship and and the fabric.

THE SEVENTEENTH CENTURY

After the Reformation, religion remained central to the life of King's College but the chapel itself did not. The history of the chapel in the early years of the Reformation is obscure. Between 1559 and 1569 it was saved from damage or destruction on what may have been as many as three occasions. Its treasures were either sold or, more probably, dispersed for safekeeping among local Catholic families. Nevertheless, collegiate worship may have continued there, albeit irregularly.[1] At some time after the Reformation of King's College, however, possibly in 1574 when the college acquired the deanery of Aberdeen and the principal as a result acted as minister to Old Aberdeen,[2] the chapel lost this role. As the college laws of the seventeenth century show, its place came to be taken partly by the college 'schools [classrooms]', partly by the parish church. Daily private morning and evening devotions took place in the students' rooms; public morning and evening prayers, in the public school on the east side of the college; prayers and readings accompanied dinner and supper in the hall above it. On Sundays, staff and students assembled in the public school and processed to St Machar's, where they occupied the 'college loft [gallery]'; afterwards, the students were examined on the sermons and lessons in their four private schools.[3] The chapel was used for worship, however, in 1642 and 1645, when Principal William Guild treated it as a parish church, preaching there mid-week to the college and an unenthused congregation from the town.[4] It was also used in 1676, when the college ordered that morning prayers should be held there, although these were again held in the public school by 1690.[5]

   The chapel's principal function in the seventeenth century was as a venue for offical church and academic gatherings. The Synod of Aberdeen met there intermittently from around 1627 until 1662 and regularly thereafter;[6] the Presbytery of Aberdeen also used it when meeting in the Old Town.[7] In 1640 John Forbes, professor of divinity, appeared there before a committee of the General Assembly, to defend his refusal to sign the Covenant;[8] and in 1694 Episcopal clergy from north of the Tay assembled there to compose their 'Protestation and Appeal' against Presbyterian rule, for presentation to the Assembly's commissioners.[9] Among academic events, elections to the chair of divinity, established in 1619 under the patronage of the Synod of Aberdeen, were held there from at least 1642;[10] it may have been used during the visitation of the college by royal commissioners in 1664;[11] and Principal George Middleton chose it for his public lectures on theology in 1685, although public theological lectures by his predecessors, John Row and Alexander Middleton, and public lectures on other subjects by his colleagues, James Scougall and William Black, were given in the public school.[12]

The chapel continued to be used, as it had been before the Reformation, for burials, burial services and the reception of the dead. Principal Walter Stewart was buried there in 1592; Peter Udny, subprincipal, in 1601; Andrew Strachan and John Cruickshank, laymen, in 1604, and Henry Scougal, professor of divinity, in 1678;[13] and when the Countess of Huntly died in Old Aberdeen in 1638, her corpse lay in the chapel for ten days before being taken to the New Town.[14] In 1669 and 1686 the college set fees for receiving corpses there before burial — with or without the tolling of bells.[15]

Despite the limited role which the chapel played in college life, its fabric was a constant source of concern. There were comprehensive surveys in 1620 and 1638, but they seem to have been exceptional;[16] more commonly, repairs were undertaken as they became necessary and when they could be afforded, apparently on the initiative of the principal or the common procurator (the member of the academic staff who administered college funds), often without reference to their colleagues in rectoral or college meetings. The crown tower proved the heaviest burden but, as a symbol of royal patronage and a recognized feature of the region's architectural heritage, it was one which the college resolutely shouldered.[17]

The main changes to the interior of the chapel in the seventeenth century were the introduction of the bishop's desk in place of the high altar in 1627 during the chancellorship of Bishop Patrick Forbes 1618–35 and the removal of the organ case and its painted Virgin from the loft in 1642. Together, these changes enabled the Synod to meet there in an orderly fashion, its principles uncompromised.[18] Other work included repairs to 'the door under the organs' around 1666, and to 'the folding seats in the church' and the 'desks in the kirk' in 1675.[19] The interior seems to have been neglected in later years: it was used as a lodge for masons hewing stone for the New Work (Cromwell Tower) in 1657–58; there are payments for 'dighting the redd [cleaning out the rubbish]' before functions there in 1680 and 1695.[20] Security measures, like the 'grait lock' added to the west door in 1653, and college laws against defacing *subsellia* (seats or stalls) were among several steps taken to protect the chapel interior.[21] The quantity of graffiti carved by seventeenth-century students on the woodwork suggests that they were less than effective.[22]

In the seventeenth century the 'knock [clock]' and the bells in the crown tower regulated the college day;[23] the latter supplemented by the smaller bell hung at the east end of the chapel around 1660.[24] The college entrusted the maintenance of the clock, in the second half of the century at least, to William Forsyth, a smith in the Old

Town, and Patrick Kilgour, a watchmaker from the New, who regulated and oiled it, providing it with 'towes [ropes]' and new cords.[25] Work on the bells included renewing their ropes, replacing their 'tongues [clappers]', mending the 'reavelling' [railing] around them and securing the steps that led up to them; it, too, was entrusted to 'Smith Forsyth' and other local tradesmen.[26] Ringing the bells was the duty of the janitor from at least 1643: a college law of that time, however, suggests that his role was sometimes usurped by rowdy students.[27]

THE EIGHTEENTH CENTURY

In the eighteenth century the chapel was used intermittently for public worship. In 1712 it was reported that, under Principal George Middleton, 'those of the Episcopal persuasion in the old town do possess [it] for worship and sermon on Sundays while throughout the week the presbyterian professor of theology teaches his lessons there'; the Government suppressed the services soon afterwards.[28] In 1720 Principal George Chalmers and the professor of divinity, David Anderson, held a series of 'Discourses on Catachitical Doctrine' in the chapel.[29] Their successors may have done something similar in the 1740s and may also have used it, instead of the public school, for morning prayers.[30] Finally, Principal John Chalmers permitted John Wesley to preach there in 1761, 1766 and 1770.[31]

The chapel continued to accommodate elections to the chair of divinity and the award of doctorates in that subject.[32] It also came to be used for graduations in arts. During the seventeenth and early eighteenth centuries, these had been held in the public school.[33] In 1760, however, the chapel was said to be used for 'giving degrees'; there are payments in 1764 and 1765 for 'upputting a desk in the Church for the Graduation' and for other, possibly related works; while the use of the chapel for graduation in 1764 is mentioned specifically in the *Aberdeen Journal*.[34]

A second change in function transformed the nave. The original college library on the south side of the chapel had been rebuilt in 1725–26, but the new structure was soon seen to be unsuitable for its purpose and unsoundly built. The possibility of replacing it was explored in the 1750s and 1760s, but it was not until 1773 that the college was presented with an affordable scheme.[35] As a result, the library and the classrooms below were demolished and the books housed in the nave. Described only two years earlier as 'neglected and disused',[36] it was now converted into a galleried hall:

> a noble room . . . nearly the one half of the church . . . and very high in the roof. In the west end is a large Gothic window, and from the centre of the wall below, begins a screw stair, spreading to both sides of the room, and leading to the galleries, which occupy the whole length and go across the east end (Fig. 16.20).[37]

The college recreated the demolished classrooms by partitioning the public school, which could no longer be used for college prayers and assemblies. As a result, the choir of the chapel, now blocked off from the converted nave, was equipped with pews and became the public school, where the college held morning prayers and assembled before processing to St Machar's on Sundays.[38] This arrangement continued for some fifty years.[39]

When it was not being used for church and academic purposes, the chapel provided much-needed storage space. In 1724, for example, 'big tables' were kept there, and in 1768, beds for the students' rooms.[40] A more unusual item was a kayak, formerly exhibited in the lobby of the public school, which was set up in the chapel in 1747.[41]

In 1700 the upkeep of the chapel became the responsibility of the aedilis or master of works, a newly-created post held by a member of the academic staff.[42] Commitment to maintenance was regular throughout the century.[43] In addition to work on the masonry and windows, payments were made in 1713 for re-hanging 'the hearse [candle-holder] . . . bing verie dangros vork',[44] and in 1745–46 for work to 'the college organ'.[45]

From the early eighteenth century onwards, the servicing of the chapel clock — 'furnishing her with oil and ropes' — was contracted out annually to a local clockmaker; later it was entrusted to the college 'officer [sub-janitor]'.[46] It was, however, something less than reliable: John Mowat, one of the first contractors, noted that 'in the first year I entred [1719–20] . . . she stoped to number of twenty times'.[47] In 1796 the college decided to replace the clock, which 'after all never goes right'.[48] The sub-janitor was also responsible for ringing the recast bells: they sounded daily at eight, nine and eleven a.m., noon, and three, four and nine p.m.; on the birthdays of Bishop Elphinstone and the monarch; and on special occasions, such as the 'Rejoicing for the Battle of Culloden'.[49]

THE NINETEENTH AND TWENTIETH CENTURIES

During the nineteenth and twentieth centuries, the chapel regained some of its former importance: first, in a purely religious role; subsequently, as a symbol of the university's pride in its heritage. The process of recovery was initiated by Alexander Murray, who bequeathed to the college in 1793 money for a series of religious lectures for the spiritual benefit of the students, accompanied by divine service, to be held in the chapel on Sunday mornings.[50] In 1821, when they eventually implemented the bequest, the trustees went further: 'by appointing divine service to be performed both morning and evening in the College Chapel at the same hours as in the Parish Church, they will extend the benefit to be derived from the institution, promote the views of the Founder, and wholly remove any grievance or indecorum resulting from the processions to Church'.[51] The grievance, namely of academic staff who had to supervise the processions, had provoked a constitutional crisis in the college in 1818; the indecorum was to survive in the collegiate memory for many years.[52] The plan was supported in Senate, not least because student numbers were now too great for the space reserved in the east gallery of St Machars. Principal William Black, however, doggedly opposed it: 'By a simple process the purest wine may be converted into vinegar, the best medicine into poison, a Lectureship on the Principles of pure and undefiled Religion into an ill-constructed Chapel of Ease'.[53] Yet another constitutional crisis was only resolved by appeal to the chancellor and rector. Finally, however, the choir, refurbished by the trustees at a cost of almost £500 but retaining most of the original furniture, was re-opened for the lectures and services in 1824.[54]

Thereafter, the chapel continued to house elections to the chair of divinity,[55] but it ceased to function as the public school. The original school was reopened and used for assemblies, examinations and graduations until at least 1847; it was demolished in 1860.[56]

In 1860 King's and Marischal were 'fused' into the University of Aberdeen. Teaching in arts and divinity was sited at King's and work began on a new library to support it. After a decade of frustration and confusion, in which the University wrestled with the Universities' Commissioners, the Treasury and the Board of Works, the new library was opened on the site of the demolished public school.[57] The books which were shelved — and ultimately heaped — in the nave were transferred there in 1871, and in 1873 the chapel, now in use again for graduations in arts,[58] was 'liberated from end to end to subserve its original purpose'.[59] The process of liberation, carried out on the initiative of Principal Peter Colin Campbell and under the supervision of the Board of Works, attracted little attention at the time; nevertheless, the changes made were far-reaching and some, such as the relocation of the choir screen and the removal of the organ gallery, were later roundly criticized.[60] At the same time, John Webster of Edgehill contributed a new west window, by Clayton & Bell of London, 'equal to anything heretofore produced in England in that branch of art'.[61] In this way, the practice of enriching the chapel through private benefaction, in abeyance since the Reformation, was resumed.

The chapel may have been liberated but it was not much loved — at least, by the students. The choir was cold and uncomfortable, the sermons long, the pews rarely filled.[62] Those who did love it had to admit that it looked 'bare, ugly, and disappointing' and reflected poorly upon the university's concern for its heritage.[63] It was this group, led by men like John Webster,[64] who began to press for improvements. In 1886 'friends of the university', represented in Senate by William Milligan, professor of biblical criticism, offered to provide a new organ.[65] Then in 1889, George Reid, already energetically promoting the artistic heritage of the region,[66] virtually bounced the university into a major restoration scheme.[67] Both initiatives were approved: partly because they would enhance the chapel as a venue for events like graduation in arts;[68] partly because they were to be achieved through private funding;[69] partly — and most importantly — because they had behind them the full and irresistible force of the long-established professor and newly appointed principal, William D. Geddes.[70] The university was by then beginning to plan the redevelopment and extension of Marischal College: the future of the Old Town site was implicitly, if not yet explicitly, threatened. To Geddes and those, like P. J. Anderson,[71] who shared his sentimental attachment to King's, the restoration and improvement of the chapel were the means to affirm the pre-eminence of the older foundation and its right to be the centre of teaching in the arts.[72] Elsewhere, however, the plan was received coolly. Even J. M. Bulloch, Anderson's protégé, was in two minds: 'Unless something more radical is done, the undergraduates will not be in the slightest degree benefitted . . . Of course, if this chapel is to be considered only as a show-room for 'Arry on tour, the finer its ecclesiastical upholstery the better.' Others had no such reservations: 'Is this the most needed way of spending [£3,000] at King's College?'[73]

In the years immediately following the opening of the restored chapel in November 1891, the criticisms seemed justified. Attendances at chapel did not improve — in fact, they remained lower than those at Marischal.[74] Ultimately, however, the aspirations of Webster, Reid and Geddes were realized. The chapel, as a simple but venerable symbol of antiquity, proved an effective counterweight to the grandeur of the Mitchell Hall. At the same time, it became, in effect, a shrine, to be glorified over the next fifty years by a new generation, led by William Kelly and Douglas Strachan. It was not until 1945, when the first university chaplain was appointed,[75] that the chapel took on a revitalized role as a centre of spirituality and pastoral care.

Notes

[1] D. Stevenson, *King's College, Aberdeen, 1560–1641: From Protestant Reformation to Covenanting Revolution*, Quincentennial Studies in the history of the University of Aberdeen, Aberdeen, 1990, 8, 13, 15.

[2] Stevenson, 1990, 53.

[3] *Fasti*, 225–55; C. A. McLaren, 'Discipline and Decorum: the Law Codes of the Universities of Aberdeen' in *Scottish Universities: Distinctiveness and Diversity*, J. J. Carter and D. J. Withrington (eds), Edinburgh, 1992, 129–30, 135–36.

[4] J. Spalding, *Memorialls of the Trubles in Scotland and in England, AD 1624–AD 1645*, ed. J. Stuart, Spalding Club, 2 vols, Aberdeen, 1850–51, II, 141, 185, 453, 457.

[5] AUL, MS K 37, fol. 37^r; *Fasti*, 366.

[6] *Selections from the Records of the Kirk Session, Presbytery and Synod of Aberdeen*, ed. J. Stuart, Spalding Club, Aberdeen, 1846, lxiii.

[7] Stevenson, 1990, 54.

[8] AUL, MS 635A, Diary or Spiritual Exercises of John Forbes of Corse, 1624–47, pp. 222–23.

[9] G. Grub, *Ecclesiastical History of Scotland*, 4 vols, Edinburgh, 1861, III, 335; *Miscellany of the Spalding Club*, 2, ed. J. Stuart, Aberdeen, 1842, 163.

[10] AUL, MS K 55/3, fol. 3^r; *Fasti*, 158; Spalding, *Memorialls*, II, 300; the first occupant was examined *in magno auditorio collegii* in 1620 and the second, *in auditorio Theologico*, in 1634; P. J. Anderson, 'Collections towards a Bibliography of the Universities of Aberdeen' in *Studies in the History and Development of the University of Aberdeen*, ed. P. J. Anderson, Aberdeen University Studies, 19, Aberdeen, 1906, 392, 397, hereafter *Studies*, 1906.

[11] A session took place immediately after a meeting of the Synod: *Fasti*, 321. The chancellor's visitation of the university in 1638 was held in 'the session house of the college kirk', presumably the 'chapterhouse now turned to a private school' on the south side of the chapel: *Fasti*, 285; James Gordon, *Abredoniae Utriusque Descriptio: A description of both touns of Aberdeen*, ed. C. Innes, Spalding Club, Edinburgh, 1842, 22.

[12] AUL, MS K 38, pp. 6, 8; *Fasti*, 244, 435.

[13] *Officers and Graduates of University & King's College, Aberdeen, MVD–MDCCCLX*, ed. P. J. Anderson, New Spalding Club, Aberdeen, 1893, 40, hereafter *Officers*; Orem, 1791, 191; P. J. Anderson, 'Notes on heraldic representations at King's College, Old Aberdeen', *PSAS*, 1888–89, XXXIII, 80–86; Sir W. D. Geddes, *Notes on the Restoration of King's College Chapel*, Aberdeen, privately printed, Aberdeen, 1892, 9–10; Kelly, 1949, 61–62.

[14] Spalding, *Memorialls*, I, 90.

[15] AUL, MS K 37, fol. 21^v; K 38, p. 16.

[16] *Fasti*, 280–85, 410–11.

[17] See Chapter 16.

[18] Kelly, 1949, 63; J. Gordon, *History of Scots Affairs, from MDCXXXVII to MDCXLI*, ed. J. Robertson and G. Grub, Spalding Club, 3 vols, Aberdeen, 1841, III, 218; Spalding, *Memorialls*, II, 124.

[19] AUL, MS K 255/33, 'Mr Alexander Middleton's comptes from January 63 to February 66', p. 13; MS K 278/2/30. It is not clear whether repairs to 'the loft in the kirk desk' in 1655 and the 'new door to the kirk loft' in 1661 refer to the chapel or the 'college loft' in St Machars: MS K 256/42/1, p. 10; 256/42/2, p. 8; *Fasti*, 603, 606. It should be noted, however, that work on 'the college loft in the parish kirk' is recorded independently: MS K 256/42/2, p. 2; *Fasti*, 605.

[20] AUL, MS K 275/5/57,67; K 55/1, fol. 3ᵛ; see also C. McLaren, 'New Work and Old: Building at the Colleges in the seventeenth century', *AUR*, 1990, LIII, 211; AUL, MS K 55/3, fol. 3ʳ; K 55/16, p. 19.

[21] AUL, MS K 256/42/1, p. 2; K 278/2/30; K 3, p. 21; K 265/1, p. 2; K 130, fol. 3ʳ; *Fasti*, 234, 599.

[22] AUL, MS U 593, A. Savours, Drawings of the graffiti on the stalls in King's College Chapel, 1953; Eeles, 1956, pls 72–78. An examination of some 40 dated inscriptions covering the period 1586–1687 produces distinctive clusters in 1610, 1623 and 1625. Students in these clusters who can be positively identified are: 1610, George Annand, Andrew Mancur, William Mancur, William Gordon major, all of the class of 1608–12; 1623, Thomas Molyssoun, of the class of 1621–25; James Douglas, John Urquhart, Robert Williamson, all of the class of 1622–26; 1625, Thomas Gilzean, Hugh Irving, Alexander Barclay, all of the class of 1623–27.

[23] *Fasti*, 226, 233, 243.

[24] AUL, MS K 256/42/2, p. 2; *Fasti*, 605.

[25] AUL, MS K 256/42/1, p. 2; K 54/10, p. 6; K 54/13, p. 11; K 55/4, pp. 4, 7; K 55/8, p. 22; K 55/10, p. 8; K 55/15, p. 19; K 55/17, p. 19; *Fasti*, 601, 602.

[26] AUL, MS K 256/42/1, p. 8; K 256/42/2, p. 4; K 278/7/23; K 55/18, p. 18; *Fasti*, 603, 605, 606.

[27] AUL, MS K 265/1; *Fasti*, 421.

[28] Historical Manuscripts Commission, *13th Report, Portland MSS*, 10 vols, 1891, X, 250; Grub, 1861, III, 359.

[29] AUL, MS K 41, fol. 50ʳ; Orem, 1791, 185.

[30] According to the recollection of Principal Roderick Macleod in 1813: AUL, MS K 49, p. 302.

[31] J Wesley, *Works: Journal and Diaries*, W. R. Ward and R. P. Heitzenrater (eds), 6 vols, Nashville, 1988–95, IV, 468; V, 43, 228.

[32] It was probably used for this purpose in the seventeenth century, but the awards of 1711 and 1714 are the first to specify the place: *Studies*, 1906, 420, 421.

[33] Orem, 1791, 177–78, 182; T. Middleton, *An Appendix to the History of the Church of Scotland*, London, 1677, 42–43. In printed graduation theses, the location is given as: *in publico auditorio* 1624, 1629; *in publico acroaterio* 1625; *in acroaterio* 1633; *in auditorio maximo* 1637; *in publico asceterio* 1681. *Studies*, 1906, 392, 394, 396, 399, 409–10.

[34] AUL, MS K 257/20/4/48; K 257/20/5/9; R. Pococke, *Tours in Scotland 1747, 1750, 1760*, ed. D. W. Kemp, Scottish History Society, Edinburgh, 1887, 207; *Aberdeen Journal*, 16 April 1764.

[35] AUL, MS K 47, pp. 51–57. The condition of the 1726 building, the fire which was thought to have destroyed it, the plans submitted for the new building, and the building project itself, are described in: J. R. Pickard, *History of King's College Library, Aberdeen, until 1860*, 4 vols privately printed, Aberdeen, 1979, III, 236–43; D. M. Walker, 'The rebuilding of King's and Marischal Colleges, 1723–1889', *AUR*, LV, 1993, 2, no. 190, 123–45.

[36] Orem, 1832 edn, 68.

[37] F. Douglas, *A General Description of the East Coast of Scotland*, Paisley, 1782, 190.

[38] [T. Gordon], 'University and King's College of Aberdeen' in *Statistical Account of Scotland*, ed. Sir J. Sinclair, 21 vols, Edinburgh, 1791–99, XXI, 90. The use of the chapel for this purpose had been foreshadowed by James Byres, whose plan for the west front of 1767 showed the chapel remodelled as 'a common hall for prayers': AUL, MS K 252; Walker, 1993, 126.

[39] In a survey of 1822, the 'Public School and the Library' are described as 'the Old chapel divided': AUL, MS K 50, p. 128; Geddes, 1892, 6.

[40] AUL, MS K 257/19/2/18; K 257/20/8/13.

[41] AUL, MS K 257/6/4/38. It was seen there by a visitor to King's in the 1750s: information from Marischal Museum, where the kayak is now kept.

[42] AUL, MS K 39, p. 6. Payments for work to the chapel nevertheless appear principally in procuration accounts until 1752–53; thereafter, there is a regular, separate series of aedilis accounts, beginning in MS K 59, p. 7. After the installation of the library in the nave, interior and exterior work on this part of the fabric was charged to the library accounts: MS K 61, pp. 161, 167.

[43] See Chapter 16.

[44] AUL, MS K 255, box 28, procuration accounts instructions, 1712–13. For cleaning the hearse: MS K 57/7, p. 6; K 257/5/2/14.

[45] AUL, MS K 57/24, p. 7, K 257/6/3/26, 27.

[46] Beginning AUL, MS K 56/7, fol. 6r.

[47] AUL, MS K 57/3, p. 6; K 257/2/1/55. For other repairs: K 257/19/7/12, 26; K 257/20/7/13; K 257/20/11/5; *Records of Old Aberdeen*, ed. A. M. Munro, New Spalding Club, 2 vols, Aberdeen, 1899, 1909, I, 184, hereafter *Records of Old Aberdeen*.

[48] AUL, MS K 48, fol. 96[r]. It was not until 1809, however, that it was replaced by John Gartly; his clock was converted to an electrical system in 1866: MS K 49, p. 218; U 370/1, p. 331.

[49] AUL, MS K 45, fol. 4[r]; K 257/2/2/2; K 257/6/3/7; K 257/8/5/27.

[50] Murray A. M. 1746, DD, 1784 refers to the principal, John Chalmers, as his 'venerable cousin'; he was also a class-fellow of the sub-principal, later principal, Roderick Macleod: *Officers*, 77; AUL, MS K 49, p. 302.

[51] AUL, MS K 50, pp. 92–94.

[52] AUL, MS K 49, pp. 418–24, 428–43; Macpherson, 1889, 26. A more decorous picture is given by J. Logan around 1825: *Records of Old Aberdeen*, II, 304.

[53] AUL, MS K 49, p. 96.

[54] AUL, MS K 98, Minutes of the Murray Trustees, 1813–61, unfoliated, 7 December 1822.

[55] AUL, MS K 140, 'Proceedings of delegates in elections .. of Professors of Divinity, 1795–1887'.

[56] AUL, MS K 52, pp. 473–74; W. Walker, *Reminiscences Academic, Ecclesiastic and Scholastic*, Aberdeen, 1904, 14–15; Sir W. D. Geddes, 'Notes on King's College Quadrangle as it stood before 1860', *Scottish Notes and Queries*, 11, 1898, 113–15; R. S. Rait, *The Universities of Aberdeen: A History*, Aberdeen, 1895, 241.

[57] AUL, MS U 399, Memorial to Treasury, 3 December 1867; I. G. C. Hutchison, *The University and the State: the Case of Aberdeen 1860–1963*, Quincentennial Studies in the History of the University of Aberdeen, Aberdeen, 1993, 6–7.

[58] AUL, MS U 373/2, pp. 26, 29.

[59] Acting Committee for King's College Chapel Improvement Scheme, *Statement*, Aberdeen, 1889, 4, hereafter *Statement*, 1889; see Chapter 16.

[60] Geddes, 1892, 7; Macpherson, 1889, 31.

[61] AUL, MS U 399, John Webster to Lord Henry Lennox, Chief Commissioner of Public Works, 30 June 1874. See Chapter 23.

[62] AUL, MS U 370/2, pp. 261, 275–76; *Alma Mater*, I, 1883–84, 209; II, 1884–85, 19; IV, 1886–87, 28; VIII, 1890–91, 27.

[63] *Statement*, 1889, 15.

[64] Geddes, 1892, 8.

[65] AUL, MS U 370/3, p. 258; Geddes, 1892, 7. Services had previously been accompanied on a harmonium, introduced by John Christie, professor of church history: Geddes, 1892, 7; *The Fusion of 1860: a record of the centenary celebrations and a history of the United University of Aberdeen, 1860–1960*, ed. W. D. Simpson, Aberdeen University Studies, 146, Edinburgh, 1963, 220. Christie's daughter became the chapel's first permanent organist: *Alma Mater*, IX, 1891–92, 55; see Chapter 15.

[66] *Aberdeen Journal*, 23 September 1889.

[67] AUL, MS U 370/4, p. 19; Geddes, 1892, 8; *Aberdeen Journal*, 27 September 1889. Reid's silly and potentially divisive evocation of the sixteenth-century chapel filled with 'youthful collegians from the Mearns and Buchan with a sprinkling of shock-headed bajans from the wilds of Mar and Badenoch' was not reprinted in the *Statement*, 1889.

[68] W. D. Geddes, *Organ for King's College Chapel*, Aberdeen privately printed, Aberdeen, 1887; *Statement*, 1889, 4.

[69] AUL, MS U 370/3, pp. 258; U 370/4, p. 19.

[70] Geddes, 1892, 8.

[71] Hon. Secretary of the Improvement Scheme Committee; self-termed 'annalist' of the University; shortly to become Rector's Assessor 1891 and Librarian 1894.

[72] From information generously provided by Mrs M. Pryor, who will address these issues in her forthcoming thesis.

[73] *Alma Mater*, VII, 1889–90, 6, 71.

[74] *Alma Mater*, IX, 1891–92, pp. 9, 11, 26, 185, 195; X, 1892–93, 36.

[75] *Senate Minutes*, XIV, 1944–47, 58, 70–71.

CHAPTER FOURTEEN

POST-REFORMATION WORSHIP

By Henry R. Sefton

Only for a very short period of its history has King's College Chapel been used for the worship for which it was designed. For about two hundred years it was not used as a chapel at all. This calls for some explanation.

The Estates of Parliament passed an act in 1560 forbidding the celebration of mass. This edict was evaded for some years in the north-east and mass was almost certainly said in the chapel for, uniquely among the Scottish universities, King's College strongly resisted the Reformation. But the deprivation of the principal, Alexander Anderson and other members of the academic staff for refusing to subscribe the new Confession of Faith in 1569 would have brought the saying of mass in the chapel to an end.[1] In an attempt to blacken the reputation of the last Catholic principal, seventeenth-century writers accused Anderson of selling off the chapel treasures, running down the college he knew would succumb to reform. According to Middleton in 1677, 'For the hatred he bore to the reformed religion, [Anderson] . . . sold the ornaments, books and other furniture'.[2] There is no contemporary evidence that he was a common embezzler, while efforts to transfer church treasures to those who would appreciate them also took place at the cathedral where the Catholic Earl of Huntly was entrusted with the plate and vestments.[3] After 1569, daily prayers at the university continued to be offered but they were of a very different style and were said not in the chapel but in the college hall.

Of the three college chapels extant in Scotland in 1560 only one, St Leonard's College Chapel in St Andrews, continued to be regularly used for worship. This was because it was also a parish church and the parishioners of St Leonard's parish continued to worship there until 1761. In that year the building was declared unsafe and the parishioners of St Leonard's were removed to St Salvator's College Chapel where a gallery was provided for the students of the United College of St Salvator and St Leonard. This arrangement lasted until 1904 when a new church was provided for St Leonard's parish.[4] In Old Aberdeen the ancient cathedral was recognized as the parish church and so there was no need for the Snow Kirk (the medieval parish church) or King's College Chapel as places of worship.

The Reformed Church recognized two kinds of corporate worship — parish and family. The proper place for parish worship on the Lord's Day was the parish church and so it was right for students, as for everyone else, to attend there. In Old Aberdeen the students went to St Machar's. The students of Marischal College attended the West Kirk of St Nicholas. In both churches galleries were assigned to their use.

Family prayers would be offered in the home. By analogy the daily prayers of the college were said in the common hall. There was no provision for a chapel in Marischal College. In King's College the chapel was redundant as a place of communal worship and was put to other use, as was St Salvator's Chapel in St Andrews. When in 1773 the common hall of King's was divided into 'schools', or lecture rooms, the eastern part of the chapel was made the common hall and so daily prayers were said there.[5]

Bishop Elphinstone's charter had required the Principal of King's College not only to teach theology but also to preach the Word of God to the people six times a year.[6] This would be done from the ambo in the rood-screen which faced the nave or western part of the chapel. When Principal William Guild attempted to revive the preaching in 1642 he encountered opposition. It seemed strange that there should be preaching 'outwith Maucher Kirk' and that men, women and girls should be brought among young scholars and students. 'His auditoures war few, who had littell feist of the doctrein, and at last himself wyreit, and shortlie gave over this weiklie sermon moir foolishlie nor it began'. This revival 'schortlie decayit to his disgrace, as he justlie deserviit'.[7] When in 1720 Principal George Chalmers attempted to follow Guild's example he met with as little support.[8] Principal Chalmers was however admitted to the first charge of St Machar's and held that in conjunction with the principalship until his death in 1746.[9]

Thus until 1824 the students of King's College in their scarlet gowns were marched in procession to St Machar's each Sunday. It would seem, however, that the procession was not always as disciplined as it ought to have been. It was not uncommon for students to break ranks and disappear down the closes that abutted on to the High Street of Old Aberdeen. Some were detected and were brought back to the procession but others made their escape. This unruly student behaviour was well known and deplored by at least one alumnus of King's College, the Revd Alexander Murray (MA 1746, DD 1784). It was one of the considerations which led him to found the Murray Lectureship.[10]

After some years as a schoolmaster Alexander Murray was licensed as a preacher by the Presbytery of Strathbogie and was appointed to preach at Glenlivet. Four years after his ordination by the Presbytery of Aberlour he resigned and went to England. In 1763 he was sent by the Society for Propagating the Gospel in Foreign Parts to serve as their missionary at Reading, Pennsylvania. He died in Philadelphia in 1793.[11] His legacy to King's College was 'for the encouragement in the first place of a clergyman to preach a course of lectures in their College church on Sunday mornings'. But the will goes on to make it clear that 'this donation is also intended to remove in some measure the uncommon grievance and indecorum of their processions to the Parish Church'.[12]

It should be made clear that the Murray Lectures were not to be academic lectures but the kind of lectures which were at that time part of the ordinary parish worship of the Church of Scotland. They were almost indistinguishable from a sermon but were more directly related to a particular portion of Scripture than a sermon might be.

During the nineteenth century the practice of 'lecturing' gradually ceased, leaving the sermon as the only address at a service.[13]

Dr Murray's long absence from Scotland and his having become an Episcopalian clergyman may account for the terms of another passage in his will: 'In this unprejudiced critical age it were to be wished that this famous seminary would agree upon a form of public prayer and worship with or without responses and instrumental music to be read at these lectures as is common in all other countries to move the youth to the greater solemnity and order.'[14] Responses were not then part of the worship of the Church of Scotland nor was instrumental music.

Because of a life-rent Dr Murray's legacy was not available until Session 1824–25.[15] The eastern part of the chapel was made ready for the delivery of the lectures and the accompanying Sunday worship. For two sessions the duties of the lectureship were undertaken by members of the College (Drs Mearns and Forbes, Professors Paul and Scott) so that the income from Murray's foundation might be made available for the repair of the college buildings. But from Session 1826–27 the lectures were given by recently licensed preachers awaiting a call to a parish. Dr Murray had stipulated that 'two of these lectures at least shall be printed, published and presented to the Trustees by the Lecturer every year before he receives his salary, and afterwards collected by them into volumes in abstract or at length after the manner of the Hon. Robert Boyle's Lectures'. Three volumes of Murray Lectures in the University Library testify to the observance of this condition.[16]

In 1860 on the union of King's and Marischal Colleges, the Professors of Church History, Systematic Theology and Biblical Criticism became permanent lecturers on the Murray foundation. This arrangement caused considerable controversy and required an Act of Parliament to validate it. The Revd Stephen Ree (MA 1872, BD 1876) tartly comments: 'The effect of this scheme was to practically obliterate this valuable foundation, whose existence and purpose became almost unknown to the students — a result scarcely compensated by a substantial augmentation of the salaries of these three professors.'

The professors fulfilled their duties as Murray lecturers by conducting in rotation public worship in the college chapel on Sundays. According to Stephen Ree the services 'were not of a specially attractive nature'. Instrumental music was excluded and for a time even a choir was unknown. Whatever their gifts as scholars and teachers the professors were not pulpit orators. There was a strong suspicion that they frequently used old sermons delivered elsewhere 'as evidenced by rural illustrations and by references that presupposed a more varied and a more highly-organized congregation than that found in the college chapel'.[17]

The Revd James Cooper (MA 1867, DD 1892) gives a more favourable opinion on the preaching of one of these professors, William Milligan, Professor of Biblical Criticism 1860–93. Cooper admits that Milligan's morning sermons were sometimes 'a little too flowery' but those he delivered at the afternoon service were models of what expository sermons ought to be.[18] They were, it would seem, the kind of lectures envisaged by Dr Murray. Arts students belonging to the Church of Scotland and living in Old Aberdeen were then required (and very properly in Cooper's view) to attend twice every Sunday. According to Stephen Ree, practice was laxer. Although a roll was called at the beginning of each service by censors who were the bursars of the tertian class, absentees were not called to account. Attendance was quite good in the bajan year but tailed off in subsequent years. Ree describes the accommodation provided for the students as 'inadequate, uncomfortable and mean' and the internal condition of the chapel as 'a disgrace to the University'.[19] The student magazine *Alma Mater* ran a series of articles in which the poor attendance of students was blamed on the preaching monopoly of the Divinity professors and the quality of their sermons. A typical comment: 'The Rev. Professor's voice and style are as repellent as his religious views.'[20]

The reports prepared by Charles Dankester, Sacrist of King's College 1891–1918, show that there were considerable changes after the renovation of the chapel in 1891. Professor Milligan preached the special sermon at the re-opening service (to which students in gowns were admitted by the east door in the quadrangle — others had to obtain tickets) but the Divinity monopoly was broken. Distinguished preachers from other denominations were also invited and the Sunday morning services began to attract a large outside congregation as well as more students. According to Dankester, the largest congregation was on 19 November 1899 when 727 were present to hear the Revd R. J. Watson of Liverpool. The Sacrist notes that it was a splendid day and that the collection amounted to £10 8s. 5d. for soldiers' wives left behind during the South African War.[21] By this time the Students' Representative Council was complaining that students were crowded out of the accommodation reserved for them.[22]

Prior to 1891 the chapel services consisted of preaching and little else. Charles Dankester reports that the first Communion service was held in the winter session of 1892. James Cooper records that the celebrant, Professor Milligan, was convinced that 'the most pressing need of the Church of Scotland was the revival of the weekly eucharist'. Appropriately an 'altar-table' was erected in the chapel in Professor Milligan's memory in 1898.[23] The sacrist reports twice yearly Communion services thereafter. His summary of chapel services during the period 1891–1911 includes eight marriages, six christenings and two ordinations (Professor Gilroy in 1895 and Professor Curtis in 1903). The annual kirking of the S.R.C. dates from this period. The enhancement of music in the chapel is described in Chapter 15.

The Dankester reports are so detailed that a chapter could be written on them alone. For each Sunday he gives the name of the preacher, the text, the Scripture lessons and the reader's name, the psalms and hymns sung, the amount of the collection with a note of each coin, the weather including the wind direction and temperature, a list of staff and the staff wives present and a note of the reasons for absence, and whether or not candles, and later electric lights, were used. The version of the Bible used in the readings is also recorded. All this is written in a large copper-plate hand. Charles Dankester was a Cornishman who identified himself completely with King's College and became something of a legend in his own life-time. *Alma Mater* referred to the 'Lex Dankestris' and a student penned a limerick:

When I came as a Bajan to King's,
I heard some most horrible things:
They told me that Dankey
Was a pal of old Sankey
And wrote quite the most of the hymns.[24]

Dankester's reports were prepared for Sir George Adam Smith, Principal of the University 1910–35. As a minister of the United Free Church of Scotland he took a keen interest in the worship of the chapel and regularly preached there. The economist and poet, Alexander Gray, Professor of Political Economy 1921–34, has testified to Sir George's power as a preacher: 'Although his utterances were the fruit of profound scholarship and thought, the final result was always a message within the grasp of ordinary men and women — and ordinary students.' The principal's beautiful voice was itself a benediction.[25] The Divinity professors continued to share in the Sunday services and also led daily prayers in the chapel until the appointment of the first full-time chaplain to the University in 1947.[26] Current religious practice in the chapel is described in Chapter 25.

Notes

[1] David Stevenson, *King's College, Aberdeen 1560–1641: From Protestant Reformation to Covenanting Revolution*, Aberdeen, 1990, 13–17, 24, 48.

[2] T. Middleton, *An appendix to the History of the Church of Scotland*, London, 1677, page following p. 38, titled p. 25; Andrew Strachan, *Panegyricus Inauguralis*, Aberdeen, Raban, 1631, 26, also mentions his alienating college valuables.

[3] *Fasti Aberdonenses*, xxviii, nn. 2 and 3; Stevenson, 1990, 13–14.

[4] Ronald G. Cant: *The College of St Salvator*, Edinburgh, 1950, 201–02, 213–15, 220–22.

[5] [T. Gordon], 'University and King's College of Aberdeen' in *Statistical Account of Scotland*, ed. Sir J. Sinclair, 21 vols, Edinburgh, 1791–99, XXI, 90. See Chapter 13.

[6] Eeles, 1956, 169.

[7] J. Gordon, *History of Scots Affairs from MDCXXXVI to MDCXLI*, J. Robertson and G. Grub (eds), Spalding Club, Aberdeen, 1849, II, 141.

[8] AUL, MS K41, fol. 50ʳ; Orem, 1791, 185.

[9] Hew Scott, *Fasti Ecclesiae Scoticanae: the succession of ministers in the Church if Scotland from the Reformation*, 8 vols, Edinburgh, 1915–28, VI, 20; VII, 367. Hereafter Scott, *Fasti*.

[10] *Fasti Aberdonenses*, 209; Macpherson, 1889, 26ff.

[11] Scott, *Fasti*, VI, 341ff.

[12] *Fasti Aberdonenses*, 209; Macpherson, 1889, 26f.

[13] William D. Maxwell, *A History of Worship in the Church of Scotland*, London, 1955, 97f, 102f.

[14] *Fasti Aberdonenses*, 209; Macpherson, 1889, 27.

[15] The Murray Bequest began to pay for repairs to the chapel in 1821, but the first lectureship was awarded in the session for 1824–25. AUL, MS K 98; Notes on the History of King's College, AUL, MS K 138.

[16] 'Discourses on the subject of pure and undefiled religion in the Chapel of the University and King's College, Aberdeen, at the lecture founded by Alexander Murray'. AUL, Lambda Murr 1, 2, 3.

[17] *Aurora Borealis Academica*, ed. P. J. Anderson, Aberdeen, 1899, 161–63.

[18] *Aurora Borealis*, 1899, 182.

[19] *Aurora Borealis*, 1899, 162.

[20] R. D. Anderson, *The Student Community at Aberdeen 1860–1939*, Aberdeen, 1988, 52.

[21] AUL, MS U556.

[22] Anderson, 1988, 52.

[23] Scott, *Fasti*, VII, 377; *Aurora Borealis*, 1899, 187.

[24] *The Fusion of 1860*, ed. W. Douglas Simpson, Edinburgh, 1963, 321.

[25] Simpson, 1963, 154.

[26] Simpson, 1963, 32, 319.

CHAPTER FIFTEEN

MUSIC AND MUSICIANS SINCE 1891

By ROGER B. WILLIAMS

Music played an important part in the life of the chapel once again after a new organ was installed in 1891.[1] Elisabeth Christie, fourth daughter of the Professor of Church History, who had taken lessons in both London and Paris, became Organist and Director of Music in King's College chapel after two other applicants retired before the audition at St Machar's Cathedral.[2] A voluntary chapel choir was formed, singing from the gallery. At first the choir was unrobed, but distinctive royal purple gowns and black trenchers ordered by Senatus, were worn for the first time in September 1906 for the Quatercentenary celebrations.[3] At first services were held on Sunday during the winter term only, but from 1900 services were also held on Sundays in May and June.[4] Miss Christie described the job in modest terms: 'music was of the most elementary description and no self-respecting organist would have dreamt of applying for the post'.[5] But some idea of the musical standards achieved may be deduced from the success she and the choir achieved at the Glasgow Competitive Festival.[6]

The distinguished Bach scholar and historian C. S. Terry had taken over the University Choral and Orchestral Society on his arrival in Aberdeen in 1898.[7] He and musicians of the calibre of Sir Frederick Bridge of St Paul's Cathedral and Sir Edward Bairstow of York Minster, 'practically adopted us and gave us recitals and encouragement in every direction'.[8] In 1922, after thirty years, Elisabeth Christie resigned and Albert Adams, FRCO of Cults, was appointed.[9] From 1898 there had been a separate organist at Marischal College,[10] but in March 1935, after the death of the incumbent Mr Nesbit, both posts were combined.[11] After the resignation of Albert Adams in 1937,[12] in quick succession, a second year Arts student Alastair David Macdonald (1937),[13] Alexander Hendry, FRCO (1938)[14] and Willan Swainson, FRCO (1940)[15] were appointed organists. After long and distinguished service to the university as Director of Music, developing not only performance but laying secure academic foundations for the MA degree in music, Willan Swainson was succeeded by Reginald Barrett-Ayres as organist in 1956,[16] a post which he held until his death in 1981. Subsequently Dr Roger B. Williams has held the post.

The organ of 1891 was built by Norman Brothers and Beard of Norwich and comprised two manuals and fifteen stops, with a hydraulic blowing mechanism.[17] A third manual and nine more stops were prepared for. The money required for the organ was raised within four weeks from 'purely voluntary sources'.[18] In 1899 an anonymous benefactor gave £200 to complete the organ to the original design, 'provided that the required balance was subscribed by the public'.[19] The final total of money raised came to £489 11s. 6d., £10 more than the cost of the work.[20] In 1912, the organ was rebuilt by Hilsdon,[21] and three years after repairs in 1928, the organ was cleaned, some additions made, and an electric blower was installed.[22] By the late 1940s there was talk of a replacement organ being necessary.[23] Although the proposals are no longer extant, the John Compton Organ Company Limited, W. Walker & Sons Ltd,[24] and Rushworth & Dreaper[25] were all involved, as were the distinguished organists Geraint Jones[26] and Sir Thomas Armstrong.[27] In 1952 the organ was pronounced unfit for use[28] and over the next few years it proved to be very unreliable.[29] Four years later a Compton electronic organ was obtained but the Chapel Committee kept up the pressure to replace the worn-out pipe organ.[30] The Committee was rewarded in 1958 when Harrison & Harrison of Durham was contracted to build a new organ. The Court Minutes of 12 January 1960 carry an appreciation from the Chapel Committee of the newly completed instrument.[31] However, the problems were by no means over, and it appears likely that overheating in the chapel led to problems with the new instrument. For many, the basic tonal design was flawed, and the separation of the console from the pipes does not present an instrument of integrity. Professor Peter Williams,[32] then of Edinburgh University, was called in to advise and in 1983 a detailed report was received,[33] though the financial climate precluded taking the matter any further. Cleaning, some renovation work and considerable revoicing was carried out at the end of 1991.[34]

The chapel choir has always been made up of volunteers. In the early 1980s, however, the former Principal Professor McNicol instituted two organ and eight choral scholarships open to any student of the university. The scholars sing at the university chapel services and rehearsals, at concerts in which chapel choir takes part, and for graduations.

It is almost impossible to give a comprehensive idea of what the repertoire of music for the chapel services has been over the last hundred years. Payments were made to Andrew Milne, James Barron and James Valentine for leading Psalmody in the chapel in the 1860s and 1870s.[35] Other sources hint at the central place of hymns and psalms,[36] particularly metrical versions of the latter. From the well-worn state of The Oxford Church Anthem Book we may guess at some of the repertoire. Willan Swainson performed the Passions by J. S. Bach on a regular basis and made a special feature of the chorales. The BBC has broadcast services from the chapel from the late 1930s through to the present day.[37] Changing tastes in church music were readily reflected in many new compositions of the 1960s by Reginald Barrett-Ayres and this tradition continued with a series of broadcasts in the late 1980s featuring many items from the newly produced supplement to the Church Hymnary — *Songs of God's People*. Specially commissioned music was performed for the Queen Mother's Graduation in 1983, and for the Quincentenary celebrations in 1995, honorary doctor and Aberdeen composer Judith Weir, and former assistant organist and lecturer in the music department Peter Inness, were both invited to write new pieces. In 1997 George McPhee, Master of Music and organist of Paisley Abbey, was commissioned to write an anthem for St Machar's Day based on a text from Bishop Elphinstone's

Aberdeen Breviary. Various organists, assistants and students have contributed to renewing the repertoire which is now probably as wide-ranging as it has ever been. Medieval plainchant is frequently used in the penitential seasons, while for more joyous occasions a small orchestra is sometimes added to the choir. One of the more recent traditions, dating from the late 1970s, is the annual performance of the Coronation Anthem, *Zadok the Priest*, by Handel, at the Founder's Day Service. The chapel choir gives an annual concert for the Alumnus Association in December, while the university carol service, sung on the final Wednesday of the autumn term, is now held in St Machar's Cathedral. Recently the chapel choir has performed Handel's *Messiah*, Bach's *St John Passion*, Fauré's *Requiem*, Vivaldi's *Gloria*, Monteverdi's *Beatus Vir* and Haydn's *Insanae et Vane Curae*. The chapel is used regularly for concerts in the University Music series, and has included many memorable appearances by Aberdeen's first professional music group, the Yggdrasil Quartet. Organ recitals, lunchtime concerts and several recent recordings and broadcasts show that music is very much alive in the university chapel at the end of the twentieth century.

The acoustics of the chapel are excellent. Not only is speech clear but music of many different types sounds very well. Music was an important part of the initial function of the chapel and both medieval plainchant and polyphony sound particularly fine in the building. The original choral priests sang from the choir stalls with an organ on the screen. In Elisabeth Christie's day the chapel choir sang from the gallery as they have done until recently. Today, unless a very full congregation is expected at the university service, the choir once more sits in the choir stalls, a siting which also achieves the best balance with the organ. Solo instruments sound well in the building, especially harpsichord and guitar and recent concerts using baroque instruments have been particularly rewarding. The old wood of the stalls and the ceiling add warmth and resonance, while the mix of glass, plaster-work, tiled floor and the well-proportioned space enable the sound to carry truthfully to all parts of this very special building.

Notes

[1] Minutes of the University Court of the Univerity of Aberdeen (hereafter Court Minutes), 10 November 1891.

[2] E. C. Brown, *The Kildrummy Christies*, Aberdeen, 1948, 75.

[3] Court Minutes, 12 June 1906; 28 November 1906.

[4] Court Minutes, 10 April 1900.

[5] Brown, 1948, 75.

[6] Brown, 1948, 77.

[7] A. Shiel, *Tribute to Charles Sanford Terry (1864–1936)*, programme booklet for University Concert, 21 March 1999, University Music, University of Aberdeen, 1999, 2.

[8] Brown, 1948, 77.

[9] Court Minutes, 9 May 1922.

[10] Court Minutes, 8 November 1898.

[11] Court Minutes, 9 July 1935.

[12] Court Minutes, 13 July 1937.

[13] Court Minutes, 12 October 1937.

[14] Court Minutes, 8 March 1938.

[15] Court Minutes, 14 May 1940; 9 July 1940; 11 September 1940.

[16] University Calendar 1956/57.

[17] Court Minutes, 4 November 1895.

[18] Court Minutes, 10 November 1891.

[19] Court Minutes, 16 April 1899.

[20] Court Minutes, 10 July 1900.

[21] Court Minutes, 12 December 1911.

[22] Court Minutes, 10 November 1931.

[23] Court Minutes, 25 July 1946; 9 December 1947; 9 November 1948; 14 June 1949; 13 June 1950; 10 October 1950; 9 October 1951.

[24] Court Minutes, 9 December 1947; Organ File — letter from J. W. Walker & Sons Ltd, 13 May 1965. The Organ File is kept by the Estates Section of the university.

[25] Court Minutes, 9 December 1947; 8 June 1954.

[26] Court Minutes, 10 March 1953.

[27] Court Minutes, 8 June 1954; 6 July 1954.

[28] Court Minutes, 15 January 1952; 12 February 1952.

[29] Organ File letters: December 1953; April 1955; May 1955.

[30] Court Minutes, 11 December 1956.

[31] Court Minutes, 12 January 1960.

[32] Organ File, January 1983.

[33] Organ File Report, 15 May 1983.

[34] Organ File, January 1992.

[35] Vouchers for payments in AUL, MS U 1358. I am very grateful to Mary Pryor for drawing this reference to my attention.

[36] Court Minutes, 11 January 1910; 10 November 1914; 10 February 1931.

[37] Court Minutes refer to broadcasts in February 1939; May 1941; March and April 1946; the most recent broadcasts have been on Radio 4, 21 February and World Service, 7 March 1999.

CHAPTER SIXTEEN

POST-REFORMATION BUILDING: THE CROWN TOWER AND OTHER REPAIRS

By JANE GEDDES

The chapel building has enjoyed a relatively uneventful history ever since the Reformation. The following account presents none of the architectural and artistic fireworks which feature in the earlier chapters. In fact, what makes King's Chapel exceptional in Scotland, is precisely what did *not* happen. The lead roof was not immediately stripped for scrap, the interior was neither gutted nor reconstructed according to later fashions. Blessed by neglect, lack of funds and periodic bouts of essential maintenance, it remains fundamentally as Bishop Elphinstone intended and one of the finest pre-Reformation church interiors in Scotland.

'This chapel was richly adorned in the time of Popery, but was spoiled of all its rich ornaments at the beginning of the Reformation.'[1] Probably two violent and dangerous moments, in 1560 and 1568 passed like furious waves over the chapel, wreaking destruction on the cathedral instead. This was due to the robust defence put up by Principal Alexander Anderson who forcibly repelled the looters who 'would have taken away the lead and bells'.[2] As mentioned in Chapter 14, Anderson, a devout Catholic, may also have sold off the chapel treasures to prevent their destruction.[3] The other major loss, probably in the seventeenth century, was the magnificent bronze tomb of Bishop Elphinstone.[4] A certain lack of ideological fanaticism can be detected: there is a notable absence of axe or scorch marks on the surviving fabric; one misericord even retains the sacred IHS letters. An image survived on the old organ until 1640 'painted in a course draught, the pourtraichte of some woman, nobody could tell who, and had hung ther half brockne and wholly neglected for many years: this was brockne downe and complained upon as a thing very intollerable in the churche of a colledge'.[5] A year later, the medieval organ 'of fyne wanescot' was removed.[6]

Although the chapel has been costly to maintain, the building has had the capacity to accommodate many different functions, thereby ensuring its survival. The east end served as a synod meeting room from the early seventeenth century, the west end was used as a stone carving lodge for masons constructing the New Work or Cromwell Tower in 1657–58; and was later converted to a library before the whole interior reverted to religious use in 1873.[7]

On the outside, four areas have demanded serious attention over the centuries: the crown tower, the spirelet, the windows and the south wall. On the inside, the main changes concern the chancel and nave arrangements, the organ loft and the glass. The external changes were primarily due to maintenance; those on the inside reflect the evolving functions of the building.

THE TOWER: THE CROWN

The daring architecture of the crown tower has required a continuing financial commitment. Even during the centuries when the chapel fell out of ecclesiastical use, the crown stood as a symbol of the university's loyalty to the king. In return, the king was occasionally petitioned to contribute towards its upkeep.

After the first hundred years, a difficult period with fluctuating finances, the commissioners in 1619 found that the 'maintenance of the edifice of the said universitie wes cleane neglected, quhairthrow the haill place is become ruinous'. The physical decay mirrored the moral condition: 'lamentable hethenism and sic lowsnes as is horrible to record'.[8] Little seems to have been done because the next visitation, in 1623, is more specific and urgent. By this time the west windows of the tower needed to be replaced, the west window of the church needed new glass, other windows needed masonry repairs and the 'heid of the gryt stepill sould be mendit in steane, lead and tymer as the samen was abefoir'.[9] Perhaps nothing was done, because the great gale of 1633 brought the crown down.[10] Dr William Gordon, mediciner, was responsible for organizing the repairs in 1634 and the name of the mason, George Thomson, is carved on the west side of the crown.[11] With great difficulty, the university raised funds for the restoration, gaining contributions from the town, cathedral congregation and sheriffdom, and eventually sending a representation to King Charles I in 1634 asking for tax relief.[12]

To what extent is the present crown a replica of Elphinstone's design? (Fig. 16.1). The replacement received general approval but was certainly not identical. Spalding, who knew both, considered the new crown was 'little inferior to the first'.[13] Gordon, in 1661, considered it was 'restored in a better forme and conditione'.[14] Middleton, in 1677, said it was 'afterwards built more stately'.[15]

Boece, writing in 1522, is quite clear in his description of the original tower shortly after it was built: 'the bell tower is of great height surrounded by stone work arched in form of an imperial crown over the leaded roof'.[16] In other words, the arches themselves constituted and symbolized the closed imperial crown and there is no mention of the second crown on top at this date. The next description equally clearly emphasizes the literal crown we see today. It was written by John Forbes the rector of the university in July 1634, after the terrible storm damage. The work had come to a standstill for lack of funds when barely a quarter of the repairs were complete. Thus, Forbes' description must refer to the old crown because the new one did not yet exist. He calls the steeple 'a most curious and statlie work of hewn and corned [carved?] stones; representing to the view of all beholders *a brave pourtrait of the royall diademe*'.[17] The diadem must therefore refer to the literal crown above the arches. Spalding's description of 1640 corroborates this: 'putting up on the stepill . . . ane staitlie croune, throwne down be the wynd abefoir'.[18]

WEST ELEVATION
OF UPPER PART OF TOWER.

CHAPEL AND TOWER, KING'S COLLEGE
ABERDEEN UNIVERSITY.   Nº 4.

Fig. 16.1.   The Crown, by J. C.
Watt, 1885 (Copyright: University
of Aberdeen)

Since Boece, in 1522, is so specific that the crown was made up by the arches alone, was he overlooking the second crown, was it a solid shape or was the design not yet complete? Because of this ambiguity, Kelly even proposed that the original crown of four ribs was topped by a steeple, like St Giles, Edinburgh and St Nicholas, Newcastle, but he chose to ignore Forbes' description of the royal diadem (Figs 4.15, 4.16).[19]

This problem can be examined by looking first at the surviving stonework and then at the Scots and English regalia.

An inspection of the stonework shows that the four great arches are still substantially constructed of the yellow sandstone which makes up the majority of the original building. The repairs and replacements are equally clear: the copings on the arches, and practically all the sculpture (pinnacles, and the entire top crown with the blind arcade around its supporting drum) are made of a greyish stone speckled with a few granulations. These are presumably the additions and reinforcements from 1634. However behind the grey, blind arcading on the drum there is a core of yellow sandstone blocks which looks like part of an original drum. Certain stones making up the diadem itself look freshly cut and are probably Kelly's or more recent repairs. They are a similar greyish colour to the 1634 work.

Five critical details distinguish the Aberdeen crown: the circlet or head band is decorated with pairs of little gems alternating with single large diamonds; the circlet bears alternating crosses patée and fleurs-de-lis, with a 'pearl' on a scallop between each of them; there are four open arches; the arches are covered by a sequence of small scrolls or curled leaves; and the design is topped by an orb and cross. Tracing the development of these features through the sixteenth and seventeenth centuries indicates how the design began and how it reached its expression in 1634 on the tower.

Both James III and James V are depicted on coins with an imperial crown.[20] In the *Book of Hours of James IV and Margaret Tudor* (1503), James is painted wearing a delicate imperial crown (Col. Pl. IV).[21] The circlet is decorated with alternating large and small sprigs of foliage with gems on the head band and pearls on top of the small sprigs. The two arches are low, each bearing two crockets and topped by a very small orb and pearl. This crown has no connection with the one at Aberdeen. The crown from James IV's arms of 1504 on the west front of the chapel has fleurs-de-lis and crosses patté on the circlet but shows a solid bonnet, not arches, above (Fig. 10.2).

James V kept the arches on the crown of Scotland, remodelled after 1539 (Fig. 16.2).[22] This has a circlet of gems, heightened by ten fleurs-de-lis and ten crosses fleury alternating around the upper edge of the circle. In between the crosses and fleurs-de-lis is a scalloped, pearl-topped band.[23] The two arches are decorated with oak leaves. They rise sharply upwards and then dip in the middle to support a celestial orb and cross patée. Here then is a source for three Aberdeen features, namely the scallops between the crosses and fleurs-de-lis, scrolly leaves applied to the arches, and the orb and cross. Other expressions of James V's imperial crown appear on the heraldic ceiling of St Machar's Cathedral (*c.* 1520 and very schematic),[24] on his towers at Holyrood Palace,[25] and on the fountain at Linlithgow Palace (Fig. 4.17). The fountain crown, dated by a stamped drainpipe to 1538, has several points of comparison with Aberdeen.[26] Where the Aberdeen crown rests on a solid drum, the Linlithgow crown perches on four slender columns. Where the four Aberdeen diadem arches soar precariously through open space, the two Linlithgow arches rest on a solid semidome of stone, representing the velvet bonnet of the true crown. The Linlithgow circlet has a cable moulding around the bottom and alternating crests of fleurs-de-lis and a type of splayed cross.[27] So, based on the models of James IV's arms at King's and the Linlithgow fountain, it is possible that the first Aberdeen crown had a solid top or bonnet, thereby allowing Boece to extol the open 'imperial' arches below.

Walker asserted that the 1634 stone crown was based on a fresh model which he identifies as that of Charles I.[28] The English state crown of Charles I, destroyed in 1649, was depicted by Daniel Mytens and Van Dyck (Fig. 16.3). This crown, existing in the reign of Henry VIII (1509–47), had crosses patée, fleurs-de-lis and two arches, all studded with jewels. On top of the arches was an orb surmounted by a cross.[29] This crown introduces the cross patée around the crest.

Fig. 16.2.   The crown of Scotland, crafted by John Mosman, 1540 (Crown Copyright: courtesy of Historic Scotland)

While the two real crowns provide some aspects of the model for Aberdeen, it is unlikely that any stone mason either around 1520 or 1634 knew what they looked like. More likely sources are coins or heraldic blazons. The silver ryal of Mary and Henry Darnley (1565–67) shows the Aberdeen features of a circlet bearing alternating crosses patée and fleurs-de-lis, with a 'pearl' on a scallop between each of them; two (not four) open arches; arches covered by a sequence of small scrolls or curled leaves; and the orb and cross on top.[30] The arms of St Margaret, painted in 1542, show the following features: a circlet studded with geometric gems, including diamonds alternating with pairs of 'pearls'; cresting with alternating crosses patée and fleurs-de-lis, each separated by a scalloped 'pearl' topped band; scrolled motifs on the three arches. The arches are topped by a cross without an orb.[31] On the painted arms and badges of Charles I, the crown has a circlet of circular gems alternating with pairs of 'pearls'; the crest alternates crosses patée and fleurs-de-lis with a tiny pearl between each, while the clearly painted four arches are topped by curly scrolls drawn in the same bold manner as on the tower and they are topped by a cross.[32] The heraldic crown of Charles I on the lead panels of the chapel steeple (Fig. 16.4) is almost exactly this type, having the circlet crests, multiple arches, orb and cross. Thus, while all these

Fig. 16.3. State crown of Charles I, 1631, by Daniel Mytens (By courtesy of the National Portrait Gallery, London)

crowns share several features, the scalloping on the crest appears in James V's reign. The four arches themselves are an artistic and functional device. Real crowns tend to have two arches at most. The imperial crown made for the Delhi Durbar of George V in 1911 has three arches, but that was unusual.[33] On the other hand, four arches would add stability to an architctural feature and are commonly shown in heraldry.[34]

In conclusion, it is impossible to be sure what the original crown looked like, but a comparison with other contemporary stone models suggests it may have had a solid bonnet on top. The regular sequence of cross patée, pearl on scallop and fleur-de-lis was not yet established for the circlet, although it probably had some form of cross and fleur-de-lis. The new design of 1634 clearly incorporated a few changes. I would suggest that these included the geometric arrangement of gems on the circlet, plus the present cresting sequence and multiple open arches which are only shown in Scots heraldry after 1542. Likewise, the Baroque chunkiness of design with multiple arches topped by prominent scrolls only becomes fully evident on the painted arms of Charles I and a close parallel is evident on the adjacent steeple.

THE TOWER: MAINTENANCE

Apart from its crown, the other feature to note is that the tower originally had a pitched roof under the crown: hence the need for the doorways in the pinnacles to provide circulation around the parapet. These doorways are also found at St Giles,

Fig. 16.4.   Steeple detail, north-east panel

Fig. 16.5.   Steeple detail, north-east panel

Edinburgh. The pitched roof is shown in the *c.* 1640 painting, and is described in the survey of 1638 where there is a discussion about repairing the roof as 'a platt, or an upstanding ruiff as abefoir' (Col. Pl. I).[35] By 1658 the roof was leaking badly, 'the timber frame of the steeple began to rot and the stonework to rive; the college were necessitate to remove the timber frame and to platform the great steeple and lay it with lead'.[36] Hence James Gordon's view of *c.* 1660 shows the new flat top to the tower (Fig. 4.6).

Maintenance was frequent but seemingly ineffective. Repairs to the masonry and lead are recorded at least six times between 1669 and 1690.[37] Barely eighty years after the great storm and rebuild, Orem reports that in 1719 the tower was again failing. 'The masters of the college are fearing the falling down again of this crown, which is one of the best monuments that is in the nation; whereanent they are asking advice from the King's mason what way it must be supported from falling'.[38] The accounts for this episode, in spite of providing minute details about workmen's activities like making cranes, barrows and nails, give little clue about the nature of the repairs. A great deal of effort was expended on erecting form-work or shuttering under the arches.[39] Maintenance of the masonry and lead on the tower continued for most of the century.[40] A new buttress was added in the south-east corner in 1773–74.[41] Inside the tower, there were repairs to the floor and stair, and the ground floor was paved in 1780–81.[42] The masonry and roof of the chapel were repaired in 1713–15, 1726–27 and 1788–90, and the lead of the spire in 1715.[43] Between 1792 and 1794 the roof and spire caused serious concern: the parapet wall and lead were removed, the roof slated, and the spire — after careful consideration — repaired and retained.[44] Between 1884 and 1887 the base of the tower was sealed off, only accessible through the sacrist's lodge, in order to create a fire-proof strong room.[45]

By the 1960s a serious crack had developed down the north-east corner of the tower, the only angle without a buttress. The repairs, put in hand by James Kelman, involved inserting reinforced concrete collars inside the tower, tying a phospher-bronze band around the parapet, and pressure grouting the masonry.[46] The cause of this damage, and presumably so much more in the past, was failure of the mortar and pointing, in soft sandstone exposed to the full fury of North Sea weather.

The Little Steeple

The little steeple or flèche was part of the original design, marking the internal division of the chapel at the rood screen. It was warmly appreciatd by Francis Douglas in 1782: '. . . one of the most elegant small spires I have ever seen . . . the sheet-lead is very prettily gathered about the root of it. Perhaps you may think me too minute in this; I can only say that I went to some distance and enjoyed the prospect of it for a good while' (Fig. 4.6).[47]

By 1638 the 'litle stipill' needed repairs to both its lead and timber but the university was very short of money.[48] Then, in 1641, Charles I founded the Caroline University, uniting Marischal and King's. This act was designed specifically to increase the revenue of the colleges by diverting money from the bishopric's funds. Most unusually in such a foundation charter, it is specified that the extra money was to be used for upgrading the library and 'for a full repairing of the said auld college in ruiff leid sklait work lofting and uther places necessar'.[49] Presumably there had been no funds to remedy the roof defects listed in the survey of 1638.[50] Eventually in 1656 'the prikket [spire] upon the college kirk the timber work being all together rotn and the leads decayed was inteerly rebuilt',[51] and William Kerr was paid for gilding the weather vane, presumably when the steeple was complete.[52]

These dates are interesting because of the embossed designs on the six lead panels at the base of the steeple (Fig. 16.5). Charles I had been executed in 1649 and the principal in 1655–56 was John Row, a supporter of Cromwell. The lead panels each bear the initials CR, and the remainder of the design alternates the bough-pot of lilies, symbolizing the Virgin and three fishes in a fret pattern. The lilies and fish were Bishop Elphinstine's personal insignia and are used on the first seal of the university. Above the lilies is a crown between fleur-de-lis and thistle; above the fish is a crown between two thistles.[53] At the top is a border of abstract geometric motifs.

Innes and Macpherson, unaware of the documented dates, assumed that the initials CR referred to Charles II (1660–85).[54] Kelly noted that on the lead itself are the words 'W. Scot 1655 FECIT' and reached the unlikely conclusion that the CR panels were actually made in the Interregnum, with second-hand moulds.[55] William Scot was a wright working with lead and iron for the university between 1652 to 1657.[56]

A close inspection of the panels, made possible by reslating the chapel roof in 1999, may provide a different explanation. In contrast to the accomplished cast royal initials, the embossed 'W S' below are decidedly coarse and irregular. Moreover, the remainder of the inscription, 'cot 1655 FECIT', although neatly formed, is merely scratched on the surface. The spacing of the letters is clearly an after thought: W S is fairly symmetrical but the rest is squeezed into the bottom right corner of the panel. It is possible, therefore, that the magnificent CR panels were cast to commemorate the founding of the Caroline University in 1641, or more specifically the accompanying royal grant to pay for the roof, and were then re-used when Scot rebuilt the rest of the steeple in 1655–56.

ARRANGEMENTS AT THE EAST END

The changes here have been crucial to the survival of the building. Because the layout could be adapted without too much destruction, the chapel remained in use after the Reformation and was therefore periodically repaired.

Although mass was banned in 1560, worship perhaps continued for a short while, until all the altars were presumably swept away. It was Bishop Patrick Forbes who converted the east end into a meeting room for the synod of the diocese. His own chair was installed in 1627 against the east wall (Fig. 16.6) and it was flanked by seats painted with the name of each presbytery represented at the meetings.[57] Douglas remarks waspishly in 1782 'On the east . . . are a parcel of modern pews, for the occasional accommodation of the clergy, as clumsy as the most orthodox presbyterian could desire'.[58] The area must have been dim and gloomy as windows on the north side were progressively walled up (see below). In 1821, orders were given to get the chapel plaster lathed.[59] This must have primarily applied to the east end since the nave at this stage was sheathed in book cases. This order serves as a reminder that the internal dimensions of the building are no longer precisely what they were at the beginning. It also provides a terminal date for the painted masonry lines on the plaster. The walls were further strapped and plastered in 1873 when the library was removed and the stalls shifted westwards.[60]

1824 marks the start of a new era for the chapel. Thanks to the Murray Bequest, religious worship resumed in the choir but it took about seventy years to recolonize and decorate the whole building.[61] The east end was still dominated by Bishop Forbes' chair because it was used for academic functions like graduations.[62] The step up to the altar, banned in 1641 but still surviving, was removed in 1824 to make the liturgical space more acceptable.[63] The wooden ceiling at the east end was restored with 'the new carving not as rich as what remained of the old'.[64] At this point the five great paintings, illustrating royal biblical subjects, were brought over from the hall vestibule to decorate the chapel (Col. Pls VI–VIII).[65]

In 1844 Bishop Stewart's pulpit, made for St Machar's Cathedral in the 1530s, was restored and installed on the north wall of the chapel.[66] After 1873 when the choir

Fig. 16.6.   The east end of the chapel, 1928
(Copyright: University of Aberdeen)

Fig. 16.7.   Peter Udny's tomb
slab. (Copyright: University of
Aberdeen)

stalls were moved one bay westwards, there was more space to fill at the east end. Rowand Anderson suggested in 1889 that the pulpit be moved one bay further east, to its present position level with Elphinstone's tomb, and the space between the old stalls and the pulpit should be 'filled with two rows of fixed oak pews, treated in the same style as the old stalls'. More stalls and panelling were to be erected around the apse, to accommodate the senatus.[67] The students' seating never materialized because photos from 1891 show plain chairs east of the stalls.[68] However, Anderson's range of stalls from the east end of the chapel, made on a pattern relating to the panels on Bishop Forbes' chair, were moved in 1932 to fit against the north and south walls where they are today, with Kelly making a few extra to fit.[69] Forbes' chair was eventually put in store in 1931, to make way for the restoration of the east window.[70] The chair was rebuilt by the south door after the Second World War. A communion table was discussed in 1889, and the present table was made later in memory of William Milligan, Professor of Biblical Criticism from 1860 to 1893.

Behind the table is a remarkable survival, rescued from the floor in 1932. It is a black marble altar slab, still bearing three of the original five consecration crosses (Fig. 16.7). It was re-used after the Reformation as a tomb for Peter Udny, the sub-principal from 1593 to 1601. This tomb may provide a clue to the gradual and reluctant demise of Catholicism in the chapel. The inscription includes the phrase 'I have learnt and I have taught Thy wounds, O Christ'.[71] The consecration crosses already on the slab came to symbolize the five wounds of Christ. William Elphinstone, Prebendary of Clatt, paid in 1512 for a mass of the five wounds of Christ to be said on the highest loft of the crucifix, 'every week for ever'.[72] Perhaps these services continued privately as late as 1601, with Udny creeping to the top of the pulpitum to perform them with a few students. Perhaps someone like Udny remained resolutely seated on the IHS misericord when the other images were taken down.

THE FENESTRATION

The windows suffered numerous changes as part of the east end of the chapel subsided into swampy ground, new access was provided through the east end, glass fell out and panels were simply walled up. Probably the only windows now in a reasonably original condition are the short mullions on the south side, and the great west window. The documentary evidence does not always make it clear whether recommendations or instructions were carried out.

In 1623 the north windows were to be 'sett and harlett with lyme and the steane wark of the second wastmost window sould be teine out and fillit with glass as the rest of the saidis windowis was . . . and the east window sould be takine doun within six fuittis of the soill, and fullit with glass'.[73] The east window may have been blocked due to subsidence at an early stage and this repair may never have been carried out because by 1627 the bishop's chair was set axially in front of the east window when the choir was converted to a synod house. Certainly by 1657–58 the east end was damaged by the provision of access to the 'timber muses', a passage leading from the chapel to the 'new work', now known as the Cromwell Tower.[74] The 'muses' are illustrated in Gordon's drawing of 1660, together with their pinnacled stair turret (Fig. 4.6). This structure was removed around 1821–25 when the east end reverted to a chapel.[75] The east end was again disturbed when Henry Scougal's mort was moved there from the north-east wall of the apse.[76] Orem records the blocking in 1715[77] of a window which Macpherson identified as the north-east. Macpherson's father recalled all the north windows being blocked by the early nineteenth century, except for the upper part of the two in the nave which were used to light the library.[78] An order was given in 1821 to 'build up all the windows with the exception of the large Gothic window in the court and of the window opposite and similar to it, looking into the Principal's garden'. At the same time a window (presumably the one blocked in 1715) was to be opened 'on the north east side of the master's desk to correspond with the one on the south east of the same, [?] not now to be built up'.[79] Perhaps this was not carried out until money from the Murray Bequest became available in 1821, because at that point the two angled windows of the apse were filled with wooden tracery. Macpherson's father recalled that previous tracery 'was all in the same heavy style, and in harmony with the other old windows'.[80]

When the library was removed in 1873, slow steps were taken to reglaze the chapel, beginning at the west end in 1874.[81] Following the offer of Professor Hugh Macpherson's family to present a stained glass window, it was decided to replace the

Fig. 16.8. The east end today, showing Kelly's reconstructed tracery of the east windows

'altogether incongruous' tracery in the side windows of the apse with a more suitable design of flamboyant mouchettes above three lancets, in 1882 (Fig. 16.6).[82] These only lasted until Kelly began to excavate the jambs of the east window in 1931.[83] Although the south jamb had been damaged by the timber muses, he found enough evidence to reconstruct the medieval tracery in the east window and the two adjacent windows were altered to correspond (Fig. 16.8).[84] The tracery of the Robertson Smith Memorial window (north side, first bay from the east) was reconstructed by Marshall Mackenzie in 1896 (Col. Pl. XIII).[85]

THE LIBRARY EPISODE

The library, jewel house, charter room and vestry were originally situated abutting the south wall of the chapel, hence the high level rectangular windows on the south side. This extension was completed by Bishop Stewart[86] and is illustrated with its flat lead roof in James Gordon's drawing of 1660 (Fig. 4.6). The block was completely rebuilt in 1725–26, with class rooms on the ground floor and library above, due to the generosity of an old alumnus, Dr Fraser.[87] However, this library was soon too small and poorly maintained. Elaborate plans were made to create a domed neo-classical western library range, stretching out from the quad almost to the line of the High Street.[88] This scheme, apparently designed by James Byres, involved reducing the chapel tower to two stories and refacing the south wall of the chapel to match the arcaded loggia on the opposite side of the quad. The chapel itself would remain as a 'common hall to hear prayers'. As a result of the 'kind suggestion of a visiting professor from a neighbouring university' this drastic and ambitious scheme was scrapped.[89] Further proposals for improving accommodation in the west range showed more consideration for the exterior of the chapel. By 1773, it was decided to convert the west end of the chapel into a library. John Adam's design of that year involved duplicating the west façade of the church on the south side of the tower (Fig. 16.9).[90] Inside the chapel, his proposed library conversion of the west end illustrates a cosy Georgian fireplace and therefore presumably a chimney across the entrance to the rood screen.[91] However, in the end, parsimony prevailed and the university decided to use the stone from Fraser's library to build more manses, and to simply shift the library into the west end of the chapel, installing a gallery, staircase and wall-to-wall presses, sign posted with latin and greek titles painted in gold (Fig. 16.10).[92]

Macpherson claims his parents recalled Fraser's library being burnt down, with the books only being saved by 'throwing them into the nave of the chapel' which was then 'neglected and disused'.[93] There seems to be no record of this fire; on the contrary, the move was systematically and carefully carried out, with the chapel well prepared to receive the books.[94] Thereafter, the south side of the chapel was faced in granite (Col. Pl. V). The coats of arms previously found on the walls of the library were shifted to the new south wall of the church.[95] Eventually, after forty years in which the south side of the chapel was unencumbered, John Smith designed the new wing which abuts the south side of the tower, forming the entrance to the quad, in 1824.[96]

THE GEDDES-ANDERSON RESTORATION OF 1891

The removal of the library in 1870 at last released the entire chapel for ecclesiastical use, but it took time and careful planning to raise funds and conduct the preliminary research. The principal Dr Peter Colin Campbell arranged for H.M. Office of Works to take responsibility for repairs to the chapel in the 1870s, when the building, at last, could be reviewed as a whole.[97] At this stage, in 1873, the stalls were moved one bay westward. The west end of the ceiling was restored, following the warning by Billings of its serious decay in 1845.[98] The first true and accurate survey of the building was produced by James Cromar Watt in 1884 (Figs 4.1, 4.3–5, 16.1). His prize-winning drawings were published by *The Builder* in 1885.[99] They provided the detailed structural understanding required for subsequent work.

The building was now in sound condition and ready for its transformation to high Victorian taste. Thanks to the historical awareness of Principal William Geddes and sensitivity of the architect Rowand Anderson, the surviving fabric was treated with utmost respect.

Fig. 16.9. Proposed west façade of the college, by John Adam, 1773. AUL K525 H (Copyright: University of Aberdeen)

Fig. 16.10. The west end of the chapel, in use as a library, in 1845, by R. W. Billings (Copyright: University of Aberdeen)

Public support for improvements initially came from the desire to install a decent organ in 1886. As funds rolled in, a more extensive programme became feasible. Norman Macpherson was asked by the principal to record family memories about the college, passed down through three generations, much of which he was able to corroborate through the archives.[100] The new scheme respected and enhanced Bishop Forbes's arrangements in the apse since the chapel was still used for academic functions. The step was restored to the chancel. Panelling and fifteen professorial stalls for the senatus were added at the east end, to blend with Bishop Forbes' desk (Fig. 16.6).[101] Thanks to the detective work of Macpherson, the loft and canopies over the screen were reinstated (Fig. 6.5).[102]

Dramatic but reversible innovations included laying a bright heraldic tile and stone floor throughout the chapel and painting the ceiling and walls.[103] Principal Geddes provided the inspiration behind the choice of heraldry on the floor, carved emblems on the stalls and edifying inscriptions all over the ceiling. He also approved of the painter Mr Powell of Lincoln who was allowed a 'much richer gamut of colour' for a scheme that was both 'effective and beautiful'. The large background panels on the ceiling were painted in red and green, 'subdued to ecclesiastical softness'.[104] The ashlar lines on the walls were obliterated, being replaced by dazzling flowers and decorative patterns on both the walls and ceiling (Fig. 6.5).

The Ecclesiological Society of Aberdeen was not entirely satisfied with the work. There was a complaint about allowing Bishop Forbes' chair to remain the focus of the east end; a suggestion that the blocked east window space be filled with mosaic because the Cromwell Tower allowed so little light to enter; and disappointment about the modern furniture which 'is of the meanest possible description and the seats are so uncomfortable as to positively deter the students from attending'.[105]

The Kelly Restoration of the 1930s

Dr William Kelly was responsible for the last campaign of alterations to the chapel.[106] He opened up and restored the east window in 1932, picking his way through masonry fragments in the jambs, to arrive at what he considered to be the original design (Fig. 16.8). As a consequence Bishop Forbes' seat was moved to the south side of the chapel. The professors' stalls around the apse were moved westwards to flank the north and south walls[107] and the minister's desk, reader's desk and lectern installed. Bishop Stewart's pulpit was restored.[108] Kelly designed the two south doors with their bronze handles in 1932.[109] The bright floor tiles and roof painting were judiciously removed.[110] Kelly transformed what was little more than a lobby west of the rood screen into the University War Memorial, dedicated in 1928. Its dignified oak panels with heraldic and symbolic decoration are carved with the names of the fallen.[111] The space, originally part of the medieval nave, became the ante-chapel. Kelly's longer term ambitions were to reinstate the embattled parapet around the chapel and convert the slate roof to its original lead.[112]

During this phase, Henry Wilson's monument for Bishop Elphinstone finally arrived in Aberdeen, much larger than the commissioning committee had intended.[113]

A mock up of it was tried on the site of the original tomb in 1928 (Fig. 16.6), but it was then installed in the ante-chapel where it remained until 1947 when it was removed to its present position outside the west door. Kelly meanwhile inserted the bronze lettering on the tombs of both Elphinstone and Hector Boece.[114]

Ther have been no major alterations since the 1930s. Strenuous maintenance has continued on the tower and roof, new lighting and moveable chairs have been installed throughout. The long term threat to the building now is the delicate condition of the exterior sandstone which requires continuous monitoring and periodic replacement. This is particularly sensitive in areas where the stone is carved: the consecration crosses on the north side, the dedication inscription and the oldest heraldic panels on the west front.

Notes

[1] I would like to thank Charles Burnett, Richard Fawcett and Colin McLaren who have contributed generously to this research. Orem, 1791, 173.

[2] David Stephenson points out that the exact order of events is not clear (*King's College, Aberdeen, 1560–1641: From Protestant Reformation to Covenanting Revolution*, Aberdeen, 1990, 8, 13–14, 127 nn. 5–6). According to Thomas Middleton, a mob of reformers came up from the Mearns, looted the Black and Grey Friars churches in the town, proceeded to St Machar's where they destroyed the ornaments and jewels, and removed the roof lead and bells in December 1559 or early 1560 (*An appendix to the history of the Church of Scotland . . . with the foundation of the universities and colledges*, London, 1677, 9). However, a specific task force to remove lead and bells from the cathedral was sent by the Earl of Moray in 1568 (*Register of the Privy Council of Scotland*, 38 vols, Edinburgh, 1877–1970, 1545–69, 608–09). This team would have been better equipped than the earlier mob, for the heavy lifting required. A. Strachan, *Panegyricus inauguralis*, 1631, 27) and Middleton (1677, 25 (follows printed page 38)) merely state that Anderson repelled reformers or plunderers who wanted to take the college lead and bells. It is only John Kerr in 1725 (*Donaides*, Edinburgh, 17) who says the Mearns mob of 1559 attacked the lead and bells of both cathedral and college, as if it were single incident.

[3] See p. 165.

[4] See pp. 115–31.

[5] J. Gordon, *History of Scots affairs from MDCXXXVII to MDCXLI*, J. Robertson and G.Grub (eds), Aberdeen, Spalding Club, 1841, III, 218.

[6] J. Spalding, *Memorialls of the trubles in Scotland and England A.D. 1624–A.D. 1625*, Spalding Club, Aberdeen, 1850–51, I, 124.

[7] See Chapter 13.

[8] *Fasti*, Royal Visitation 1619, 276.

[9] *Fasti*, Visitation 1623, 282–83. The survey which produced this evidence was carried out on 13 June 1620. *Fasti*, 281.

[10] *Fasti*, Representation to the King, 1634, 309–10; Spalding, *Memorialls*, I, 31.

[11] *Fasti*, Visitation 1634, 395; Spalding, *Memorialls*, I, 257.

[12] *Fasti*, 309; *Extracts from the Council Register of the Burgh of Aberdeen, 1625–42*, ed. C. Innes, Scottish Burgh Records Society, Edinburgh, 1871, 59, 29 May 1633; James Gordon, *Abredoniae Utriusque Descriptio: A description of both touns of Aberdeen*, ed. C. Innes, Spalding Club, Edinburgh, 1842, 23.

[13] Spalding, *Memorialls*, I, 31.

[14] Gordon, *Abredoniae*, 23.

[15] Middleton, 1677, 25.

[16] Boece, 95. '*Habet campanile, immensa altitudine sublatum, cui lapideus arcus instar imperialis diadematis, mira arte fabrefactus, plumbeam supra tectoram adhibetur*'.

[17] *Fasti*, 309–10.

[18] Spalding, in 1640, referring the the death of Doctor Gordon, medicinar, who rebuilt the steeple. (*Memorialls*, I, 257).

[19] Kelly, 1949, 47.

[20] For instance, James III's silver groat of 1484–88, James V's silver groat of 1526–39, in Seaby's Standard Catalogue of British Coins, part 4, *Coins and tokens of Scotland*, compiled by P. F. Purvey, London, 1972,

48, 55. A recent survey of imperial crown iconographs is in R. A. Mason, 'This Realm of Scotland is an Empire?' in *Church, Chronicle and Learning*, ed. B. Crawford. Edinburgh, 1999, chapter 4.

[21] Vienna, Österreichische Nationalbibliothek, Codex Vindobonensis 1897, fol. 24ᵛ. Facsimile with a commentary by F. Unterkircher, *Das Gebetbuch Jakobs IV von Schottland un seiner Gemahlin Margaret Tudor*, Codices Selecti 85, Graz, 1987.

[22] C. J. Burnett and C. J. Tabraham, *The Honours of Scotland*, 1993; J. Skelton and W. H. St John Hope, *The Royal House of Stuart*, London, 1890, 3. On the ceiling of St Machar's Cathedral made around 1520, James V is represented heraldically by closed crown. David McRoberts, 'The Heraldic Ceiling of St Machar's Cathedral, Aberdeen', *Friends of St Machar's Cathedral*, Occasional Papers No. 2, 1981, 9–10.

[23] This arrangement is also depicted on the crown of Henry VII of England (1485–1509). J. H. and R. V. Pinches, *The Royal Heraldry of England*, London, 1974, xvi.

[24] David McRoberts, 'The Heraldic Ceiling of St Machar's Cathedral Aberdeen', *Friends of St Machar's Cathedral*, Occasional Papers No. 2, Aberdeen 1981, 1–12.

[25] The towers were built between 1528 and 1532. The imperial crowns perched on top of their conical roofs, illustrated by James Gordon of Rothemay in 1647, look as though they are made of iron or wood.

[26] See Chapter 4.

[27] Not a true cross patée as the arms appear to be more pleated than splayed.

[28] R. S. Walker, 'The Crown of King's', *AUR*, 30, 1942–44, 307–10.

[29] M. R. Holmes, 'The Crowns of England', *Archaeologia*, LXXXVI, 1937, 82–84 (73–90).

[30] Seaby's Standard Catalogue of British Coins, part 4, 1972, 63, no. 5424.

[31] Sir David Lindsay of the Mount's *Armorial*, 1542, ed. D. Laing, Edinburgh, 1878, 21.

[32] From a manuscript in the Society of Antiquaries of London, in Pinches, 1974, 175.

[33] Holmes, 1937, pl. XIX.

[34] The arms of the queens of James V and those of Charles I, Pinches 1974, 160, 174.

[35] *Fasti*, 410. This survey of 1638 reveals that only four years after the storm damage repair, the chapel roof was still defective: 'the haill soll of the bake batalling and sputtis of leid of the kirk be all lifted, of new casting and laid again'.

[36] AUL, MS K 269, a copy made in 1717 of the minute book 1634–69.

[37] Repairs to the masonry and lead, in 1669, 1665–66, 1672, 1686–87, 1688–89, 1690–91: AUL, MS K 37, fol. 19r; K 54/6, p. 5; K 54/10, p. 9; K 55/8, p. 23; K 55/9, p. 20; K 55/11, p. 19.

[38] Orem, 1791, 174.

[39] AUL, K 41, King's College Minutes, IV, 1716–22. On 25 August 1718 the king was petitioned to provide help 'for the low and sinking condition of this college and the ruinous condition of our fabric, particularly of the cupola' (fol. 28). On 14 October 1718 the masters received advice from Mr McGill architect about 'cuming (shuttering) the cupola of the steeple' (fol. 29). On 9 June 1719, the principal managed to obtain funds from the king for the repairs (fol. 36).

[40] For example: AUL, MS K 56/1, p. 17, K 56/2, p. 12, K 56/3, p. 13, K 278/9/21–3 for 1700–04; K 257/1/2/2, 257/1/2/13, 257/1/2/15, for 1715; K 57/16, p. 6, K 257/5/2/19 for 1737–38; K 58, p. 71, K 257/18/13,14, K 257/19/8/76 for 1755–56; K 58, p. 209, K 257/20/5/13, K 257/20/6/5 for 1765–66; K 60, p. 177 for 1776–77; K 61, p. 149 for 1783–84; K 61, p. 161 for 1789–90.

[41] AUL, MS K 60, p. 7; K 257/10/1; K 257/18/24.

[42] For example: AUL, MS K 257/19/7/49; K 257/20/3/6; K 257/20/6/2; K 257/20/9/9; K 257/20/11/3; K 61, p. 143.

[43] AUL, MS K 255, box 28, Procuration accounts instructions, 1712–13; K 56/13, fol. 13ʳ, K 257/1/2/2; K 257/1/2/13; K 257/1/2/15; K 57/8, p. 7; K 257/3/1/10; K 61, pp. 159, 161.

[44] AUL, MS K 48, fols 24ʳ, 56r; K 61, p. 167.

[45] AUL, MS U 399.

[46] J. Kelman, on tape recording, AUL, Interview no. 23(i), 3 April 1985. Side one.

[47] F. Douglas, *A General Description of the East Coast of Scotland, from Edinburgh to Cullen, including a brief account of the Universities of St Andrews and Aberdeen*, Paisley, 1782, 189–91.

[48] Report by George Pyper, wright and plumber, 15 June, 1638. *Fasti*, 410.

[49] *Fasti*, 153.

[50] *Fasti*, 410. See above, note 48.

[51] AUL, MS 2379/1/10/2, p. 2.

[52] *Fasti*, 602.

[53] P. J. Anderson, 'Note on the heraldic representations at King's College, Old Aberdeen', *Proceedings of the Society of Antiquaries of Scotland*, XXIII, 1888–89, 85.

[54] *Fasti*, lix; Macpherson, 1889, 31.

[55] Kelly, 1949, 74. The W S inscription is on the bottom of the north-east panel.

[56] *Fasti*, 600, 601, 602, 608. On the south side of the steeple is an inscribed plaque, 'J. Blaikie & Son plumbers Aberdeen 1832'.

[57] See Chapter 17. Described by Orem in 1724: 'the bishop's seat or pulpit is in the east end thereof wher the altar stood formerly, with the presbytery desks on every side thereof'. Orem, 1791, 173. W. Kennedy, *Annals of Aberdeen from the reign of William the Lion to the end of the year 1818, with an account of the city, Cathedral, and University of Old Aberdeen*, London, 1818, II, 397, mentions the presbytery inscriptions.

[58] Douglas, 1782, 155.

[59] AUL, MS K 138. *Notes on the history of King's College*, Christie. Minutes of 11 September 1821.

[60] AUL, MS U 201. King's College Chapel Improvement Scheme, Minute Book 1889–93. Rowand Anderson, Report on the fabric, 19 July 1889.

[61] See Chapter 14.

[62] AUL, MS U 201. King's College Chapel Improvement Scheme, Minute Book 1889–93. The seating before the 1891 improvements can be seen in Eeles, 1956, pl. 1. The pulpit was moved one bay further east in 1891.

[63] Fig. 16.6. W. Geddes, 'Notes on the restoration of King's College Chapel, 1891', *Transactions of the Aberdeen Ecclesiological Society*, 6th year, 1891 (1892), II, 62.

[64] Macpherson, 1889, 34.

[65] Macpherson, 1889, 28. See Chapter 19.

[66] See Chapter 11. W. R. H. Duncan, 'The Restoration from 1867 to 1975', in *The Restoration of St Machar's Cathedral*, J. H. Alexander *et al.*, Aberdeen, 1991, 3; Macpherson, 1889, 30.

[67] AUL, MS U 201, Rowand Anderson's report on the fabric, 19 July 1889. Fifteen professorial stalls were made to go around the apse. The cresting above the stalls depicted the attributes of the seven virtues, twice: the scales for justice; a thistle for courage; compasses for prudence; a victory wreath for faith; an anchor for hope; a flaming heart for love; and alpha-omega for the last stall. Panels on the back of the stalls show Christological emblems: a lily; palm; rose; trefoil; vine; olive; wheat; and pot of lilies. W. Geddes, 'Notes on the restoration of King's College Chapel, 1891', *Trans. Aberdeen Ecclesiological Society*, 1890–93, II, 66, 72.

[68] Eeles, 1956, pl. 2.

[69] AUL, U 662, Aberdeen University Court, Edilis Committee 1936–38, 27 January 1932.

[70] Kelly, 1949, 64.

[71] Kelly, 1949, 61–62. In the centre of the slab is the Udny armorial shield; around the cardinal points of the shield are the letters 'MPVS', Magister Petrus Udneus Subprimarius. Above, in Latin, is the inscription 'Safe I lie down again weary of the wicked world. And I have learnt and I have taught the wounds of Christ'. Below the shield, in Greek, 'all glory to God'. Around the rim is a partially obliterated inscription in Latin, 'Dominus Petrus Udnevs, vir undequaque humanissimus [inclytae hu]ius Academiae olim sub-primarius fatis cessit 24 Aprilis, AD 1601'. W. Geddes, 'Notes on the restoration of King's College Chapel, 1891', *Trans. Aberdeen Ecclesiological Society*, 1890–93, II, 66; P. J. Anderson, 'Notes on heraldic representations at King's College, Old Aberdeen', *PSAS*, XXIII, 1888–89, 84–85.

[72] Eeles, 1956, 75.

[73] *Fasti*, Visitation of 1623, 282; Survey of 1620, *Fasti*, 281.

[74] Orem, 1791, 183. AUL, MS K 269 describes the leading of the timber muses in 1668–69. An account of the New Work is in C. A. McLaren, 'New Work and Old: Building at the Colleges in the seventeenth century', *AUR*, LIII, 1989–90, 208–17.

[75] In 1821 the executors of the Murray Trust began to pay for repairs to the chapel, making it ready for services in 1824. AUL, MS K 98. Kelly, 1949, 60.

[76] Orem, 1791, 191; Macpherson, 1889, 28; Kelly, 1949, 59. In the 1889 scheme, it was proposed to move Scougal's mort back to the north side of the apse. AUL, MS U 201. King's College Chapel Improvement Scheme, p. 7.

[77] Orem, 1791, 173.

[78] Macpherson, 1889, 11. This arrangement is sketched in Macpherson's reconstruction drawing of the nave as a library, pl. LXIII.

[79] AUL, MS K 138. *Notes on the history of King's College*, Christie. Minutes of 11 September 1821.

[80] Macpherson, 1889, 11.

[81] See Chapter 23.

[82] AUL, U 399. Letter including the design, from W. Robertson to Office of Works, 27 April 1882. AUL, A 5/26, drawings of tracery, 1882.

[83] Minutes of the University Court, X, 15 January 1924–10 July 1928, Aberdeen, 1931, 416. Edilis Committee Report, 18 January 1927: the east window to be opened up and filled with sheet glass until the stained glass commission by Douglas Strachan was ready. This window was to be dedicated to the memory of Professor Harrower and was part of the same embellishment campaign as the Founder's Tomb.

[84] Kelly, 1949, 60, 66, 67. AUL, A 5/19, A 6/21, Kelly's east window drawings.

[85] AUL, U 622, Aberdeen University Court, Edilis Committee, 1890–96, 2 September 1896.

[86] Orem, 1791, 183.

[87] AUL, MS K 42, fols 21^r, 21^v, 22^v. The eighteenth- and nineteenth-century schemes are discussed in detail in D. M. Walker, 'The Rebuilding of King's and Marischal Colleges, 1723–1889', *AUR*, 1993, LV, 2, No. 190, 123–45. J. R. Pickard, *History of King's College Library, Aberdeen, until 1860*, 4 vols, Aberdeen, 1987, III, 119, 124–25.

[88] AUL, K 252 A-D.

[89] AUL, MS K 47, p. 181.

[90] AUL, K 252 H.

[91] AUL, K 252 I.

[92] Pickard, 1987, III, 242–43; citing AUL, New Charter Chest, Sh. 21, No. 39, *Receipts for reparation of the Library and Schools, 1773–1774*, now AUL MS K 257/21 and /39.

[93] Macpherson, 1889, 23–24. Pickard ponts out that there is no evidence for the fire, apart from reports of stuffy chimneys in Fraser's library. Pickard, III, 236, 242–43.

[94] AUL, MS K 47, Minutes XII, 1770–89, pp. 181–82; AUL, New Charter Chest, Sh. 21, No. 39; cited in Picard, 1982, III, 236, 242–43.

[95] Macpherson, 1889, 23; the coats of arms were gilded and painted by John Norrie, 16 December 1773: AUL, New Charter Chest, Sh. 21, No. 39.

[96] Walker, 1993, 131–32. AUL, MS K 50, p. 128, 237.

[97] Macpherson, 1889, 30–31. This explains why there is a detailed plan of the chapel by the Office of Works from 1882 (AUL, A 5/14), and why the ambo was temporarily removed to the Scottish parliament house cellar in Edinburgh.

[98] R. W. Billings, *The Baronial and Ecclesiastical Antiquities of Scotland*, Edinburgh, 1845–52, I, 2.

[99] Original drawings: AUL, A 5/1 elevations, 106; A 5/2 west elevation 108; A 5/3 tower 107; A 5/4 choir stall canopies 109; A 5/5 doors of choir 110; A 5/6 plan 105. RIBA Silver medal competition, 1885, medal of merit and premium awarded, *The Builder*, 6 June 1885. The preliminary drawings for this project are at the Royal Institiute for British Architects, London, listed under James Cromer Watt (*sic*), made in 1884. The documents are Y6/56/1–43. I would like to thank Rosemary Mackay for this reference.

[100] Macpherson, 1889, 3.

[101] W. Geddes, 'Notes on the restoration of King's College Chapel, 1891', *Trans. Aberdeen Ecclesiological Society*, 1890–93, II, 74–75.

[102] AUL, MS U 201. King's College Chapel Improvement Scheme, p. 7. See Chapter 6.

[103] Relaying the floor with a damp proof membrane entailed lifting the entire choir stalls for the second time, and treating them for rot. Ecclesiological Notes, *Trans. Ecclesiological Society of Aberdeen*, 5th year, 1890 (1891), 63. The floor had been previously 'pathmented' [paved] around 1740, AUL, MS K 57/18, p. 6, K 257/5/4/26–8.

[104] Geddes, 1890–93, 66–68, 74–75. The shields on the floor tiles referred to pre-Reformation personae: St Margaret, James IV, Margaret Tudor, Elphinstone, Dunbar, William Stewart, J. Leslie, Boece, R. Maitland.

[105] *Trans. of the Aberdeen Ecclesiological Society*, 4th year, 1889 (1890), 73.

[106] Summarized by W. D. Simpson, 'Memoir of Dr Kelly', in Kelly, 1949, 10–11.

[107] AUL, U662, Aberdeen University Court Edilis Committee. Stalls to be moved, 27 January 1932.

[108] See Chapter 11.

[109] AUL, U 662, Aberdeen University Court Edilis Committee. Stalls to be moved, 28 November 1932. The previous south-east door was an elaborately carved medieval survivor, rescued from St Machar's Cathedral. Macpherson, 1889, 27.

[110] AUL, A5 /50/15, 10 May 1932.

[111] See Chapter 22.

[112] On his restoration of the north-east buttress, Kelly has inserted the springers for the eventual replacement of the parapet. Kelly, 1949, 11.

[113] See Chapter 24.

[114] W. D. Simpson, 'The Founder's Memorial', *AUR*, July 1931, XVIII, no. 54, 214.

CHAPTER SEVENTEEN

THE DESK OF BISHOP PATRICK FORBES

By Charles J. Burnett Esq., Ross Herald

The chronological range of woodwork in King's College Chapel is remarkable for its interest. A period of some four hundred years intervene between the creation of the choir stalls and the installation of the modern war memorial.[1] During this period the chapel underwent several changes of function. These changes in turn required new furniture and fittings, not all of which have survived.

A good example of furniture from the early middle period of the chapel's existence is the desk made for Bishop Forbes in 1627. This has not survived in its original location or form.[2] Originally the desk took centre place in the chapel, located where the high altar once stood in front of the central apsidal window (Fig. 17.1).[3] This had been blocked up. The desk was on a high plinth and appeared to be entered from either side. It was flanked by pews, each of which was painted. This setting was created by Bishop Forbes for meetings of the synod of his diocese, where each presbytery was identified by its name painted on the appropriate pew.

In 1823, when the chancel reverted to a place of worship, the desk was no longer appropriate. The canopied back was retained with a modern pulpit installed in front, in 1828. This is visible in Fig. 17.1. The front and lower back section of the bishop's desk were removed to the north side of the chapel to form a new seat. In 1844, when Bishop Stewart's pulpit arrived from the cathedral, it was lacking a base, so the desk section was installed under it — 'quite incongruous' according to Macpherson. By 1891, the panels were enclosing a box-like seat linked to the base of the pulpit.[4] Although Macpherson illustrates the desk as a complete piece of furniture in 1889 (Fig. 17.2), this must be a proposed reconstruction because he pleads for the various pieces of the desk to be united in 1889, and they are clearly still apart in the pre-1891 photo. The assembly must have taken place after this date. In 1931 the central apsidal window of the chapel was opened up and restored, whereupon the opportunity taken to remove Bishop Forbes's desk and place it in storage.[5]

Sometime after the end of the Second World War, the desk was brought back in to the chapel and set against the south wall adjacent to the south-east door. It was given a new plinth, 15cm high, along with a new oak front, side and seat. The oak front, incorporating the three old panels, was given a top rail with denticulated moulding; a side unit on the east was made with two panels copied from the old front panels; and the supporting side of the new seat incorporated an old panel (Fig. 17.3).[6]

The high back consists of nine old panels and three new panels behind the seat. It terminates in a hanging canopy, 38cm deep, which is divided by four balusters at the

Fig. 17.1.   The east end
of the chapel after 1823
(From Kelly, 1949)

front to form a larger central panel flanked by four smaller panels carved with
foliacious relief decoration. There are two matching panels on either side of the
canopy. The upper part of the larger central panel suffers from some loss of carving as
have the flanking and side panels. The junction between vertical back and curving-
out canopy has an elaborately carved moulding which appears to be held in place
with nine wrought iron nails.

The canopy central panel is carved with an inscription in Greek which reads in
translation: SALVATION TO OUR GOD AND TO THE LAMB. APOCALYPSE,
7.10 (Fig. 17.4). On either side of the inscription is a right and left hand holding a
bough of laurel which has been torn out by the root and above is a flattened oval ring.
The meaning of this symbolism adjacent to a specific quotation from the Bible is
unclear.

The nine old panels which form the back of the stall are arranged in three groups
of three, each group different in design from the other. The lower panels are
decorated with relief-carved rectangles with straight sides and double-curved tops and

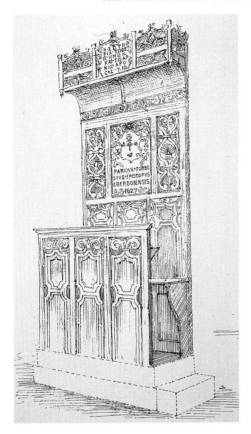

Fig. 17.2. Reconstruction of Bishop Forbes' desk by N. Macpherson, 1889

bottoms. Each rectangle contains a plain elongated oval (Fig. 17.5, the panel incorporated in the desk seat support is the same).

The middle panels are more elaborately carved with curved and straight lines which terminate abruptly at the foot of each panel as though each had been cut from a taller panel to provide the required height (Fig. 17.7).

The upper three panels are both taller and carved differently from those below (Fig. 17.7). There is a central large panel flanked by two narrow panels. The central panel is carved with the shape of a multi-curved shield surmounted by a mullet which has foliacious carving on either side in the manner of heraldic mantling. At the foot of the panel is the date 1627 flanked by two scrolls. The space between shield and date carries the faint outlines of a former inscription now planed off: PATRICUIS.-FORBE/SIUS.EPISCOPUS/ABERDONENSIS. This may have been removed in 1828 when the desk was converted for use by a preacher and seems a remarkable piece of university vandalism.

The only painted decoration on the desk is the Arms of Bishop Forbes contained within the multi-curved shield. The original paint has faded and darkened with age but still discernible is a cross paty fitched between three bear heads muzzled,

Fig. 17.3.   Bishop Forbes' desk, 1999

Fig. 17.4.   Bishop Forbes' desk: the canopy front with Greek inscription

Fig. 17.5.   Bishop Forbes' desk: the lower row of panelling

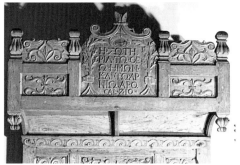

surmounted by a mitre. Traces of paint can be seen all over the central panel and on the other five upper panels which leads to the conclusion the desk had originally been painted overall. This fits in with the fact that the former named presbytery pews of *c*. 1627 were also painted.

Final evidence of the desk's alterations and changes is the distinctive break line which separates the lower six panels from the upper six. The latter, plus the canopy, are finer work and set in stiles with moulded inner edges. Old and replacement oak are all of pegged construction.

Of the twenty original carved panels making up Bishop Forbes's desk, ten have shallow, very stylized, three-line decoration in a debased Mannerist style. The remaining ten panels located on the upper half of the desk, including the Greek inscription and the armorial panels, have linear relief decoration in quite a different style. They appear to be the work of another hand.

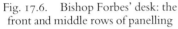

Fig. 17.6.   Bishop Forbes' desk: the
front and middle rows of panelling

Fig. 17.7.   Bishop Forbes' desk: the painted
arms and inscription of 1627

This is not surprising as Aberdeen had a group of post-medieval wood carvers and furniture makers which has been described as 'a school of wood carvers [flourishing] from the middle of the sixteenth to the last quarter of the seventeenth century'.[7] A characteristic of the school is the production of panels, carved in a debased Mannerist style, either employed as wall covering or incorporated in the construction of furniture. The group of twenty chairs held at Trinity Hall, the headquarters of the Aberdeen Incorporated Trades, are well known and have been described in print.[8] Of these, twelve are decorated with carved motifs typical of the Aberdeen school. Throughout the north-east there are other examples which can be ascribed to this group of associated craftsmen. At Crathes Castle, seat of the Burnetts of Leys, there is an oak bed with heraldic tester, dated 1594, commissioned by Sir Alexander Burnett of Leys and his wife Katherine Gordon; there is a bench in St Nicholas' Kirk, Aberdeen dated 1607 with characteristic carving of the school (Fig. 17.8); there is a canopied oak dresser of 1613;[9] we have the bishop's desk in the chapel; St Nicholas' Kirk possesses another bench made in 1677 (Fig. 17.9); a group of one hundred and four panels in St Mary's Aisle below the east Kirk of St Nicholas dating from 1606 to c. 1700;[10] four panels incorporated in the modern oak choir pews of East St Nicholas' Kirk (Fig. 17.10), and within the Elders' stalls in the apse of the same kirk, and finally another large group of surviving panels in Greyfriars' Kirk, Aberdeen, contain thirteen panels exhibiting the decorative style of the Aberdeen school (Fig. 17.11).

This large surviving group of carved work has not been fully appreciated, or described in detail, by recent scholars with the exception of Learmont who restricted his study to the Trinity Hall chairs. Further study may throw light on source material

Fig. 17.8.   Bench from St Nicholas'
Kirk, Aberdeen, 1607 (Photo:
Scottish Domestic Architecture, 1922,
pl. 96)

Fig. 17.9.   Bench from St Nicholas'
Kirk, Aberdeen, 1677 (Photo: *Scottish
Domestic Architecture*, 1922, pl. 96)

for the elaborate designs which in several instances employ elaborate curves, fleurs-de-lis, ermine spots, and grotesque animal heads, some bird-like, others elephantine in appearance.[11]

A superficial overall inspection places the episcopal desk of Patrick Forbes within this corpus of work. There can be no doubt the desk was made in Aberdeen, and constructed from standard carved panels, apart from the armorial panel and Greek inscription panels which were 'one-offs'. For example, four panels in East St Nicholas' Kirk are all around 66.5 x 42cm, as are four panels in Greyfriars' Kirk; six panels of Bishop Forbes's stall are 42 x 28cm; four panels in the St Nicholas' Kirk bench of 1677 are 49 x 24cm. Although not exactly the same size there is a consistency. Panels in Greyfriars' and St Nicholas' Kirks range from 37 x 26cm to 67 x 42cm. None is as tall as the three panels at the desk front belonging to Bishop Forbes, i.e. 81.5 x 27.5cm.

The canopy with inscription and square balusters on the bishop's desk has precedents. Another example, carved twenty-nine years before in 1598, was located in Parton Kirk, Kircudbright. The carved canopy proclaims FEIR THE LORD AND HONOUR HIS HOUS.[12] The oak dresser of 1613, already mentioned, has a canopy which overhangs a greater distance.

This prolific school of seventeenth-century wood carvers was producing ranges of fairly standard panels which could be adapted for desks, beds, dressers, wall covering and doors. It also had access to a range of more exotic and fashionable pattern books for specially commissioned work. The design and range of products may be compared both with those of James Fendour and his team, working a hundred years earlier, which supplied gothic panels for stalls, canopies, seats and ceilings at St Nicholas', St

Fig. 17.10. Two panels from the choir pews, St Nicholas' Kirk, Aberdeen (Photo: William Bailey)

Fig. 17.11. Two panels from the apse of Greyfriars' Kirk, Aberdeen (Photo: William Bailey)

Machar's and King's, and the workshop which produced panels for the pulpit and Master of Hospital's chair. All these testify to the high standard of native craftsmanship to be found in Aberdeen.

Although the desk of Bishop Forbes does not have the visual impact of the chapel choir stalls, nevertheless it is a very fine unique example of a specialist piece of furniture made in Aberdeen during the first half of the seventeenth century.

Notes

[1] See Chapters 6 and 22.

[2] Macpherson, 1889, 20, 21, 30.

[3] Illustration of the chapel after 1823, from Kelly, 1949, fig. 27.

[4] Macpherson, 1889, 21, 30. Photo before 1891 in Eeles, 1956, pl. 1. Rowand Anderson proposed the reconstruction in 1889: Rowand Anderson's *Report on the Fabric, 19 July, 1889*, in AUL, MS U 201.

[5] Kelly, 1949, 64.

[6] The overall dimensions of the desk are now, height 308cm, width 122cm, depth (front panel to back panel) 92cm.

[7] D. Learmont, 'The Trinity Hall Chairs, Aberdeen', *Furniture History*, 1978, No. 14, 1–8.

[8] Learmont, 1978, 1–8.

[9] In Invery House, Banchory, in 1922, see pl. 102, *Details of Scottish Domestic Architecture*, The Edinburgh Architectural Association, 1922.

[10] A. M. Munro, 'The Monumental Inscriptions, and Carved Woodwork, in St Mary's Chapel, Aberdeen', *Transactions of the Scottish Ecclesiogical Society*, 1905–06, 301–14. An architect involved with the restoration of this chapel in 1898 was Dr William Kelly who was largely instrumental in creating King's College Chapel as we know it today: Kelly, 1949, 6.

[11] Printed pattern books, produced in northern Europe, such as *Architectura* by W. Dietterlin, Nuremberg, 1598, and *Perspective*, by J. Vredeman de Vries, Leiden, 1604, are two possible sources for the more exotic details in Aberdeen school carving.

[12] Now exhibited in the new Museum of Scotland, Edinburgh, accession number, NMS H.KL.2.

CHAPTER EIGHTEEN

THE SUNDIAL

By John S. Reid

The King's Chapel sundial looks down on sacrist, student, professor and tourist alike as they hasten across the quadrangle, or tarry awhile in conversation or reflection (Fig. 18.1, Col. Pl. V). It is so centrally placed and so quietly appropriate that many who notice it perched 9.5 metres above the terrace beside the south chapel wall can be excused for thinking that it has been there from the beginning.[1] It is tempting to speculate that it was commissioned as the master dial that kept the college bells right with the sun and right with the world; that it had, perhaps, additional symbolic relevance: *tempus fugit* and we should use our allotted span wisely.

There can be a real danger of associating historical survival with significance. No documentary or pictorial evidence has been found that supports any functional interpretation of the origin of the King's dial. Indeed, the records are conspicuous in their silence on the topic, even on matters of routine maintenance. This lack of evidence is consistent with the plain idea that the dial has been erected as a simple architectural ornament. Ornaments carry with them their own story and the dial certainly deserves a second look by all who pass through the quadrangle.

The King's dial is a square sandstone slab, 0.6 metres (2ft) on each side, mounted close to the top of the widest of the chapel buttresses facing the quadrangle.[2] Its location is shown clearly on James C. Watt's architectural drawing of 1885 (Fig. 4.4). The dial has been designed as a south-facing wall dial, within reasonable error.[3] Measurement shows that the line of the buttresses faces some 5° East of South. The dial is marked with hour lines from six a.m. to six p.m.,[4] the hours being shown with arabic numerals. Most of these are somewhat unusually sloped to lie along the hour lines, in the manner of roman numerals on many long-case clock faces. The quarter-hours are shown by shorter sub-divisions. These broadly marked, gold painted, lines give the face a rather cluttered appearance from the ground. The gold paint hides the weathered lines of the original dial carving.[5]

Time is read anti-clockwise around the face, the time being marked by where the shadow of the top, sloping edge of the gnomon falls. (All sundials have a gnomon, whose shadow marks the time.) The shadow edge is hard to see against the dark base, not only because the dial is high off the ground but also because the gnomon's heavily pierced design allows bright light into the shadow region. If this feature were original, it would be further circumstantial evidence that the dial is mainly decorative. The height is the greatest available in order that the winter sun can reach the dial over the roof on the opposite side of the quadrangle, which it does for some hours every day

Fig. 18.1.   The sundial

even in December. (The taller mid-nineteenth-century buildings that now form the remainder of the present quadrangle, the Cromwell Tower excepted, post-date the sundial.)

Sundials have an ancient origin, traceable to Babylonian civilization. The Old Testament books of 2 Kings and Isaiah both include the same oblique reference to a sundial.[6] The ancient dials, though, differed from the 'modern' dial on the chapel wall. In so much as dividing the day into hours was important in earlier times, the ancient dials embodied division of daylight into 'temporary' hours, twelve of which filled the time between sunrise and sunset, whatever the season of the year. This practice was carried into the Christian era and it was not uncommon, for example, for Anglo-Saxon churches to include wall dials so marked.

From the thirteenth century onwards, the advent of mechanical tower clocks publicly displaying time highlighted the difference between the variable length of temporary hours during the year.[7] This difference becomes more conspicuous the further north one goes. The anonymous response to this public mechanization of time was the design of a dial that showed equal length hours for all seasons. The 'secret', which is at the heart of all modern dials, is to incline the gnomon so that it is oriented parallel to the earth's axis. As the sun changes its altitude with the seasons at a given time of the day, the shadow edge moves parallel to itself. It therefore shortens and lengthens but does not change its angle on the dial. The face can therefore be marked out in hours of equal intervals.

The sundials with which we are all familiar are therefore comparatively 'modern', with the roots of their design in the anonymous fifteenth-century inspiration of the inclined gnomon. The first book in English on modern dialling was printed about one hundred years after the foundation of King's.[8] No such dials earlier than the sixteenth century are known in Britain. Notwithstanding the absence of the south wall buttresses when King's Chapel was built (see, for example, Gordon's picture of the 1660s, Fig. 4.6), the history of sundialing mitigates against any association of the chapel dial with the early history of King's College. Besides, the foundation documents assign to the sacrist responsibility for maintaining the college clock, which struck the hours.[9] The mechanization of time reached King's before the modernization of sundials that is embodied in the chapel design.

Even the brilliant innovation of the inclined gnomon did not make the simple sundial into a really accurate instrument. There are good astronomical reasons why 'solar time', the time recorded by a dial, can vary by up to twenty minutes in some months of the year from the reading of an accurate watch. In winter and summer a dial is slow by a watch, in spring and autumn, fast. It is on this account that even the most carefully set sundial seems at times to show '1-ish' or '2-ish', lacking precision, like a clock with a missing hand. Setting a watch by a sundial is no guarantee that it will be 'on time'. There is inevitably some disappointment that the chapel dial is so high off the ground and a natural wish to have it closer so that it can be read more accurately. As far as reading the right time is concerned, the dial is not badly placed. On top of this, a wall dial serves a community, a horizontal dial, an individual.

The recent removal of rainwater guttering that hid some of the dial from the near half of the quadrangle has made the dial more visible than it has been for over half a century. When you look up, you will see a dial in plain style, its simplicity and materials reminiscent of the oldest dated vertical dials in Aberdeen, which are cut in to the projecting sandstone gables of 22–24 Upper Kirkgate. These are small declining dials dated 1694. The chapel dial is less sharp than the twin metal dials on Provost Skene's house, near Marischal College, that was completed in the second half of the seventeenth century, or the metal Townhouse dial originally erected in 1730.[10] Unfortunately, dating sundials by style is unreliable. Too few were erected for a 'style' to have much currency. Personal taste and purpose were almost all.

The most likely story, consistent with the sparse facts, is that the dial was erected in its present site as part of the decorative accompaniment to the granite cladding and buttressing of the south wall, following the demolition of the abutting library and sacristy in 1773.[11] The wide buttress top, which differs from that of all the other buttresses, is suitably designed to take the dial, which aesthetically balances the large heraldic shield of James IV lower down. The dial's workmanship, material and appearance are quite consistent with an earlier date, as indeed is the weathering that has in places almost obliterated the original subdivision lines. References as early as 1700–02 in the accounts to a dial or 'dyall' could refer to the college clock face, but they are suggestive that the sundial, like the shields below it, pre-dates the buttressing.[12] Time seems to have obliterated any record of its origin.[13] The dial should be enjoyed for what it is: a symbol of College rather than Chapel, an appropriate and simply presented architectural ornament that links scholarship with Nature in a way that everyone can appreciate.

Notes

[1] At the time of writing, even the British Sundial Society supposed the dial had been in its present position since the foundation. Their records follow the standard description in D. MacGibbon and T. Ross, *The Castellated and Domestic Architecture of Scotland from the Twelfth to Eighteenth Century*, 5 vols, Edinburgh, 1887–92, v, 358, which includes major errors.

[2] The dial slab has been squarely recessed into the granite buttress stonework.

[3] The gnomon is a comparatively modern replacement of thin sheet metal. Whether its design replicates earlier gnomons is not known but the angle of its inclination to the vertical is 29.5°, appropriate to a latitude of 60.5°, instead of the expected 33°.

[4] The chapel tower prevents the sun shining on the dial in the late afternoon.

[5] The sandstone has been black painted and subsequently covered in parts in a gunmetal grey, perhaps for the purpose of making the shadow more visible or for filling in some of the irregularities of the stone surface.

[6] 2 Kings 20.9–11; Isaiah 38.7–8.

[7] Clepsydra and sandglasses showed the effect in earlier times.

[8] Thomas Fale, *Horologiographia: the art of dialling*, printed by Thomas Orwin, London, 1593. AUL, Special Collections have editions of 1626 and 1627.

[9] Eeles, 1956, 179 quotes the duty of the sacrist in the foundation document and again, 221, in Bishop Elphinstone's second charter. The 1542 inventory more explicitly includes '*horologium magnum ferreum, cum malleo fereo ad horas signandas pondens*', and no sundial.

[10] MacGibbon and Ross, 1887–92, v, 366 describe the Town Hall dial. It can be seen in its nineteenth-century location in Union Street as a blackened metal plate with gold lettering and a pierced gnomon, roman numerals, fine subdivisions, and calendric lines.

[11] See Chapter 16.

[12] E.g. AUL, MS K 56, 1700–02, Part 4, Second Section, articulus secundus, refers in 1702 to 'colouring of the King's armes and dyall, £12'. As the King's arms were a stone plaque on the wall, this suggests that the dial was also a stone plaque, and not necessarily a clock face. AUL, MS K 257/6/6/34 refers to 'mending and fixing the Dial plate' in 1748. No picture showing the dial has been traced which is earlier than the nineteenth century, although there is some ambiguity in Gordon's illustration of the 1660s (Fig. 4.6). On the old library, the windows are all shown with cross-hatching, but the westernmost rectangle is shown as a solid, possibly an heraldic plaque or the dial. William Orem's extended description of King's College in 1725 makes no mention of a sundial (Orem, 1791, 172–92). In contrast, the 1771 description of St Machar's says 'It had a great clock and sundial in the time of the Popish Clergy' (Orem, 1791, 66).

[13] No unambiguous record has been found associating the sundial with the chapel prior to its present eighteenth-century location.

CHAPTER NINETEEN

KINGS FOR KING'S: THE OLD TESTAMENT PAINTINGS

By ELIZABETH BRACEGIRDLE

The five 'Black Paintings' that have hung largely unnoticed in King's College Chapel since the beginning of the nineteenth century are a remarkable survival.[1] By style they clearly belong to the mid-seventeenth century and to the tradition of the craftsmen painters who gave us the painted ceilings that are such an important feature of Scottish art in the late sixteenth and early seventeenth centuries. The ceilings are not sophisticated in execution, perhaps, but they are vivid and inventive. So are these paintings. But they are large in size, painted on canvas and so are quite unlike anything else that survives from the period. It is their dirt and discoloration that has given them their nickname of 'The Black Paintings'. They were hung so high in the chapel that in their darkened condition they were quite invisible till three of them were taken down for a conservation assessment.[2]

Very little is known about them. No documentation has yet been discovered which could explain the circumstances surrounding their origin. Professor Macpherson in 1889 recounts how the paintings were brought into the chapel in 1823, having previously hung in the vestibule to the old hall. The sacrist and janitor, 'John and Davie', rescued the paintings when they were removed from the vestibule, had them 'varnished by the village painter', and arranged their installation at night in the chapel over the stalls and over the west door.[3]

ICONOGRAPHY

Macpherson identified the subject matter of the paintings as five episodes from the Old Testament: *David and Goliath* (1 Samuel 17.39–51); *David and Abigail* (1 Samuel 25.14–41); *The Judgement of Solomon* (1 Kings 3.16–28); *Solomon and the Queen of Sheba* (1 Kings 10.1–13); *Jephthah and his Daughter* (Judges 11.29–39) (Col. Pls VI–VIII).[4] Macpherson's identifications make sense except in the case of the last named which seems more likely to be *The Entry of Saul and David into the Cities of Israel* described in 1 Samuel 18.6–7. Jephthah was indeed greeted by his daughter coming out of his house 'with timbrels and with dances' as is happening in the scene represented here, but as a consequence of this encounter, Jephthah was forced to sacrifice his only child as a burnt offering (Col. Pl. VIb). This subject is hard to explain if these paintings were in any way connected with celebration as seems likely from the arguments set out below. On the other hand 1 Samuel 18, describes the

CONSTRUCTION AND STYLE

Each of the King's paintings has a narrow decorative border, at the top edge and a wider border along the bottom. The upper borders use an acanthus motif.[11] The lower borders consist of fruit and flower swags, supported at points by nude figures though there are considerable variations in detail. The florid nature of the designs for the lower borders could suggest a date later rather than earlier in the seventeenth century, when such patterns became more fashionable.[12] The original support for all five paintings is canvas of 'a coarse plain weave'.[13] The canvases for *The Judgement*, *Solomon and the Queen of Sheba*, *The Entry of Saul and David* and *David and Goliath* are composed of three sections with horizontal seams, whereas the canvas for *David and Abigail* is composed in two vertical sections with a vertical seam approximately central, so that in this way *David and Abigail* differs from the other four.[14] The lower border of *David and Abigail* is a later addition.[15] The lower border of *David and Goliath* is part original and part replacement, the replacement being added obliquely. The later canvas is much finer in texture than the original.[16]

In *The Judgement* and *David and Abigail*, the original paint layers appear to have been thinly applied to a pinkish-brown ground.[17] In addition to this it is possible in some areas, for example around the hand of Saul, to see a painted red brown under drawing. Around some of the masonry details, for example the steps of Solomon's throne in *Solomon and the Queen of Sheba*, a fine black outline is visible. The original paint layers were necessarily thin in order to coat the coarse grain of the canvas. However some paint, for highlights in particular, is applied more thickly.

Overpainting carried out during an earlier restoration is seen in all five paintings.[18] The overpainting is associated with canvas inserts used to repair tears and with areas of infilling. These areas are significantly smoother than the original paint layers and are easily detectable. Dirt and discoloration of varnish make it difficult to see just how the artist or artists handled colour and light. Colours used include browns, creams, white, a red, pink, a yellow, a blue and a blue green. Colours in some of the flesh areas, faces in particular, are unusually bright, incorporating strong reds and pinks. This is particularly true of *Solomon and the Queen of Sheba*.

All five paintings, as far as can be seen, use a degree of chiaroscuro, with areas of deep shadow contrasting with highlighted areas, particularly on drapery, armour, tree leaves and flesh. In all five the light source is external and comes from the left. There is an occasional hint of subsidiary light sources, for instance a suggestion of reflected light along the jaw line of the Queen of Sheba. This technique can be see in the unicorns of the arms of Scotland in the birth room of James VI at Edinburgh Castle, painted by John Anderson of Aberdeen in 1617.[19] A shadow on the forehead of Saul created by his turban suggests quite a subtle understanding of light, although in other areas, for instance on the figure of David in *David and Goliath*, handling of light is much less sophisticated. Effective tonal modelling can be seen in some areas, for instance of the arms, hands and face of Saul, but not in others.

Poses and gestures of figures represent the artist's interpretation of the original pattern. In some cases these poses and gestures seem to be competently interpreted, exemplified by the two female figures in *The Judgement*. In other cases there are misunderstandings, demonstrated by the left arm of the executioner in *The Judgement* (Col. Pl. VIIb).

All the paintings make some attempt to create a sense of pictorial space and recession. *The Judgement* and *Solomon and the Queen of Sheba* both appear to use linear perspective by locating the episode on a tiled floor. In neither case do orthogonals meet at a single vanishing point: the vanishing points are approximate rather than precise. Aerial perspective is used to some degree in all the paintings. It is used most successfully in *Saul and David entering the cities of Israel*, *David and Abigail* and *Solomon and the Queen of Sheba*. The faces of the lions in *Solomon and the Queen of Sheba* have an expressive and rather comic effect. This appearance is quite commonly found among the Scottish decorative art that remains to us from the late sixteenth and early seventeenth centuries, for instance the pelican from the frieze in the Green Lady's Room at Crathes Castle (1602) and the animals among the foliage in the Arbour Room at Kinneil, Bo'ness. Nearer in date would be the unicorns from the arms of Scotland in the birth room of James VI in Edinburgh Castle (1617), which have similarly cheerful expressions.

Foliage is represented distinctively in all of the paintings. In each case highlighted leaves are painted against the green tree form in fan-shaped clumps using light dabs of paint. In *David and Goliath* this can only be seen in the foreground foliage and is hard to observe.

The uneven quality of the paintings indicates that more than one hand was involved in their creation. For instance facial features in *The Entry of Saul and David* are far more distinctively and subtly executed than those in *Solomon and the Queen of Sheba* (Col. Pls VIb, VIII). Handling of drapery in *The Judgement of Solomon* is more sophisticated than that in *Solomon and the Queen of Sheba* (Col. Pls VIIb, VIII). This might mean that they were produced at different times, or that a team of painters was drafted in because the pictures had to be produced quickly. There are also common features, such as representation of foliage in all the paintings using characteristic fan-shaped dabs of paint.

A thistle appears in the foreground of *David and Goliath*. The thistle had long been established as the national flower of Scotland and had indeed been used in a rather similar context in the altarpiece painted for the Scottish congregation at Elsinore in the late fifteenth century where it is clearly a declaration of Scottishness. The thistle, together with a harp, rose and fleur-de-lis is also found on the King's College silver mace, dated 1650.[20]

The Artist

There were a number of competent artists working in Aberdeen throughout the mid-seventeenth century. Painters at this time in Scotland belonged to a subdivision of the Incorporated Trade of Wrights and Masons. They had to go through the process of becoming a burgess in order to work as a painter.[21] A strong contender would be John Anderson, a highly regarded decorative artist (*fl.* 1599–1649).[22] George Jamesone

(1589/90–1644) could be considered, but the technical differences between Jamesone's known work and the King's paintings make this a very unlikely proposition.[23] There are other possibilities among Aberdeen craftsman burgesses, depending on which date is favoured, for example, Andrew Melville (1611–34), Andrew Strachan (fl. 1616–73) or Patrick Alexander (fl. 1666–70).[24] There is also evidence that artists moved around to work on different commissions. John Anderson came from Aberdeen and worked in Edinburgh; John Sawers the Younger worked in Edinburgh and Glasgow; the Englishman, Valentine Jenkin (fl. 1617–34) worked in Glasgow, Stirling and Falkland.[25] It is also possible that the paintings could have been produced elsewhere, say for the coronation in Edinburgh in 1633, and brought back to Aberdeen as left over 'party decorations'. There is a record dated 8 July 1633 of a payment made 'for carying of the kinges fyve pictures out of the abay [presumably Holyrood] to Leith'.[26] These five pictures are unknown but such an origin cannot be ruled out.[27] The 1633 decorations were in fact dominated by the humanist intellectual agenda of the Toun's College (later Edinburgh University; see below), while the King's College paintings, with their royal theme, are more appropriate for King's College itself.

KINGSHIP

The stories from the books of Samuel and Kings were an appropriate compliment to the Stuart kings seen as perpetuating the divinely ordained role of biblical figures such as David and Solomon. James himself was referred to as the British Solomon, an identity to which Charles I was heir. But stories of Biblical kings were also appropriate to celebrate the institution itself, King's College. The Stuart kings' own public imagery, such as that used in masques, was designed to provide a 'seamless tradition which linked the old authorities — biblical and imperial — with the new'.[28]

In addition to these biblical types, the antiquity and legitimacy of the Scottish kingship was celebrated on several occasions by portrait series of the monarchs of Scotland put up in their honour by their loyal subjects. James VI's lineage was demonstrated by the genealogy of the Kings of Scotland (possibly portraits or just names) erected as a decoration for his 1579 entry into Edinburgh.[29] For the coronation of Charles I in Edinburgh in 1633, 109 portraits of Scottish Kings were created by George Jamesone commissioned by the city;[30] these were copied by de Witt for Holyrood Palace, after the Restoration; and a few survivors of what might have been other such series exist at Marischal College, Aberdeen.[31]

THE OCCASION

There was a European custom to adorn streets and buildings lavishly for festivities associated with monarchy. Temporary mountains and triumphal arches were commonly constructed and major artists were often involved in the design and execution. Rubens was put in charge of designing a massive programme of civic decorations, including temporary triumphal arches, for the entry into Antwerp of the Cardinal-Infante of Austria in 1635.[32]

Edinburgh transformed its streets and gateways with painted architecture, scenery and allegories on numerous occasions. The entry of James VI in 1579 was particularly elaborate. All the inhabitants were instructed to hang 'tapestrie and ares works' [tapestry from Arras] on their forestairs. The west port 'presentit unto him the Wisdom of Solomon . . . that is to say King Solomon was representit with the twa women that contendit for the young chylde and the servant that presentit the sworde to the king with the chylde'. At the salt market, a genealogy of the Kings of Scotland was erected and at the east port, the conjunction of the planets. 'The haill streits was spred with flowres, and the forehowsis of the streits be the whilks the king passit war all hung with magnifik tapestrie, with payntit historeis, and with the effegeis of noble men and wemen.'[33]

When James returned to Edinburgh in 1617, the wisdom of Solomon was again recalled in the panegyric delivered to him at the west port by John Hay: 'Who will not, with the Queen of Sheba, confess that he has seen more wisdom in your Royal Person than report hath brought to foraine ears'.[34] The painted decorations were ordered to be executed by John Anderson of Aberdeen, John Sawers (fl. 1591– d. 1628) and James Workman.[35]

However, it was for the coronation of Charles I in 1633 that the new College of Edinburgh began to make its contribution to the content of the civic decorations.[36] A major structure was Mount Parnassus 'reared up on a vast frame of timber'.[37] This was filled with books and populated with portraits of Scottish academic worthies, including Bishop Elphinstone.[38] The aim of this expensive splendour was to focus the attention of the king on the needs of the new Edinburgh College which James VI had sponsored but never properly endowed.[39] On the Tolbooth 'stod an vast pageant arched above, having on an large map the pourtraits of 109 Kings of Scotland',[40] as mentioned above, by George Jamesone of Aberdeen.[41] As with almost all these decorations, 'by an fatal neglect, all were lost in a very few years thereafter, except a few pourtraits of the Kings' and a small number do indeed survive in private collections to this day.[42]

In Aberdeen, for Charles I's coronation, poems were produced and the market cross was hung with tapestry.[43] For the safe return of Charles II in May 1660 the council ordered 'his maiesties loft in the old church to be all hung over with tapestrie in the best manner can be devysit', the market cross was once more draped and musicians played on top of it. The tapestries came out yet again for the coronations of Charles II in April 1661[44] and James VII in 1685.[45] At St Nicholas Kirk, four large embroidered hangings from the Restoration period still survive.[46] All these examples show the way in which tapestry and 'payntit historeis' were used for temporary celebrations to promote the public image of the monarchy.

The loyalty of Aberdeen to the crown was demonstrated on many occasions in the mid-seventeenth century. The university principal between the difficult years of 1640 and 1651 was Doctor William Guild (1586–1657) who had been a chaplain of Charles I. He refused to condemn episcopacy in 1638 and was openly loyal to the king, which was the reason for his deposition by Cromwell in 1651.[47] Guild was also related by marriage to both the Anderson and Jamesone families who included in their number the artists John and George respectively.[48] Another remarkable Aberdonian of the period was Alexander Jaffrey (1614–73). He was known as a Covenanter, but was instrumental in bringing Charles II to Scotland in 1650, being one of the Scottish Commissioners who went to the Hague to approach Charles regarding his religious principles.[49] Jaffrey's attitude was not untypical in that his argument with the monarchy was primarily religious rather than political. Jaffrey was provost of Aberdeen in 1635–36, 1638 and 1641. It was with Jaffrey that George Jamesone went to London for a few months in 1633, following the Scottish Coronation of Charles I. Jaffrey accompanied Sir Paul Menzies, then provost of Aberdeen, to the coronation of 1633 where Menzies was knighted. Jamesone's first known portrait is of Menzies, with whom he may also have been connected by marriage.[50] Either of these men might have been involved with the creation of the paintings.

Loyalty to the crown was further demonstrated by the reception of Charles II in Aberdeen twice during the Interregnum. The first time was the 7 July 1650 when he stayed at Pitfodels Lodging in the Castlegate.[51] It was probably for this occasion that the university, in a hasty burst of royalist fervour, commissioned the creation of the mace with its regal insignia.[52] The second visit spanned a few days in the spring of 1651.[53] On both occasions the costs were covered by the City of Aberdeen, as demonstrated by the council accounts.[54] So the existence of royalist iconography in Aberdeen during the Commonwealth is not incongruous, representing the loyalty of both the town and university. The period c. 1633 to c. 1660 would seem to be a probable window for the production of the King's paintings, in view of the royalist and artistic connections held by leading lights of the time.

The question that is harder to answer concerns the way in which these paintings were intended to function. There are two size categories into which the five paintings fall, two being significantly wider than the other three. This suggests that the commission was site specific, although the originally intended site is unknown.

But were these easel paintings or were they painted hangings or cloths produced to decorate a particular space in celebration of a specific event?[55] The scale of the paintings their decorative borders, their bold style and the coarseness of the canvas all suggest that they were temporary painted hangings or cloths, remnants of a phenomenon once extremely common but now extremely rare: temporary creations produced to celebrate an event, often enthusiastically recorded at the time but then disposed of. It is most likely that they were originally free hanging like tapestries and were put on stretchers at a later date.[56] Damage to the lower borders indicated by the need to replace them (see above) may be a symptom of this.

There are four festive occasions when they might have been made. The first was 1633, the date of the Scottish Coronation of Charles I. The second was 1641 when King Charles, 'out of his pious dispositioune and princelie cair to literatour and religionne' granted the revenues of the Bishopric of Aberdeen to support the colleges of King's and Marischal.[57] Although the two colleges were to be united and known henceforth as 'King Charles university of Aberdeen', King's College benefited most with two-thirds of the revenue and Marischal with only one-third. This occasion might well have given rise to an acknowledgement of the monarch's wisdom, power and justice, particularly since the money for King's College was to free it from debt and restore the fabric of the buildings.[58] The third opportunity was the visit paid by Charles II to Aberdeen in 1650 during the Interregnum, when the mace was hastily created to honour him. The fourth is 1660, the Restoration, shortly before the end of the era of the Caroline University. An example of decorative painting which celebrates the Restoration was the astral ceiling, destroyed by fire in 1987, at Cullen House, Banffshire.[59] Here, peace in heaven mirrors true peace on earth which can only exist when the divinely ordained king is enthroned.[60]

In the end, the iconography is perhaps the best indicator of the pictures' original purpose, although two different explanations are proposed, the first by Duncan Macmillan. Kings for King's seems at first sight to be the guiding principle. Certainly the examples of the royal entries for which we do have evidence make it clear that the iconography, and the accompanying rhetoric too, was in each case elaborate and carefully thought out as one might expect in the age of the emblem book. Here we have two pictures of Solomon, one that celebrates his royal wisdom in *The Judgement* and the other his royal grandeur as he receives the Queen of Sheba. These were an appropriate celebration of kings in general, and in particular of the college's founder James IV and his descendants, especially Charles I who had continued to support it. Thus Solomon also provided an iconography by which the eponymous King's College could pay itself a reflected compliment. Indeed, the dedication inscription on the west front of the chapel specifically associates the building with Solomon's Temple.[61] On their own these two pictures could fit any of the royal occasions we know of, and one should remember the possibility that the paintings in fact relate to more than one of them. The tapestries were clearly brought out on several occasions, and the pictures might have enjoyed the same treatment, their number being added to as occasion demanded.

This might apply to the two Solomon pictures, but in the three pictures where David is either present or is the actual protagonist, the iconography seems too specific for such a general use. It is notable that in the David scenes, he is not yet king. When Charles II visited Aberdeen in 1650, he was not yet crowned king either and he was also, like David, a young man of only twenty. His coronation at Scone took place five months later on 1 January 1651. It was also for his visit in 1650 that, however hurriedly, the College commissioned a mace. If they had time to do that, then they also had time to commission paintings like these, particularly considering the evidence that they were painted by several hands and therefore quickly. That being so, and considering their general uniformity in spite of individual differences, it seems more likely that all five were painted for the same occasion and that they were part of the same programme of symbolism as the mace.

Taken together, the David pictures do seem to fit that occasion very well. With David and Goliath, for instance, it would not need much imagination in a royalist city to identify the leaders of the Commonwealth with the Israelites' most deadly foe, the Philstines, nor indeed to see Goliath reincarnate in the person of Cromwell.

David and Abigail is even more apposite. Although Abigail rather casually became David's wife, the main point of the story is how, after her previous husband, Nabal, had refused to help David in exile and a fugitive in the wilderness, Abigail had come to his aid and brought him supplies, no less than 'two hundred loaves, and two bottles of wine, and five sheep ready dressed, and five measures of parched corn, an hundred clusters of raisins, and two hundred cakes of figs'. Here is generous support of a fugitive which neatly draws attention to the city of Aberdeen's parallel support of Charles. With all this loaded on five asses and without telling her husband Abigail then went to find David in the wilderness: 'And when Abigail saw David, she hasted and lighted off her ass and fell before David on her face, and bowed herself to the ground.' That is the moment portrayed here. Crucially, it is a moment of recognition of potential royalty in the young David, even in adversity. Finally, to add to that, Dr William Guild and the learned professors of Aberdeen might have found it hard to resist the emblematic conjunction of those two initial letters 'Ab' in Abigail and Aberdeen.

There is a an apparent puzzle, however, with the Saul and David picture. Like David and Goliath, it is a story of victory in the struggle of the Israelites against the Philistines and so it is generally an appropriate image. On the face of it, too, Saul's triumphal return from the war was a suitable archetype for all royal entries, and it may be we should take it at face value as just that. The problem is that it was because the Israelite ladies, as they welcomed Saul and David, tactlessly sang 'Saul has slain his thousands / And David his ten thousands', that Saul 'was very wroth' and David had to flee. If it is indeed part of the narrative, then perhaps the anxious face at the window is that of Jonathan anticipating trouble. This figure is distinguished from the others by pose, colouring and dress. He could be a contemporary personality observing the biblical scene, mindful of its significance. Perhaps the intention here was to boost Charles's image as a new David in implicit contrast to the lack of success of his unfortunate father, not a point that could be made too bluntly in the circumstances. More simply, it seems clear that the point in two of these three pictures is to celebrate Charles through David as hero in the struggle against the Philistines and even as uncrowned king. In the third painting, David and Abigail, the additional point is that Aberdeen as Abigail recognises Charles and offers him succour in his adversity.

The case for Charles II's visit to Aberdeen in 1650, argued above by Duncan Macmillan, is persuasive, but the case preferred by Elizabeth Bracegirdle, for the Restoration of Charles II in 1660 should not be ruled out. According to the second proposal, the five scenes function as a chronological cycle, beginning with the episodes of the young uncrowned David/Charles II. David/Charles is acknowledged and greeted by Abigail/Aberdeen in 1650, at a time when he is barely recognised elsewhere. The entry into the cities of Israel does not represent a triumph over the Philistines but a premature welcome of David/Charles at Scone in 1651. There are two leaders in this picture and the older one, Saul/Cromwell will spend many years persecuting his younger rival, forcing him into exile. This scene could only be understood with hindsight, perhaps indicated by the anxious face at the window,

Jonathan warning of troubles to come: David and Charles had many years of struggle following this happy occasion. David and Goliath is, of course, the eventual triumph of young Charles over Cromwell and the Commonwealth. The final two scenes represent the fulfilment of kingship: Solomon in judgement between the true and false church (an interpretation close to the interests of the broadly episcopalian university) and his recognition by Sheba at the end, the Restoration in 1660.

The King's College Chapel paintings are a unique survival of temporary 'painted cloths', from a period when there is little enough evidence of artistic activity in Scotland at all. While a conclusive date is not possible, the paintings nevertheless represent a document in the story of Aberdeen's loyalty to the crown. As paintings they attest to the continuing energy of the decorative tradition of the craftsmen painters widely seen on painted ceilings, but not at all hitherto in the form of painted canvas. It was a tradition that underpinned the achievement of Scottish artists in the eighteenth century and the survival of such important works on canvas from this date provides a link between that remarkable achievement and the painted ceilings of the earlier seventeenth century.[62] In view of their rarity, it is to be hoped that some day conservation and cleaning will allow them to lose their nickname of the 'Black Paintings'.

Notes

[1] This article by Elizabeth Bracegirdle, has benefited from generous contributions to the iconography and conclusion from Duncan Macmillan. She would like to acknowledge the considerable support given by Jane Geddes in the writing of this chapter as well as the advice given by Duncan Thomson and Anthony Wells-Cole of Temple Newsam House, Leeds. Sizes of paintings and catalogue numbers from Marischal Museum Catalogue. ABDUA:31852, *David and Goliath*, oil on canvas, 245 x 179cm (measurement from Marischal Museum Catalogue); ABDUA:31853, *The Entry of Saul and David into the Cities of Israel*, oil on canvas, 245 x 216cm (measurement from Marischal Museum Catalogue); ABDUA:31855, *David and* Abigail, oil on canvas, 241 x 173cm (sight size, Meredith, 1998); ABDUA:31851, *The Judgement of Solomon*, oil on canvas, 240 x 195cm (sight size, Meredith, 1998); ABDUA:31854, *Solomon and the Queen of Sheba* (this name is given in the Marischal Museum Catalogue), 259 x 214cm (incl. frame), (measurement from Marischal Museum Catalogue).

[2] The condition of all the paintings is poor. Clare Meredith carried out conservation assessments on two of them, *The Judgement of Solomon* (Col. Pl. VIIb) and *David and Abigail* (Col. Pl. VIIa), in May 1998. Meredith, 1998, refers to the unpublished conservation survey she produced for Marischal Museum. This assessment revealed different problems in each case. These included various amounts of damage to both the original support and paint layer. Common to all the paintings is the discolouration of a varnish layer, and accumulation of dirt in the grain of the coarse woven canvas. The paintings have been given new stretchers on at least two occasions, and have also been lined. It is feasible that varnishing, application to stretchers and lining were all undertaken at the same time in the nineteenth century, possibly at the instigation of 'John and Davie'.

[3] Macpherson, 1889, 28–29. They were removed to Marischal Museum in 1999.

[4] Macpherson, 1889, 28.

[5] R.-A. D'Hulst and M. Vandenven, *Rubens: the Old Testament*, Corpus Rubenianum, London, 1989, 146.

[6] Anthony Wells-Cole, *Art and Decoration in Elizabethan and Jacobean England*, Yale, 1997, 195; *Rubens and his Engravers*, Colnaghi Exhibition Catalogue, 1977; C. G. Voorhelm Schneevoogt, *Catalogue des etampes gravés d'après P. P. Rubens*, Haarlem, 1873, 7, no. 51.

[7] Wells-Cole, 1997, 194–95 and 122.

[8] Macpherson, 1889, 28–29. Macpherson did not recognize the original source.

[9] This wording is used in an engraving by Hendrick Goltzius of the Judgement of Solomon. F. H. W. Hollstein, *Dutch and Flemish Etchings, Engravings and Woodcuts*, Amsterdam, 1949–, VIII, 19.

[10] E. Bracegirdle, 'Ornamented Dwellings', *Inferno*, ed. S. Alexander, P. Cottrell, S. Penman (eds), IV, St Andrews, 1997, 44.

[11] This is a commonly used motif. It is shown in Sebastiano Serlio, *The Book of Architecture*, New York, 1970 (facsimile of 1611, London edition), Book III, fols 50 and 60. The acanthus motif was used in a dado band in the painted decoration of the Arbour Room, Kinneil, probable date 1570s.

[12] As seen for example in the in the work of Johan Jacob von Sandrart (1627–99), F. W. H. Hollstein, *German Etchings, Engravings and Woodcuts, 1450–1700*, Amsterdam, 1954–, XL, 99, no. 116.

[13] Clare Meredith made this observation regarding *The Judgement* and *David and Abigail*, Meredith, 1998. The same sort of canvas seems to have been used for the other three paintings as well.

[14] Clare Meredith observed the composition of the canvases for *The Judgement* and *David and Abigail*, Meredith, 1998. The other three seem to conform to the pattern of *The Judgement*.

[15] Meredith, 1998.

[16] Meredith, 1998.

[17] Meredith, 1998.

[18] Clare Meredith observed the presence of overpaints in *The Judgement* and *David and Abigail*, Meredith, 1998. Similar effects are visible in the other three.

[19] Apted and Hannabuss, 1978, 23–24.

[20] See Chapter 20.

[21] Apted and Hannabuss, 1978, 1–5.

[22] Apted and Hannabuss, 1978, 23.

[23] Duncan Thomson, *The Life and Art of George Jamesone*, Oxford, 1974, 53–54.

[24] Apted and Hannabuss, 1978, 22.

[25] Apted and Hannabuss, 1978, 23, 82, 52.

[26] Thomson, 1974, 68, reproducing Scottish Record Office, Accounts of the Master of Works, vol. XXV, fol. 45^v.

[27] It seems likely though that one of them was the Rembrandt self-portrait now in Liverpool that was given to the king in 1633 by the Earl of Lothian. His coronation would seem to be the most likely occasion for such a gift to his sovereign by one of his leading Scottish supporters and one who also shared his taste for paintings.

[28] Tim Benton, *Seventeenth-Century Culture: A Changing Culture, 1618–1689*, Open University, 1980, A203, Block 2, 26.

[29] *Documents Relative to the Reception at Edinburgh of the Kings and Queens of Scotland 1561–1590*, ed. Sir Patrick Walker, 1822, 23.

[30] Duncan Thomson, 1974, 27, 95–101. The surviving 26 paintings from this series were at Newbattle Abbey in 1971, but are now dispersed.

[31] Another series, now lost, was painted for Campbell of Glenorchy, also around 1633, not extant (Thomson, 1974, 29). Aberdeen University holds early series of royal portraits: James II, ABDUA:30620; James III, ABDUA:30089; James IV, ABDUA:30262; James V, ABDUA:30088. Another series is: Mary, ABDUA:30108; James VI, ABDUA:30628; Charles I, ABDUA:30039; Charles II, ABDUA:30041. In addition there are Mary, ABDUA:30626; James VI, ABDUA:30090; Charles II, ABDUA:30619.

[32] John Rupert Martin, *The Decorations for the Introitus Ferdinandi*, Corpus Rubenianum XVI, London, 1972.

[33] *Documents Relative to the Reception at Edinburgh of the Kings and Queens of Scotland 1561–1590*, ed. Sir Patrick Walker, 1822, 23, 30–31. When James VI brought Queen Anne to Edinburgh in 1589, the town made ready all things 'upon the walls, ports, croce, trone . . . with all payntings and other furnitoures', Walker, 1822, 36. M. Lynch, 'Court ceremonial and ritual during the personal reign of James VI', in *The Reign of James VI*, Julian Goodare and Michael Lynch (eds), East Linton, 2000, 75 ff.

[34] W. Maitland, *The History of Edinburgh*, Edinburgh, 1753, 59.

[35] Apted and Hannabuss, 1978, 23.

[36] E. McGrath, 'Local Heroes: the Scottish Humanist Parnassus for Charles I', in *England and the Continental Renaissance, essays in honour of J. B. Trapp*, E. Chaney and P. Mack (eds), Woodbridge, 1990, 257–70.

[37] Thomas Craufurd, *History of the University of Edinburgh from 1580 to 1646*, Edinburgh, 1808, 120–22. This pageant is also described extensively in Walker, 1822, 69 155.

[38] In Chapter 7, it is tentatively suggested that the portrait now owned by Lord Elphinstone might have been rescued from this occasion.

[39] McGrath, 1990, 260, 269.

[40] Craufurd, 1808, 121.

[41] Thomson, 1974, 50–51.

[42] Craufurd, 1808, 123.

[43] *Extracts from the Council Register of the Burgh of Aberdeen, 1625–42*, ed. C. Innes, Scottish Burgh Records Society, Edinburgh, 1871, 60.

[44] *Extracts from the Council Register of the Burgh of Aberdeen*, 187, 197.

[45] Alexander Keith, *A Thousand Years of Aberdeen*, Aberdeen, 1972, 271.

[46] J. Cooper, 'Pictorial Decorations', *Proceedings of the Aberdeen Ecclesiological Society*, 2, 5th year, 1890 (1891), 2–5. The subjects are *The Finding of Moses, Esther before Ahaseurus, Susannah and the Elders* and a version of *Jephthah and his Daughter*. (In the latter scene, somewhat similar to the King's *David and Saul*, with dancing girls, Jephthah is rending his clothes as specified in the text.) They are reputed to be by Mary Jamesone, daughter of George Jamesone, based on the evidence that they were sold to the City of Aberdeen by her third husband, George Adie in 1688 for £400 Scots. How he actually acquired the hangings in the first place is not known.

[47] Keith, 1972, 244.

[48] Keith, 1972, 241–48.

[49] Keith, 1972, 252.

[50] Thomson, 1974, 80.

[51] *Extracts from the Council Register of the Burgh of Aberdeen*, 114. Perhaps this visit was not lavishly served by the town: the accounts ask 'to prowyd fit lodgings . . . as may be best haid on so short advertisementis'; William Kennedy, *Annals of Aberdeen*, London, 1818, 226–27; *Accounts of the Burgh of Aberdeen, Discharge 1649–50*, ed. John Stuart, Miscellany of the Spalding Club, Aberdeen ,1852, 167–68.

[52] See Chapter 20; *Fasti*, lxiii.

[53] *Accounts of the Burgh of Aberdeen, Discharge 1649–50*, ed. John Stuart, Miscellany of the Spalding Club, Aberdeen, 1852, 168–69.

[54] Keith, 1972, 244.

[55] 'Painted cloths' were extremely common in the sixteenth and seventeenth centuries, but the survival rate has been small. Extant examples include a set in the original chapel at Hardwick Hall (Wells-Cole, 1997, 275–89). Tessa Watt also discusses this medium of decoration in *Cheap Print and Popular Piety, 1550–1640*, Cambridge, 1991.

[56] Perhaps by Macpherson's 'John and Davie', Macpherson, 1889, 28.

[57] *Fasti*, 1567, 150–54.

[58] See Chapter 16.

[59] Bracegirdle, 1997, 46, 48. It is possible that the iconography of this ceiling could be linked with the kind of imagery presented at court masques such as *The Triumph of Peace* written by James Shirley and *Coelum Britannicum*, written by Thomas Carew, both dating form 1634 and designed by Inigo Jones (1573–1652). Stephen Orgel, *The Illusion of Power: Political Theatre in the English Renaissance*, University of California Press, 1975, 77–87.

[60] Stephen Orgel and Roy Strong, *Inigo Jones: the Theatre of the Stuart Court*, University of California Press, 1973, I, 50. Martin Butler, 'Courtly Negotiations', in *The Politics of the Stuart Court Masque*, David Bevington and Peter Holbrook (eds), Cambridge, 1998, 36–37. 'The agenda to which [masques] were tied was specifically that of the legitimation of sovereignty, whether overtly in terms of the praise of kingly wisdom, or implicitly in terms of the gestures of obedience and social solidarity which their performances rehearsed'.

[61] See Chapter 5.

[62] As late as 1771 Fuseli wrote of Alexander Runciman that he was 'the best painter among us here in Rome'. That would not have been so if Runciman had not been trained in the decorative tradition by the Nories. Fuseli in a letter to Mary Moser, see Duncan Macmillan, *Painting in Scotland: the Golden Age*, Oxford, 1986, 52 quoting J. T. Smith, *Nollekens and his Times*, London, 1806.

CHAPTER TWENTY

THE SILVER MACE OF KING'S COLLEGE

By Stuart Maxwell and George R. Dalgleish

The King's College mace was described in detail by A. J. S. Brook in a paper on Scottish maces in the *Proceedings of the Society of Antiquaries of Scotland.*[1] 95cm long (3ft 1½ins) and weighing 55oz 1dwt., it has a bowl-shaped head under an imperial crown closed by four beaded arches which support an orb and cross; it has a plain cylindrical shaft which has two chased moulded bands with acanthus leaves above and below; the shaft ends in a domed finial which also has acanthus leaves (Fig. 20.1). The bowl is closed by a circular plate on which are embossed the Stuart royal arms, with 'GOD SAVE THE KING' in raised letters beneath (Fig. 20.2). The bowl has two embossed cartouches supported by winged cherubs; one bears the emblem of the Virgin, a pot with three lilies, the earliest arms of the college (Fig. 20.3), the other the arms of Bishop Elphinstone, argent a chevron sable between three boars' heads gules. On the bowl of the crown are embossed 'gems' and a harp, thistle, rose and fleur-de-lis. Around the shaft's upper band, in raised letters, is 'WALTERUS MELVIL FECIT ANNO 1650'.

In form it resembles other maces of the time, including three of the maces of the Court of Session, one of which was made by Edward Cleghorn of Edinburgh in 1653–54 or 1659–61[2] and most notably that of Marischal College (undated and by an unknown maker but probably made in 1671, when it was purchased in London).[3] However, the earliest example in Scotland of a mace incorporating a crown head and the royal arms is that made for the City of Edinburgh in 1617 by George Robertson, goldsmith in Edinburgh. The Town Council ordered the mace on 16 December 1616, to be ready in time for the King's visit which started on 25 May the following year. The design of the mace incorporates the town arms along with the crown and the arms of James VI, and it was carried at the official celebrations that accompanied the monarch's visit. James, on his entry into Edinburgh, was presented with two silver keys and 'ten thousand merks in double angellis of gold and [a] gilt baissin . . . to put the same in'.[4]

There may be simple coincidence in operation, but it is more likely to be significant that the King's College mace was made in the same year as another royal visit, that of Charles II. Innes indeed suggests 'that it must have been provided to do honour to the visit which Charles II made to Aberdeen, 7th July, 1650, or on the 25th February following, while he was still King in Scotland'.[5] Its maker, Walter Melvil, is also recorded as having been paid £67 Scots for the provision of two ceremonial silver keys, presumably for presentation to Charles.[6] It would seem at least plausible that

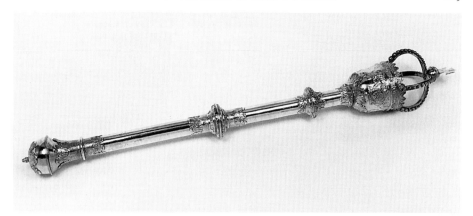

Fig. 20.1. The King's College mace, made by Walter Melvil, Aberdeen, 1650 (Copyright: Trustees of the National Museums of Scotland, 1999)

Fig. 20.2. The mace bowl, showing the Stuart royal arms and the motto 'God Save the King' (Copyright: Trustees of the National Museums of Scotland, 1999)

Fig. 20.3.   The mace bowl showing the early arms of the college (Copyright: Trustees of the National Museums of Scotland, 1999)

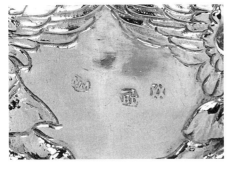

Fig. 20.4.   The mace bowl showing the maker Walter Melvil's mark, the Aberdeen town mark, and the 'tryer' William Anderson's mark (Copyright: Trustees of the National Museums of Scotland, 1999)

when presented with the problem of how to adequately mark the royal visit, the magistrates of Aberdeen, and their chosen craftsman, turned for a precedent to the visit of Charles' grandfather to Edinburgh some thirty-three years before. The fact that the motto 'God save the King' appears so prominently, something which is unusual on other maces, also points to the mace being made specifically for the royal visit, to emphasize the college's loyalty to the Crown (Fig. 20. 2).

The mace first seems to have been recorded in an 'Inventory of the silver plate and other utensills of the College', 31 March 1738: '1 Imp: The Silver mace which was to be carried in all the publik solemnityes of the College'.[7] It was first published over 100 years later in *Fasti Aberdonensis*, where the editor, Cosmo Innes, suggests that, although made in Aberdeen in 1650, it was possibly an imitation of the old mace[8] described in the 1542 chapel Inventory as 'the Rector's mace, of silver, with the arms of the King and of the Founder'.[9] Despite this superficial description seeming to echo the existing mace, there is no doubt that it owes more to the secular tradition of bell-headed maces, as represented in Scotland by the mace of the City of Edinburgh, the High Court maces and the mace of Marischal College,[10] than to the great ecclesiastical tabernacle type maces of St Andrews and Glasgow Universities.[11] It is probable that the mace referred to in the 1542 list followed this ecclesiastical tabernacle form, and that Walter Melvil simply incorporated the descriptive references to the arms into his new mace (Fig. 20.3). As has been suggested, the use of a form representing secular royal power may be significant. (Two maces are listed in the 1542 register of the College's silver. Brook speculates that one of these may have been given by Bishop Elphinstone.[12] The representation in 1650 of the earliest arms and those of the founder may signify that while the earlier mace was not then extant, its decoration was remembered.)

Brook points out that the silver of the rod, which has a wooden core, is inferior to that of the decorated parts, but both are below the quality of silver specified by Act of Parliament, 'xi denniers fine'. He also notes it had been in a 'much dilapidated condition before it was recently repaired'. The results of Brook's assay are somewhat ironical, given the care which the maker, Walter Melvil, took to ensure that not only would he be recognized as its author, but that it would be marked in a way which fully complied with national and local laws regarding the quality of silver offered for sale. As well as having Melvil's name and the date of manufacture as part of the decoration, in a manner more resembling bells of the time than pieces of silver, the mace head also has his maker's mark , the Aberdeen town mark, and the mark of William Anderson, 'tryer', or assayer, stamped in two separate places (Fig. 20.4).

Walter Melvil became one of the most important seventeenth-century goldsmiths in Aberdeen. He was admitted as a goldsmith burgess on 10 October 1649, having possibly served his apprenticeship under William Anderson.[13] An active member of the Incorporation of Hammermen, becoming their Deacon in 1662, he also played a role in the burgh's affairs, being elected one of the Trades representatives on the Council in 1663.[14] He was the maker of some important pieces of silver, including the Strathnaver Cup, 1653; the medal attached to the Aberdeen Grammar School silver arrow in 1664 by George MacKenzie; the beakers for Leochel Cushnie church; and the beaker presented to Ellon Kirk, which curiously is dated 1642, seven years before Melvil was admitted as a goldsmith.[15]

Alongside Melvil's mark are stamped the Aberdeen town mark — the simple contraction 'ABD' and the mark of William Anderson. Anderson was a goldsmith in his own right, although there is no entry for his admission as a goldsmith burgess, which must have been about 1630.[16] However, his mark appears on the mace in his capacity of 'tryer', or assayer of gold and silver made in the town. The Council appointed him to this office on 7 November 1649, having 'taking to their consideratioun the insufficiencie of silver maid within this brughe'. They were very specific about the correct marking of silver that he was to test. If he tested it and found it to conform to the national legal standard of the time, i.e. 11 parts silver to one part alloy,[17] he was to stamp it with 'his mark and the townes mark'.[18] The fact that the metal used for the mace is not of the correct quality, despite being marked and therefore presumably tested by the 'tryer', would possibly suggest that the accuracy of the assay method used by Anderson was deficient. It is perhaps significant that there is no 'assay groove' on the mace. This is the visible scrape where the necessary sample of silver is removed if the quality is to be tested by the 'fire assay' or cupellation method. This is a simple analytical refining method which produces an accurate indication of the amount of pure silver in the item tested. This method was certainly available in the seventeenth century, and indeed other pieces made by Melvil and tested by Anderson have this groove. However, there was another method of testing in use at the time, that of the touchstone. This is less accurate but is much quicker,[19] and although national legislation specified cupellation, it is possible that Anderson used the touchstone method. The overall quality of the design and workmanship of the mace has the feel of being rushed and it is possible that both the maker and 'tryer' were responding to an urgent demand to have the mace ready for a special occasion.[20]

Notes

[1] We would like to record our grateful thanks to Neil Curtis of Marischal Museum for giving us access to the mace, to Joyce Smith for her excellent photographs and to Godfrey Evans for reading this note in draft and making constructive comments. A. J. S. Brook, 'An account of the Maces of the Universities of St Andrews, Glasgow, Aberdeen, and Edinburgh, the College of Justice, the City of Edinburgh etc', *PSAS*, XXVI, 1891–92, 492–95 and pl. X.

[2] Brook, 1891–92, 509–11 and pl. XII.

[3] Brook, 1891–92, 498.

[4] *Extracts from the Records of the Burgh of Edinburgh, 1604–1626*, ed. M. Wood, Edinburgh, 1931, XII, 158.

[5] *Fasti*, lxiii.

[6] Dr I. E. James, *The Goldsmiths of Aberdeen*, Aberdeen, 1981, 37.

[7] AUL, MS K 103, p. 148.

[8] *Fasti*, lxiii.

[9] Eeles, 1956, 21, 44; *Fasti*, lxii, 571.

[10] Brook, 1891–92, 484ff.

[11] Brook, 1891–92, 440–84.

[12] Brook, 1891–92, 495.

[13] James, 1981, 35–37.

[14] James, 1981, 37.

[15] The Strathnaver Cup was presented by George Gordon, Lord Strathnaver to Marischal College, Aberdeen, where it is still in the museum. George Mackenzie's medal is attached to Aberdeen Grammar School's silver arrow archery prize. The communion beakers for Leochel Cushnie still belong to the parish church. The beaker given to Ellon church by 'John Midletoune, burges and baxter' of Aberdeen is on loan from the Ellon Kirk Session to the National Museums of Scotland.

[16] James, 1981, 29.

[17] *Acts of the Parliaments of Scotland*, Vol. II, 1555, c34, p. 449.

[18] James, 1981, 31.

[19] The metal to be tested is drawn across a piece of dense, hard black stone, leaving a smear of silver. This is then visually compared with a smear from a piece of silver of known composition.

[20] A similar context has been suggested for the 'Black Paintings', Chapter 19.

CHAPTER TWENTY-ONE

THE LATER ARMORIALS

By Charles J. Burnett Esq., Ross Herald of Arms

The original armorials of the chapel were discussed in Chapter 10. This chapter examines the later heraldry, both on the outside and around the memorial chapel in the nave.

The Exterior

The later exterior heraldry is no longer attached to its original location. There are eleven carved panels in total. Two decorate the east side of the chapel tower and nine are positioned along the south side of the chapel, facing the quadrangle (Col. Pl. V).

Six of the panels are placed on buttresses mimicking the arrangement of royal panels on the west front, but all are of different periods and vary in style of heraldic display. This not only gives a clue to the date of execution but suggests a sequence of events which can only be postulated.

The reason for this variety lies in the architectural changes to the south side of the chapel. By 1545 a combined sacristy, jewel house, and library had been erected adjacent to the chapel, extending eastward from the tower to the fourth buttress of the chapel. It was two stories high and completed during the episcopacy of Bishop William Stewart (1532–45) who was also chancellor of the university. At some stage during the late seventeenth century an heraldic scheme of seven panels was probably erected on the south wall of this lean-to structure. The arms were those of Bishop William Elphinstone (1483–1514), Bishop Gavin Dunbar (1518–32), Bishop William Stewart (1532–45), Bishop Patrick Forbes (1618–35), and the supposed royal arms of James IV, King of Scots. These panels will be described in due course. The remaining two panels, carved by a different mason, feature the arms of Hector Boece, first principal of the university (1505–36) and Robert Maitland, Dean of Aberdeen (1565–79).

The lean-to structure fell into disrepair, the seven panels were removed and the building was rebuilt and enlarged in 1725–26 by Dr James Fraser, royal librarian. The seven panels may have been re-incorporated in his new building. Apart from the financial contribution made by James Fraser, it is possible additional assistance was received from Colonel John Buchan of Cairnbulg who died in the year the new building was completed. As a former student he may have given money to his Alma Mater so his arms were also included in the new building. Also placed in position after 1730 were the arms of Simon, eleventh Lord Lovat. These seem a remarkable choice but, apart from being Dr James Fraser's chief, he may have wished to support his clansman with financial aid for the university library. There is no proof that he did so, but how else can one explain the presence of his arms? The good Dr Fraser died in 1731 and thereafter a grateful university caused the tenth commemorative panel, to be erected in his memory.

In 1773 Dr Fraser's building was demolished, and once again all the heraldic panels were saved and placed in storage. In due course the south front of the chapel was refaced in granite with supporting buttresses and at least nine heraldic panels were incorporated without any attempt at chronological order.[1] Finally, after 1840, a tenth heraldic panel was placed above the chapel tower east doorway, bearing the arms of John Simpson of Shrubhill, a generous benefactor to the university who died in 1840. In 1891 the eleventh panel, to Bishop Forbes, was erected.

A blazon and comments on the eleven panels, which have been tinctured and gilded in recent times, now follows in their present location reading from left to right, that is from the eastern face of the chapel tower to the east end of the chapel:

1.   Bishop and Chancellor Patrick Forbes (Col. Pl. IXa)[2]
Azure, three bear heads couped Argent muzzled Gules between a Latin cross Or, shield surmounted by a *mitra pretiosa* with mantling doubled Argent and Azure, above the initials PF, below on a riband the motto ROSIS CORONAT/SPINA (The thorn crowns with roses.)

This panel was carved in the seventeenth century with later additional lettering on the dexter CB.AD/MDCXXXV on the sinister AE.S.LXXI (d. 1635, his age 71).

2.   John Simpson of Shrubhill (Col. Pl. IXb)
Argent, on a chief indented Azure, three crescents of the first, the shield surmounted by the crest of a goshawk Proper rising, on a wreath (should be Argent and Azure) flanked by mantling of the liveries, above the initials IS, below on a riband the motto ALIS NUTRIOR (I am fed by my wings).

This is a nineteenth-century heraldic carving which makes use of the Petra Sancta system of dots and lines to denote tinctures. The colour of the chief is represented by the horizontal lines. The shield is flanked by lettering OB.AD MDCCXL (d. 1840).

3.   Bishop William Elphinstone, Founder of the University (Col. Pl. IXc)
Argent, a chevron Sable between three boar heads erased Gules. Shield surmounted by a *mitra pretiosa* with mantling doubled Argent and Sable, above, the initials WE, below on a riband the motto NON CONFUNDAR (I shall not be confounded).

The knotted ends of the mantling is typical of late seventeenth-century Scottish heraldic carving, and the initial W rather than V confirms the later date. Again, at a later date additional lettering flanks the shield, OB.A. MDXVIV (d. 1514).

4.   Bishop and Chancellor Gavin Dunbar (Col. Pl. IXd)
Argent, three cushions within a double tressure flory counter flory Gules. Shield surmounted by a *mitra pretiosa* with mantling doubled Argent and Gules, above, the initials GD, below on a riband the motto SUB SPE (Under hope). Additional inscription on dexter side of panel OB A MDXXXI (d. 1531).

5.   Bishop and Chancellor William Stewart (Col. Pl. Xa)

Or, a fess chequy Argent and Azure surmounted of a bend engrailed Gules. Shield surmounted by a *mitra pretiosa* with mantling doubled Or and Gules, above, the initials WS, below on a riband the motto VIRESCIT VULNERE VIRTUS (Her virtue flourishes by her wound).

Additional inscription on dexter side of panel OB A MDXLV (d. 1545).

Panels 3, 4 and 5 were carved by one mason who used the same design of mitre and terminated the mantling with a knot and tassle. Panel 1 was probably carved at a slightly later date by another craftsman.

6.   James IV, King of Scots (Col. Pl. Xb)

Or, a lion rampant (should be armed and langued Azure) within a double tressure flory counter flory Gules. Shield surrounded by a collar of thistles, with flower heads placed outwards, from which is suspended a St Andrew Badge, and is surmounted by an imperial crown bearing the crest of a crowned lion sejant Gules holding a sword in the dexter paw and a sceptre in the sinister, and is flanked by the letters IA 4R, and above on a riband the motto IN DEFENCE. The shield is supported by two imperially crowned unicorns Argent gorged and chained Or with tails curving upwards, holding a banner. That on the dexter bears the royal arms of Scotland and on the sinister the unicorn carries the national flag of Scotland. The supporters stand on a debased strapwork panel bearing the motto NEMO ME IMPUNE LACESSIT.

This panel was cut in the late seventeenth century after 1680.[3] Unicorn supporters were uncrowned in the reign of James IV, their tails were couée, the second royal motto NEMO ME IMPUNE LACESSIT was not adopted until the reign of James VI, and the first royal motto was always spelt IN DEFENS during the reign of James IV. According to Anderson this panel was originally placed above the outer gate of King's College.[4]

7.   Principal Hector Boece (Col. Pl. Xc)

Argent, a saltire and chief Azure. Shield within a debased strapwork cartouche, above, the initials HB.

As on the other contemporary panels, at a later date additional lettering has been carved, in this case on either side of the shield: OBMD/ADXXXVI (d. 1536).

8.   Robert Maitland, Dean of Aberdeen (Col. Pl. Xd)

Or, a lion rampant Gules couped in all the joints Sable (should be armed and langued Azure). Shield within a similar debased strapwork cartouche as 7, above, the initials RM.

On either side of the shield later carving DEC/MAD/ABD/LXXIX (Dean of Aberdeen until 1579).

These two panels were carved by the same mason during the seventeenth century. The manner in which the debased strapwork cartouches have been carved is typical of that century.

9.   Dr James Fraser, royal librarian (Col. Pl. XIa)

An oval shield within a strapwork cartouche, quartered 1st and 4th, Or, three antique crowns Gules (incorrectly tinctured should be gold crowns on red), 2nd and 3rd, Azure three fraises Argent. Above, flanking the cartouche, the letters IF, below a panel partially obscuring the cartouche. The panel bears the inscription: A.D.MDCC.XXIV/VIR NUNGUAM SINE LAUDE/NUMINANDUS IACOBUS FRA/SERIUS IUD UNICUS MUSA/RUM FAUTOR ALMAM SUA/MATREM ABERDONENSEM/AEVI INIURIA PARTIM LABAN/TEM PARTIM IACENTEM SOL/ LUS FERE RESPEXIT EREXIT/PROVEXIT (A.D. 1724. A man never without praise named James Fraser, unique arbiter, patron of the Muses. When his kindly Aberdonian mother (The University) was, through the injury of an age, partly-collapsing, partly-lying in ruins, almost alone, he turned back to her, drew her up and led her forth.)

This panel is a good example of Aberdonian thrift! There are no records that James Fraser was armigerous although he used an armorial seal bearing Fraser's arms. The arms are actually for someone named Grant. The original identification has been covered with a plain slab partly covering the cartouche and used for the laudatory inscription. The letters IF were carved on the original as part of the adaptation.

10.   Simon Fraser, eleventh Lord Lovat (Col. Pl. XIb)

Quartered shield, 1st and 4th, Azure three cinquefoils, Argent, 2nd and 3rd, Gules, three antique crowns Or. Above the shield a baron's coronet surmounted by a helmet, flanked with mantling (incorrectly tinctured) above, on a wreath (incorrectly tinctured) the crest in the form of a stag head. The shield is supported by two harts Proper which stand on a motto scroll at the foot of the panel carved with the words IE SUIS PREST (I am ready).

This panel is carved in an archaic style and could be of the eighteenth century or earlier. Whatever period, it is specifically the arms of a Lord Lovat and not, as has been suggested, representative of the Fraser of Lovat family.[5]

11.   Colonel John Buchan of Cairnbulg (Col. Pl. XIc)

Argent, a garb Azure, banded Gules between three lion heads erased Sable, langued of the Third, within a bordure embattled of the Second. Above the shield an Esquire's helmet with mantling (incorrectly tinctured). On a wreath (incorrectly tinctured) is set for crest a demi-lion Sable holding a branch with leaves Proper. Above the crest the letter C and flanking the shield, which is set on a debased strapwork cartouche, the letters IB. Below the shield on a riband is the motto FORTIOR QUO MITIOR (He is the stronger who is the better man).

This panel has been repaired before being tinctured at some time after 1888. Anderson's description indicates that the lion head charge in base had disappeared.[6] The panel was carved soon after 1724 but the stone mason retained a remarkable archaic style which matches the spirit of the earlier panels.

King's College Chapel has been subject to restoration twice since P. J. Anderson wrote his article in 1888. In 1891 work was supervised by Dr (later Sir) Robert Rowand Anderson, and in 1931 Dr William Kelly was responsible for re-opening the east window in the apsidal end of the chapel.[7] The heraldic panel of Bishop Forbes must have been erected on the east side of the chapel tower during the 1891 restoration when repairs were also made to damaged and weathered panels such as that to Colonel John Buchan of Cairnbulg.

THE INTERIOR

This section examines the significance of the heraldry chosen for the war memorial, constructed in the nave in 1929.[8] The architect, Dr William Kelly, knew the chapel intimately and produced a sympathetic and sensitively designed scheme featuring the names of university members who fell in the First World War (Fig. 22.1). Additional names were added after the Second World War. The memorial takes the form of oak panelling round three walls with an elaborate cornice inspired by the medieval choir stalls. The cornice is decorated with fifteen heraldic medallions with a title panel over the west entrance door incorporating five more armorial ensigns. The medallions feature the Burgh arms of communities in the north-east, the Highlands and Islands, from which the fallen students came. These are now historic in themselves since the passing of the Local Government (Scotland) Act 1973 altered the whole pattern of local administration in Scotland. Most of the burghs featured on the war memorial have ceased to exist. The arms will be described in a clockwise direction starting at the south-west door which leads from the quadrangle:

1.   Royal Burgh of Inverbervie, Kincardineshire
Azure, a rose Argent, barbed and seeded Proper.
   Arms granted on 4 June 1929 specifically for display on the University War Memorial.

2.   Burgh of Stonehaven, Kincardineshire
Per fess: in chief paly of six Or and Gules, in base Azure.
   Arms granted 18 October 1929, again for display on the War Memorial.

3.   City and Royal Burgh of Aberdeen
Gules, three towers triple-towered within a double tressure flory counter flory Argent.
   Arms granted 25 February 1674. Aberdeen in one of four burghs in Scotland which possess two coats of arms. The second coat showing St Nicholas is seldom used.

4.   Royal Burgh of Inverurie, Aberdeenshire
Azure, two castles in fess Or, masoned Sable, windows and portcullis Gules.
   Arms granted 7 November 1930.

5.   Burgh of Peterhead, Aberdeenshire
Vert, a chief paly of six Or and Gules
   Arms granted 29 November 1929. The similarity of design with Stonehaven is by reason of both burghs having once belonged to the 5th Earl Marischal of Scotland, the man who founded Marischal College, Aberdeen.

Fig. 21.1.   Detail of the War Memorial, the University and the Nations

6.   Burgh of Fraserburgh, Aberdeenshire
Quarterly: 1st and 4th, Purpure, three fraises Argent; 2nd and 3rd, Gules, a lion rampant Argent, armed and langued Azure.
   Arms granted 12 March 1930.

7.   Royal Burgh of Banff, Banffshire
Gules, the Virgin Mary with her Babe in her arms Or.
   Arms granted 24 November 1673.

8.   Burgh of Grantown-on-Spey, Morayshire
Gules, between three antique crowns Or, a fess undy of five Argent and Azure.
   Arms granted 24 June 1930.

9.   Royal Burgh of Elgin, Morayshire
Argent, Sanctus Aegidious habited in his robes and mitred, holding in his dexter hand a pastoral staff and in his sinister hand a clasped book all Proper.
   Arms granted 9 October 1678.

10.   Royal Burgh of Inverness
Gules, Our Lord upon the Cross Proper.
   Arms granted 9 February 1900.

11.   Royal Burgh of Dingwall, Ross & Cromarty
Azure, the sun in its splendour between five mullets Or.
   Arms granted 31 March 1897.

12.   Royal Burgh of Tain, Ross & Cromarty
Gules, Saint Duthacus in long garments Argent, holding in his dexter hand a staff garnished with ivy, in the sinister laid on his breast a book expanded Proper.
   Arms granted c. 1673.

13.   Royal Burgh of Dornoch, Sutherlandshire
Argent, a horseshoe Azure, having seven horsenails Or.
   Arms granted 20 June 1929.

14.   Royal Burgh of Kirkwall, County of Orkney
Party per fess wavy Or and Azure: ancient three-masted ship of the First, sails furled, masts and rigging Proper, flags and penons Gules, each having a canton of the Second charged with a Saint Andrew's Cross Argent.
   Arms granted 11 November 1886.

15.   Burgh of Lerwick, County of Zetland
Or, in the sea Proper, a dragon ship Vert under sail, oars in action; on a chief Gules, a battle-axe fess ways Argent.
   Arms granted 20 April 1882.[9]

   Over the west door is a commemorative panel bearing the arms of the University of Aberdeen (Fig. 21.1):

Quarterly: 1st, Azure, a bough-pot Or charged with three salmon in fret Proper, and containing as many lilies of the garden, the dexter in bud, the centre full blown, and the sinister half-blown, also Proper, flowered Argent, issuant downwards from the middle chief amid rays of the sun a dexter hand holding an open book, likewise Proper (for King's College, Old Aberdeen),
2nd, Argent, a chief paly of six Or and Gules (for the 5th Earl Marischal),
3rd, Argent, a chevron sable between three boar heads erased Gules (for Bishop William Elphinstone),
4th, Gules, a tower triple-towered Argent, masoned Sable, windows and port of the Last. (for the City of Aberdeen)
Arms granted 1888.[10]

In each corner of the panel is a shield of arms representing the four nations of the University:
Dexter chief: Moray: Azure, three mullets Argent
The ancient armorial ensigns of the province of Moray.
Sinister chief: Buchan: Azure, three garbs Or.
The arms of the ancient Earldom of Buchan held by the Comyns before 1314.
Dexter base: Mar: Azure, between a bend six cross crosslets fitched Or.
The arms of the ancient Earldom of Mar, now held by Margaret, 31st Countess of Mar.
Sinister base: Angus: Argent, a lion passant guardant Gules, imperially crowned Or.
The armorial ensigns of Gillibride, Earl of Angus c.1135, and now borne by David Ogilvy 13th Earl of Airlie KT.

There are two further tinctured coats at a high level carved on the back of the organ case, dexter the arms of King's College and sinister the quartered coat of the University of Aberdeen.

This heraldic scheme in the Chapel, though restrained, is as important as the more elaborate approach made by Sir Robert Lorimer in the Scottish National War Memorial within Edinburgh Castle. This was formally opened on 14 July 1927, two years before Dr Kelly's University War Memorial was installed. Whereas Lorimer used burgh heraldry to indicate where the associated Scottish Regiments drew their recruits, Dr Kelly made his scheme pertinent to the burghs which sent their young people to Aberdeen for their further education.[11] There are obvious parallels between the two schemes but each acknowledge the symbolism and decorative qualities of heraldry.

Notes

[1] For the architectural context, see Chapter 16. After the demolition of Dr Fraser's library, the arms were repainted and gilded by John Norrie, AUL, New Charter Chest, Sh. 21, No. 39, account for 16 December 1773.
[2] The arms of Bishop Forbes, although carved in the seventeenth century, are not mentioned by Anderson, suggesting they had not been erected in this location in 1888. P. J. Anderson, 'Note on Heraldic Representations at King's College, Old Aberdeen', *PSAS*, XXIII, 1888–89, 80–86.

[3] In that year Sir George Mckenzie of Rosehaugh published the first printed book on Scottish heraldry, *Science of heraldry*. The engraved frontispiece shows the royal arms of Scotland with the shield surrounded by a collar of thistles exactly as carved on the King's College panel.

[4] Anderson, 1888–89, 80–86.

[5] L. J. Macfarlane, *A Visitor's Guide to King's College*, 2nd edn, Aberdeen, 1992, 15.

[6] Anderson, 1888–89, 80–86.

[7] Kelly, 1949, 64.

[8] See pp. 233–35.

[9] See R. M. Urquhart, *Scottish Burgh and County Heraldry*, London, 1973, for a list of pre–1973 Scottish Burgh arms.

[10] J. B. Paul, *An Ordinary of Arms*, Edinburgh, 1893, 23, 32, 52, 220.

[11] *The Scottish National War Memorial* (Edinburgh, 1932) with an introduction by General Sir Ian Hamilton GCB, DSO.

CHAPTER TWENTY-TWO
THE ARTS AND CRAFTS FURNISHINGS

By Elizabeth Cumming

The years immediately after the First World War witnessed the final flowering of the Arts and Crafts Movement in Britain. Not only were sculptors in demand for figural work to commemorate the fallen, but metalsmiths and architectural woodcarvers were needed to provide public and private memorials to enable the country to mourn the loss of so many. In Scotland, town squares and kirkyards were equipped with crosses and obelisks, and in many churches brass and bronze plaques were placed in chancels. Such commissions were usually handmade using traditional techniques to provide the sense of care and humanity demanded by the country. In the designs, too, a mix of modernity with tradition satisfied a quest for security and continuity with the past. Nearly all the designs, including the essential lettering, were the work of leading traditionalist architects — and in many cases, indeed, that of a relatively new professional, the conservation architect.

The two Aberdeen architects who contributed to this field were Alexander Marshall Mackenzie (1843–1933) and William Kelly (1861–1944). Marshall Mackenzie is now celebrated as the architect of the extension in the 'Skyscraper Perpendicular' Gothic style to Marischal College (1893–1906).[1] His memorial work included the moderno-classical War Memorial and Cowdray Hall (opened 1925) — Aberdeen's civic war memorial — and, on a smaller scale, interior plaques and panelling. In the latter, Marshall Mackenzie adopted a traditionalist approach in order to bind the present to the past. His oak work at Pitsligo, for instance, was 'in keeping with the early seventeenth-century oak work in the Laird's loft'.[2] William Kelly also believed in the need to harness such design to an awareness of past glories. As the architect who designed the university's war memorial — the panelling of the ante-chapel at King's — and oversaw the twentieth-century restoration of the entire chapel, he, more than any other, was the man who shaped the building as we know it today.

In many respects Kelly was the direct heir of William Smith (1817–91), in whose office he trained from 1877 to 1883,[3] and from whom he learned the precision of visual scholarship.[4] While practising in a number of styles, from the classical revival buildings of Aberdeen Savings Bank in Union Terrace and George Street to the Gothic of St Ninian's Church, Kelly was principally concerned with intellectual clarity, visual restraint, and a command of materials. Douglas Simpson, Kelly's biographer, emphasizes Kelly's mastery of proportion and skill in colours. In his discussion of the George Street bank, he comments how the two portions of the building are united by the use of extremely subtle materials: 'a podium of dull-polished Kemnay granite banded with

Rubislaw granite, also dull-polished'.[5] For Kelly, beauty of design and craftsmanship could only be created through a union of respect for the past, based necessarily on academic scholarship, with a scrupulous selection of materials. This devotion to tradition in terms of style and fabric was, however, only one side to his Arts and Crafts practice. In Kelly's best domestic work in Aberdeen, such as the 1890s granite villas in Rubislawden North and South, the architect 'exacted a disciplined workmanship of the highest order from the masons, carpenters, plumbers and painters'. Moreover, most of these houses were 'enriched with Morris wall-papers and furnishings, William De Morgan tiles, leaded glass-work and other features designed to have them as artistically satisfying as he could make them'.[6] Yet, while he was an academic who sought to bring beauty to his city, Kelly was a man whose career also embraced the social meaning of Arts and Crafts belief: in the post-war years, as the city's Director of Housing, he was able to design cottage housing schemes for all.[7]

Like community housing, war memorials are intended to be shared by the whole of society. The memorial woodwork which lines the ante-chapel at King's was the result of ten years of negotiation and design from initial university proposal[8] to consecration at the service on Armistice Day, 1928.[9] The 1890s work by the Edinburgh office of Sir Robert Rowand Anderson[10] and in turn that of Kelly through the 1920s and early 1930s, was aided by a set of fine measured drawings by James Cromar Watt (1862–1940) in 1884 (Figs 4.1, 4.3–5, 16.1). Watt had also been articled to Smith from 1879. These drawings, which include elevations, plans, and details such as canopies and doors, had won him the coveted prize of the Royal Institution of British Architects and were published by the leading London architectural journal *The Builder* in 1885.[11] But in drafting his designs, Kelly also referred to his own recent work at other memorials. At St Ninian's Church, for instance, two central oak panels in the chancel bear the names of the congregation killed in the war in raised, carved and gilded lettering, edged with a moulding carved with ivy, the badge of the Gordon Highlanders in which regiment the men had all served. Two shields bear a St Andrew's Cross and the Arms of Aberdeen. The entire memorial is topped by a five-bay modern Gothic canopy whose tracery provides a sense of shelter and delicacy of form.

Kelly adopted all these ideas in his design proposals for King's.[12] His oak screening lines three of the four walls of the ante-chapel with the rood screen placed against the fourth, east wall (Fig. 22.1, 21.1). Twenty-eight panels were needed for the names of the 341 members of the university — graduates, alumni, staff and students — who had fallen in the Great War.[13] These were framed in stiles carved with leaf motifs of seven Scottish trees or plants: the oak, maple (or Scotch plane), the hazel, the hawthorn, the rowan, the dog rose, and the bramble. The end of each group is enclosed in vine moulding, and the screen topped with a cornice and final cresting which echoes the top rail of the Gothic rood screen, as well as developing that sense of bittersweet beauty and containment achieved at St Ninian's. Fifteen medallions, showing the coats of arms of burghs to which most of the dead belonged, furnish the cornice.[14] The walls are lined simply, in contrast to the elaborately carved stalls such as the recent work at the Thistle Chapel or Dunblane Cathedral. As Kelly was to

Fig. 22.1.   The shrine on the south wall (1929–30) designed by Kelly to house
The Roll of Service

remove Rowand Anderson's 1890s chapel stalls in 1931 for alteration, 'simplification' and rebuilding, so he here designed a more modern Gothic interior within which the visitor can meditate.[15] Unlike Lorimer's Scottish National War Memorial (1924–27), however, this scheme does not attempt to inspire awe through grandeur. The figural carving introduced into the scheme — two painted figures of St Andrew and St Michael the archangel occupy niches either side of the west entrance door — is on a domestic scale. Nearby, a recess contains a medieval holy water stoup: above, Kelly displayed the old ambo which had originally projected from the top of the rood into the nave. The work progressed through late 1923 and 1924, and by the spring of 1925 only the lettering remained to be carved.[16] Apart from the list of names of the fallen, Kelly proposed two inscriptions for the memorial, one running along the stile above their names, the other above the west entrance door.[17] The second inscription is a particularly fine example of Scottish 1920s lettering.[18] The inscription panel bears centre the crest of the University of Aberdeen and at the four corners, the coats of arms of the 'four nations of the University: Moray, Buchan, Mar and Angus'.[19] By combining heraldry and fine lettering, the architect again adopted a traditionalist approach.[20] His choice of raised gilt letters set in incised ground relates to the foundation inscription on the west front (Fig. 5.1).

The name tablets were consecrated on Armistice Day in 1928.[21] The memorial was however still incomplete. Only in April 1929 did the War Memorial Committee finally recommend Douglas Strachan's design for the war memorial window on the north wall, first suggested in 1922 (Col. Pl. XV),[22] and propose that a recess be made in the south wall for the purpose of 'holding a special bound copy of the Roll of Service' (Fig. 22.1).[23] This recess provides intimacy for the visitor with what is effectively a miniature chapel to house the Book of Remembrance. Fine panelling is fitted with gilt-bronze figures of Peace and Mercy in a medieval style. Later still, in July 1934, bronze handles made by the Birmingham Guild Ltd were fitted to the doors of the chapel.[24] The War Memorial was now complete.

The university's War Memorial Committee had met throughout the 1920s. Its members — all architects or artist-craftsmen at the forefront of the Arts and Crafts Movement in the city — included Marshall Mackenzie, Kelly, Strachan, Harry Townend and James Cromar Watt. As noted above, Watt, one of Scotland's leading Arts and Crafts enamellers at the turn of the century, possessed a detailed knowledge of the building. Like Kelly, he had absorbed Smith's intellectual rigour and, in order to seek out historic church buildings and fittings, he travelled extensively in Europe, sometimes with his friend Douglas Strachan.[25] Watt enjoyed dialogue and collaboration with fellow artists and designers. In the 1890s he had been involved in the reconstruction of the Chapel of St Mary of Pity in the East Parish Church of St Nicholas where he worked closely with the English glass artist, Christopher Whall.[26] At King's College Chapel he encouraged Henry Wilson (1864–1934) in his fine sculpted bronze monument (1912–26) to Bishop Elphinstone.[27] Had it been made to the appropriate dimensions, it would have been a magnificent modern centrepiece and Wilson and Watt's vision for the chapel would have been realized.[28]

As Kelly had received an honorary doctorate in 1919, so the university also honoured Watt in 1931. Both these designers were inspired by the subtleties of natural materials. Like Kelly at the George Street Savings Bank, Watt's design for a university mace shows a Ruskinian love of natural stones whose colours were to be 'reddish ochre to grey green', 'veined brown and white', 'flesh to grey green' and 'dull green and greyish salmon'.[29] A religious man, like Kelly, his iconography is at times imbued with formal Christian symbols.[30] The colours, too, that he created were equally symbolic. Blood red enamels vividly decorate the brass alms dish which he made for King's College Chapel and presented in 1934 (Col. Pl. XId). Set with rock crystals, the dish is also decorated with the enamelled coats of arms of the founders of King's and Marischal Colleges, and of the burghs of Old and New Aberdeen. The dish is an object of both beauty and utility, and, like Kelly's work, it bears an inscribed message. Placed on the communion table at the east end of the chapel — in fact near the spot where Wilson's effigy of Elphinstone should have modernized the space — the dish's fine gilt inscription encourages visitors, including graduands, to play a democratic and generous role within society — to share their property, and perhaps also their knowledge and spiritual wealth.[32] At either end of King's College Chapel, the work of Kelly and Watt thus confirms and celebrates the value of craft in the modern age.

Notes

[1] National Monuments Record of Scotland, *Aberdeen on Record: Images of the Past: Photographs and Drawings of the National Monuments Record of Scotland*, Edinburgh, 1997, 43.

[2] Caption to the photograph of the panelling, *c.* 1920, in two albums of photographs of Scottish war memorials compiled between 1919 and 1921 by Thomas Greenshields Leadbetter of Spittal Tower: collection New College Library, University of Edinburgh.

[3] AUL, MS 2393.

[4] Kelly, 1949, 17. Simpson (p. 2) points out how Kelly admired the work of past Aberdeen architects John Smith and Archibald Smith not only for their 'taste, skill and scholarship' (attributes Simpson also perceived in Kelly himself) 'in the adaptation of classic forms . . . to modern uses' but, importantly, for their 'success in training a school of craftsmen unrivalled for the accuracy and beauty of their work'.

[5] Kelly, 1949, 4.

[6] Kelly, 1949, 7. These houses included Kelly's own home at 62 Rubislawden North (1896).

[7] These included Torry Garden City (1919). See *Aberdeen on Record*, 1997, 48. Kelly and his practice partner James B. Nicol were involved also in designs for the Sick Children's Hospital (1926–28) and the Royal Infirmary (1927–36).

[8] University of Aberdeen, *Minutes of the Senatus Academicus*, VIII, Aberdeen, 1920, 248. The meeting of 17 December 1918 states that 'the Principal referred to the question of a War Memorial, and proposed that the Senatus should take the initiative in suggesting the matter to the University Court, the General Council, and the Students Representative Council'. He suggested this might take two forms, the first being a 'complete Roll of those who have served in His Majesty's Forces' and 'some monument in the University Buildings to those who have given their lives for their country and its cause, in such form as may be considered most suitable'. The provision of memorials at King's College Chapel and in the Quadrangle of Marischal College were approved by the Senatus Academicus on 9 July 1919, but the University Court asked to present detailed plans of any 'suggested alterations to the University Buildings before the Scheme is definitely approved'. On 3 February 1920 the principal was able to report that subscriptions totalling £1,527 had been received.

[9] University of Aberdeen, *Minutes of the Senatus Academicus*, X, Aberdeen 1932, 207. It was agreed by the Senatus Academicus on 30 October 1928 that the 'war memorial tablets' would be consecrated 'at the

Service on to be held on Armistice Day': there were subsequent complaints that this service had been insufficiently advertised.

[10] Rowand Anderson designed new furnishings for the chapel in the early 1890s, including choir stalls for university professors at the east end. These were taken down, reworked and resited by Kelly in 1931 (see Chapter 16; Kelly, 1949, 64). Anderson's work continued into the 1900s: the minute of the University Court meeting on 12 April 1904 makes reference to Messrs James Garvie & Sons of Aberdeen as having carried out woodwork to Rowand Anderson's designs for the restoration of the chapel and states that the dado of carved oak woodwork in the ante-chapel has yet to be completed. Completion would be 'largely paid for by Lady Geddes' (the widow of Sir William D. Geddes, late principal of the university). The designs by the Rowand Anderson office also included minor metalwork such as a silver vase (AUL, MS U 1494 A5/44) to hold three or five lilies to be made up by Wakely & Wheeler, 27 Red Lion Square, London, and a design for a mace holder and hook for the chancel (AUL, MS U 1494 A5/38).

[11] AUL, MSS A5–7.

[12] The War Memorial Committee, established by the Senatus Academicus, presented Kelly's proposals for approval on 30 May 1922. University of Aberdeen, *Minutes of the Senatus Academicus*, IX, Aberdeen, 1928, 210. The cost was estimated at £2,242 'but reserving the question of the door shown in the south wall . . . the plans to be carried out in British oak off the tool'. The same meeting intimated a proposal to 'fill in' (reglaze) the north window in the ante-chapel and 'recommended the scheme proposed by Mr (Douglas) Strachan' for his war memorial window. It was also intimated that Dr Kelly's proposals would necessitate the removal of some existing memorials and that 'in view of the finances available', the Memorial be limited to the proposal in the ante-chapel.

[13] Of the 2,852 members of the university who served in the war, 341 were killed. They were commemorated in the *University of Aberdeen Roll of Service in the Great War 1914–1919*, edited by Mabel Desborough Allardyce and published by the university in 1921. This handsome volume included detailed biographies of all and photographs of most of those whose had died.

[14] University of Aberdeen, *Minutes of the Senatus Academicus*, X, Aberdeen, 1932, 289. The meeting of the Senatus Academicus held on 30 April 1929, after the dedication of the memorial, noted that the War Memorial Committee had changed two of these medallions: Tain replaced Dornoch and Inverurie the arms of Nairn. The changes reflected the proportional number of dead who came from these towns.

[15] Kelly, 1949, 64.

[16] University of Aberdeen, *Minutes of the Senatus Academicus*, IX, Aberdeen 1928, 468. On 28 October 1924 members of the Senatus Academicus were informed that most of the carving of the memorial was complete, and 'all the panelling, except the doors and the step or bench, has been framed up, and is ready to be glued'.

[17] University of Aberdeen, *Minutes of the Senatus Academicus*, IX, Aberdeen, 1928, 586. The inscription is given in Latin following a debate at the meeting of the Senatus Academicus held on 27 October 1925. The War Memorial Committee had cast even votes on the issue of the language: at this meeting a Latin inscription was favoured by 12 votes to 10. In translation this inscription (from The Epistle to the Hebrews, 11.33–34; 12.1) reads 'They through faith conquered kingdoms, exercised justice, quenched the force of fire. Out of weakness they grew strong, they became powerful in war, they routed the armies of foreigners. Therefore let us also, since we have so great a cloud of witnesses placed over us, lay aside every encumbrance and the sin that presses around us, and let us run with steadfastness the race that lies before us'. (Translation from Leslie Macfarlane, *A visitor's guide to King's College, University of Aberdeen, Aberdeen*, 1992, 17).

[18] Kelly regarded the quality of the lettering as challenging and vitally important. In an evening class to printers in March 1938, he said that 'the Roman alphabet . . . is the greatest thing of its kind ever invented and brought to perfection' and referred to the 'pre-eminent strength of character and beauty of the forms, and the rhythmic combination of these into words and groups of words'. In memorials, 'one of the chief points to be attended to in setting out carved inscriptions is to have, if possible, each and every word placed so as to bridge and overlap the spaces between words' (quoted in Kelly, 1949, 8). The inscription here reads 'TO THE GLORY OF GOD IN MEMORY OF THE SONS OF THIS UNIVERSITY WHO GAVE THEIR LIVES FOR THEIR KING, THEIR COUNTRY AND THEIR HOMES IN THE SACRED CAUSE OF JUSTICE AND FREEDOM DURING THE GREAT WAR MCMXIV MCMXIX' and it was subsequently amended to include the dead of the Second World War: their names are listed on the lower panels of the memorial. 'WAR' thus reads 'WARS' and 'MCMXIX' is now 'MCMXLV'. The war memorial now commemorates 524 members of the university who gave their lives in the wars.

[19] As given in Macfarlane, 1992, 17.

[20] Kelly was also responsible for the lettering for other memorials including those to Edward Henry Cardinal Howard, in the Fitzalan Chapel, Arundel, and to Sir John Frederick Bridge at Glass parish church: Kelly, 1949, Figs 12, 32, pp. 7–9.

[21] The service was held on Sunday 11 November and was conducted by the Very Reverend Principal, Sir George Adam Smith, DD, who himself had lost sons in the war. The *Aberdeen Press and Journal* reported on 12 November that 'there was a large congregation which overflowed into the ante-Chapel, where the dedication took place . . . the Principal recalled the facts on which the service rested — facts, simple, yet stupendous, terribly tragic yet glorious, shaking the world, yet only to redeem it from one of the greatest material and moral disasters by which mankind was ever threatened'. The university 'acknowledged the service of the committee charged with carrying out that project, and especially the genius of the architect, Mr William Kelly, and the careful skill of Mr Gibbon and the craftsmen under him who had prepared the panels and carved the names'.

[22] On 30 May 1922 the War Memorial Committee had intimated to the Senatus Academicus that it was proposed 'to fill in the North Window in the Ante-Chapel' and recommended 'a general scheme proposed by Mr Strachan'; University of Aberdeen, *Minutes of the Senatus Academicus*, IX, Aberdeen, 1928, 210.

[23] University of Aberdeen, *Minutes of the Senatus Academicus*, X, Aberdeen, 1932, 289. Meeting held on 30 April 1929.

[24] The south-east door replaced an ancient specimen covered with delicate medieval tracery which had been rescued from the cathedral in the early nineteenth century. Macpherson, 1899, 27, pl. LXVII. AUL, U662, Aberdeen University Court Edilis Committee. Door handle designs: AUL, U714, 29 November 1932; 23 June 1934.

[25] Many of his drawings from these tours are with Aberdeen Art Gallery.

[26] Christine Rew, *A Vivid and Individual Art: Enamels by James Cromar Watt*, Aberdeen, 1992. This catalogue is one of the few publications on this designer and craftsman of the Arts and Crafts movement in Scotland. Watt was celebrated for his enamelled jewellery, often set with opals, pearls and gemstones chosen and worked with the most scrupulous care. His work aimed at a perfection of form and materials. It was known beyond Aberdeen through his participation in group exhibitions across Scotland and he also contributed to the Scottish Section of the International Exhibition of Decorative Arts in Turin in 1902. In recognition of his contribution to British enamelling, his work was included and illustrated in Henry Cunynghame's treatise, *European Enamelling*, London, 1906.

[27] Henry Wilson had received an architectural training and practised primarily in building design and the crafts. Apprentice, and the successor to the practice of J. D. Sedding, one of the most important London architects and theorists of the late nineteenth century, Wilson pursued excellence in all the work he designed and made, which included both sculpture and the crafts of silversmithing and enamelling. His instructional book on *Silverwork and Jewellery* was published in 'The Artistic Crafts Series of Technical Handbooks', ed. W. R. Lethaby.

[28] See Chapter 24. The sculpture unfortunately was found to be too large for its intended site in front of the altar on its arrival in Aberdeen in 1927. It occupied the centre of the ante-chapel from 1930 to 1946 when it was moved outdoors. Denied its intended interior site, this important and fine sculpture has lost much of its impact, value, and intellectual relevance, and the chapel design lacks the richness which such 'new sculpture' would have provided.

[29] AUL, MS 2053. This document is his design for the mace which was made for the univerity S.R.C.

[30] Rew, 1992, 5, notes that Watt's sketchbooks (Aberdeen Art Gallery) contain drawings of Christian symbols.

[31] The Senatus Academicus noted at its meeting on 30 January 1934 that 'J Cromar Watt, Esq., LL.D., has presented an Alms Dish for use in the University Chapel'.

[32] In translation the dish's inscription reads 'If much has been given to you, distribute it generously. If little, devote yourself willingly to sharing even that little'.

CHAPTER TWENTY-THREE

THE STAINED GLASS

By Jane Geddes

The great traceried windows of King's Chapel were originally filled with stained glass, adding to the colour provided by the vestments and hangings. While Boece in 1522 merely refers to Bishop Elphinstone providing the window glass (*vitrinis*), Strachan adds in 1631 that the windows were coloured.[1] Gordon mentions in 1661 'all the church windows of old wer paynted glass; and ther remains as yit a pairt of that ancient braverye'.[2] As late as 1818 'some of the original panes of painted glass still remain' in the choir.[3] Today only two original pieces survive, a pair of small, yellow-stain quarries set in the tracery of the west window. As noted in Chapter 16, the glass suffered numerous assaults which included the deliberate walling up of certain windows and attacks from students with stones, snowballs and tennis balls.[4] As a result, the glazing is now predominantly late nineteenth- and early twentieth-century.

The incentive to begin reglazing came in 1870 when the library was removed from the west end of the chapel, the pulpitum was shifted one bay west to enlarge the choir in 1873, and the western bays effectively became an ante-chapel. Dr John Webster, an honorary graduate of the university and Lord Provost of Aberdeen donated the glass of the west window, made by Clayton and Bell.[5] (Letters refer to the windows on Fig. 23.1.)

CLAYTON AND BELL: WEST WINDOW (J, 1875) AND CAMPBELL WINDOW (F, 1880)

J. R. Clayton and Alfred Bell ran one of the most successful glazing firms in London, producing work for architects like G. E. Street and George Gilbert Scott. With their increasing popularity, more work was delegated to workshop staff.[6] Products like the King's west window became standardized, with a repetition of colour schemes, decorative designs and figures.[7] The iconography of this window sets the theme for the remainder in the chapel, tying in predominantly biblical narrative rather than theology, with aspects of university history (Col. Pl. XII).[8] The left panel shows Samuel teaching the law to young prophets (1 Samuel 19.20). Above are medallions of King James IV and Bishop Elphinstone. The next panel shows several prophets with Alisha cutting timber by the Jordan (2 Kings 6.4), a reference to the construction of King's College, with Andrew Melville and the Earl Marischal above. The third panel shows Christ disputing with the doctors in the Temple (Luke 2.46), with Bishops Patrick Forbes and Gilbert Burnet above. The last panel shows Paul being

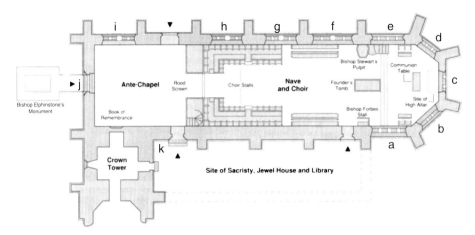

Fig. 23.1.   Plan of chapel showing numbering of the windows

instructed by Gamaliel (Acts 22.3) with Principal G. Campbell and Dr James Beattie above.

The second window is dedicated to Peter Colin Campbell, Principal and Vice-Chancellor, 1855–76. It depicts the visit of the Queen of Sheba to Solomon (1 Kings 10.1–13), and the adoration of the Magi, three kings worshipping Christ. An extraordinary 'crown tower' is in the background. The coats of arms at the bottom are, on the left, the University of Aberdeen, and on the right Principal Campbell.

HARDMAN AND CO.: THE MACPHERSON WINDOWS (1883)

Professor Hugh Macpherson proposed to present two new windows for the sides of the apse in 1882.[9] He had strong personal ideas for their design and style: 'We have no wish to commit ourselves to Clayton and Bell and think it would be well that some other artists should have the chance of showing what they can do!'[10] He chose John Hardman and Co. of London and Birmingham, asking for six apostles in each window. The glaziers, brimming with their own iconographic schemes, had to politely point out to their patron that 'the twelve apostles in simply two rows of figures is generally monotonous'.[11] Macpherson won and Fig. 16.6 shows the result.

When it was proposed to install the Harrower window in the central east bay in 1934, the new glazing scheme by Douglas Strachan was conceived as a triptych and the two Macpherson/Harding windows were removed, to the consternation of Macpherson's family.[12]

MORRIS AND CO.: ROBERTSON SMITH WINDOW (E, 1897)

This window was dedicated to the memory William Robertson Smith, professor of Hebrew (1846–94). The commission to Morris and Co. in 1879 was executed by

Edward Burne-Jones and a team of workshop painters (Col. Pl. XIII).[13] The four figures, Isaiah, Ezekiel, Jeremiah and Daniel were originally designed for St Eustachius the Martyr, Tavistock in 1875. About this commission Burne-Jones comments in his account book of 1875 '4 major prophets on a minor scale designed I regret to say with the minimum of ability'.[14] Although this window is a typical late product of the Morris studio, with a lot of the detail added by assistants, it is a period piece with the added advantage of providing swathes of clear, warm light on the north side of the chapel. It is not universally appreciated: in 1984 a substantial endowment was presented by Dr William Lillie in order to 'be used for the preservation and adornment of the chapel at King's College with the suggestion but not express condition that when the sum is sufficiently accumulated it be used to replace the Robertson Smith window by a more pleasing memorial to the great scholar'.[15]

DOUGLAS STRACHAN, GEDDES WINDOW (A, 1903); PIRIE WINDOW (H, 1912); WAR MEMORIAL WINDOW (I, 1920); HARROWER WINDOW (C, 1934); SOUTH-EAST APSE WINDOW (B, 1938); NORTH-EAST APSE WINDOW (D, 1938)

The seven windows by Douglas Strachan (1875–1950) were made between 1903 and 1938. They provide the chapel with a visual unity and also allow viewers to explore the artistic development of one of the great Scottish glaziers of the twentieth century. In contrast to the Victorian workshop glaziers, Strachan said, 'I have never consciously repeated myself, nor ever consciously not repeated myself in my work'.[16]

Douglas Strachan attended Robert Gordon's College, Aberdeen and spent one session at the life school of the Royal Academy, Edinburgh.[17] In 1897 he met James Cromar Watt, the Aberdeen draftsman and enamellist[18] and they travelled around the Mediterranean on a drawing tour together. His first commissions were for large murals in Aberdeen[19] and society portraits. He resented the fashionable slickness required for the portraits[20] and began to explore the abstract qualities of pure colour which could be found in glass. As a result, with the encouragement of William Kelly, he produced a window for the chapel of St Mary in the undercroft of St Nicholas' church, Aberdeen. Here, Cromar Watt had designed the communion table and Christopher Whall had made another window. Strachan was strongly influenced by Christopher Whall who believed in the artistic integrity required by a true artist craftsman: supervising or executing every stage of the production from the first sketch to firing and fixing the lead. Whall's search for better materials led him to the firm of Britton and Gilson in Southwark where in 1888 a new glass of rich jewel-like translucency had been developed. These technical improvements can be seen in King's Chapel where Strachan's glass gleams vibrantly compared with the flat, solid blocks of colour produced by Clayton and Bell and Burne-Jones.

In 1913 Strachan won the competition for windows in the Peace Palace at the Hague, and his international reputation was secured. The architect Sir Robert Lorimer was a keen promoter of Strachan's glass, commissioning him to work in the National War Memorial, Edinburgh in 1924.[21] However Lorimer overturned many of Strachan's colour schemes in order to improve lighting on the sculpture.[22] So it is principally at Paisley Abbey (east window, 1931), Winchelsea church, East Sussex (1928–33) and at King's Chapel that the integrity of Strachan's work can be appreciated.

The evolution of Strachan's style can be fully explored at King's. In the Geddes and De Gurbs windows (1903, 1904) the figures are literal portraits, closely delineated (Col. Pl. XIVa). He makes extensive use of the variable texture of the glass itself to deflect the light. Rich colour tones of blue and purple intensify each other. The lead lines are handled with a medieval feeling for the size of pane and structure of the figures. He subtly varies the thickness of the lead to enhance certain features. In the Pirie window (1912) he is still absorbed by individuals, narrative and historic detail, to an almost Pre-Raphaelite extent (Col. Pl. XIVb).

By 1921, with the War Memorial window, Strachan's style had broken free from the constraints of linear detail and single lights. The design, spread across the entire window, explodes into a swirl of symbolic colour (Col. Pl. XV). Transmitting only the cool northern light, powerfully energetic bands of blue are punctured by stabs of red, which highlight the sombre brown/green soldiers. The figures, memorials of the mass slaughter, are no longer portraits but allegories. In its rich symbolism of both form and colour, the window anticipates the designs of other early 1920s memorials, such as the Apollyon window in the Martin Hall, New College, Edinburgh (c. 1922).[23]

The three apse windows present a challenge to any artist because their light is severely compromised by the Cromwell Tower immediately behind, but Strachan could cope with this. These windows (1934 and 1938) represent Strachan's mature style (Col. Pl. XVI). He has reverted to a dense narrative composition but the figures are now elongated and schematic. Intense colours, cooled by the use of white or clear glass, enhance each other. Bold lead lines around small panes add movement to the compositions. This style had already developed when Strachan made the windows for the Scottish National War Memorial in 1927. At King's, the three east windows work together. Although they are set in triple lancets, a loose circle embraces the width of each window. On the east window, dark blues and reds in the lower part of the composition give way to soaring white and yellow at the top, rising above the crucifixion. With its cool tones, the glass cannot and is not required to glow. The north-east window is similarly cool but light. But its pair, on the south-east cant, catches the glancing morning sun and gleams with red and gold.

In all his King's windows, Strachan maintains a thread of meaning: a link between the eternal truths of the Bible and personalities and events at the university. In the Geddes window (1903, a) the coming of Christ is personalized by a portrait of Sir William Geddes in his Vice-Chancellor's robes representing the magus Balthazar. On the De Gurbs window (1904, g) the coronet of Stephen Baron De Gurbs, a university graduate, is depicted beneath the Presentation at the Temple. The Pirie window (1912, h) shows the life of Bishop William Elphinstone. On the left panel, James IV's ambassador presents the supplication for founding the university to Pope Alexander VI; next, the Elphinstone is shown supervising the construction of the great hall; the third panel shows Elphinstone presenting the Aberdeen Breviary to James IV; and the right panel shows the bishop's burial in King's Chapel. On the War Memorial window (1920, i) allegorical figures of prudence, fortitude and justice ride out to combat evil against the background of King's and Marischal College. The enormity of this theme led Strachan to abandon his tendency to depict portrait faces in favour of anonymous symbolic figures. The three apse windows create a harmony of colour. The central Harrower Memorial window (1934, c) is appropriately Christ the King, conqueror of death. Bishop Elphinstone kneels at his feet, along with St Andrew, St Machar (patron saint of the cathedral) and St Nicholas (patron saint of New Aberdeen). The south-east and north-east windows are a pair (1938, b and d). They are packed with symbolic detail, a creation cycle to the south and a cosmic hymn of praise to the north.[24]

Concerning the iconography of these windows Strachan wrote cheerfully to the principal,

> . . . my friend Kelly who has seen the designs wrote to me some days ago expressing doubts about the soundness of my theology and saying that after a second day of cogitation he was still wondering 'how the Theologians would take it' — 'it' being the little death of Abel in the south east window. Now Mr Kelly has always been a dab at Theology, whereas I—! my ignorance of it is so abysmal that I do not even understand, or have ever been able to memorise its scale of values: that will give you some ideas.[25]

However, Strachan was well aware of the power art has to impart spiritual meaning and equally how the church can challenge artists to work on a higher plane. He wrote 'The church owes a debt to art and art a debt to the church'.[26]

Strachan enjoyed a cordial relationship with the university, receiving an honorary LL.D. in 1923. He addressed the principal as 'My dear Fyfe' and his correspondence is in a decidedly jocular vein.[27] He refunded the Court for what he considered excessive payment for the Harrower window, and he presented the German madonna to the chapel in 1944.[28]

WILIAM WILSON, MERSON MEMORIAL WINDOW (K, 1963)

William Wilson, a close follower of Douglas Strachan, was inspired to develop in Strachan's style after seeing the National War Memorial.[29] This window is dedicated to Captain William Merson of the Gordon Highlanders who was killed in France in 1916. On the left are the arms of Aberdeen University and the badge of the Gordon Highlanders. On the right is St Andrew. Wilson's eclectic use of colour and the predominant use of diamond lights on an otherwise small design tend to minimize the impact of this window, but it enhances the theme of the Memorial Chapel.

Notes

[1] I would like to thank Elizabeth Cumming for commenting on this chapter. Boece, 95; '*vitrinas coelaturas*', A. Strachan, *Panegyricus inauguralis*, Aberdeen, 1631, 10.

[2] James Gordon, *Abredoniae utriusque descriptio. A description of both touns of Aberdeen*, Spalding Club, Edinburgh, 1842, 23.

[3] Wm. Kennedy, *Annals of Aberdeen*, London, 1818, vol. 2, 397.

[4] For example: AUL, MS K 256/42/1, p. 6; K 278/2/45; K 255/43, Miscellaneous vouchers; *Fasti*, 245.

[5] L. Macfarlane, *A Visitor's guide to King's College*, Aberdeen, 1992, 30.

[6] AUL, U 399, letter from John Webster to Lord Henry Lennox, 30 June 1874, concerning the commission to Clayton and Bell: 'they are well known as being at the head of their profession and the beautiful windows in St Michael's Church,Cornhill may be referred to as sufficient evidence of their skill'. AUL, U 399, coloured tracing for the west window by Clayton and Bell. Also letter from Office of Works, London, 18 August 1879, giving approval for the Campbell window by Clayton and Bell.

[7] Martin Harrison, *Victorian Stained Glass*, London, 1980, 31–32.

[8] The iconography of all the glass is explained in detail in Macfarlane, 1992, 23–32.

[9] AUL, U 399, W. Roberston to Office of Works, 27 April 1882: Macpherson's gift of the glass required the windows to be fitted with new stone tracery.

[10] AUL, U 399, H. Macpherson to Office of Works, 16 February 1882.

[11] AUL, U 399, J. Harnmann, letter, 31 December 1882. Their letter explains the iconography in great detail.

[12] AUL, Minutes of the University Court, XII, 11 October 1932–35, October 1936, Aberdeen, 1939. January 1934, p. 194. AUL, MS U613, Letter from Frances Macpherson, 19 March 1938; letter from Kelly to Frances Macpherson, 22 March 1938, apologizing for the difficulty in contacting the Macpherson family about the removal of the windows.

[13] A. C. Sewter, *The Stained Glass of William Morris and his circle — a catalogue*, Yale, 1970, II, 5.

[14] Sewter, 1970, II, 185. The same designs are also used at Jesus College Cambridge, Arbroath Old Parish Church and St Stephen Broughty Ferry. Sewter comments (I, 50) that these prophets 'lack altogether the power of the Jesus College evangelists, their forms being almost smothered in voluminous drapery and their excessively small hands twisting rather weakly'.

[15] Dr Lillie donated £14,000. Aberdeen University Finance Department, trust fund accounts.

[16] Considerable information for this section has been gleaned from Jill Runcie, *Douglas Strachan, and the windows he designed for St Machar's Cathedral and King's College, Aberdeen*, unpublished MA dissertation in History of Art at Aberdeen University, 1997. I would like to thank Jill for allowing me to use her work. Gordon Webster, 'Douglas Strachan, L.L.D; H.R.S.A.', *British Society of Master Glass Painters*, XIV, 1964, 43.

[17] Basic information about his life and commissions in *Dictionary of National Biography, 1941–1950*, L. G. Wickham Legg and E. T. Williams (eds), Oxford, 1959, 846.

[18] See Chapter 22.

[19] The Trades Hall and Music Hall. *The Journal of Decorative Art*, December 1899, 10–11.

[20] Glasgow School of Art Archives, DIR, 9, D. Strachan to W. Hutcheson, 9 February 1935, Glasgow School of Art Archive.

[21] Sir Robert Lorimer, 'Memorial Stained Glass Windows', *Country Life*, 13 November 1915, 641–44. A. C. Russell, *Stained Glass Windows of Douglas Strachan*, Aberlemno, 1994, lists all his known windows.

[22] Douglas Strachan to Sir John Stirling Maxwell, 8 October 1931. Glasgow City Archives, Maxwell of Pollok Muniments, T-PM/122/1/38.

[23] E. Cumming, 'Patron and Artist: Grace Warrack and Douglas Strachan', *The Yearbook of the Scottish Society for Art History*, Edinburgh, 1988, 52.

[24] Minutes of the University Court, XII, 11 October 1932–5 October 1936, Aberdeen, 1939. January 1934, p. 194, includes detailed description of the iconography by Strachan.

[25] AUL, MS U613, Strachan to Fyfe, 24 February 1938.

[26] D. Strachan, 'Modern art and the future', *AUR*, June 1918, 193–207.

[27] AUL, MS U613, Strachan to Fyfe, 24 February 1938.

[28] See Chapter 12.

[29] F. Pearson, *William Wilson 1905–1972*, The Trustees of the National Galleries of Scotland, Edinburgh, 1994.

CHAPTER TWENTY-FOUR

HENRY WILSON AND ELPHINSTONE'S MONUMENT, 1912–31

By John Thomas

The modern monument to Bishop Elphinstone has its origins in the restoration and adornment of the chapel, begun under the principalship of Sir William Geddes (1885–1900).[1] The founder's tomb at that time consisted of two stone slabs, set above the pavement, and ideas to mark his memory included a window, panelling in the ante-chapel, and a statue, but in 1909, the scheme of re-creating the original tomb, as known from the 1542 inventory, was considered. By March 1910, a sub-committee entrusted with the task of producing a monument was considering sculptural ideas which were the work of English artist Henry Wilson (1864–1934); a contract to produce the final work was made with him on 20 March 1912 (Fig. 24.1).[2]

The committee included architects A. Marshall Mackenzie and William Kelly, stained-glass artist Douglas Strachan, and local artist and architect James Cromar Watt; a vital additional member was John Harrower, Professor of Greek in the years

Fig. 24.1.   General view of Bishop Elphinstone's monument

Fig. 24.2.   Collotype by
Henry Wilson (Copyright:
University of Aberdeen)

1886–1931. These men had the immensely difficult task of producing a monument
(despite seemingly endless difficulties and delays lasting over more than twenty years)
working with an artist who was given to procrastination, requests for extra payments,
and who produced a work far larger than stipulated (and did not himself erect on
site — which seems to be the work of James Cromar Watt); between them, however,
sculptor and committee produced a work which is arguably one of the finest personal
funerary monuments created in the twentieth century, and one which bears
comparison with such monuments of any age.

     Henry Wilson was the quintessential figure of the Arts and Crafts Movement.
Trained at an art school, he worked as an architect, but from 1900, increasingly turned
to jewellery, metalwork, and sculpture. His introduction to the University of
Aberdeen might have come by way of Cromar Watt, who may have met Wilson
when a student of architecture, in London, in the late 1880s.[3] Wilson's workshop was
at Platt, Borough Green, Kent, but the bronzes which compose the monument were
sculpted in Venice, and cast there by Munaretti of Murano. The contract stipulated
completion by 31 May 1913, but the sculpture was not unveiled until 1931.[4] The
delays were due to the war, Wilson's serious illness around 1915, but more, perhaps,
a seeming inability on his part to regard time, and the requirements of a contract, to
impinge on — and possibly compromise — the creative process. Perhaps a future
biographer of the artist will explain the events concerning this commission, his
constant requests to the committee for more money and time, with reference to his

Fig. 24.3.
Love

personality, and observe them in his dealings with other patrons. In the end, it was an exasperated committee, perhaps prevented from foreclosing on the artist by the favourable reports of Harrower (who saw some of the bronzes in Venice), and the investment of effort that had already been made, who paid the founder for the bronzes, had them shipped directly to Aberdeen (against Wilson's wishes), and erected. A mock-up placed on the site of the original tomb (Fig. 16.6) proved that the new memorial was too large for the main body of the chapel. So, initially the work was set in the ante-chapel, but in the end its excessive size caused its re-siting (1946) outside the chapel's western door.[5]

The process of designing the monument involved around three or four different forms of recumbent effigy supported by piers and/or sarcophagus, with representations of Virtues set beneath the effigy. Three possible stages are discernible, 1) that known from a photograph of a model;[6] 2) that seen in a colour-washed drawing formerly at the Royal Institute of British Architects Drawings Collection;[7] and 3) that seen in a collotype (Fig. 24.2).[8] A further evolution takes the 'collotype scheme' to the monument as we have it. There may well have been other stages in the process, not now readily recoverable.

The second stage, the RIBA drawing, shows an angel sitting above Elphinstone's head, his wings enclosing the upper part of the effigy; clearly Wilson had been

The Elphinstone Monument - Bronze Figures

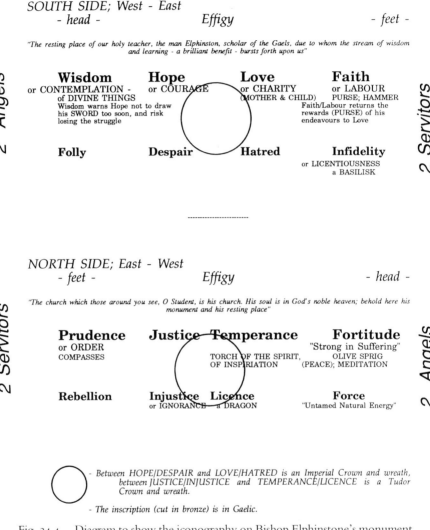

SOUTH SIDE; West - East
- head -   Effigy   - feet -

"The resting place of our holy teacher, the man Elphinston, scholar of the Gaels, due to whom the stream of wisdom and learning - a brilliant benefit - bursts forth upon us"

2 Angels

Wisdom
or CONTEMPLATION -
of DIVINE THINGS
Wisdom warns Hope not to draw
his SWORD too soon, and risk
losing the struggle

Hope
or COURAGE

Love
or CHARITY
(MOTHER & CHILD)

Faith
or LABOUR
PURSE; HAMMER
Faith/Labour returns the
rewards (PURSE) of his
endeavours to Love

2 Servitors

Folly   **Despair**   **Hatred**   **Infidelity**
or LICENTIOUSNESS
a BASILISK

NORTH SIDE; East - West
- feet -   Effigy   - head -

"The church which those around you see, O Student, is his church. His soul is in God's noble heaven; behold here his monument and his resting place"

2 Servitors

Prudence
or ORDER
COMPASSES

Justice Temperance
TORCH OF THE SPIRIT,
OF INSPIRATION

Fortitude
"Strong in Suffering"
OLIVE SPRIG
(PEACE); MEDITATION

2 Angels

Rebellion   **Injustice Licence**
or IGNORANCE   a DRAGON

Force
"Untamed Natural Energy"

- Between HOPE/DESPAIR and LOVE/HATRED is an Imperial Crown and wreath,
  between JUSTICE/INJUSTICE and TEMPERANCE/LICENCE is a Tudor
  Crown and wreath.

- The inscription (cut in bronze) is in Gaelic.

Fig. 24.4.   Diagram to show the iconography on Bishop Elphinstone's monument

influenced by Alfred Gilbert's Clarence tomb, Windsor (1892–98), where there is a similar angel at the head, or that at Hawarden, Clwyd (William Richmond, *c.* 1901–06), where an angel's wings enfold W. E. Gladstone and his wife.

The Virtues and Vices (the Inventory specified the original presence of Faith, Hope, Charity/Love, and also Justice, Prudence, Fortitutde and Temperance) are perhaps the most fascinating and beautiful aspect of the monument. While of partly ancient origin, such figures for long featured in the history of Christian art. The sculpture's scheme of figures and ideas, and their arrangement, was seemingly complete by Wilson's memorandum of June 1915.[9] It reveals that Wilson had recast the traditional Virtues as the Elohim, the seven creative spirits about the throne of God, the 'sevenfold aspect of divine power', and this transformation betrays a little of that mystical, esoteric, interest present in *fin de siècle* art. (Faith, Hope and Charity are also to be seen on the only comparable contemporary sculpture, Gilbert's Queen Alexandra memorial, London, 1926–32.)

Together, the Virtues and Vices produce friezes of figures, yet are sculpted completely in the round (Fig. 24.3); they are formally and symbolically linked by swords, and limbs, the Vices squeezed beneath them with often-amazing contortion (Fig. 24.4). The effigy, with its contrasting, peaceful immobility, may appear comparatively insignificant, until it is realised that the Virtues are Elphinstone's monument, issuing directly from his life and works.

Whatever the the stylistic nature of the sixteenth-century monument, in its re-creation, Henry Wilson chose to work in a broadly classical tradition, his Virtues looking back to Victorian and neo-classic reflections of Antique art (and very much present is the inspiration of Michelangelo). Similarities with such precedent as Henry VII's tomb (1511–18) are no accident, for Wilson created a fitting successor to the traditions of late medieval and Renaissance funerary sculpture, both in the grandeur and delicate detail of his work, and also in its dramatic presentation of humanist philosophical values and ideals.

Notes

[1] This chapter is an abridgement of John Thomas, 'The Elphinstone Monument at King's College, Aberdeen', *AUR*, LVI, 1992, 315–33. This article provides more detailed references and early photographs of the monument.

[2] AUL, U 1161, Minutes 20 March 1912.

[3] In 1908 Wilson had been commissioned by William Kelly to make the ceremonial staff for the university. Letter, Kelly to Wilson, 16 August 1906, Royal College of Art, London, HW–5.

[4] AUL, U 1161, Minutes 9 December 1911.

[5] AUL, U 701/3, folder for years 1945–48.

[6] AUL, 560, item 2, 'an early suggestion for the monument'. Photograph of a model showing a recumbent figure on pillars.

[7] *Catalogue of the drawings collection of the Royal Institute of British Architects*, ed. Jill Lever, T-Z, Gregg International, 1984, 251, (Henry Wilson, drawing 2). The Wilson drawings at the R.I.B.A. are in the process of transfer to the Victoria and Albert Museum.

[8] AUL, MS 2054. This folder includes many early photos of the monument in various stages, with comments by James Cromar Watt.

[9] W. D. Simpson, H. Wilson, and H. Townend, 'The Founder's Memorial', *AUR*, XVIII, 1930–31, 213–21. Typed copies of the memorandum in AUL, MS 2054.

CHAPTER TWENTY-FIVE

THE CHAPEL TODAY, 2000

By GILLEAN MACLEAN

Today King's College Chapel once again houses a worshipping community, albeit a very different one to that described in the early years following its foundation. Instead of eight full-time chaplains there is only one, currently a woman. Alexander Murray's legacy of the 1793 has been built on and extended by Professors of Divinity and, since 1947, the serving chaplains to the university.[1]

Each weekday in term time begins with an act of worship. Morning prayers, like all of the present-day services in the chapel, are open to students and staff of all denominations of the Christian Church. Members of other faiths, seekers and the simply curious are also given a warm welcome. The leading of prayers is today shared by the chaplain (a Presbyterian minister of the Church of Scotland), the assistant chaplain (a priest of the Scottish Episcopal Church) and the chaplain appointed by the Roman Catholic Church. The form is not something that would have been recognized by those early eighteen students, although the numbers attending are similar. The difference is that no one is coerced into attending and the chapel certainly could not house the present university community of around 12,000 students and some 3,000 staff. The liturgy currently in use is a hybrid of many traditions, both ancient and modern, Roman Catholic and Protestant. Morning prayers, as in past times, are followed by a simple breakfast.

Each Sunday morning sees the main act of university worship. This service is presided over, in normal circumstances, by the chaplain to the university. The choir, academics and clergy attending process in, preceded by the sacrist carrying aloft a replica of the King's College mace. The congregation may sit only when the mace is lowered into its housing in the stalls. Preachers come from as wide a range of theological persuasions as possible. They are invited by the chaplain in consultation with the university Chapel Committee whose job it is to oversee the use of the chapel and offer encouragement and advice to the chaplain and her team.

Congregations are now a mixture of students, all grades of staff, local people and visitors and an attempt is made to offer in the choice of preachers as wide a canvas of opinion as possible. A recent partial-revival of the tradition of 1826 has seen a termly invitation to preach offered to candidates for the ministry of the Church of Scotland.

Although the current chaplain is a Presbyterian, the form of service incorporates responses and a corporate confession and an attempt is made to represent other worshipping traditions. Sunday morning service is followed each week by informal communions. Professor Milligan, a great exponent of more frequent communion, would have been delighted.[2]

Christ's College, the body supervising training of students for the ministry, holds a weekly service on a Friday lunch time, the purpose of which is to familiarise students with current practices of worship, to stimulate theological debate and to draw together the community. The service incorporates the sacrament of communion and is usually presided over by staff of the Department of Divinity with Religious Studies.

Further, a weekly Eucharist is celebrated on Wednesday by the chaplain to Anglican students, who is also a lecturer in Zoology. This too is open to all members of the university Christian Community.

Regular Roman Catholic masses are held in Elphinstone House on the High Street. The General Act of 1560, banning all mass, still largely holds in King's College Chapel although on the occasion of the university quincentenary (1995) special arrangements were made and a mass celebrated at which only the celebrant and the assistant received. A further mass is planned for the chapel's quincentenary on 2 April 2000 and it is hoped that the Roman Catholic members of the congregation will be able to take part fully. Nuptial masses are also permitted. In this new age of supposed tolerance, and as we enter the third millennium, the wisdom of retaining the ban on the mass is actively being discussed by the chaplain and the Chapel Committee.

Other services, such as evening services or weekly prayer meetings encompassing a wide range of traditions, change according to the needs and composition of the student community. Each year brings new ideas and demands from all parts of the globe reflecting the diversity of age and culture of our students.

Throughout the university year there are a number of major events in the life of the chapel and its many congregations. In 1928 the space to the west of the rood screen, by then little more than a lobby, was dedicated as the university war memorial, and is now designated as the ante-chapel. The names adorning its walls are now sadly too numerous to recite during the course of the remembrance service. The many students of the university Cadet Units attend, as do their senior representatives, and wreaths are laid for those who died during both world wars and all conflicts since. The Kirking of the Students' Representative Council remains an annual event.

Founder's Day is another event that is celebrated in the chapel and on a Sunday in February the community gathers. The principal reads aloud the names of the founding fathers of our institution together with a selection of those more recent benefactors who continue to support the life of the university.

In mid-March a special service is held to honour the business community of Aberdeen city and members of the Incorporated Trades of Aberdeen (an ancient institution connected with the university since the days of William Guild) are invited to attend. The pulpit fall now in use in the chapel, replacing the one gifted in 1908 by women students, was presented to the chapel by the Aberdeen Guild of Weavers and stands today as a reminder of the warm and co-operative relationship between the university and the local business community.

During 1998 the chapel hosted ninety-eight marriages and eight baptisms. In 1994, the year when Aberdeen University celebrated the centenary of women's matricula-tion, the current chaplain was ordained by the Presbytery of Aberdeen — the first woman chaplain and the first woman to be ordained in King's College Chapel. In

1998 the current assistant chaplain was ordained priest of the Scottish Episcopal Church by the bishop of the diocese.

Not all weddings in the chapel are conducted by members of the chaplaincy team and wedding parties are encouraged to bring their own priest or minister if they have one.

Graduation ceremonies do not normally take place in King's College Chapel and the chaplain or a member of her team is required to offer prayers, both in Latin and in English, at the event in Marischal College's Mitchell Hall. Graduation Services are, however, held in the chapel, and graduands and their families travel by bus from the campus at King's into the town where the culmination of their years of hard work will be recognized in the conferring of their degree.

Sadly the chapel has also been used in present times for funerals and memorial services. Students, staff and alumni of the university may request its use and bring their own minister in consultation with the chaplain. In the event of a student death it is now common practice for the chaplain to preside over a service of thanksgiving for their life, allowing the whole community to share in the bereavement process.

The role of the chaplain today is a wide-ranging one of which an oversight of the chapel services is only a part. She works hand-in-hand with the other student support agencies within the university, visiting students in hospital or in their homes as necessary. She spends many hours in listening to an increasing diversity of problems and tries to provide opportunities for retreats and discussion. She is assisted by a team of chaplains, most of whom are unpaid and all, apart from her Roman Catholic colleague, are part-time and seconded by their denominations. The team, along with a small group of student helpers, form a vital support role within the university community and help to foster a spirit of co-operation between the institution and its neighbours.

A plaque placed in the ante-chapel by Principal Thomas Murray Taylor (1897–1962, appointed Principal and Vice-Chancellor in 1948, and died in office) bears these lines,

> Here one may
> Without much molestation
> Be thinking what he is
> Whence he came
> What he has done
> And to what the King has called him.

The conclusion to this process of thought today may be very different from that in Principal Taylor's time and certainly from that in Bishop Elphinstone's time. However, the opportunities for exploring the human spirit and its relationship to the divine will continue to be offered by those whose role it is to take King's College Chapel and its diverse congregations into the next millennium.

Notes
[1] Revd Alexander Murray (MA 1746, DD 1784): Founder of the Murray Lectureship. See Chapter 14; *Fasti*, 209. Murray's will of 1793, executed in 1824–25, provided for a clergyman to preach in chapel.
[2] Hew Scott, *Fasti Ecclesiae Scoticanae*, Edinburgh, 1915–28, VII, 377.

CHAPTER TWENTY-SIX

A BIBLIOGRAPHY OF KING'S COLLEGE CHAPEL, ABERDEEN

By Myrtle Anderson-Smith

Notes

Some items are listed under more than one heading

MS references are to manuscripts held in the University of Aberdeen, Directorate of Information Systems and Services: Historic Collections, Special Libraries and Archives, King's College, Aberdeen AB24 3SW

ABDUA references are to paintings and objects held in the University of Aberdeen, Directorate of Information Systems and Services: Historic Collections, University Art Collection, Marischal Museum, Broad Street, Aberdeen AB10 1YS

Published material can be located in University of Aberdeen libraries by use of the On-line Public Access Catalogue, URL: http://webpac.qmlib.abdn.ac.uk/webpac.html

I   **Sources specifically relating to King's College Chapel, King's College, or the University of Aberdeen**

1.1   **Archival sources**   Arranged chronologically by the period described

1.1.1   **King's College archives** 1494/5–1860

Charters, Writs and Related Papers in the Old Charter Chest, MS K 256/1–52	1494/5– 1766
Arranged by shuttle and item; Inventory, MS K 106, and Summary list	
Papal Bull, MS K 256/43/2	1494/5
See below 1.2.1 1494, Innes; 1.3.1 Eeles	
Foundation Charter, MS K 256/48/2	1505
Contains many directions for conduct of services	
See below 1.3.1 Eeles	
Second Foundation Charter; MS K 256/48/3; copy *c.* 1850, MS K 102	1529–31
Contains many directions for conduct of services	
See below 1.3.1 Eeles	
Inventory of Rectorial Visitation of King's College 1542, MS K 256/ 23/1	1542
See below 1.2.1 1494, Innes; 1.3.1 Eeles	
Liber Rationum Collegii Regalis Aberdonensis, MS K 2	1579–1653
Economist's accounts	
Senatus Minutes, MS K 36–52	1634–1860
Intermittent references, e.g. 1718–19, work on steeple; 1773, April–May, fitting up nave as library	
Compts of the Buildings Procuration, MS K 256/42	1652–1700
Procuration Accounts, MS K 54–65	1658–1850
Incorporating Aedilis Accounts	
Intermittent references, e.g. K 56, Accounts for 1700–02, 4th part, Section 2, Art. 2: 'To colouring of Kings armes & dyall £12.0.0'; 'To work about the bells . . . placing of bells in the steeple'; non-specific payments for 'work about the Colledge'	
Related Procuration Vouchers, MS K 278/1–12, for 1623–1763, incomplete	
Aedilis Accounts, MS K 257/18–20	1658–1776
Intermittent references, e.g. /18/1 The new work of King's College 1658–63: diary of work, workmen, sources of stone, payments, etc.; /18/5 Repair of cupola of steeple, 1718; /18/14 Pointing of steeple, 1755–56; /19/1 Repair of the Crown, 1719	

Gordon, Thomas, Manuscript collections, MS K 269   1658–69
  Notes from Senatus Minutes *re* 17th-century damage and repairs to steeple
  and roof

Correspondence, legal papers, vouchers, *etc.* in the New Charter   1713?–1890
  Chest, MS K 257
  Arranged by shuttle and item; Inventory, MS K 106, and Summary list

Christie, John, Notes on the History of King's College, *c.* 1880,   1722–1831
  MS K 138
  The main part provides a selective guide to the contents of the Senatus
  Minutes, 1722–1831, plus summary notes from various King's College
  records on all aspects of its history,
  e.g. brief notes on the history of the Crown Tower
  1792 Aug 16: consideration of the roof of the Church and Library
  1821 April 2: report of a Commission of the Senatus and Dr Murray's
  Trust, including need for repairs to Chapel, recommendations *re* conduct
  of services

Murray Trustees, Minutes, MS K 98   1813–61
  1821, Restoration of worship to the Chapel

Procuration Accounts, MS K 66   1815–52
  'Disbursement for buildings' is an annual heading; but entries for the
  Chapel are mainly 'for winding up College clock'; 1849–50 'for cleaning
  of same'.

Correspondence, legal papers, *etc.*, including Procuration Accounts
  instructions, MS K 255

1.1.2   **University of Aberdeen** 1860–   **archives and manuscripts**

Senatus Minutes and related papers, MS U 370   1860–
  Intermittent references

King's College Chapel, MS U 399   1872–87
  Correspondence with HM Office of Works *re* refurbishment of the
  Chapel in 1872–73 after removal of the Library; Professor Macpherson's
  proposal to present stained glass windows, 1874–83; construction of a
  Strong Room/ Treasury/ Muniments Room in the base of the Crown
  Tower, 1884–87

Macpherson, Norman, Letters to Sir William Geddes, Principal of   1888–89
  Aberdeen University, MS U 618
  Respecting preparation and publication of a paper on King's College
  Chapel

Anderson, R. Rowand, architect, To the Improvement Committee   1889
  of King's College Chapel, Draft report on building, recommendations, estimates, 19 July 1889, MS U 1119

King's College Chapel Improvement Scheme, Minute Book,   1889–93
  MS U 201
  With printed reports. Includes print of MS U 984, *see below* 1.4.1
  See also below 1.2.1 published edition

Edilis Committee, Minutes, MS U 662/1–7   1890–1936
   Intermittent references

Dankester, Charles H., Sacrist, King's College Chapel Annual   1891–1918
   Reports, 1891/92 — 1917/18, MS U 556. 9 vols
   Detailed weekly records of sermon texts and themes, lessons, readers,
   those present, register of attendance, amount of offering, general remarks,
   complaints, weather; with scrapbook items, orders of service, programmes

Geddes, William D., Notes on the Restoration of King's College   1891
   Chapel, MS U 605
   Annotated copy with letters, newspaper cuttings, and other papers
   See also below 1.2.2 published edition

Notes on a carved oak figure in King's College Chapel, with   1903
   memorandum as to its history by Anthony B. Miller, MS U 556/2.
   4 leaves
   MS and typescript

Elphinstone Tomb Committee, Minutes, MS U 1161   1909–31
   With correspondence, accounts and other related papers inserted

Wilson, Henry, Designs for Reconstruction of the Tomb of Bishop   191–?
   Elphinstone in King's College Chapel, MS 2054. 1 parcel
   Photographs, prints, newscuttings, typescript notes, with annotations by
   James Cromar Watt, the donor

Papers and Correspondence relating to the Bishop Elphinstone   1927–31
   Tomb, MS U 701. 2 folders

Chapel Correspondence, MS U 714. 1 folder   1928–46
   Re acccounts, refurbishment, services, etc

War Memorial Committee, Minute [of meeting] held on 25th April,   1929
   1929, MS U1494/A5/50/14. 4 leaves
   Typescript

Minute of Meeting of the Committee appointed by the Court on   1932
   10th May 1932 to report on the Treatment of the Walls of King's
   College Chapel, held on the 18th June, 1932, MS U 1494/A5/50/
   15. 4 leaves
   Typescript

King's College Chapel. Dr J. E. Crombie Memorial Tablet,   1934
   MS U 1494/A5/45/1–15
   /1:   Letter to Doctor Kelly from the Carrick Pursuivant, 22 August 1934
   /2:   Letter from H. J. Butchart, Secretary of University of Aberdeen to
         Dr. Kelly, 31 August 1934
   /3:   Note with drawings from William Kelly to Mr Ross, 21 Nov. 1934
   /4–14: Drawings. For details of drawings, *See below* 3 Plans 1934
   /15:   Letter to Doctor Kelly from the Carrick Pursuivant, 3 August 1934
          'Re Dr J.E.Crombie Tablet'. 3 leaves, with sketch design of revised
          plan on verso of leaf 3

Edilis & Lands Committee, Minutes, MS U 662/8–10   1936–47
   With Contents list in each vol., including entries: King's College Chapel
   Later Edilis papers are in the Estates Office; papers for the late 1950s and
   early 1960s were destroyed by a flood in the basement of Elphinstone Hall

Strachan, Douglas, Correspondence relating to the Chapel Windows,   1938
    with reference in particular to the Commemoration of Hugh
    Macpherson, MS U 613

Chapel Committee, Minutes, MS U 893   1939–52
    Mainly relating to services and other uses of the Chapel

Eeles, Francis C., Correspondence and other papers relating to King's   1931–54
    College Chapel, etc., MS U 596. 1 box
    Drafts of his book *See below* 1.3.1 Eeles

Ferguson, Alexander S., 'The Monument to William Elphinstone',   *c.* 1944
    MS 2622/1
    Typescript article and correspondence with F. C. Eeles

Hay, George, Letter to Dr W. Douglas Simpson, 5 August, 1952, and   1952
    acknowledgement, *re* 'rough draft plan of the King's College
    Chapel', MS U 1494/A6/4
    See below 3 1952 for plan

Estates Office, File 92/92: King's College Organ   1953–92

Scottish Episcopal Church, Diocese of Aberdeen and Orkney.   1953–57
    Register of services held in King's College Chapel, Aberdeen,
    according to the rites and ceremonies of the Scottish Episcopal
    Church, MS 3320/16. 3 pages
    Records date, day, hour, service, celebrant, no. of communicants

Kelman, James, Aberdeen University Oral History Archive, Inter-   1968–78
    view 23, 1985, MS 3620
    Transcript of recorded memories of the University Buildings Officer
    1968–78

1.2   Primary printed sources

Arranged chronologically by the period described

1.2.1   King's College and University of Aberdeen printed records

Fasti Aberdonenses: Selections from the Records of the University and King's   1494–1854
    College of Aberdeen, 1494–1854, ed. Cosmo Innes (Aberdeen:
    Spalding Club, 1854)
    The historical introduction in the 92 page preface includes an account of
    the development of the 'fabric', including the Chapel, on pp. lvi–lxiv,
    citing and quoting from various early descriptions; with contemporary
    descriptions by the editor.
    The table gives a detailed summary of the College records reproduced,
    arranged chronologically; including
    I   Privileges and endowments
    II   Laws
    III   Visitations, 1549–1718
    IV   Collegiate visitations, 1634–1753, including recasting of bells in
         1700, pp. 438–9
    IX   Register of all the silver, brass . . . and other goods of King's College,
         James Strachan rectorial visitation, 1542

X   Selections from the accounts, including, Principal Row's Accounts 1652–57, relating to the 'edifice', and those of 1659–61; Alex Middleton's accounts 1663–66, including building work
Indexes of names and of places
Some transcripts and translations are not full and accurate: *See below* 1.3.1
Eeles, p. vii

King's College, Inventory, 1542, in F. C. Eeles, *King's College Chapel*   1542
(Edinburgh: Oliver & Boyd, 1956), pp. 4–69
A register of all the silver, brass and iron vessels, copes and other ornaments of the church, altars, vestments, curtains, carpets, cushions, and books of King's College, Aberdeen, contained in the church, bell tower, hall and rooms of the college, compiled in a visitation made by James Strachan, Rector, 1542
Description, transcription, translation of the Latin section, commentary

Douglas, William, *Academiarum Vindiciae* . . . (Aberdeen: Brown,   1659
1659)
The dedication contains a description of the King's College buildings

University of Aberdeen Court, *Minutes*   1861–
Index in each volume

University of Aberdeen, *Statement in Reference to the Buildings of the*   1865
University of Aberdeen (Edinburgh: J. Hughes, 1865). 31p.
A statement, with documentation, of the repairs and extensions agreed to by the Treasury in December 1855, and of the work carried out from 1858 until abandoned in 1863, stressing the urgent need for a new Library and the restoration of the Chapel

King's College Chapel Improvement Scheme, with covering letters   1889–92
Including: Report of architect, R. Rowand Anderson; with print of plan; Donors and subscribers to King's College Chapel Improvement Fund, 1st and 2nd lists; Organ for King's College Chapel, Aberdeen, invitation to subscribe; Public meeting in favour of the improvement and restoration of King's College Chapel; Interim report
See above 1.1.2 MS U 201, archival copy

King's College Chapel Schemes for Restoration and Improvement. I. Organ   1894
fund. II. Chapel fund. List of subscribers and balance sheets (Aberdeen, 1894)

University of Aberdeen Senatus Academicus, *Minutes*, Vol. 5–   1894–
Index in each volume. References to Chaplaincy, e.g. establishment of, 14 (1944–47), 58, 70

1.2.2   **Other contemporary records**

Strachan, A., *Panegyricus Inauguralis* (Aberdeen: Raban, 1631)   1631
Describes the building benefactions of Elphinstone, Dunbar and Patrick Forbes

Kerr, John, *Donaides: sive Musarum Aberdonensium de eximia Jacobi*   1725
Fraserii, J.U.D. In Academiam Regiam Aberdonensem munificentia
Carmen Eucharisticum. Notis illustratum, quibus strictim perscribitur
Historia Universitatis & Collegii Regii Aberdonensis, a primaeva ipsius

Institutione, ad nostra usque tempora perpetua serie (Edinburgh: Ruddiman, 1725)
Reprint: *Donaides, John Ker (1728) and a Poem in Imitation of Donaides [David Mallock] (1725)*, introduction by Irma S. Lustig, and a translation by Barrows Dunham, The Augustan Reprint Society publications 188 (Los Angeles: Clark Memorial Library, 1978)
With an introduction, translation and notes
Also in *Musa Latina Aberdonensis* Vol.3 Poetae minores, ed. William Keith Leask (Aberdeen: New Spalding Club, 1910), 189–208
Text, translation and good footnotes by the editor
An allegorical tribute to James Fraser, benefactor, incorporating a poetic description of the vicissitudes in the development of King's with periods of expansion and of neglect, naming the persons involved

Gregory, William, 'Account of the University and King's College of   1845
Aberdeen', *The Statistical Account of Aberdeenshire*, Appendix, (Edinburgh: Blackwood, 1843)
With two paragraphs on the Chapel and Tower, pp. 1160–61

Scottish Universities Commission 1858, *General Report of the Commis-*   1863
sioners under the Universities (Scotland) Act, 1858 (Edinburgh: HMSO, 1863)
Records unseemly use of the Chapel, p. xxii

'The Proper Position for an Organ in the Chapel of King's College,   1890
Old Aberdeen', *Transactions of the Ecclesiological Society of Aberdeen*, 1, 4th year, 1889 (1890), 10: illus
Report of meeting subject
With an Ecclesiastical note, 'Restoration of King's College Chapel', p. 73

Geddes, William D., *Notes on the Restoration of King's College Chapel,*   1891
Aberdeen (Aberdeen, 1892)
See also above 1.1.2 MS U 605 archival copy
Reprinted from *Transactions of the Ecclesiological Society of Aberdeen*, 6th year, 1891 (1892), 61–81: illus
'The following paper is an attempt to set forth in order the chief features of the Restoration, with a view to shew not merely the details of the decoration introduced, but to indicate briefly the principles by which those in charge of the restoration were guided, and the limitations or conditions under which the work had to be accomplished . . .', Introduction

Walker, R. S., 'The Bombing of King's College Grounds', *Aberdeen*   1942
University Review, 29 (1941–42), 132–34
Brief mention of no damage to the Chapel

1.3   **Secondary works**   Arranged alphabetically by author or title

1.3.1   **Books**

Aitken, W. H., *Crown and Tower: the Story of Aberdeen University* (Aberdeen: Jolly, 1895)
With a description of the Chapel and Tower on pp. 40–48

Anderson, P. J., *Historical Notes on the Libraries of the Universities of Aberdeen* (Aberdeen: University Press, 1893)
Chronological list, including references to the Library in the Chapel in 1751, 1773, 1837, 1844

Billings, Robert William, *The Baronial and Ecclesiastical Antiquities of Scotland*, illustrated by Robert William Billings, architect, (Edinburgh: Blackwood, 1845–52). 4 vols.
Vol. 1 contains 'King's College Chapel': 4 pages of text [by John Hill Burton], with 4 illustrations: Chapel West Front, Interior Stallwork, Library in Chapel, Geometric tracery
Brief architectural-historical description of the exterior and interior, including a warning about dampness in the roof tracery

Bulloch, John Malcolm, *A History of the University of Aberdeen, 1495–1895* (London: Hodder & Stoughton, 1895)
Chapel of King's College, pp. 43–50

Carter, Jennifer and Colin A. McLaren, *Crown and Gown 1495–1995: an Illustrated History of the University of Aberdeen* (Aberdeen: Aberdeen University Press, 1994)

Eeles, Francis C., *King's College Chapel Aberdeen: its Fittings, Ornaments and Ceremonial in the Sixteenth Century*, Aberdeen University Studies 136 (Edinburgh: Oliver & Boyd, 1956); xxvi, 270 pp., 78 plates: illus; Index
'An ecclesiological study . . ., with special reference to its medieval internal arrangements' commissioned by the University Court, [Preface, p. vi]
The ground-work of the volume is a revised and accurate text and translation of the Latin portion of, and explanatory commentary on, the 1542 Inventory of King's College, together with a new transcription and translation by Gordon Donaldson of the Foundation documents
Main divisions: The 1542 Inventory, Translation and Commentary; The Building; Liturgical Rules for the College Church, with Commentary; Appendices.
Notable illustrations of the choir stalls

The Fusion of 1860: a Record of the Centenary Celebrations and a History of the United University of Aberdeen, 1860–1960, ed. W. D. Simpson, Aberdeen University Studies 146 (Edinburgh: Oliver & Boyd, 1963)
Contains scattered references to the Chapel, Chaplaincy and Choir, esp. pp. 220, 234–5

Macfarlane, L. J., *King's College, Old Aberdeen: a Guide and History* (Aberdeen: University of Aberdeen, 1982)
2nd edn revised, 1992 as *A Visitor's Guide to King's College, See below*
Supersedes W. Douglas Simpson, *King's College, Old Aberdeen: an Introduction and Guide*, 1973, and *King's College Chapel Windows*.

Macfarlane, L. J., *A Visitor's Guide to King's College, University of Aberdeen*, 2nd edn revised (Aberdeen: University of Aberdeen, 1992)
Succinct description of the present buildings and the history of their development, with many coloured illustrations, and a bibliography of the buildings and monuments, p. 38

Macfarlane, Leslie J., 'The University from 1505 to 1514: the Buildings', in *William Elphinstone and the Kingdom of Scotland 1431–1514: the Struggle for Order*, Quincentenary edn (Aberdeen: Aberdeen University Press, 1995), pp. 326–36: illus.
The most thorough account of the King's College buildings in the earliest period; includes a plan of the Chapel with seating arrangements in 1514

Macpherson, Norman, *Notes on the Chapel, Crown, and other Ancient Buildings of King's College, Aberdeen* (Edinburgh: Neill, 1889)
Reprinted from *Archaeologia Scotica*, 5 (1889)

Rev. edn, with some changes in footnotes (Aberdeen: D. Wyllie, 1890); 17 plates
Historical and contemporary descriptions, giving documentary sources, and incorporating memories of himself, his father, who took special charge of the restoration in 1823, and of his grandparents.
Kelly: 'some of his views are of more than doubtful validity';
but Eeles maintains that the work is of permanent value, remarkably accurate for its period, though more has been discovered since

Pickard, J. R., *A History of King's College Library to 1860* (Aberdeen: J. R. Pickard, 1987)
Vol.1: 1569–1699. Vol.2: 1700–1799. Vol.3: 1800–1860. The Library was adjacent to or in the Chapel until 1870
Useful detailed listing and analysis of sources

[Pirie, George], *King's College, Aberdeen* (Aberdeen: Aberdeen U.P., 1885?)
Another edn 1904
A descriptive pamphlet for visitors

Rait, Robert S., *The Universities of Aberdeen: a History* (Aberdeen: J. G. Bisset, 1895)
Identifies his sources. Includes Slezer's drawing of Old Aberdeen, 1693, *See below 2.4*
Chapter 19 is devoted to the buildings, with the Chapel described on pp. 234–40, and its history on pp. 244–46. This chapter was offprinted as

Rait, Robert S., *King's College Buildings: a Descriptive Account* (Aberdeen: Aberdeen Journals, 1895)
For update *see below* 1.3.2

Stevenson, David, *King's College, Aberdeen, 1560–1641: from Protestant Reformation to Covenanting Revolution;* with a translation of the New Foundation by G. Patrick Edwards, Quincentennial Studies in the History of the University of Aberdeen (Aberdeen: published for the University of Aberdeen by Aberdeen University Press, 1990)
Brief references to the Chapel in Reformation and Covenanting times, pp. 12–15

Studies in the History and Development of the University of Aberdeen, ed. P. J. Anderson, Aberdeen University Studies 9 (Aberdeen: The University, 1906)
With chapter on The Buildings, and Collections towards a Bibliography of the Universities of Aberdeen, by P. J. Anderson, still the most comprehensive bibliography, revised and reissued as Edinburgh Bibliographical Society Publications 8 (1907)

A Tribute offered by the University of Aberdeen to the Memory of William Kelly, LL.D, ARSA; ed. W. Douglas Simpson, Aberdeen University Studies 125 (Aberdeen: Aberdeen University Press, 1949
Essays by William Kelly: II. Scottish Crown Steeples [with account of the building of that of King's College Chapel, pp. 42–48]. III. King's College Chapel (1932), pp. 49–62. IV. Some Further Notes on King's College Chapel; The Little Steeple; George Pyper, and William Scot (1938), pp. 63–75
With 10 photographs featuring the Chapel

Walker, Robert, and Alexander M. Munro, *Handbook to City and University. Part 1: The University*, University of Aberdeen Quatercentenary Celebrations, September 1906 (Aberdeen: The University, 1906)
Description of the Chapel on pp. 77–80, with photographs of the Chapel in 1895 and 1906

1.3.2   **Articles**

Alma Mater: Aberdeen University Magazine (Aberdeen), 1–67, 1883–1965

Features regular series of 'Chapel notes', in the 1900s reduced to 'Chapel statistics' and 'Chapel preachers' — a list for the new session; also occasional features, e.g. 9 (1891–92), 11: Editorial on the resumption of services after refurbishment, 55: 'In the Chapel again'

Anderson, P. J., 'Notes on Heraldic Representations at King's College, Old Aberdeen', *Proceedings of the Society of Antiquaries of Scotland*, 23 (1889), 80–86; 166–84: illus

Anderson, P. J., 'The Old Stalls in King's College Chapel and their Occupants', *Scottish Notes and Queries*, 8 (Dec 1894), 97–98: illus

Anderson, P. J., 'Views of King's College', *Scottish Notes and Queries*, 8 (March 1895), 145–47: illus
Succinct descriptions of the buildings at different periods, based on extant views, which are reproduced
Reprinted in

Anderson, P. J., 'Views of King's College, Old Aberdeen, 1660–1860', *Crown and Tower*, ed. for University Union Bazaar by J. S. Shewan, Alex Brown, C. I. Beattie (Aberdeen: Adelphi Press, 1896), 29–35

Anderson, P. J., 'Views of King's College', *Scottish Notes and Queries*, 10 (Dec 1896), 107–08: illus

Cooper, James, ['Pictorial Decorations of the Seventeenth Century in Aberdeen Churches'], *Transactions of the Ecclesiological Society of Aberdeen*, 2, 5th year, 1890 (1891), 5–6
With Ecclesiological notes: Need for restoration of King's College Chapel, 63

Edwards, G. Patrick, 'William Elphinstone, his College Chapel, and the Second of April', *Aberdeen University Review*, 51 (1985–86), 1–17: illus
An explanation of the foundation inscription

Eeles, F. C., 'The Inventory of King's College, Aberdeen, 1542', *Scottish Notes and Queries* Series 2, 2 (12), (June 1901), 183–5; 3 (1), (July 1901), 11–13

'The Elphinstone Tomb', *Aberdeen University Review*, 16 (1928–29), 239–41
Concerning the re-erection of the monument in the ante-chapel

Fawcett, Richard, 'The Architecture of King's College Chapel and Greyfriars Church, Aberdeen', *Aberdeen University Review*, 53 (1989–90), 102–26: illus.

Geddes, W. D., 'The Ambo in King's College Chapel', *Scottish Notes and Queries*, 2 (11), (April 1889), 161–62: illus

[Gordon, Thomas], 'University and King's College of Aberdeen. Transmitted to Sir John Sinclair, Baronet, by the members of the University, anno 1798', *Statistical Account of Scotland*, Vol. 21, Appendix (Edinburgh, 1799), 51–104
Describes current use of Chapel, p. 90

'Graduate', 'Chapel Lighting', *Alma Mater*, 30 (30 Oct. 1912), 34–35

Henderson, G. D., 'Elphinstone's Birthday Celebrations in the Eighteenth Century', *Aberdeen University Review*, 18 (1930–31), 255–57
Refers to the ringing of the College bells

Kelly, William, 'King's College Chapel', *A Tribute offered by the University of Aberdeen to the Memory of William Kelly LL.D, ARSA*, ed. W. D. Simpson (Aberdeen: AUP, 1949), 49–62

'Having lately been engaged on certain works at the East end of the Chapel, I should like to tell you something of what has been done, and of what has been found, and to recapitulate briefly the story of some parts of the Chapel from its foundation until now', p. 49

Kelly, William, 'Some Further Notes on King's Chapel: The Little Steeple, George Pyper, and William Scot', *A Tribute offered by the University of Aberdeen to the Memory of William Kelly LL.D, ARSA*, ed. W. D. Simpson (Aberdeen: AUP, 1949), 63–75
About 17th-century repairs

Leslie, G. A. Y., 'King's College in 1818', *Aberdeen University Review*, 5 (1917–18), 143–44
Mentions use of the Chapel for the Bursary Competition

Macfarlane, L. J., 'King's College, Aberdeen: the Creation of the Academic Community, 1495–1532', *Aberdeen University Review*, 56 (1995–96), 211–22
References to the Chapel on pp. 213 and 216

Macfarlane, Leslie J., 'King's College Chapel', *Aberdeen University Review*, 48 (1979–80), 239–47: plan
Bibliography on p. 247
The early period is revised and expanded in his *William Elphinstone. See above* 1.3.1

Macfarlane, Leslie J., 'A Synopsis of the Building Programme at King's College Chapel, University of Aberdeen, 1500–1988', The Buildings of the University of Aberdeen, Aberdeen University, 1987–88
Prepared for the Quincentennial History Conference: The Buildings of the University, Aberdeen, October 1987
Typescript

McLaren, Colin A., 'New Work and Old: Building at the Colleges in the Seventeenth Century', *Aberdeen University Review*, 53 (1989–90), 208–17

Neil, W., 'The Dedication of the War Memorial: sermon', *Aberdeen University Review*, 35 (1953–54), 1–7

Rait, Robert S., 'The Buildings: King's College, 1500–1900', *Studies in the History and Development of the University of Aberdeen*, ed. P. J. Anderson (Aberdeen: Aberdeen University, 1906), 369–78: The Chapel
This updates, but does not supersede, his 1895 book, *see above* 1.3.1

'Restoration of King's College Chapel Organ', University of Aberdeen *Newsletter*, (April 1992), 1

Simpson, W. D., H. Wilson and H. Townend, 'The Founder's Memorial', *Aberdeen University Review*, 18 (1930–31), 213–21
Deals with its reconstruction, the symbolism, and the memorial as a work of art

Stewart, Alasdair M., 'Three Danzig Beakers in Old Aberdeen', *Aberdeen University Review*, 47 (1977–78), 303–07: illus
Descriptions of the Thomson and Specht communion cups presented to King's College in 1643
See below 1.4.2 Clarke, Six Photographs; 1.4.4 Danzig beakers

Thomas, John, 'The Elphinstone Monument at King's College, Aberdeen: its Construction in the Sixteenth Century and Reconstruction (1909–31) by Henry Wilson', *Aberdeen University Review*, 54 (1991–92), 315–33: illus.

Walker, David M., 'The Rebuilding of King's and Marischal Colleges, 1723–1889' *Aberdeen University Review*, 55 (1993), 123–45: illus
Describes plans for and affecting the Chapel

Walker, R. S., 'The Crown of King's', *Aberdeen University Review*, 30 (1942–44), 303–12: illus
> Considers the design, builder, place in architectural history and historical development

Walker, R. S., 'The Oldest View of King's College', *Aberdeen University Review*, 31 (1945–46), 26–27: illus

1.3.3   Dissertations

Runcie, Jill, *Douglas Strachan, and the Windows he Designed for St Machar's Cathedral and King's College*, Aberdeen. Unpublished dissertation for the Master of Arts degree in History of Art, University of Aberdeen, 1997

Sweet, Sallyanne, *Bishop Elphinstone's Choir Stalls in King's College, Aberdeen*. Unpublished dissertation for the Master of Arts degree in History of Art, University of Aberdeen, 1996

1.4   Visual and aural material   Arranged chronologically by the period depicted

1.4   Illustrative material
> A comprehensive file of photocopies is held in Special Libraries and Archives, DISS: Historic Collections, University of Aberdeen

1.4.1   Drawings and prints

Crown and Tower, eds James Shewan, Charles J. Beattie, Alexander W. Brown (Aberdeen: Taylor & Henderson, Adelphi P., 1896)   1660–1860
> With reproductions of a series of views of King's College 1660–1860, with accompanying text by P. J. Anderson, pp. 29–35
> Reprinted from *Scottish Notes and Queries* March 1895

Anderson, P. J., 'Views of King's College', *Scottish Notes and Queries*, 10 (7), (Dec 1896), 107–8: illus   1811, 1850

Interior of King's College Chapel. After a painting by J. B. Gillanders. Andw Gibb & Co. Lithos., 3 Queen St. Abdn, MS U 1494/A7/1
> Print, 19 x 13.5 cm

King's College Chapel, MS U 399   1874–83
> Correspondence with HM Office of Works *re* Professor Macpherson's proposal to present stained glass windows, 1874–83; with coloured tracings of window designs

King's College Chapel: Proposed Plan of Restoration, MS U 984   1889
> Original plan, mounted, by R. Rowand Anderson, architect, Edinburgh; 2 litho prints by And. Gibb, Aberdeen: longitudinal section, cross section, plan. Scale $1\frac{1}{4}''$ to 10′.

Robertson, Annabella, Six Photographs of Drawings of the Carved Oak Screen in King's College Chapel, and the medal awarded for the drawings, MS U 594   1903

Wilson, Henry, Designs for Reconstruction of the Tomb of Bishop Elphinstone in King's College Chapel, MS 2054. 1 parcel   191–?
> Photographs, prints, newscuttings, typescript notes, with annotations by James Cromar Watt, the donor

Aitken, John M., Drawings of five shields with coats of arms of local   1919?
counties for the Aberdeen University War Memorial, 1914–1918,
MS U 573

Savours, Ann, Drawings of graffiti on stalls in King's College Chapel,   1953
1953, MS U 593. 1 file

1.4.2   **Photographs**

Wilson, G. W., Glass plate negatives held by Photographic Unit,   186–?–190–?
DISS: Historic Collections, University of Aberdeen.
King's College Chapel:
Exterior: College & Chapel, C1372; Chapel, Ab56 (print); Chapel from
Quadrangle, C1359, C1367, B293, E5, E2147, E644, E644X; Chapel from
College Bounds, A1059, F109, F109X, G5; Graduation groups, A339, A3236
Interior: Looking West, E1624, F1988; Choir stalls, C1356, C1356X

Carved Stalls, King's College Chapel, Aberdeen. 170. G.W.W.,   n.d.
MS U 1494/A6/2
Mounted photograph; 28.5 x 38 cm

King's College Chapel. Aberdeen. 160. G.W.W., MS U 1494/A6/3   n.d.
Mounted photograph of Crown Tower and quadrangle side of Chapel;
28.5 x 38 cm.

[King's College Chapel, Quadrangle side], MS U 1494/A/6/1   n.d.
Photograph, in framed paper mount; 16 x 21.5 cm

[King's College Chapel and Crown Tower, Quadrangle side],   n.d.
MS U 1494/A7/34
Photograph; 16.5 x 16 cm

[King's College Chapel, from the North in snow], MS U 1494/A/53   189–?
Photograph mounted on card; 20.5 x 25 cm

Walker, Robert, and Alexander M. Munro, *Handbook to City and*   1895
University. Part 1:The University, University of Aberdeen Quatercentenary Celebrations, September 1906 (Aberdeen: The University, 1906)
Description of the Chapel on pp. 77–80, with photographs of the Chapel
in 1895 and 1906

Robertson, Annabella, Six Photographs of Drawings of the Carved   1903
Oak Screen in King's College Chapel and the medal awarded for
the drawings, MS U594

Elphinstone Tomb Reconstruction Photographs, MS U 560^2.   1910?
1 album

Wilson, Henry, Designs for Reconstruction of the Tomb of Bishop   191–?
Elphinstone in King's College Chapel, MS 2054. 1 parcel
Photographs, prints, newscuttings, typescript notes, with annotations by
James Cromar Watt, the donor

Coat of arms: DWG 1635, MS U 1494/A5/7   193–?
Stamped: Photo by A. J. B. Strachan, 416 Union Street, Aberdeen. Ref.
no. 1/44223
Plainer than A5/8

Coat of arms: DWG 1635. GP Fecit, MS U 1494/A5/8   193–?
> Stamped: Photo by A. J. B. Strachan, 416 Union Street, Aberdeen. Ref.
> no. 2/44223
> More ornate than A5/7

King's Coll[ege] Chapel: 4 photographs of carving, with ruler,   1932
mounted on one card, MS U 1494/A5/49
> Annotated: 'William Kelly 1932'; 'a later version see other sheet'. Cf:
> A6/9

King's College Chapel: 3 photographs of carving detail, with ruler: a,   1932
b, c. William Kelly, 1932, MS U 1494/A6/9
> Mounted on one card. Cf: A5/49.

King's Coll[ege] Chapel, Aberdeen: 7 photographs of exterior,   1932
mounted on one board, MS U 1494/A6/36
> 3 photographs of windows; 'N corbel ?for Lenten veil'; 'One of the 5
> existing Consecration Crosses'; 2 of the North Elevation Jan. 1932,
> showing work in progress at the East end

[King's College Chapel]: 4 photographs, mounted on one card,   1932
MS U 1494/A/6/11
> Part of Quadrangle side with SE door, Feb. 1932, J. H. B.; Passageway
> between Chapel and Cromwell Tower, with supporting timbers Jan.
> 1932, J. H. B.; S. Corbel . . . Lenten veil. ap. 1932 J. H. Ball; The Stoup,
> ap.1932 J. H. Ball,

King's College Chapel: 5 photographs, mounted on one card,   1932
MS U 1494/A6/7
> War memorial window, J. H. Ball, April 1932; SE court . . .; Sir R. R.
> Anderson's panelling 1891 . . .; The Fleche, JHB Aug 1932; 2 of the new
> pinnacles — photo by John Rennie, mason, 1932

Haffit of Desk from St. Machar's Cathedral, MS U 1494/A7/32   1934
> 'William Kelly, 62 Rubislawden North, Aberdeen April 1934'; photo-
> graph mounted on card
> This is now a desk end in King's College Chapel

Clarke, G. A., Six Photographs of Andrew Thomson's 1643 commu-   193–?
nion cup, MS U 554
> *See below* 1.4.4 Danzig beakers; *See above* 1.3.2 Stewart

Clarke, G. A., Twenty-eight Photographs of the Chapel, taken   1936
during the Restoration, 1936, MS U 555/1

Clarke, G. A., Six Photographs of King's College Chapel, March,   1939
1939, MS U 555/2

A Tribute offered by the University of Aberdeen to the Memory of William   1949?
Kelly, LL.D, ARSA; ed. W. Douglas Simpson, Aberdeen Univer-
sity Studies 125 (Aberdeen: Aberdeen University Press, 1949)
> Essays by William Kelly
> With photographs: King's College Chapel — detail of War Memorial;
> Inscription on West Front; West Front; Plan showing original arrange-
> ment; View of Crown; View from North-East; Consecration Crosses;
> View from South-East; The Quadrangle between 1825 and 1865; Interior
> looking East, after 1823.

Eeles, Francis C., Some Illustrations for *King's College Chapel*, (1956),   1955?
MS U 598
See above 1.3.1 Eeles, Francis C., *King's College Chapel Aberdeen*, plates
1–56, 72–78, *and next item*
With 1 mounted sepia print of the Chapel after installation of the organ

Eeles, Francis C., *King's College Chapel Aberdeen: its Fittings, Ornaments*   1955?
and Ceremonial in the Sixteenth Century, Aberdeen University
Studies 136 (Edinburgh: Oliver & Boyd, 1956)
Notable sequence of photographs of the choir stalls, and other features,
plates 1–56, 72–78

Davidson, I. W., Photographs of the Bronze Figures on the   1955
Elphinstone Cenotaph, MS U 560[4]

Thomas, John, The Elphinstone Monument: 12 photographs repro-   1990?
duced in or relating to his article, MS 3415
See above 1.3.2. Thomas

1.4.3   **Aural records**

Religious Service in King's College Chapel: BBC broadcast on 2   1958
long play records, March 1958, MS U 1065

Kelman, James, Aberdeen University Oral History Archive, Inter-   1968–78
view 23, 1985, MS 3620
Recorded memories of the University Buildings Officer 1968–78.

1.4.4   **Other material**

Danzig beakers, ABDUA:36869–36870
Two silver communion cups
See above 1.4.2 Clarke, Six Photographs, 193–?; *and* 1.3.2 Stewart

Six plaster casts of masons' marks on King's College Chapel,
MS U 597, 1 box

Paintings

William Elphinstone, ABDUA:30005

The Judgment of Solomon, ABDUA:31851
David and Goliath, ABDUA:31852
The Entry of David and Saul into Jerusalem, ABDUA:31853
Solomon and Queen of Sheba, ABDUA:31854
David and Abigail, ABDUA:31855
The five Biblical paintings hung in the Chapel during the period 1870s to
1990s

2   **Other material containing significant references to King's College Chapel**

2.1   **Archival sources**   Arranged chronologically by the period described

Aberdeen City Archives, Council Register, vols 51–61   1624–1753
Contain records of contracts for work at King's College
See below 2.2 *Extracts from the Council Register*

Tough Kirk Session Records,   1735
  Bell book: records the transfer of a bell from King's College Chapel in
  1735
  See below 2.2 1735 'Inventories of Ecclesiastical Records of North-Eastern
  Scotland'
  Original in National Archives of Scotland [formerly SRO], CH2/356/3

Royal Institute of British Architects, London. James Cromer Watt   1884
  [*sic*]. Preliminary Drawings and Rubbings of King's College
  Chapel, RIBA Y6/56/1–43
  See below 3 1884 Chapel and Tower, Drawings Nos. 1–6 by James C. Watt

Royal College of Art, London, Henry Wilson Archive, HW–5:   *c.* 1906–31
  Correspondence
  Includes correspondence with P. J. Anderson, J. R. Cooper, J. Harrower,
  D. Strachan, J. Cromar Watt relating to the Elphinstone Monument

2.2   **Primary printed sources, including contemporary accounts**
       Arranged chronologically by the period described

Halyburton, Andrew, *The Ledger of Andrew Halyburton, Conservator of*   1497
  the Privileges of the Scotch Nation in the Netherlands, 1492–1503, ed.
  C. Innes, Series of chronicles and memorials (Edinburgh, HM
  General Register House, 1867)
  Building equipment ordered by Bishop Elphinstone in 1497, pp. 183–84

Munro, A. M., *Records of Old Aberdeen*, 1498–1903, Vol. 2 (Aberdeen: 1498–1903
  New Spalding Club, 1909)
  Scattered references, e.g. p. 205: Walter Stuart buried in the Chapel;
  pp. 253–55: Epitaphs and inscriptions in King's College Chapel: texts,
  with brief note
  pp. 296–98: J. Gordon's description of the Chapel
  p. 308: J. Logan's manuscript description of the pulpit later transferred to
  King's College Chapel from St Machar's Cathedral *See below* 2.4 Logan

Boece, Hector, *Episcoporum Murthlacen. & Aberdonen . . . Vitae* [Paris: 1522
  Prelio Ascensiano], 1522
  Contemporary account of the buildings erected by Elphinstone and
  Dunbar and of the service arrangements:
  Brief mentions of Bishop Elphinstone's building and organisation of the
  College, fol. 29; bequest to the College, fol. 33; burial before the altar,
  fol. 34
  Reprinted, with a translation by James Moir, *Hectoris Boetii Murthlacensium*
  et Aberdonensium Episcoporum Vitae (Aberdeen: New Spalding Club, 1894);
  with plate of the Chapel interior. Above references, in translation, on
  pp. 93–96, 106–07, 109

Spalding, John, *Memorialls of the Trubles in Scotland and England A.D.*   1624–45
  1624 — A.D. 1645, ed. John Stuart (Aberdeen: Spalding Club,
  1850–51). 2 vols
  Vol. 1, p. 31: reference to the steeple being blown down in 1633 and
  replaced; various references to King's College as meeting place of
  Assemblies in the Covenanting period

Vol. 2, pp. 124, 141, 185, 453, 457: references to preaching in the College kirk

Aberdeen Town Council, *Extracts from the Council Register of the Burgh of Aberdeen*, ed. John Stuart, Scottish Burgh Records Society publications 8–9 (Edinburgh: Scottish Burgh Records Society, 1871–72)   1625–1747
Spine title: Extracts from the Records of the Burgh of Aberdeen. Vol. 1 1625–1642. Vol. 2 1643–1747
Includes records of licences and contracts of work, etc

Chalmers, David, *Davidis Camerarii Scoti De Scotorum Fortitudine, Doctrina & Pietate, ac de Ortu & Progressu Haeresis in Regnis Scotiae & Angliae* (Paris: Baillet, 1631)   1631
Pp. 56–59 contain the earliest account of the discipline of King's College, the Chapel on p. 57
Quoted in *Collections for a History of the Shires of Aberdeen and Banff*, ed. Joseph Robertson, (Aberdeen: Spalding Club, 1843), 211–14

Gordon, James, *History of Scots Affairs, from M DC XXXVII to M DC XLI*, eds Joseph Robertson and George Grub, (Aberdeen, Spalding Club, 1841). 3 vols   1637–41
Scattered references, e.g. v.3, 218: the breaking down of the old organ in the Chapel

Gordon, James, *Abredoniae Vtriusque Descriptio. A Description of both Touns of Aberdeen*, ed. Cosmo Innes (Edinburgh: Spalding Club, 1842)   1661
Good contemporary description of King's College on pp. 23–25, with plan of the Old Toun, incorporating a keyed plan of King's College. The volume also contains a reproduction of Slezer's 'The Prospect of Old Aberdien'
Also in *Records of Old Aberdeen*, ed. A. M. Munro, Vol. 2 (Aberdeen: New Spalding Club, 1909), 296–99
A new translation by Rev. John Milne

Middleton, Thomas, *An Appendix to the History of the Church of Scotland .. with the Foundation of the Universities and Colledges . . .* (London: printed by E. Flesher, for R. Royston, 1677)   1677
On p. 38: reference to Bishop Elphinstone's work; p. 39 to Principal Alexander Anderson (1557–69)'s loss of furnishings, etc, and to repulsing of Reformers seeking lead and bells
See below 2.2 Orem (1791), p. 142

Camden, William, *Camden's Britannia* newly translated into English: with large additions and improvements, published by Edmund Gibson (London: printed by F. Collins for A. Swolle, 1695)   1695
With very brief details of the Chapel on p. 952

Macky, John, *A Journey through Scotland in Familiar Letters from a Gentleman here to his Friend Abroad*, vol. 3, 2nd edn (London, 1732)   1723; 1732
The Chapel is described on pp. 106–07

Orem, William, *A Description of the Chanonry of Old Aberdeen, in the years 1724 and 1725, by William Orem, Town Clerk of Old Aberdeen*, Bibliotheca Topographica Britannica 3 (London: J Nichols, 1782)   1724–28

Half-title: With a few occasional corrections made by the author in 1726, 1727 and 1728.
Contents include: 'The Life of William Elphinstone, Bishop of Aberdeen; translated from Hector Boethius' Lives of the Bishops of Morthlac and Aberdeen' [includes description of the Chapel buildings, furnishings, services, pp. xxv–xxvi];
'A description of Old Aberdeen in 1771' [with a description of the King's College buildings on pp. xlii–xliv];
'Of the King's College in Old Aberdeen' [reproduced from Middleton, *see above* 2.2];
'An Account of the University and King's College of Aberdeen' [with the briefest references to the Chapel and services];
'Inventory of King's College 1542';
'Some Remarkable Passages concerning the King's College in Old Aberdeen' [with an account of the historical development of the buildings, pp. 158–61];
General index, with specific entries for King's College buildings, but not listing all references;
Reproduction of G. & W. Paterson's map of 1746
Compilation of documents, without acknowledgment of sources, together with contemporary descriptive matter
Cf.

Orem, William, *A Description of the Chanonry of Old Aberdeen, in the years 1724 and 1725, by William Orem, Town Clerk of Old Aberdeen* (Aberdeen: J. Chalmers, 1791)   1724–25
Same text as 1782 ed., except that it lacks the half title page and has a new, but less good, index.

Orem, William, *A Description of the Chanonry of Old Aberdeen, in the years 1724 and 1725, by William Orem, Town Clerk of Old Aberdeen* (Aberdeen: J. Rettie, 1830)   1724–25
Same text as 1791 edn

Orem, William, *A Description of the Chanonry of Old Aberdeen, in the years 1724 and 1725, by William Orem, Town Clerk of Old Aberdeen* (Aberdeen: A. Brown, 1832)   1724–25
Reissue of 1830 edn

'Inventories of Ecclesiastical Records of North-Eastern Scotland', *Miscellany of the New Spalding Club*, Vol.1 (Aberdeen: New Spalding Club, 1890), 163–356   1735
P. 200: Inventory of the Parish of Tough; includes entry for the 'Bell book: 1735, containing names of all those who subscribed to buy . . . one of the bells of King's College.' Original in the National Archives of Scotland [formerly SRO], CH2/356/3. *See above* 2.1 Tough Kirk Session Records

Pococke, Richard, *Tours in Scotland, 1747, 1750, 1760*, ed. Daniel William Kemp, Scottish History Society Publications 1.1 (Edinburgh, 1887)   1760
Description of the Chapel in *Tour* 1760, p. 207

Pennant, Thomas, *A Tour in Scotland MDCCLXIX* (Chester, 1771)   1771–74
One sentence description of the Chapel, p. 116

Cf: 3rd edn Warrington, 1774, p. 125
No further amendments in 1776 and 1790 edns

Douglas, Francis, *A General Description of the East Coast of Scotland,*   1782
*from Edinburgh to Cullen, including a Brief Account of the Universities of
St. Andrews and Aberdeen* (Paisley: printed for the author by
A. Weir, 1782)
Reprinted: (Aberdeen: Chalmers, 1826)
Description of King's College Chapel, with measurements, pp. 189–91 in
1782 edn; pp. 153–58 in 1826 edn

Camden, William, *Britannia; or, A Chorographical Description of the*   1789
Flourishing Kingdoms of England, Scotland, and Ireland, translated
from the edition published by the author in MDCVIII; enlarged
by the content discovered by Richard Gough (London: printed by
J. Nichols for T. Payne, 1789)
Vol. 3, p. 419 has a very brief revised and updated description of the
Chapel

Wilson, Robert, *An Historical Account and Delineation of Aberdeen*   1822
(Aberdeen: Johnston, 1822): illus
Succinct contemporary description of the buildings at King's College,
with dimensions, and a drawing of the library in the Chapel by G. Smith,
pp. 53–54

MacGibbon, David, and Thomas Ross, *The Castellated and Domestic*   1892
Architecture of Scotland from the Twelfth to the Eighteenth Century
(Edinburgh: Douglas, 1887–92). 5 vols
Vol. 5, p. 358: Description of the sundial on King's College Chapel [with
major errors]; pp. 542–43, 563: Discussion of masons and architects

MacGibbon, David, and Thomas Ross, *The Ecclesiastical Architecture of*   1897
Scotland (Edinburgh: Douglas, 1896–97). 3 vols
Vol. 3, pp. 287–96: illus, contain a detailed architectural description of
King's College Chapel. The historical development is described with
quotations from Macpherson, Spalding, Gordon, Innes

2.3   **Secondary works**   Arranged alphabetically by author or title

2.3.1   **Books**

Brown, Elizabeth Christie, *The Kildrummy Christies,* (Privately published, 1941)
By the first Chapel Organist and Director of Music, 1891–1921; pp. 47, 75–78 contain
references to the Chapel organ and choir

Brown, Elizabeth Christie, *Personal Memoirs,* (Privately published, 1954)
Many references to music in the Chapel on pp. 10–44

Dennison, E. Patricia and Judith Stones, *Historic Aberdeen: the Archaeological Implications
of Development,* The Scottish Burgh Survey (Edinburgh: Historic Scotland, 1997)
King's College Chapel on pp. 101–06: illus

Fawcett, Richard, *Scottish Architecture from the Accession of the Stewarts to the Reformation,
1371–1560,* The Architectural History of Scotland (Edinburgh: Edinburgh University Press, 1994)

In chapter 5: Rural and academic collegiate churches, King's College Chapel is considered on pp. 161–66

Kennedy, William, *Annals of Aberdeen from the Reign of King William the Lion to the end of the year 1818, with an account of the City, Cathedral, and University of Old Aberdeen* (London: printed for A. Brown, Aberdeen, 1818), 2 vols
Based on the use of Town and University archives and with acknowledgement to the Statistical Account
Fairly detailed descriptions of the Chapel and Tower in Book V, ch. iii, pp. 396–400; with a list of the coats of arms
Appendix with reproductions of early documents

Milne, John, *Aberdeen: Topographical, Antiquarian, and Historical Papers on the City of Aberdeen* (Aberdeen: 'Aberdeen Journal' Office, 1911)
Pp. 195–217 contain material on King's College Chapel

Rettie, James, *Aberdeen Fifty Years Ago*: being a series of twenty-one engravings of buildings in and that were about Aberdeen (Aberdeen: Smith, 1868)
Description of the Chapel, on pp. 123–25; illus, with reference to the bells; derivative.

Stanley, Arthur Penrhyn, *Christian Institutions: Essays on Ecclesiastical Subjects* (London: J. Murray, 1881)
Reference to the ambo in the Chapel on p. 55

2.3.2　**Articles**

The principle local newspapers are

Aberdeen Journal, 29 Dec. 1747/4 Jan. 1748– , weekly until 1957; daily from 25 Aug. 1876–30 Nov. 1922, when it became the *Aberdeen Press and Journal*, 1922–
Typescript index to 1748–1861 in Special Libraries and Archives, DISS: Historic Collections, University of Aberdeen, contains a few references under Old Aberdeen; thorough search will reveal more

Aberdeen Daily Free Press, 6 May 1853–30 Nov. 1922, when it became the *Aberdeen Press and Journal*

Aberdeen Herald, 1832–76

Duncan, Walter, 'Restoration from 1867 to 1975', *The Restoration of St Machar's Cathedral* (Aberdeen: Kirk Session and Friends of St Machar's Cathedral, 1991), 3–8
On p. 3 he describes Bishop Stewart's pulpit and its transfer to King's College Chapel in 1844

Eeles, F. C., and Ranald W. M. Clouston, 'The Church and Other Bells of Aberdeenshire, part III', *Proceedings of the Society of Antiquaries of Scotland*, 94 (1960–61), 272–300
King's College on pp. 286–89

Geddes, W. D., 'Local Aspects of the Fine Arts. II. Old Aberdeen,', *Transactions of the Aberdeen Philosophical Society*, 1 (1884), 15–30: illus
A talk delivered on Nov. 11, 1873. The Chapel is described on pp. 16–23

Richardson, J. S., 'Fragments of altar retables of late medieval date in Scotland', *Proceedings of the Society of Antiquaries of Scotland*, 6th series (1927–28), 197–224
Pp. 199–200 refer to King's College Chapel

2.4   **Visual material**   Arranged chronologically by the period depicted

Gordon, James *Abredoniae Vtriusque Descriptio. A Description of both Touns of Aberdeen*, ed. Cosmo Innes (Edinburgh: Spalding Club, 1842)   1661
Plan of the Old Toun, incorporating a keyed plan of King's College
The volume also contains a reproduction of Slezer's 'The Prospect of Old Aberdien' , *see below*

Slezer, John, *Theatrum Scotiae, containing the Prospects of their Castles and Palaces, together with those of the most considerable towns and colleges, the ruins of many abbeys, churches, monasteries and convents, within the Kingdom* (London: Abel Swalle, 1693)   1693
Facsimile reprint, (Turriff: Heritage Press, 1979)
Plate 20: Facies Civitatis Aberdoniae Vetus. The Prospect of Old Aberdien

Cordiner, Charles, *Remarkable Ruins, and Romantic Prospects, of North Britain: ancient monuments, and singular subjects of natural* history (London, Mazell, 1788–95). 2 vols   1765
1 plate: King's College, Aberdon [from the NW], drawn by C. Cordiner, engraved by P. Mazell

Logan, James, [The Old Pulpit in St Machar's Cathedral], no. 5 in a set of 6 watercoloured drawings, MS 3598/5   1808?
Earlier than the drawing in his Collectania Ecclesiastica, *see below*, with ms marginal notes by W. Kelly

Logan, James, Collectanea Ecclesiastica in Provincia Abredonensi, 1819, MS 2928/1–3.   1819
With illustrations in Vol. 3: Bishop Stewart's Pulpit, and Panels from Bishop Stewart's Pulpit, reproduced in *next item*

Logan's Collections, ed. James Cruickshank, (Aberdeen: Third Spalding Club, 1941),   1819
Plate 7: 'The old pulpit in St. Machar's Cathedral, now reconstructed in King's College Chapel' ,
p. 126: 'Panels from the old pulpit in St Machar's Cathedral'. *See below next item*, photographs

Bishop Wm Stewart's Pulpit, St. Machar's Cathedral, drawn by James Logan, MS U 1494/A7/47   1819
3 photographs of details of Logan's drawing, mounted on one card, annotated, 'William Kelly, 62 Rubislawden N., Aberdeen'; '24 May 1932'

Wilson, Robert, *An Historical Account and Delineation of Aberdeen* (Aberdeen: Johnston, 1822): illus   1822
Succinct contemporary description of the buildings at King's College, with dimensions, and a drawing of the West Front of the Chapel and Crown Tower by G. Smith, pp. 53–54
The drawing is reproduced in James Rettie, *Aberdeen Fifty Years Ago, see above* 2.3.1

Nichol, J. & D., *Aberdeen Illustrated in Nine Views, with explanatory remarks, plan of the town, and several vignettes*, Cities and Towns of Scotland 1 (Montrose: Nichol, 1840)   1840

Plate 7: King's College, Aberdeen

Billings, Robert William, *The Baronial and Ecclesiastical Antiquities of*   1845
Scotland; illustrated by Robert William Billings, architect, (Edinburgh: Blackwood, 1845–52). 4 vols.
Vol. 1 contains 'King's College Chapel', 4 illustrations: Chapel West Front, Interior Stallwork, Library in Chapel, Geometric Tracery

'King's College, by Sir George Reid'; *Scottish Notes and Queries*, 12   1881
(1),(July 1898), frontispiece

Watt, James C., 'Chapel and Tower, King's College, Aberdeen   1885
University', *The Builder*, 1885
Six plates of architectural drawings awarded the medal of merit and premium award in the R.I.B.A. Silver Medal Competition 1885. Also published in the *Edinburgh Architectural Association Sketch Book*, Vol. 1, new series (1886), plates 4–9 *See also below* 3 1884 Chapel and Tower, Drawings Nos. 1–6 by James C Watt.
Preliminary drawings in R.I.B.A. archives, *see above* 2.1.

3   Plans

1773   Building plans for the New Work, MS K 252
Plans F to I show the Chapel

1871–1952   King's College Chapel, Aberdeen, Plans and Drawings,
MS U 1494/A5, A6, A7
Listed below. Titles and annotations are transcribed from the original as closely as possible

Date	Title [or description]	Plan number
	'Annotations on the plans'; Format; Size in cm	
	Notes	

Dated plans

1871–2?	Canopies No. 2, 3, & 4 on both sides	A6/13
	'Traced from a drawing . . . the C. of Works, about 1871 or 2'; Tracing; 38 x 29	
1876–7?	Section of Canopy. Scale: $\frac{11}{16}''$ to 1'	A6/67/2
	'Drawn by John Melville Keith, c.1876 or 7', 'William Kelly, 62 Rubislawden North, Aberdeen'; print mounted on card; 30.5 x 22.5	
188–	[Ground plan of Chapel]	A7/58
	'Traced from JCW's plan of 188[–]'; Tracing; 36.5 x 52	
188–?	King's College Woodwork. Charles Carmichael	A6/68
	'158'; 'Stalls, King's College'; 56.5 x 34.5	
188–?	King's College Woodwork. Charles Carmichael	A6/71
	'159'; 56 x 39	
	Details of carving	

1882	King's College Woodwork. Charles Carmichael. [Window] Scale: 4″ to 1′ 'Aug. 1882'; 56.5 x 38.5	A6/69
1882	King's College Woodwork. Charles Carmichael. [2 windows?] 'Aug/82'; 56.5 x 38.5	A6/70
1882	King's College Chapel Aberdeen. Drawings of proposed new tracery for two east end windows. Note: this drawing is made to the curve of the southmost window. Outside elevation. Section. Inside elevation. Plan. Scale: $\frac{1}{2}$″ to 1′. H.M. Office of Works &c Edinburgh 15 Novr. 1882. 'J.T.' 'W.W.Robertson'; Linen backed; 50 x 67	A5/26
1883	Measurements of Crown Kings College Tower. Oct. 1883 + Front Elevation of S.W. Buttress Tracing mounted on paper; 36 x 50.5 On verso: drawing of battlement	A7/54
1883	Kings College, Old Aberdeen. Upper part of Lantern Tower from measurements taken October 1883 JCW Scale: $1\frac{1}{2}$″ to 1′; 76 x 57	A7/56
1883?	Measurement of Crown Kings College Tower, [including] Front Elevation of battlement. On verso: 'C Carmichael mens. & delt.' 'Charles'; Tracing mounted on paper; 50 x 36	A7/55
1883–84	Crown of Tower, King's College, Aberdeen. Half plan at D. Half plan at C. Half plan at B. Half plan at A. Charles Carmichael, Del. March 1884. Measured October 1883. Scale: $\frac{1}{2}$″ to 1′ 65 x 50	A6/59
1883–84	Crown of Tower, King's College, Aberdeen. [With] plan of Soffit. Section on line CD. Charles Carmichael, Del. March 1884. Measured October 1883. Scale: $\frac{1}{2}$″ to 1′ 65 x 50	A6/60
1883–84	Crown of Tower, King's College, Aberdeen. West Elevation. Charles Carmichael, Del. March 1884. Measured October 1883. Scale: $\frac{1}{2}$″ to 1′ 65 x 50	A6/61
1883–84	King's College, Aberdeen. West Elevation of Chapel and Tower. [With] plan of Chapel, and Window, Charles Carmichael, 1884 Scale: $1\frac{7}{8}$″ to 10′; 64.5 x 48	A6/62
1884	King College Chapel Aberdeen. No. 1. South Elevation. Plan at Ground Level. Scale: $1\frac{1}{4}$″ to 10′. H.M.	A5/14

Office of Works &c. Edinburgh Novr. 1882 & Jany. 1884
'J.T.'; Linen backed; 66.5 x 48.5

1884	King College Chapel Aberdeen. No. 2. East Elevation. Section on line A.B on plan. Plan of Upper part of Chapel. Scale: $1\frac{1}{4}''$ to 10'. H.M. Office of Works &c. Edinburgh Novr. 1882 & Jany. 1884 'J.T.'; Linen backed; 66 x 48.5	A5/15
1884	Kings College Chapel Aberdeen. No. 3 West Elevation. Section on line C.D on plan. North Elevation. Scale: $1\frac{1}{4}''$ to 10'. H.M. Office of Works &c. Edinburgh Novr. 1882 & Jany. 1884 'J.T.'; Linen backed; 67 x 48.5	A5/13
1884	Arrangement [within King's College Chapel] c1872–1891. Traced from plan belonging to HM Office of Works. Signed 'J.T.' & dated Novr. 1882 & Jany. 1884. Scale: $1\frac{1}{4}''$ to 10'. William Kelly, June 1932; Linen; 26 x 48.5 [See also A5/17 Tracing with additional information]	A5/16
1884	Chapel and Tower, King's College Aberdeen University. No. 1. [Drawing] From the North-West. West Elevation. Ground plan. Plans at A, B, C, D. Scale: $1\frac{1}{4}''$ to 10' 'James C. Watt Decr. 1884'; Linen mounted; 67.5 x 99.5 For Drawings Nos 1–6, *see above* 2.1 RIBA, for Preliminary sketches; 2.4 Watt, James C. for published versions	A5/6
1884	Chapel and Tower, King's College Aberdeen University. No. 2. [Drawing], From the North. North Elevation. South Elevation. Section. Window next Tower, South Elevation. [Main] scale: $1\frac{1}{4}''$ to 10' 'James C. Watt Decr. 1884'; Linen mounted; 67.5 x 99.5	A5/1
1884	Chapel and Tower, King's College Aberdeen University. No. 3. [Drawing] From the South East. Sections and plans. Scale: $\frac{1}{2}''$ to 1' 'James C. Watt Decr. 1884'; Linen mounted; 100 x 67	A5/3
1884	Chapel and Tower, King's College Aberdeen University. No.4. West Elevation of Upper part of Tower. Scale: $\frac{1}{2}''$ to 1' 'James C. Watt Decr. 1884'; Linen mounted; 100 x 67	A5/2
1884	Chapel, King's College Aberdeen University. No. 5. Sketch of canopies of stalls, about quarter full size 'James C. Watt Decr. 1884'; Linen mounted; 67 x 99	A5/4
1884	Chapel, King's College Aberdeen University. No. 6. Sketch (about one eighth full size) of East side of Centre part of Screen 'James C. Watt Decr. 1884'; Linen mounted; 101.5 x 67.5	A5/5

1884	Chapel and Tower, King's College Aberdeen University. No. 3. [Elevations, sections, plans, illustration: From the South East]. Scale: $\frac{3}{16}''$ to 1'. Vol. 1. New Series. Plate No. VI; 29 x 19 Print, from *Edinburgh Architectural Association Sketch Book*?; Cropped copy of A6/58/7, with added ms measurement.	A6/58/6
1884	Chapel and Tower, King's College Aberdeen University. No. 3. [Elevations, sections, plans, illustration: From the South East]. Scale: $\frac{3}{16}''$ to 1'. James C. Watt [. . .]. Vol.1. New Series. Plate No. VI; 45 x 28.5 Print, from *Edinburgh Architectural Association Sketch Book*?; Cropped copy at A6/58/6, with added ms measurement	A6/58/7
1884	Chapel and Tower, King's College Aberdeen University. No. 4. West Elevation of Upper Part of Tower. Scale: $\frac{3}{16}''$ to 1'. Vol. 1. New series. Plate No. VII 45 x 28.5 Print, from *Edinburgh Architectural Association Sketch Book*?	A6/58/5
1884	Chapel, King's College, Aberdeen University. No. 6. Sketch of East Side of Centre part of Screen. Vol. 1. New Series. Plate No. IX 45 x 29 Print, from *Edinburgh Architectural Association Sketch Book*?	A6/67/4
1885?	Chapel and Tower, King's College Aberdeen University. R.I.B.A. Silver Medal Competition, 1885. Medal of Merit and Premium Awarded. Measured and Drawn by Mr James C. Watt. C. F. Kell Photo-Litho London E. North Elevation. South Elevation. Illustration: From the North. Section. Window next Tower South Elevation. [Various scales] 'William Kelly, 62 Rubislawden N. Aberdeen.'; print on card; 20 x 30	A6/58/3
1885?	Chapel, King's College Aberdeen University. Sketch of Canopy of Stalls. About quarter full size. R.I.B.A. Silver Medal Competition, 1885. Medal of Merit and Premium Awarded. Measured and Drawn by Mr James C. Watt. C. F. Kell Photo-Litho & Printer, 8 Castle St Holborn, London E.C. *The Builder*, June 6, 1885 Print; 21.5 x 32.5 Cropped, but complete, copy at A6/58/8	A6/58/9
1885?	E.A.A. Sketch Book. Vol. IV plate No.-: Chapel, King's College, Aberdeen University No. 5. Printed by Messrs G. Waterston & Sons, Edinr. With pencil annotations	A7a/9
1885?	E.A.A. Sketch Book. Vol. IV plate No.- : Sketch (about	A7a/8

one eighth full size) of East Side of Centre part of Screen, Chapel, King's College, Aberdeen University No. 6. Printed by Messrs G. Waterston & Sons, Edinr.
With pencil annotations. Cf. A5/5

1886	King's College Chapel, Old Aberdeen. No. 10. Portion of Canopies to Stalls South Side of Chapel. Front Elevation. Section. Drawn by J. Melville Keith. Scale: 1″ to 1′. January 29th, 1886 (Copyright) 'William Kelly, 62 Rubislawden North, Aberdeen'; Print mounted on card; 23 x 33.5	A6/67/1
1886	[Drawing of Apse End of Chapel] 'College Chapel. Meeting of Ecclesiological Socy. June 1886'; 19 x 38	A6/77
1888?	King's College Chapel. Aberdeen. Proposed Plan of Restoration 1889. Longitudinal Section. Cross Section. Plan. Scale: 1¼″ to 10′. Andrew Gibb & Co., Draughtsmen, Lithographers & Engravers. 3 Queen St & 40 Broad St, Aberdeen 'R. Rowand Anderson, Architect' 19 St Andrew Square, Edinburgh; Stamped: Office Record Drawing No . . . ,' Kings College'; On verso: 'McIntyre, Marischal College' Duplicate at A7a/2	A7a/1
1891	King's College Chapel Old Aberdeen. Front Elevation. Plan. 16 Rutland Square Edinburgh Oct. 9th 1891. Scale: ½″ to 1′ '100'; 51 x 69 Tinted	A5/40
1892?	[King's College Chapel?] 'after 1891'; Photographic print on paper, embossed: G.W.Wilson & Co., Aberdeen; On verso: William Kelly, 62 Rubislawden North Aberdeen' 18.5 x 24.5	A6/15
1892	King's College Chapel. Aberdeen. Brass Ring for End of Chancel Rope. 16 Rutland Square Edinburgh Feb 92 'Upper part screwed on Rope knotted within clip'; '102'; 30 x 24.5 Tinted	A5/36
1892	King's College Chapel Old Aberdeen. Mace Holder & Hook for Chancel Rope. Full size. No. 44. 16 Rutland Square Edinburgh Feb 92 '101'; 69 x 51 Tinted	A5/38
1892	King's College Chapel Old Aberdeen. Panelling West of Professors Stalls. Revised Drawing. Section C.D Elevation of panelling on South Side of Chapel.	A5/42

Section A.B. Plan. Scale: $\frac{1}{2}''$ to $1'$. 16 Rutland Square
Edinburgh Feb 1892
'98'; 45.5 x 68.5
Tinted

1897	Stalls in Chapel King's College Old Aberdeen. Carving: West Elevation. Carving in Canopy panel. Elevation looking South. Scale: $1\frac{3}{8}''$ to $5'$. Measured and Drawn on the Spot by Jas. B. Fulton. June 97 With ms annotations, including 'This scale is wrong'; Print; 28.5 x 38	A5/41
1898	Stalls in Chapel Kings College Old Aberdeen. Part of Canopy at right hand side of gate. Measured and drawn on the spot by Jas. B. Fulton, June 97. Ardwinckle Studentship R.I.B.A., 1898. *The Builder*, October 1, 1898. Inx-Photo Sprague & Co. Ltd. 4 & 5 East Harding Street, Fetter Lane, E.C. Print on card; 21.5 x 30.5	A6/67/3
1911?	[King's College Chapel. Aberdeen] [Elphinstone Monument]:	A7a/10
1911?	Elphinstone Monument plan 'For the use of the Court'; Tracing paper	A7a/10/1
1911?	Elphinstone Monument Longitudinal section 'For the use of the Court'; Tracing paper	A7a/10/2
1911?	Elphinstone Monument 'Marble work No. 1'; 'Plan at 15'' above floor level The dotted line shows the lower (5'') plinth'; Tracing paper Damaged	A7a/10/3
1911?	[Elphinstone Monument] 'Marble work No. 2' South 'Plan at 2' 3'' above floor level 'Note all the parts above the 1' 3'' level from floor must be tried in position and fitted with the bronzes before being fixed'; Tracing paper Damaged; edges missing	A7a/10/4
1911?	Elphinstone Monument 'Marble work No. 3' North side; Tracing paper	A7a/10/5
1911?	Elphinstone Monument 'Marble work No. 4' South side; Tracing paper	A7a/10/6
1911?	Elphinstone Monument 'Marble work No. 5' West end. East end. Section A.B. Section C.D; Tracing paper	A7a/10/7
1911?	Elphinstone Monument 'Marble work No. 6' North West; Tracing paper	A7a/10/8
1911?	Elphinstone Monument 'Bronze work No. 7' Plan; Tracing paper	A7a/10/9
1911?	Elphinstone Monument 'Bronze work No. 8' Section; Tracing paper	A7a/10/10

1911?	[Elphinstone Monument. Drawing: South side, West side] Tracing mounted on card	A7a/10/11
1911?	'Elphinstone Tomb: suggested arrangement of west end.' Drawing; Tracing mounted on card	A7a/10/12
1911?	[3 drawings for Bishop's tomb]	A7a/13
193–?	$\frac{1}{2}''$ Detail of East Elevation — King's College Chapel 'Measured drawing by J. Fenton Wyness'; 66 x 70; Small tracing attached;	A5/29
193–?	[Drawings of details on doorway with statue] 17 x 22	A5/50/12
193–?	[Tracing of statue of bishop to flank doorway] 29 x 18.5	A5/50/10
193–?	Chapel, King's College, Old Aberdeen. Plan, to $\frac{1}{4}$ inch scale, showing suggested arrangement of floor when the Tomb is placed in true alignment and 26 inches farther east. The yellow tilework removed Tracing, tinted, mounted on card; 16.5 x 21.5	A5/52
1930	King's Coll. Chapel East window. This is a full size plan of the present jambs & mullions, as they appear to have been designed '112'; 'Superseded. Retain the ancient jambs as discovered'; '11th Feb. 1930'; Blueprint; 56.5 x 76 Tinted; Paper embossed: 62 Rubislaw Den North Aberdeen With King's College Chapel Aberdeen proposed East Window Feb. 1930; on tracing paper, attached	A5/19
1930	South window of Apse. North window of Apse. 10th Feb: 1930 '112' 'a'; 'King's College Chapel – measurements & diagrams of N & S windows of Apse; 36 x 56.5	A5/27
1930	The Shrine: Lectern for Book say 20″ x 12″ 10th Octr 1930; Niche for a figure '8th Oct. 1930, arranged this with Prof. J. Macdonald at Marischal Coll. . . . Mr Butchart & JCW also G. Reid got instructions as to walling recess'; 24.5 x 21.5	A5/50/1
1930	[Drawing of window] '118'; 'h'; 'Made 8′ 3″ Oct. 9th 1930; 39 x 20	A6/46
1930	King's College Chapel. Existing Jamb & Sill of East Window. Full Size. Section of Sole. Plan of Jamb (from full Size Templates). July 1930 '113'. 'C'; 'Superseded'; On verso: 'King's Coll. Chapel. East window, The roll contains abcd, 4 sheets'; 73.5 x 126 Tinted	A6/57

1930	[Heraldic descriptions of the coats of arms of Banff, Elgin, Inverness, Dingwall, Tain, Kirkwall, Lerwick; + other notes dated 3rd Octr. 1930] 33 x 21.5	A7/61
1930	[Drawings and heraldic descriptions of coats of arms of Dornoch, Peterhead, Fraserburgh, Grantown on Spey, Stonehaven.] 11th Nov. 1930 33 x 21.5	A7/60
1931	Elphinstone Tomb: King's College Chapel Aberdeen c. 22.5 x 102 [varying].	A5/46/1– 2,4–12

/1: Tracing of lettering: Fundator vixit MC. Cf: /9

/2: Tracing of lettering: Huius universitatis. Cf: /7

/4: Drawing of lettering: Hic Sepultus est; 'Respaced, corrected & traced 8th Sept. 1930'. Cf: /12

/5: Drawing of lettering: Fundator vixit MCCCXXI ~ MDXIIII Gulielmus Elphinstone Eps Aberdon; 33.5 x 200.5

/6: Lettering: CCCCXXXI ~ MDXIIII. North side. Feb: 9th 1931
    'VI WK copy' 'push MDXIIII to right . . .'.; Blueprint

/7: Lettering: 'Huius universitatis'. East end. 29th Jan. 1931
    'Sent 30th Jan. '; IV W.Ks copy; Blueprint; Cf: /2

/8: Lettering: 'stone eps Aberdon' South side 3rd Feb: 1931
    'III. W.Ks copy'; 'Sent 9th Feb. 1931 to Mcdonald & Creswick Ltd 20 Harrison rd Edinburgh'; Pale blueprint:

/9: Lettering: 'Fundator vixit MC'. North side Feb.7th 1931
    'V. W.Ks copy'; Pale blueprint

/10: Lettering: 'Gulielmus Elphin'. South side Jan 31 1931
    'II W.Ks copy'; Embossed: 62 Rubislawden North, Aberdeen.

/11: Tracing of letter N.

/12: Lettering: Hic sepultus est. 8th Sept. 1930
    'I W.Ks copy; .Blueprint; Cf: /4

1931?	[Tracing mounted on paper of lettering on West, South, East and North sides of Bishop Elphinstone Tomb] 'The sizes marked are for the bronze model,. . .'; 18 x 22.5	A5/50/7
1931?	[Elphinstone Monument] Diagram showing difference between the design as approved and the design of the monument as temporarily set up with wooden base $10\frac{1}{2}$' high	A6/56

'111'; 'A.M.M. W.K. J.C.W. H.T.'; 32 x 64
2 ink drawings + 2 prints mounted on one card

1931	King's College Chapel — East window. Superseded sketches, of possible arrangement & Tracery Feb. 1931 '119'. 'i'. 'V'; Includes 2 tracings pasted to card; 66 x 44	A6/45
1931	King's College Chapel. East window as existing Feb: 1931 '120'. 'j'. 'VI'; 'on trial to see how 4 lights might do'; 55 x 37	A6/48
1931	E. Window King's College Chapel. Scale: 1″ to 1′. 13th Feb:1931 '121'. 'k'. 'VIIa'. 'A'; 'Superseded by sketch marked B & inked drawing marked C.'; Linen backed; 50.5 x 29	A6/47
1931	King's Coll. Chapel E. window. 14th Feb: 1931 '122'. 'l'. 'VII' 'B'; 'sketch finally adopted for finished drawing marked C of 17th Feb; Linen backed; 31.5 x 32.5	A6/49
1931	King's College Chapel, Aberdeen. Proposed Restoration of East Window. Scale 1″ = a foot. Outside Elevation. William Kelly. 17th February 1931. Drawing C Linen; 68 x 35.5	A6/21
1931	[Detail of top of window] '123'. 'm'. 'VII' 'D'; 'Drawing C altered on suggestion of JCW 24th Feb: 1931'; Linen backed; 36 x 32.5	A6/50
1931	Drawing C King's College Chapel. Aberdeen. Proposed Restoration of East Window. Outside elevation. Scale 1″ = 1 foot. William Kelly, 17th February 1931 '124'. 'n'; 'Drawing No. 1'; Blueprint; 66.5 x 35	A6/51
1931	Drawing C King's College Chapel. Aberdeen. Proposed Restoration of East Window. Outside Elevation. Scale 1″ = 1 foot. William Kelly, ~~17th~~ 26th February 1931 '125'. 'o'; 'No. 1' 'This was the drawing supplied by the Univ. Court'; 'VII'; Blueprint; 67.5 x 35	A6/52
1931?	[Drawing of top arch of window] '116'. 'f'; On verso: measured plans and arithmetical sums, 'E. Window [..] of 13th June 1931. W.K. to Rennie & W. Tawse, Rhynie'; 56 x 45	A6/55
1931	King's College Chapel. East End. ½″ Scale. W.K. 16th June, 1931 'This was measured & plotted by RWG. The ments. were all taken again & revised, & plotted by me; See sheet I'; Tinted; On verso: 'King's College Chapel. near/west? window'; 75.5 x 58.5	A7/23

1931	King's College Chapel. East Window. Sill Courses — full size 16th June 1931 '126'. 'p'; 'original of sheets 2 & 3; 3 pieces of paper pasted together; Tinted; 77 x 124.5	A6/43
1931	Drawing of monogram: Sir A G S 'WK 24th June 1931'; Tinted; 25 x 21.5	A5/50/2
1931	Drawing No. 2. King's College Chapel. Offset mould-ing at E End full size. 30th June 1931 '127'. 'q'; 'Copy to Rhynie 10th July'; On verso: small measured drawings; 34 x 47.5	A6/42
1931	Drawing No. 2. King's College Chapel. Offset mould-ing at E. End. full size. 30th June 1931 'copy to Rhynie 10 July'; Tracing; 34 x 48.5	A7/24
1931	Drawing No. 3. King's College Chapel East Window Sole Course Full size William Kelly 30th June 1931 'Copy to Rhynie 10th July'; On verso: 'King's Coll Chapel. Some of the mason wk details'; Blueprint; 67 x 100	A5/20
1931	Drawing No. 3. King's College Chapel. East Window. Sole Courses. Full Size. William Kelly 30th June 1931 '129'. 's'; Linen backed; 68 x 97; Cf: Blueprint at A6/41	A6/39
1931	Drawing No. 3 King's College Chapel. East Window. Sole Courses. Full Size. William Kelly. 30th June 1931 '128'. 'r'; Blueprint; 67 x 92; Cf: Original at A6/39	A6/41
1931	Drawing No. 4 King's College Chapel — E. Window 11th July 1931. Scale 1″ = 1 foot. W.Kelly, 62 Rubislawden North, Aberdeen. '131a'. 'u'; 'Original & a blue to W. Tawse — Rhynie 14th July 1931'; Blueprint; 25 x 39.5	A6/35
1931	Drawing No. 5. King's College Chapel. New Work at East End. July, 1931. Scale ½″ = 1 foot. William Kelly, 62 Rubislawden North, Aberdeen '131a'. 'u'; Linen backed; 61.5 x 74.5	A6/38
1931	Drawing No. 5. King's College Chapel New Work at East End. July 1931. William Kelly 62 Rubislawden North Aberdeen 'Office copy. Copy to Mr. Tawse 23 July 1931. P.T.O.'; On verso: diagrams, 'Copy to Mr Tawse 20th August 1931. The red traced & sent to Mr Tawse 27th Aug 1931'; 63.5 x 75.5	A5/22
1931	Drawing No. 6. King's College Chapel. E. Window & new Buttress &c 21 July 1931. W.K. 62 Rubislawden N. Aberdeen, 21 July 1931 'Office copy. Copy to Mr. Tawse 23 July 1931; 44.5 x 69	A5/21
1931	Drawing No. 6. King's College Chapel. E. Window &	A6/37

new Buttress &c. July 21 1931. William Kelly. Plinth
Course. Buttress String course
'132'. 'w'; 56.5 x 76.5
Tracing at A7/68

1931	Drawing No. 6. King's College Chapel. E. Window & new Buttress &c. 21 July, 1931. Plinth Course. Buttress Stringcourse 'W. K. 62 Rubislawden N, Aberdeen, 21 July 1931'; Tracing; 45 x 61 Original at A6/37	A7/68
1931	'K. Coll. Chapel 19th Aug, 1931' [Rubbing of mason's mark?] 13.5 x 20.5	A5/9/4
1931	K. Col. Chapel 19th Aug. 1931 [Drawings of masons' marks] Two pieces of paper glued together; 26.5 x 30.5	A6/31
1931	[Altar] 'Alter Slab, used as gravestone of Peter Udny, 1601'. Plan. King's Coll. Chapel, Aberdeen. 19th August 1931 21 x 33	A7/63/1
1931	North Jamb of E. Window, from C. Bannerman's Reverse mould, 20th Aug. 1931 '134'. 'No. 7a'; 'as sent to Mr. R. 27th Aug. 1931'; Linen backed; 37.5 x 96.5; Cf: A6/34	A6/32
1931	North Jamb of E. Window, from C. Bannerman's Reverse mould, 20 Aug. 1931 '133'. 'H'. 'No. 7'; 'A copy of this on tracing paper to Mr. Tawse — 27th August 1931'; 58 x 111; Cf: A6/32	A6/34
1931	'South Side of New Buttress. 20th August 1931. Tracing to Mr. Rennie' '142'; 'Office copy'; Tracing; 15.5 x 19 'South side of New Buttress' '27th Aug. 1931' '142b'; 22 x 32.5 [Details of buttress] '142c'; 'all 1½" down'; 22 x 33 3 items pinned together	A6/12/1–3
1931	'South Jamb — E Window — King's Coll. Chapel–27th Aug. 1931' '135'. 'No. 8'; 'But left-hand — instead of right-hand as here shewn. — traced left-hand, & came to W. Tawse — 27th Aug. 1931'; Tinted; 106 x 56.5	A6/17
1931	Drawing No. 9. King's Coll. Chapel. String Course round buttress . . . full size section. 29th August 1931 22.5 x 33; Cf: A7/10, but with differences	A7/9
1931	Drawing No. 9. King's Coll. Chapel. String Course round buttress . . . full size section. 29th August 1931 22.5 x 35.5; Cf: A7/9, but with differences	A7/10

1931	Drawing No. 9. King's Coll. Chapel. Showing Course round Buttress where it is contracted from 3′ 4″ to 3′ 6″ on end elevation. Full size Section. 29th August 1931 '132'; 'a1'; Linen backed; 26 x 34	A6/24
1931	K.Coll. Chapel — Buttress Intake. Draft of drawing No. 10. 4th Sept. 1931 With tracing attached; 22 x 33	A7/12
1931	Drawing No. 10. King's College Chapel. New Buttress. Intake — full size — flush at ends. 4th Septr. 1931. W.K '133'; 'b1'; Linen backed; 29.5 x 35.5	A6/33
1931	[3 measured elevations of buttresses] 'No. 17'; 'measd. redrawn 10th Oct. 1931'; 45 x 28.5 The one on right is tracing laid on the sheet	A7/48/10
1931	[3 measured elevations and plan of buttresses] 20th & 21st Octr. 1931 'No. 17b'; Paper embossed '62 Rubislawden North, Aberdeen'; Tracing; 36.5 x 26.5	A7/48/6
1931	King's College Chapel. Upper part of new buttress, 22nd Octr.1931. WK. Scale ½″ = 1 foot 'No. 17c'; Tracing; 33 x 28; Cf. A7/48/8 Blueprint	A7/48/7
1931	King's College Chapel. Upper part of new buttress, 22nd Octr.1931. WK. Scale ½″ = 1 foot 'No. 17c'; Blueprint; 37.5 x 28; Cf. A7/48/7 Tracing	A7/48/8
1931	[Detail of stonework?] W.K. Octr. 23rd. 1931 '134'; 'c1'; 'No. 11'; Linen backed; 25 x 31	A6/26
1931	[Detail of stonework?] W.K. Oct.23rd 1931 '135'; 'd1'; 'No. 12'; Linen backed; 24.5 x 31	A6/27
1931	'e1'. at Course 'd'. W.K. Octr. 23.1931. '136' 'No. 13'; Linen backed; 29 x 27	A6/23
1931	Course f. - front side. 23rd Oct. 1931 'No. 14'; 22 x 33.5	A7/13
1931	Course f. front & side. 23rd. Octr. 1931 '137'. 'No. 14'; Linen backed; 21.5 x 43	A6/30
1931	Course 'h'. 23rd Oct. 1931 'No. 15'; 22 x 33; Cf: A6/22	A7/6
1931	Course 'h' 'g1' '23rd. Oct. 1931' 'No. 15'; Linen backed; 23.5 x 38	A6/22
1931	King's Coll. Chapel. Eaves Course on last wall. 24th Octr. 1931 '139'. 'No. 16'; 'Tracing to Mr. Rennie Same Day'; Linen backed; 33.5 x 21.5	A6/25
1931	[Detail of window tracery]. 28th Octr. 1931. '140'; 'j1'; .' No. 18'; Linen backed; 60.5 x 72.5	A6/29
1931	A small pinnacle near E. end, North side, King's	A7/48/9

College Chapel. measurements taken by Geo. Mellis. Nov. 1931
with, attached: at W. End of N. side, from measts. taken by Geo. Mellis, Nov. 1931; with, attached: at N. end of West Gable. John Rennie Sr. 1st Mch. 1932; 21.5 x 36.5

1931–32	[Measured drawing] W.K. 1931–2. Tracing; 33 x 54	A7/22
1931–32	[Unidentified] 4 pieces of scrap paper pinned together; Various sizes	A5/9/1–4
1931–32	[Elevation of pinnacle] '143'. 'm'; '28th Nov. 1931'. '16th Jan. 1932'; Tinted; 75.5 x 151.52	A6/64
1931–32	[Altar] 6 items pinned together; 42 x 60	A7/63/1–6
1932	King's College Chapel, Aberdeen [: plan]. Scale: $1\frac{1}{4}''$ to 10'. W.K. Jany. 1932 'No. 1'; Tinted; 32 x 51	A6/18
1932	Arrangement [within King's College Chapel]. Scale: $1\frac{1}{4}''$ to 10' 'Jany. 1932'; No. 2; Linen; 25.5 x 46 Cf. A5/6. Apparent tracing with additional information and tinting	A5/17
1932	P. Udny Slab. 2 of the Crosses. 6 Jan. 1932. 33 x 22	A7/63/2
1932	K.C. Chapel 7th Jan. 1932 'under Prof. Robertson Smith window'; Diagrams, text, measurements; 9.5 x 11.5	A5/9/1
1932	P. Udny slab, one of the hounds 16th Jan. 1932 Rubbing; 3.5 x 21.5	A7/63/3
1932	[Diagrams, text, measurements . . . 'Boece's tomb?'] '20th Jan. 1932; 22 x 17	A5/9/2
1932	[Diagrams, text, measurements.] 'Ht. of Organ Loft from floor' $13'\ 1\frac{1}{2}''$; '20th Jan. 1932'; 22 x 16.5	A5/9/3
1932	[Elevation of pinnacle] '144'. 'n'.; '2nd Mch 1932'; On verso: 'King's College Pinnacles'; Tinted; 78 x 152	A6/65
1932	[Outline ? elevation of altar] 8th March 1932 '$5\frac{1}{2}''$ from floor'; Tracing; 25.5 x 22.5	A7/63/5
1932	[?Altar: elevation] 'Given to Mr. Rennie 8th March 1932'; Tracing; 42 x 60	A7/63/6
1932	[Pulpit: elevation, ground plan, details] 'approved by Prof. Macdonald on Sat. 19th March, 1932, Mr. Butchart being present with me; also J. Rennie & Geo. Mellis. The false floor to be lowered at least 1 [..].' 'W.K. 19 Mch 1932'; 2 tracings mounted on one card; 44.5 x 28.5 Paper embossed: '62 Rubislawden North, Aberdeen'	A7/36

1932	[King's College Chapel. Pulpit: printed elevation and plan] 'by J. Cromar Watt'; Paper embossed '62 Rubislawden North, Aberdeen'; with additional notes; tracing of details, 'appd. 19th March 1932', Paper embossed '62 Rubislawden North, Aberdeen': tracing of elevation with realigned steps, Paper embossed '62 Rubislawden North, Aberdeen' all 3 mounted on one card; 46 x 36	A7/40
1932	[King's College Chapel Buttresses and pinnacles] 45.5 x 28.5	A7/48/ 1—10
1932	[King's College Chapel. Upper part of new buttress: 3 drawings of detail] 11th Ap. 1932 11 x 21.5	A7/48/1
1932	Bishop Wm. Stewart's Pulpit, St. Machar's Cathedral, drawn by James Logan 'William Kelly, 62 Rubislawden N., Aberdeen'; 3 photographs of drawings, mounted on one card; 'W.K.'; '24 May 1932'; with small ground plan.; 23.5 x 44.5	A7/47
1932	[Drawings of rood screen] '10th June 1932'; Tracing; 41 x 33.5	A6/6
1932	King's College Chapel. Notes from an inked in plan of the East End to $\frac{1}{4}''$ scale — not dated but about 1871–72. '10th June 1932' '11th June 1932'; .3 leaves, 2 folded; 23 x 18	A6/16
1932	Pulpit King's Coll. Chapel [drawing of canopy] June 20th 1932 Water colour; 33.5 x 22	A7/41
1932	The panels from organ screen. 23rd June 1932 33.5 x 22.5	A7/66
1932	King's Coll. Chapel — Ceiling. 29th June 1932 'try raw umber'; Watercoloured; 22 x 33	A7/64/3
1932	King's College Chapel 1932 [: Screen. Elevation] '14 July 1932'; 80 x 55	A5/35
1932	King's Coll. Chapel Ceiling rib. J.H. Ball — 28th July 1932 Tracing; 14 x 24.5	A7/64/2
1932	King's Coll. Chapel. 6th August 1932. D.L. Kelly. [Elevation of ?pillar] 64.5 x 42	A7/3
1932	Pulpit King's Coll. Chapel [2 drawings of details] 6th Sept. 1932 Water colour; 33.5 x 21.5	A7/42
1932	[Measured diagram ?for wrought iron work] 'to blacksmith' 7th Sept. 1932 33 x 22	A7/37

1932	King's College Chapel, Ceiling 3 items pinned together; 22 x 34.5	A7/64
1932?	[Measured drawing of ?altar] 33.5 x 22	A7/63/4
1933	King's Coll. Stalls /1: 'dimensions of the prayer desks St. Mary's Carden Place'. Scale 1″ = 1 ft. Nov.8, 1933 /2: measured drawing of figure seated at desk. 'K. Coll. Stalls'. Scale 1″ = 1 ft. 31st Oct. 1933 'went [. . .] H.M.M. 8th Nov. 1933' /3: series of elevations and plan. '10th Nov. 1933'. 1′ Scale 42.5 x 43.5	A7/35/1–3
1933	King's College Chapel. Proposed Desks. Novr. 1933. North side. Elevation. William Kelly. 11th Nov. 1933. Scale: 1″ to 1′ '23rd Decr. 1933'; 39 x 28	A7/27
1933	King's College Chapel. Proposed Desks. Novr. 1933. Back of seat. Front of Desk. Section. Scale: 1″ to 1′. William Kelly 13th Novr. 1933 45 x 28	A7/29
1934	Silver Bough-pot, with grid for 3 or 5 Lilies: full size. Plan. Elevation. W. Kelly Jan: 1934 '104' ; On reverse: 'Lord Meston's coat of arms on the back' and date: MDCCCCXXXI; 'The Boughpot was made by Wakely & Wheeler, 27 Red Lion Square, Holborn — London W.C.1 1934'; 'It was used in the College Chapel for the first time, on Sunday 17th March 1935. W.K.'; 'To be returned to William Kelly'; Embossed: 62 Rubislawden North Aberdeen; 55.5 x 75.5 Original, cf. Tracing at A5/43, with some differing notes	A5/44
1934	Silver Bough-pot, with grid for 3 or 5 lilies. William Kelly, 62 Rubislawden North Aberdeen, Jan: 1934. On reverse: 'Lord Meston's coat of arms on the back' and date MDCCCCXXXI; 40.5 x 76 Tracing, with ms annotations differing from those on the original; cf. Original at A5/44	A5/43
1934	[King's College Chapel. Dr J. E. Crombie memorial tablet] /1: Letter to Doctor Kelly from the Carrick Pursuivant 22/8/34 /2: Letter from H. J. Butchart, Secretary of University of Aberdeen to Dr. Kelly 31 August 1934 /3: Note with drawings from William Kelly to Mr Ross. 21 Nov. 1934. /4: Drawing of Rowan /5: Drawing of Rowan berries /6: Drawings of details 'For Dr James Edward Crombie Tablet / Oct. 1933' 'Copied & sent to Ogilvies 31 Jan. 1934'	A4/45/ 1–15

/7: [Traced drawing of pinnacle]

/8: Drawing of floral decorations '20 Nov. 1934'

/9: Drawing of 'The fleur-de-lis' ' 20. Nov. 1934'

/10: Tracing of complete plan of English Oak Tablet . . . 'W.K. 4th & 5th October 1933' 'please set out at full size & so get the divide of the vine. . .'; cf. Original at /14

/11: Tracing of drawings of details 'For the Dr. James E. Crombie Tablet. 31st Jan 1934'. 'make rough model in wax of this re-arrangement of the strengthening stub -pieces'

/12: Tracing of drawing of 'Arrangement of leaves etc. in frame: Dr. Crombie Tablet. 31 Jan. 1934'

/13: Crayon drawing of rowan berry design. '1 Sept. ' 34'

/14: Drawing of complete design of 'English Oak Tablet . . . W.K. 4 & 5 October, 1933'. 'Copied & sent to J&A O 31 Jan: 1934'; Tinted

/15: Letter to Doctor Kelly from the Carrick Pursuivant 'Re Dr J.E.Crombie Tablet' [3 leaves], with sketch design of revised plan on verso of leaf 3

/1–/15 in folder

1934	[Drawing of decorative detail] 'II'; 'Oct. 1934'; Tracing; attached to A7/51; 32 x 20.5	A7/52
1934	[Drawing of decorative detail].]. 5th Decr. 1934 'Keep these leaves as far apart as this shows'; 26.5 x 21	A7/53
1935	King's College Chapel. 8th Feb. 1935. [Detail of carving] 45.5 x 28	A7/2
1935	[2 drawings]. 12th Feb. 1935 'This . . . other end of the one [. . .]'; '2 alterations'; Tracing; 29 x 38.5	A7/30/2
1935	[5 measured drawings of decorative details] 'b' 15th Feb. 1935; 'C'; 'D' 15th Feb. 1935; 'D top of'; 'K' 31st July 1935; 'M' 31 July 1935 Sizes vary; Tracings; 23.5 x 15.5	A7/50
1935	Drawings of details of panel and elevation of [?]. 25th April 1935 '4'; 'both sides had better be measured. E & W in this niche' D.K; 30 x 35	A5/50/13
1935	The Shrine K. Coll. Chapel. 2nd. May 1935 Tracing; 53 x 33.5	A7/62
1935	[Elevation of window, with calculations] 13th August 1935 drawn. 15th August traced 33.5 x 21.5	A7/13
1935	King's College Chapel. Aberdeen. Proposed Restoration of NE window at apsidal E end. [Elevation and Section]. Scale 1″ = 1 foot. William Kelly. 23rd August, 1935 57 x 39.5	A7/20

Original, cf: Blueprint at A7a/11, Tracing at A7/18, Blueprint of tracing at A7/16.

1935	King's College Chapel Aberdeen. Proposed Restoration of NE window at apsidal E end. Scale 1″ = 1 foot 'William Kelly 23rd August, 1935. Traced 1st May 1936' Blueprint; Original at A7/20; Tracing at A7/18; Blueprint of tracing at A7/16	A7a/11
1935	King's College Chapel. Aberdeen. Proposed Restoration of NE window at apsidal E end. [Elevation and Section]. Scale 1″ =foot. William Kelly. 23rd August, 1935. Traced 1st May, 1936 'N.E'; Tracing; ; 57 x 40. Cf. Blueprint of tracing at A7/16; Original at A7/20; Blueprint at A7a/11	A7/18
1935	King's College Chapel. Aberdeen. Proposed Restoration of NE window at apsidal E end. [Elevation and Section]. Scale 1″ = 1 foot. William Kelly. 23rd. August, 1935. Traced 1st May 1936 56 x 40; With small measured diagram on verso Blueprint of tracing. Cf. Original at A7/20; Tracing at A7/18; Blueprint at A7a/11;	A7/16
1936	NE window — King's College Chapel 'Own copy': 'taken out 12th & 14th August 1936. Original to John Rennie'; On verso: NE window f.s.y. jamb insite; Tracing; 90 x 60	A5/28
1936	N.E. Window. 15th Aug. 1936. W.K. Original to John Rennie. Plan of mullion Tracing; 75.5 x 116.5	A5/24
1935	Desk King's Coll: Chapel. 31st Aug. 1935 /1: drawing of decoration; /2: tracing of decoration; /3: 3 drawings of decoration Tinted; 33.5 x 22.5	A7/26/1–3
1936	[Elevation of window] Scale: 1″ to 1′. '14th Nov. 1936. revised 16th Nov. remeasured 16th Nov. 1936'; Tracing; 57 x 39	A7/5
1937	King's College Chapel East Window 'lead lines' like painted on the temporary plate glass. The South East window. 28th July 1937 Ink tracing; 47.5 x 30.5	A7/4
1937	Full size of 'Diamond' latticing for the East window of King's College Chapel. 28th July 1937 33.5 x 22.5. Paper embossed: 62 Rubislawden North Aberdeen	A7/7
1937	King's College Chapel. The S.E.Window. outline of arch. The arch had to be taken down & when the curves were struck from centre . . . curvature. 1937 30.5 x 40.5	A7/8

1938	[Tracing of lettering for Hector Boece Tomb:] Hic Sepultus est Hector Boethius Huius Universitatis Praeses Primus A.D. MCXXXII. [2]5th May 1938. traced Monday 30th May 'altered to MDXXXVI f.s. . . . 17th Octr. 1938': On verso: 'The Boece Brass 1938–9'; 53.5 x 105	A5/55
1938	'King's College Chapel — W.R.Smith meml. window in North wall — next N.E. window'. Inside elevation. Scale: 1″ to 1′. 19th July 1938 'Tracing to W.D.S. 20th July'; 57 x 32.5	A6/20
1941	King's College Chapel. 1″ Scale Plan of Pulpit. Wm. H. Duncan meas. & det. 17th June 1941 33 x 42	A7/38
1946	King's College Chapel. University of Aberdeen. 1 inch drawing shewing Elphinstone Monument & paved recess etc. Drawing No. A/199 Pite, Son & Fairweather, Chartered Architects. 6 Queen Anne's Gate Westminster SW1 28 June 1946 With pencil addition sums	A7a/7
1952?	[King's College Chapel] On verso: '85' 'George Hay's plan of K.C. Chapel'. Scale: $1\frac{1}{4}$″ to 10′; 38.5 x 64 *See above* 1.1.2 Letter from George Hay, 1952	A6/19
1952?	[Ground plan of Chapel] Scale: $1\frac{1}{4}$″ to 10′ 'GH'; Linen; 38.5 x 65.5	A6/75
1952?	Site of Jewel House, Library, Sacristy, etc. Scale: $1\frac{1}{4}$″ to 10′ 'GH'; On verso: '721' 'K.C.Chapel'; 30.5 x 50 Brown on yellow paper	A6/5

Undated plans

Ground plans and elevations

n.d.	King's College [: ground plan]. Scale $2\frac{1}{4}$″ to 10′	A7a/12
n.d.	East End of Kings College Chapel. Ground plan. Scale $\frac{1}{4}$″ to 1 foot '43'; 56 x 44	A5/18
n.d.	Kings College Chapel. Transverse Section of Chapel, and Elevation of Screen. '$\frac{1}{4}$″ to a foot' '48'; 57.5 x 45 Tinted	A5/30
n.d.	[King's College Chapel][Rood screen] Section and Elevation on A.B. . . .. West Elevation of proposed low screen wall. Ground plan. Scale $\frac{1}{2}$ inch to a foot '51'; 'All carved work of above got from existing pieces taken from ancient high screen wall'; 46 x 65.5	A5/33

n.d.	King's College Chapel. Longitudinal Section, and inside Elevation of North Side Wall. Scale $\frac{1}{8}$ inch = one ft '50'; 48.5 x 65	A5/51
n.d.	Chapel and Tower, King's College Aberdeen University. [Printed Ground plan, West Elevation, plans of A, B, C, D. Illustration From the North West.] Scale: $\frac{7}{16}''$ to 10'. 'William Kelly, 62 Rubislawden North, Aberdeen'; 20.5 x 30 Print mounted on card	A6/58/1
n.d.	Chapel and Tower, King's College Aberdeen University. No. 4 'Septentrionale'. West Elevation of Upper Part of Tower. Scale: $\frac{3}{16}''$ to 1' 'William Kelly 62 Rubislawden N'; 30.5 x 22 Print mounted on card	A6/58/2
n.d.	[Ground plan of Choir of Chapel] 'King's College'; '1 line block Oliver & Boyd T.L.Jenkins'; Linen; 33 x 36	A6/76

Stonework

n.d.	[Elevation and plan of pinnacles] Scale: $\frac{1}{2}''$ to 2' 32.5 x 19	A6/73
n.d.	[Elevation of pinnacle] '145'; 'o'; 71.5 x 152	A6/63
n.d.	[6 drawings of detail of pinnacles, thistle and fleur-de-lis decoration] 16.5 x 22	A7/48/4
n.d.	The Consecration Crosses On verso: '19' and notes for ?mounting; 19 x 45.5 Drawings A,B,C,D,E mounted on one card	A6/74
n.d.	[Drawing of crowns on Crown Tower] Badly damaged, lower right portion missing	A7a/3
n.d.	[Outline drawing of crowns on Crown Tower] Badly damaged, top left portion missing	A7a/5
n.d.	[Slip of notes headed: Crown. NW arch inside . . .] 27.5 x 12	A7/14
n.d.	[Detail of soffit] Damaged	A7a/6
n.d.	[Details of buttress] '142c'; 'all 1$\frac{1}{2}''$ down'; 22 x 33	A6/12/3
n.d.	King's Coll. Chapel. Angle between wall & buttress '130'. 't'; on verso: Dr Kelly, 62 Rubislawden North; 56.5 x 76.5	A6/40
n.d.	[Drawing of part of round decoration] Tracing, tinted; 22.5 x 33.5	A7/70

Windows

n.d.	King's Coll. Chapel, Aberdeen. East window. [Detail of stonework? and statue figures '141'. 'No. 189'. 'k1'; 26 x 41 Linen backed	A6/28
n.d.	[Drawing of window, with details] 60 x 114	A5/25
n.d.	[King's College Chapel. Details of window + ?ground plans] '117'; 'q'; 'III';. 76 x 60.5 Blueprint	A6/44
n.d.	King's College Chapel, Aberdeen. New East Window. [Elevation and plan]. Scale: 1″ to 1′ '114'. 'd'; 'Superseded'; 112 x 84 Tinted	A6/53
n.d.	[Sketches of top arch of window] '115'. 'e'; 'See Carmelite monastery S. Queensferry p.304 III'; 28.5 x 32 Linen backed	A6/54
n.d.	S.E. Window — King's College Chapel 34 x 47 3 pieces of paper gummed together	A7/11
n.d.	[Diagram of part of top of window, with Isaiah, Ezekiel, Jeremiah, David indicated below] 'The [. . .] is about 4″ lower than the [. . .]'; 21 x 16	A7/17
n.d.	King's College Chapel. S.E. Window 53 x 78.5	A7/19
n.d.	[Elevation of a window] 34 x 18.5 Tracing	A7/21
n.d.	[Drawing of head of arched window] 39.5 x 29.5 Tracing	A7/25
n.d.	[Drawing of corner decoration] 26.5 x 29 Tracing.	A7/28
n.d.	[Drawing of corner decoration] 'The centre of ball is the centre of a circle inscribed in the spandrel'; 31 x 29.5 Tracing	A7/30/1
n.d.	[Drawing of corner and other decoration] 30.5 x 39 Tracing	A7/30/3
n.d.	[Drawing of corner decoration] 'like the 4 leaved flowers'; 32 x 28 Tracing	A7/31

n.d.	[Drawing of carved decoration at top of arch] 'Traced from G.Chalmers' fullsize — but see the photo- graph — The tracing is not consistently worked out'; 32.5 x 58 Tracing	A7/67

Woodwork

n.d.	King's College – Aberdeen. Drawing of pulpit. Scale 1″ to a Foot '99'; 54 x 36.5	A5/39
n.d.	King's College Chapel. The pulpit: proposed brackets under Canopy. 23rd Sep[. . .] 'Alteration'; [On verso: diagram of stone, with letter F; 'Sir John Fleming 2 boundary stones. Aug. 1933'; 56.5 x 62.5 Tinted	A7/39
n.d	[Lectern: views from different angles, details of carving] 21.5 x 33 With tracing 'from MS of 1521–5' attached	A7/69
n.d.	King's College Chapel. Aberdeen. Carved oak door — Plan and Elevation. Scale one inch to one ft. '47'; 'The hinged styles of door are pieced $2\frac{1}{4}$ inches in breadth, — making them 7 inches broad'; 'The Nos 1,2,3,4 & 5 refer to full sized tracings of panels herewith enclosed'; 65 x 47.5	A5/32
n.d.	Kings College Old Aberdeen Chapel Screen. Elevation & Section on line A.B. Proposed West Elevation. Ground plan. Scale $\frac{1}{4}″$ = one ft '52'; 37 x 49.5	A5/34
n.d.	[King's College Chapel, [Rood screen] Section and Elevation of West side, plan]. Scale: $2\frac{1}{2}″$ to 10′ '53'; 59.5 x 46	A5/31
n.d.	[Drawings of pinnacles and bishop] '2 tiers of pinnacles on canopy' 'pillar like Henry VII Chapel pillars'; 22 x 20.5	A5/50/3
n.d.	[Drawing of carved scroll] 22 x 16	A5/50/5
n.d.	[2 drawings of crucifix above altar, with notes from Fasti, p. 266 and p. 571] 33.5 x 22	A6/14
n.d.	[Heraldic panel: C.R.]. Scale: 1″ to 1′ Tracing mounted on paper; 22.5 x 16.5	A6/66
n.d.	Plan of Old Stalls in King's College Chapel Old Aberdeen. Scale: $\frac{3}{4}″$ to 1′ '95'; 74 x 62.5	A7/57
n.d.	[Chapel ceiling: part of ribbed vault] 'a bake of black paint about 2′ broad. page 34 Macpherson'; Tracing, tinted and gilt; 12.5 x 34.5	A7/64/1

Elphinstone Tomb

n.d.	[Drawing of tomb] 25.5 x 20	A5/50/6
n.d.	'Draft scheme for reconstruction of Founder's Tomb' Ink drawing in frame mount; Tinted; 66 x 48	A6/72
n.d.	'C' [Lettering on Bishop Elphinstone's tomb] Tracing mounted on card; 17 x 21. Cf. A5/46	A7/71

War Memorial

n.d.	[Tracing of war memorial tablet] 23 x 38.5	A5/50/11
n.d.	King's College Chapel War Memorial [: details of shields] South side Tracing; Watercolour; 27 x 43	A7/44

Miscellaneous and unidentified

n.d.	'The Shrine Ante-Chapel King's College Chapel' On verso: 'Dr W Kelly 62 Rubislaw Den North; 84.5 x 54.5 Drawing, part watercoloured, with paper and traced onlays	A5/12
n.d.	King's College Chapel. Aberdeen. Plan of rail. 1 inch scale Tinted; 37 x 51	A5/37
n.d.	[Diagram and figures] Tracing; 21.5 x 11	A5/10
n.d.	[Tracing of lettering]; 8.5 x 12.5	A5/50/4
n.d.	[Drawing of detail] 23 x 17.5	A7/48/5
n.d.	[Drawing of detail: end of two Es] 28.5 x 22.5 Tracing	A7/51

INDEX

Numbers in **bold** refer to illustrations

Col. Pl. I.   King's College, c. 1640 (Copyright: University of Aberdeen)

Col. Pl. II. Portrait of Bishop William Elphinstone, Marischal Museum
(Copyright: University of Aberdeen)

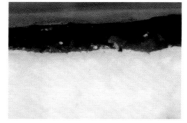

Col. Pl. IIIa.   Paint sample cross-section from landscape showing red underlayer

Col. Pl. IIIb.   Paint sample cross-section from background showing red underlayer

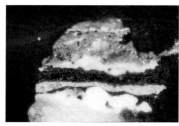

Col. Pl. IIIc.   Paint sample cross-section from dark band

Col. Pl. IIId.   Paint sample cross-section from frame

Col. Pl. IIIe.   Watercolour of Bishop Stewart's pulpit, by James Logan, 1815 (AUL, MS 2928, vol. III, fol. 14b) (Copyright: University of Aberdeen)

Col. Pl. IV.   The *Book of Hours* of James IV and his wife Margaret Tudor
(Vienna, Õsterreichische Nationalbibliothek, Codex Vindobonensis, 1897, fol. 24ᵛ.
Copyright: Bildarchiv der Ö.N.B.)

Col. Pl. V.   The south side of the chapel, showing the armorials and granite facing

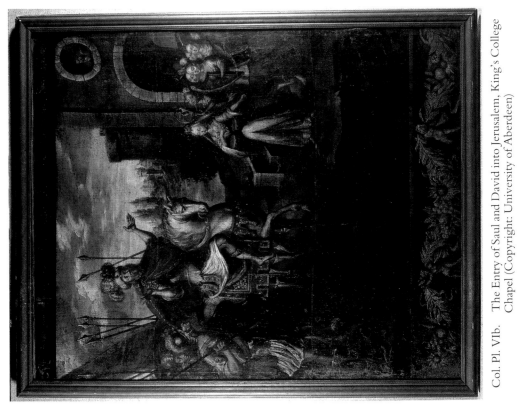

Col. Pl. VIb.   The Entry of Saul and David into Jerusalem, King's College Chapel (Copyright: University of Aberdeen)

Col. Pl. VIa.   David and Goliath, King's College Chapel (Copyright: University of Aberdeen)

Col. Pl. VIIb. The Judgement of Solomon, King's College Chapel
(Copyright: University of Aberdeen)

Col. Pl. VIIa. David and Abigail, King's College Chapel
(Copyright: University of Aberdeen)

Col. Pl. VIII. Solomon and the Queen of Sheba, King's College Chapel
(Copyright: University of Aberdeen)

a

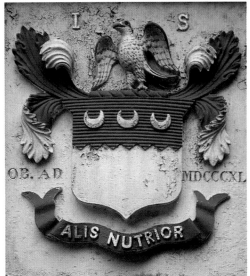

b

c

d

Col. Pl. IX. Coats of Arms: a, Bishop Patrick Forbes; b, John Simpson of Shrubhill; c, Bishop William Elphinstone; d, Bishop Gavin Dunbar

a

b

c

d

Col. Pl. X.   Coats of Arms: a, Bishop William Stewart; b, Supposed arms of James IV, King of Scots; c, Principal Hector Boece; d, Robert Maitland, Dean of Aberdeen

A. D. MDCC.XXIV.
VIR NUNQUAM SINE LAUDE
NOMINANDUS IACOBUS FRA
SERIUS I U D UNICUS MUSA
RUM FAUTOR ALMAM SUA
MATREM ABERDONENSEM
ÆVI INIURIA PARTIM LABAN
TEM PARTIM IACENTEM SOL
LUS FERE RESPEXIT EREXIT
PROVEXIT

a

IE SUIS   PREST

b

FORTIOR QUO MITIOR

c

d

Col. Pl. XI.   Coats of Arms: a, Dr James Fraser, royal librarian; b, Simon Fraser, eleventh
Lord Lovat; c, Colonel John Buchan of Cairnbulg; d, The Alms Dish, James Cromar Watt

Col. Pl. XII.   The west window (J), detail. Clayton and Bell, 1875. Panels illustrating:
Christ with the doctors in the Temple; Paul being instructed by Gamaliel. In the
medallions above (from left) are Patrick Forbes, Gilbert Burnet, Principal G. Campbell and
Dr James Beattie
(Illustration painted by Vic Davidson)

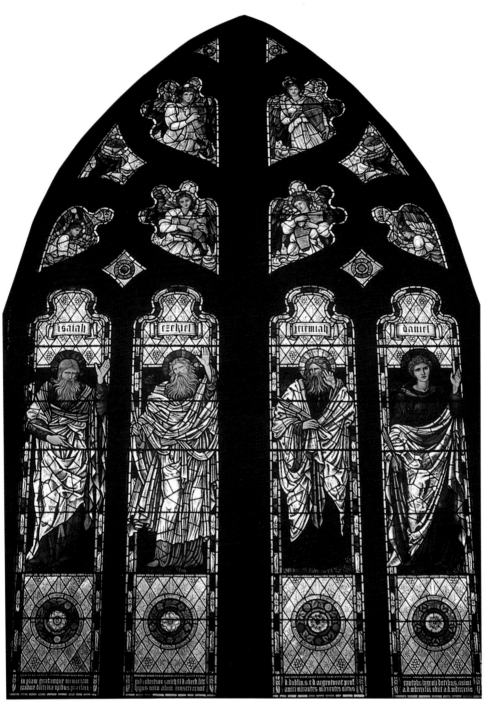

Col. Pl. XIII.   The Robertson Smith window (E). Morris and Co., 1897

Col. Pl. XIVa.   The Geddes window (A). Douglas
Strachan, 1903. Detail of Principal Geddes as
Balthazar worshipping the Christ-child

Col. Pl. XIVb.   The Pirie window (H). Douglas
Strachan, 1912. Detail of Bishop Elphinstone
building the college
(Illustration painted by Vic Davidson)

Col. Pl. XV.   The War Memorial window (I). Douglas Strachan, 1920

Col. Pl. XVI.   The Harrower window (C). Douglas Strachan, 1934